# ARCHITECTURES FOR INTELLIGENCE

*THE TWENTY-SECOND*
*CARNEGIE MELLON SYMPOSIUM*
*ON COGNITION*

# ARCHITECTURES FOR INTELLIGENCE

*THE TWENTY-SECOND
CARNEGIE MELLON SYMPOSIUM
ON COGNITION*

EDITED BY
Kurt VanLehn
*University of Pittsburgh*

**LEA** LAWRENCE ERLBAUM ASSOCIATES, PUBLISHERS
1991   Hillsdale, New Jersey          Hove and London

Lawrence Erlbaum Associates, Inc., Publishers
365 Broadway
Hillsdale, New Jersey 07642

**Library of Congress Cataloging-in-Publication Data**
Carnegie Symposium on Cognition (22nd : 1988 : Carnegie-Mellon
   University)
    Architectures for intelligence / the Twenty-second Carnegie
   Symposium on Cognition : edited by Kurt VanLehn.
        p.   .cm.
    Includes index.
    ISBN 0-8058-0405-6 (c) (ISBN 0-8058-0406-4 (p)
    1. Computer architecture—Congresses.   2. Artificial intelligence–
Congresses.   I. VanLehn, Kurt.   II. Title.
QA76.9.A73C37   1988
006.3—dc20                                        91-11395
                                                    CIP

Printed in the United States of America
10   9   8   7   6   5   4   3   2   1

# Contents

# List of Contributors

**John Allen**
*Carnegie Mellon University*

**John R. Anderson**
*Carnegie Mellon University*

**William Ball**
*University of Pittsburgh*

**Rodney A. Brooks**
*Massachusetts Institute of Technology*

**Jaime G. Carbonell**
*Carnegie Mellon University*

**Prasad Chalasani**
*Carnegie Mellon University*

**John Cheng**
*Carnegie Mellon University*

**William J. Clancey**
*Institute for Research on Learning,
Palo Alto, California*

**Oren Etzioni**
*Carnegie Mellon University*

**Michael R. Genesereth**
*Stanford University*

**Barbara Hayes-Roth**
*Stanford University*

**Eric Jenkins**
*Carnegie Mellon University*

**Craig Knoblock**
*Carnegie Mellon University*

**John E. Laird**
*University of Michigan*

**James L. McClelland**
*Carnegie Mellon University*

**Steven Minton**
*NASA Ames Research Center*

**Thomas Mitchell**
*Carnegie Mellon University*

**Allen Newell**
*Carnegie Mellon University*

**William Oliver**
*University of Pittsburgh*

**Zenon Pylyshyn**
*University of Western Ontario*

**Marc Ringuette**
*Carnegie Mellon University*

**Paul S. Rosenbloom**
*University of Southern California*

**Jeffrey C. Schlimmer**
*Carnegie Mellon University*

**Walter Schneider**
*University of Pittsburgh*

**Herbert A. Simon**
*Carnegie Mellon University*

**Kurt VanLehn**
*University of Pittsburgh*

# Preface

Given that this book is entitled *Architectures for Intelligence,* its topic might be a little obscure. It is not a book about smart buildings, nor about buildings for smart people to live in. It is not about buildings at all. It is about computing systems that exhibit intelligent behavior. Some of the authors address only man-made computing systems (i.e., computers), other authors address only biological computing systems (i.e., minds), and the remaining authors intend their observations to apply to both computers and minds.

Minds and computers change state at two vastly different rates. The information processed in the computing system changes very rapidly, whereas the basic structure of the system changes slowly if at all. Also, the system itself changes the information held in it, whereas changes to its basic structure require an external agent, for instance, when a technician installs a new disk drive or operating system on a computer or when children's normal biological development causes changes in their perception, memory, and attention. The *architecture* of a computing system describes that part of the system that remains unchanged unless an external agent changes it.

The architecture of a computer system is like the architecture of a building. The architecture is not the building itself, but a *description* of the building. Moreover, it is a *partial* description of the building. The architecture describes only the most interesting or essential aspects of the building. Similarly, the architecture of a computing system is a partial description of the fixed parts of the system. For instance, computer science classes often discuss the IBM 360 architecture. This architecture is not a complete description of the computer, but rather a description of the part of the computer that matters if you are going to try to program it. In fact, radically different computers can have exactly the same architecture. For instance, IBM sold several different computers, all of which had the 360 architecture. In general, the architecture of a computing system leaves out details about the implementation of the system and includes only a description of its basic operations and capabilities. An architecture for the mind would describe the way memory and attention operate but it would not describe how they are implemented biologically.

In principle, we could build a computer that has the same architecture as the mind. The first part of this book, chapters 1 through 7, discusses research aimed at this goal. The premise is that implementing a proposed cognitive architecture on a computer will inform us about the internal consistency of the proposed architecture and some of its operating characteristics. This should help us to evaluate it as a model of the mind, and in particular, to compare its performance with experimental data on human performance.

The research described in the second part of the book, chapters 8 through 13, explores architectures that allow large, complex computations to be performed. Although this research may ultimately help us understand the mind, it is not immediately aimed at explaining human data. Instead, these projects aim to meet a different standard for success: Does the architecture allow large, difficult problems to be solved correctly? Actually, some problems, such as robot locomotion, do not have correct solutions per se, so a less precise but more accurate statement of the criterion is: Does the architecture allow large, difficult tasks to be performed intelligently?

The final chapters in both parts of the book are commentaries. Zenon Pylyshyn discusses the Part 1 chapters, whose primary thrust is modeling the mind. William Clancey comments on the chapters in Part 2, where support for artificial intelligence is the primary concern.

All the chapters herein are based on talks delivered at the Twenty-Second Carnegie Symposium on Cognition, which was held on May 16 and 17, 1988, at Carnegie Mellon University. The exception is Herbert Simon's chapter, a comment on John Anderson's proposals, which is based on discussions during and after the symposium. I am grateful to the Cognitive Sciences Division of the Office of Naval Research for a grant supporting the Symposium, and to Betty Boal and Elaine Benjamin for running it.

*Kurt VanLehn*

# COGNITIVE PSYCHOLOGY

# 1 The Place of Cognitive Architectures in a Rational Analysis

John R. Anderson
*Department of Computer Science and Psychology,
Carnegie Mellon University*

The basic goal of a theorist in specifying a cognitive architecture is to specify the mind's principles of operation and organization much like you would specify those of a computer. Any cognitive phenomena should be derivative from these principles. As this conference gives witness, there are many cognitive architectures. This chapter will try to make some claims about the role of architectures generally in psychological theory, but it will do this by taking as examples three of the architectures which figure prominently at Carnegie Mellon University. There is the Soar architecture of Laird, Newell, and Rosenbloom (1987) my own ACT* architecture (Anderson, 1983), and the PDP architecture of McClelland and Rumelhart (McClelland & Rumelhart, 1986, Rumelhart & McClelland, 1986).

Now that there are numerous candidates for cognitive architectures, one is naturally led to ask which might be the correct one or the most correct one. This is a particularly difficult question to answer because these architectures are often quite removed from the empirical phenomena that they are supposed to account for. In actual practice one sees proponents of a particular architecture arguing for that architecture by reference to what I call *signature phenomena*. These are empirical phenomena that are particularly clear manifestations of the purported underlying mechanisms. The claim is made that the architecture provides particularly natural accounts for these phenomena and that these phenomena are hard to account for in other architectures.

In this chapter I will argue that the purported signature phenomena tell us very little about what is inside the human head. Rather they tell us a lot about the world in which the human lives. The majority of this chapter will be devoted to

1

making this point with respect to examples from the SOAR, ACT*, and PDP architectures. At the end of the chapter, I will turn to the issue of the consequences of this point for the role of cognitive architectures.

As a theorist who has been associated with the development of cognitive architectures for 15 years, I should say a little about how I came to be advocating this position. I have been strongly influenced by David Marr's (1982) meta-theoretical arguments in his book on vision which are nicely summarized in the following quote:

> An algorithm is likely to be understood more readily by understanding the nature of the problem being solved than by examining the mechanism (and the hardware) in which it is solved. (p. 27)

Marr made this point with respect to phenomena such as stereopsis where he argued that one will come to an understanding of the phenomena by focusing on the problem of how two two-dimensional views of the world contained enough information to enable one to extract a three-dimensional interpretation of the world and not by focusing on the mechanisms of stereopsis. He thought his viewpoint was appropriate to higher-level cognition although he did not develop it for that application. As recently as a few years ago I could not see how his viewpoint applied to higher-level cognition (Anderson, 1987). However, in the last couple of years I have come to see how it would apply and have realized its advantages. Before specifying its application let us briefly note three advantages of focusing on the information-processing problem and not the information-processing mechanisms:

1. As Marr emphasized, the understanding the nature of the problem offers strong guidance in the proposal of possible mechanisms. If anything this is more important in the case of higher-level cognition where we face a bewildering array of potential mechanisms and an astronomical space of their possible combinations which we must search in trying to identify the correct architecture.

2. Again as Marr emphasized, this allows us a deeper level of understanding of these mechanisms. We can understand why they compute in the way they do rather than regarding them as random configurations of computational pieces.

3. Cognitive psychology faces fundamental indeterminacies such as that between parallel and serial processing, the status of a separate short-term memory, or the format of internal representation. Focusing on the information-processing problem allows us a level of abstraction that is above the level where we need to resolve these indeterminacies.

# A RATIONAL ANALYSIS

The basic point of Marr's was that if there is an optimal way to use the information at hand the system will use it. I have stated this as the following principle:

*Principle of Rationality.* The cognitive system optimizes the adaptation of the behavior of the organism.

One can regard this principle as being handed to us from outside of psychology—as a consequence of basic evolutionary principles. However, I do not want to endorse the principle on such an evolutionary basis because there are many cases where evolution does not optimize. Of course, there are many cases where it does (for a recent discussion see Dupre, 1987). On one hand there are the moths of Manchester and on the other hand, as Simon notes in his companion article, there are the fauna of Australia. It is an interesting question just where and how we would expect evolution to produce optimization, but this is an issue that I neither have space nor competence to get into. Rather, I view the aforementioned principle as an empirical hypothesis to be judged by how well theories that embody the principle of rationality do in predicting cognitive phenomena.

On the empirical front it might seem that the principle of rationality is headed for sure disaster in accounting for human cognition. It is the current wisdom in psychology that man is anything but rational. However, I think many of the purported irrationalities of man disappear when we take a broader view of the human situation. Among the relevant considerations are the following three:

1. We have to bear in mind the cost of computing the behavior. Many think that the problem with the traditional rational man model of economics is that it ignores the cost of computation. Thus we need something like Simon's (1972) bounded rationality where one includes computation cost in the function to be optimized. For instance, in principle a rational person should be able to play a perfect game of chess told the rules of chess but this ignores the prohibitive cost of a complete search of the game tree.

2. The adaptation of the behavior may be defined with respect to an environment different than the one we are functioning in. For instance, one might wonder why human learning mechanisms do so poorly at picking up knowledge in a school environment. I think the answer is that it is not a school environment that they are adapted to.

3. One must recognize that traditional tests of human rationality typically involve normative models that make no reference to the adaptiveness of the behavior. For instance, normative models typically advocating maximizing wealth while the evidence is that there is a negative correlation between wealth

and number of surviving offspring (Vining, 1986). The implication is that one must look critically at the functions which we are trying to optimize in a rational analysis.

With these caveats it is my claim that one can use a rational approach as a framework for deriving behavioral predictions. Developing a theory in a rational framework involves the following six steps:

1. Precisely specify what the goals of the cognitive system are.
2. Develop a formal model of the environment that the system is adapted to (almost certainly less structured than the experimental situation).
3. Make the minimal assumptions about computational costs.
4. Derive the optimal behavioral function given (1)–(3).
5. Examine the empirical literatures to see if the predictions of the behavioral function are confirmed.
6. If predictions are off, iterate.

The theory in a rational approach resides in the assumptions in (1)–(3) from which the predictions flow. I refer to these assumptions as the *framing of the information processing problem*. Note this is a mechanism-free casting of a psychological theory. It can be largely cast in terms of what is outside of the human head rather than inside. As such it enjoys another advantage which is that its assumptions are potentially capable of independent verification.

What I would like to do in the majority of the chapter is to apply this rational analysis to one signature phenomenon for each of the three architectures mentioned in the introduction—SOAR, ACT*, and PDP.

## SOAR—POWER LAW LEARNING

The signature phenomenon I would like to consider for the SOAR theory is power-law learning which is referenced in many of the SOAR publications. Figure 1.1 illustrates data from the Siebel (1963) task which Rosenbloom, Laird, and Newell (1987) have simulated within SOAR. In this task subjects were presented with a panel of ten lights, some of which were lit. They had to press the corresponding fingers on their hands. Subjects saw all configurations of lights except the one in which no lights were lit. Figure 1.1 plots their performance time against the amount of practice which they had. Both scales are logarithmic. As can be seen the relationship is linear implying that the performance measure is a power function of practice. As Newell and Rosenbloom (1981) discussed, such power functions are ubiquitous. The effects can be quite extensive. The data plotted by Seibel covers 40,000 trials.

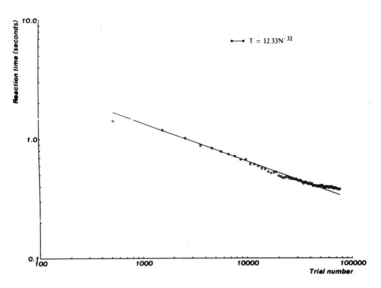

FIG. 1.1. Data from Siebel (1963) plotting time to respond against amount of practice.

In the Soar model, the power law falls out of the chunking learning mechanism plus some critical auxiliary assumptions. Chunking refers to the collapsing of multiple production firings into a single production firing that does the work of the set. In the Seibel task, subjects might chunk productions that will press subsets of lights simultaneously rather than separately. It is assumed that each chunk produces a performance enhancement proportional to the number of productions eliminated. Chunks are formed at a constant rate—either on every opportunity or with equal probability on every opportunity. The final critical assumption is that as chunks span larger and larger units the number of potential chunks grows exponentially. This is fairly transparent in the Seibel task where there are $2^n$ productions needed to encode all chunks of n lights. As a consequence of the last assumption, learning will progress ever more slowly because it takes more experience to encounter all of the larger chunks.

I have always had a number of haunting doubts about the SOAR explanation of the Seibel task. Some of these were expressed in Anderson (1982, 1983). One is that the exponential growth in chunks does not seem true of simple memory experiments (such as paired-associate learning) which produce beautiful power-law learning functions. The second is that the analysis has no place for forgetting effects which must be taking place. So we know by the time of the 40,000 trial of the Seibel task the benefit of the first trial should be fading. Third, the model has no provision for massing effects. We know that as many trials are massed together they loose their effectiveness. Note that the massing effect and forgetting effects are at odds with each other. One is optimized by massing the trials together and the other by spacing them apart.

I will offer a rational analysis of power-law learning which will also explain the forgetting and massing functions. This will be part of a larger rational analysis of human memory which is the topic of the next section.

## A RATIONAL ANALYSIS OF HUMAN MEMORY

The claim that human memory is rationally designed might strike one at least as implausible as the general claim for the rationality of human cognition. Human memory is always disparaged in comparison to computer memory—it is thought of as slow both in storage and retrieval and terribly unreliable. However, such analyses of human memory fail both to understand the task faced by human memory and the goals of memory. I think human memory should be compared with information-retrieval systems such as the ones that exist in computer science. According to Salton and McGill (1983) a generic information-retrieval system consists of four things:

1. There is a data base of files such as book entries in a library system. In the human case these files are the various memories of things past.

2. The files are indexed by terms. In a library system the indexing terms might be keywords in the book's abstract. In the human case the terms are presumably the concepts and elements united in the memory. Thus, if the memory is seeing Willie Stargell hit a home run the indexing terms might be Willie Stargell, home run, Three Rivers Stadium, etc.

3. An information-retrieval system is posed queries consisting of terms. In a library system these are suggested keywords by the user. In the case of the human situation, it is whatever cues are presented by the environment such as when someone says to me "Think of a home run at Three Rivers Stadium."

4. Finally, there are a set of target files desired by which we can judge the success of the information retrieval.

One thing that is very clear in the literature on information-retrieval systems is that they cannot know the right files to retrieve given a query. This is because the information in a query does not completely determine what file is wanted. The best information-retrieval systems can do is assign probabilities to various files given the query. Let us denote the probability that a particular file is a target by $P[A]$.

In deciding what to do informational-retrieval systems have to balance two costs. One is what Salton and McGill call the precision cost and which I will denote $C_p$. This is the cost associated with retrieving a file which is not a target.

There must be a corresponding cost in the human system. This is the one place where we will see a computational cost appearing in our rational analysis of memory.

The other cost Salton and McGill call the recall cost and we will denote it $C_R$. It is the cost associated with failing to retrieve a target. Presumably in most cases it is much larger than the precision cost for a single file or memory.

Given this framing of the information-processing problem we can now proceed to specify the optimal information-processing behavior. This is to consider memories (or files) in order of descending P[A] and stop when the expected cost associated with failing to consider the next item is greater than the cost associated with considering it or when

$$P[A]C_R < (1-P[A])C_P \qquad (1)$$

We now have a complete theory of human memory except for one major issue—how should the system go about estimating P[A]. I propose that the system should use the item's past history of usage and the elements in the current context to come up with a Bayesian estimate of that probability. A particularly transparent way of stating this is with the Bayesian odds ration formula which we can state

$$\frac{P(A|H_A\&Q)}{P(\bar{A}|H_A\&Q)} = \frac{P(A|H_A)}{P(\bar{A}|H_A)} * \prod_{i \in Q} \frac{P(i|A)}{P(i|\bar{A})} \qquad (2)$$

where $P(A|H_A\&Q)$ is the posterior probability that the memory is needed given its past history and the cues in the current context, $P(\bar{A}|H_A\&Q)$ is $1 - P(A|H_A\&Q)$, $P(A|H_A)$ is the posterior probability given just the history, $P(\bar{A}|H_A) = 1 - P(A|H_A)$, $P(i|A)$ is the conditional probability that i would be in the current context if A is needed, and $P(i|\bar{A})$ is the conditional probability if A is not needed.

This way of formulating the relationship nicely breaks up the need probability into the product of a history factor, $P(A|H_A)/P(\bar{A}|H_A)$, plus a context factor, the product involving the $P(i|A)/P(i/\bar{A})$. Note that in this context factor we are assuming the individual cues are independent of one another in order to obtain a product. I neither want to argue that this is really true nor that the human system actually acts as if it is. I am only using this as an approximation to get an indication of what the rational predictions are.

It should be pointed out that P[A] is the probability that A is needed, not the probability that A will be recalled if needed which is presumably much higher. The basic assumption in the discussion that follows is that the need probability will be monotonically related to observed dependent variables such as probability of recall and latency of recall. Elsewhere (Anderson, 1990) I have developed detailed, and I think plausible, proposals about how need probability is related to these dependent variables but the points I will make here do not really depend on this level of detail.

### The History Factor

In investigating the implications of this rational analysis for the power-law learning function, we need to focus on the history factor in the above equation. In particular, we need to specify $P(A|H_A)$. To determine this we need to know how the past history of usage of a memory trace predicts whether it will be currently used. To determine this in a truly valid objective way we would have to follow people around, determine when they use particular facts, and induce what the empirical relationship is. It is nearly impossible to imagine collecting such objective statistics in the human case but such statistics are available for other information-retrieval systems. For instance, there is data about how past borrowings from a library predict future borrowings (Burrell, 1980; Burrell & Cane, 1982). There is data about how past accesses to a file predict future accesses (Stritter, 1977). The data for these different domains are quite similar in terms of the nature of the functional relationship between past use and current use. I propose that these relationships are true of all information-retrieval systems including the human one.

The basic point of my argument might be lost in the mathematics that follows so let me state it up front: I will show that an information-retrieval system optimized in the sense defined earlier and faced with the statistics of library borrowings or file usage would produce the practice functions, retention functions, and spacing functions associated with human memory. Thus, if we accept the premise that human memory faces the same statistics as these objectively observable information-retrieval systems, we can predict its behavior with no further assumptions. The power of this analysis is that the statistics of information presentations are objectively observable and do not have to be postulated. This is in sharp contrast to a mechanistic theory where the critical structures are unobservable.

Burrell (1985) developed a model for library borrowings which provides a good analytical starting point. There are three basic assumptions in Burrell's model. The first is that the items in a system vary in their desirability. Burrell assumes that the distribution of desirability is a gamma distribution with parameter b and index v. He is able to basically show such a distribution of borrowings in the case of a library system. The second assumption that Burrell makes is that there is an aging process such that items will decay in their borrowing rate with the passage of time. Again he can empirically validate that such an aging process does occur. This means that, if we take an item from the gamma distribution with initial desirability $\lambda$, its desirability after time, t, will be $\lambda r(t)$ where $r(t)$ describes the rate of decay. Burrell uses a simple exponential decay in rate of the form $r(t) = e^{-at}$. The third assumption of Burrell is that borrowings are a Poisson process and that times until next borrowing are exponentially distributed with rate $\lambda r(t)$.

With these assumptions we can derive what I call the recency-frequency function $RF(n,t)$ which is the probability that an item introduced t time units ago and used n times over that period will be needed in the current time unit. It has the form:

$$RF(n, t) = \frac{v + n}{M(t) + b}r(t) \tag{3}$$

where n is the number of borrowings in the past and M(t) is defined

$$M(t) = \int_0^t r(s)ds \tag{4}$$

This gives us a linear relationship between number of uses, n, and need probability. This is a special case of a power function where the exponent is 1. Newell & Rosenbloom (1981) noted that such hyperbolic functions give reasonable fits to human practice functions. Under the transformation from need proba-

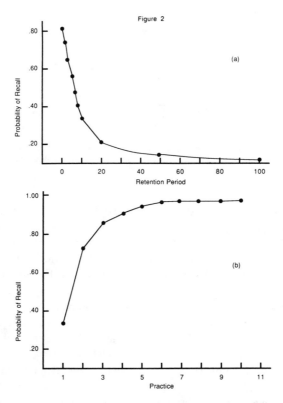

FIG. 1.2.   Relationship between probability of recall and retention interval (a) and practice (b).

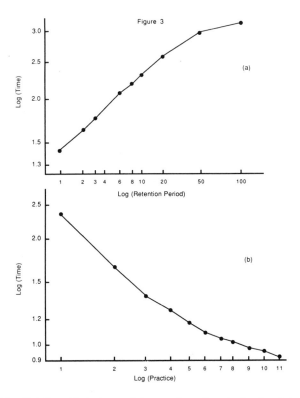

FIG. 1.3.   Relationship between latency of recall and retention interval (a) and practice (b). These are log-log plots to show the characteristic power functions.

bility to latency proposed in Anderson (1990), the power function relationship remains although there are a family of functions with different exponents.

To account for the spacing effect, I have found it necessary to augment Burrell's model with two further assumptions, both of which can be verified in the case of library systems but which were unimportant for Burrell's concerns. One is that there is variation in rate of decay. In the library system this is the distinction between the classics and the flash-in-the-pans. The second assumption is that items undergo periodic revivals in which they return to their original rate of usage. At Carnegie-Mellon, for instance, this happens when a course is offered which the book is relevant to. In my modeling I have simply assumed that there was an exponential distribution in decay rates and that revivals were also a Poisson process. Unlike Burrell's original assumptions I have no evidence that these forms are accurate for library systems or any other information-retrieval system. Therefore, these additional assumptions must be viewed as approximate.

These additional assumptions eliminate the simple closed form solutions of Equation 3 but do not upset the prediction of power-function practice. Figure 1.2

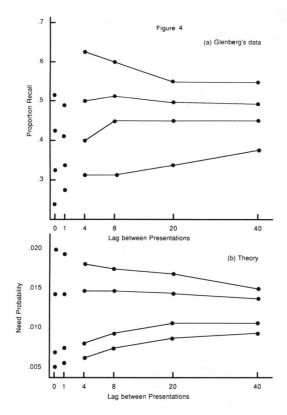

FIG. 1.4.   (a) Glenberg's data showing the interaction between retention interval and study log; (b) Predictions of the theory for Glenberg's
experiment.

illustrates the results derived from the more complex model. In addition to the
practice function, it is also the case that the theory predicts typical retention
functions. Despite the fact the decay process, r(t), is exponential the effect of the
revival component is to slow down the forgetting function to approximate the
power-function relationship that is typically obtained between delay and retention. These figures illustrate the predictions for the dependent variables of probability (Fig. 1.2) and (Fig. 1.3) but similar functions are obtained if we look at the
underlying need probability.

With these assumptions in hand, I tried to model the classic data of Glenberg
(1976) on the spacing effect. He varied the interval between two presentations of
an item and looked at the effect on the recall of the item. He showed that the
effect of the spacing interval interacted with the time between the second study
and test. His data and the predictions of the theory are shown in Figure 1.4. In
both cases at short test lags there is a negative relationship between spacing and
recall while at long test lags there is the more common positive relationship.

(Glenberg's data is a little strangely behaved at 0 and 1 study lags apparently because of inattentiveness).

Thus, we have shown that power-law learning, forgetting, and the spacing (or massing) effect can all be predicted from a single rational perspective which sees human memory as adapting to the statistics of information use. Thus, it is what is outside the human head not what is inside that is controlling the memory performance. I should emphasize that this does not deny that chunking may be one of the mechanisms the mind uses to achieve this adaptation. However, the argument is that the real explanation is in the outside world and not in the internal mechanisms.

## ACT*—THE FAN EFFECT

Now I would like to turn to the second architecture, ACT*, and consider a signature phenomenon which has played a key role in its development. This is the fan effect (Anderson, 1983). The fan effect has been most typically studied in a sentence recognition experiment where the subject is asked to study a set of sentences such as the following:

1. The doctor is in the bank (1-1)
2. The fireman is in the park (1-2)
3. The lawyer is in the church (2-1)
4. The lawyer is in the park (2-2)

In these materials we are manipulating the number of facts studied about the person and the location. Each aforementioned sentence is followed by two numbers giving its classification according to number of facts associated with subject and location.

Figure 1.5 shows the network representation that we assume in the ACT* theory that the subject sets up to encode this material. There are proposition nodes which are connected by labeled associations to each of the concepts. Note that as we increase the number of facts associated with a concept we increase the number or *fan* of arrows leading from the concept.

A typical experiment is focused on the subject's ability to recognize these sentences after they have been learned. A subject might have to recognize these sentences when mixed in with distractors like "The doctor is in the church." According to ACT*, upon being presented with a sentence such as "The lawyer is in the park" the subject activates the concepts in the sentence such as lawyer, in, and park. Activation spreads from these concepts along various network paths. The time to recognize a sentence is a function of the amount of activation reaching the proposition node. The critical additional assumption in the ACT* theory is that the amount of activation that can spread out of a node is fixed and

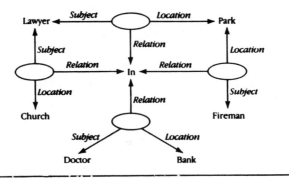

FIG. 1.5.    ACT* propositional network representation of the fan material.

that the more paths emanating out of a concept the less activation can go to any one proposition and so the slower recognition will be. Table 1.1 shows some data confirming this prediction. There we have data classified according to the fan associated with subject and with location.

## A Rational Analysis of the Fan Effect

We can extend our rational analysis of memory to accommodate the fan effect. Here we will be interested in analyzing the context factor rather than the history factor since we are manipulating properties of the memory cues that we presented to subjects. That is, we want to focus on the quantities $P(i|A)/P(i|\bar{A})$. We can rewrite these as

$$\frac{P(i|A)}{P(i|\bar{A})} = \frac{P(A|i)P(i)/P(A)}{P(\bar{A}|i)P(i)/P(\bar{A})}$$

The $P(i)$ drop out. Since $P(\bar{A})$ must be near one (there are millions of traces and no one can be very probable) it can also be ignored. To an approximation we can also ignore $P(\bar{A}|i)$. This is a good approximation to the extent that the probability of needing a trace remains low even in the presence of a predictive cue. If we allow this approximation, we get the following which is very easy to analyze:

$$\frac{P(i|A)}{P(i|\bar{A})} \simeq \frac{P(A|i)}{P(\bar{A})} \tag{5}$$

Our claims do not depend on making this approximation. It is just that they are a lot easier to see with the approximation.

In our experiments $P(A)$ is basically constant for all items and so the critical factor turns out to be the probability that the trace is relevant given a particular

## TABLE 1.1

Person-Location Experiment (A hippie is in the park)—Mean Verification Times and Error Rates for Trues and Falses

| | Trues | | | | | Falses | | | |
|---|---|---|---|---|---|---|---|---|---|
| | Number of Propositions per Person | | | | | Number of Propositions per Person | | | |
| | 1 | 2 | 3 | Mean | | 1 | 2 | 3 | Mean |
| Number of propositions per location 1 | 1.111 (.051) | 1.174 (.042) | 1.222 (.046) | 1.169 (.046) | 1 | 1.197 (.019) | 1.221 (.042) | 1.264 (.030) | 1.227 (.030) |
| 2 | 1.167 (.065) | 1.198 (.056) | 1.222 (.060) | 1.196 (.060) | 2 | 1.250 (.014) | 1.356 (.037) | 1.291 (.044) | 1.299 (.032) |
| 3 | 1.153 (.063) | 1.233 (.044) | 1.357 (.054) | 1.248 (0.54) | 3 | 1.262 (.042) | 1.471 (.079) | 1.465 (.051) | 1.399 (.057) |
| Mean | 1.144 (.059) | 1.202 (.048) | 1.267 (.054) | 1.204 (.053) | Mean | 1.236 (.025) | 1.349 (.053) | 1.340 (.042) | 1.308 (.040) |

cue. This is precisely what is manipulated by fan in a typical experiment. The more facts associated with a particular concept the less likely any one is given the concept. Basically, if the fan is n the probability is $1/n$. Anderson (1976) did an experiment that decorrelated fan and probability by manipulating the probability of testing various facts associated with a particular concept. That experiment showed conclusively that the critical factor is probability and not fan.

Thus, the fan effect is a consequence of memory using the correlation between cues and a memory's relevance to predict when the memory is needed. It may be that spreading activation is one of the mechanisms that the mind uses to compute the correlation. However, for current purposes the critical fact is that once again the explanation of the phenomena lies in what is outside of the human head and not what is inside.

## PDP—CATEGORIZATION

PDP models involve representing knowledge in a distributed form where specific experiences do not have specific encodings. On the other hand, PDP models do learning locally such that changes in strengths of connection between specific elements must underlie these distributed encodings. This leads PDP models to naturally produce generalization phenomena such that they extract central tendencies out of the experience of specific instances. In introducing PDP models, McClelland, Rumelhart, and Hinton (1986) gave a lot of play to categorization phenomena which is the identification of common categories in a set of instances. It receives more page space in their article than any other phenomenon. There is a substantial literature in cognitive psychology on categorization behavior. McClelland et al. do not actually simulate any specific experiment in this literature but rather offer a simulation of the extraction of the characteristics of the members of two gangs (the jets and the sharks) as a prototype of the experiments in the literature.

To develop a rational analysis of categorization behavior, the first thing we need to ask is what are the goals of the cognitive system in forming categories. In much of the experimental literature on categorization, one gets the feeling that the driving force behind categorization is some sort of social conformity—that we need to learn to use the same labels to describe objects as do other people. However, this clearly cannot be all of the picture, particularly because people can learn to identify categories in the absence of any labels. I think the real function of categorization is to maximize the system's ability to predict properties of objects including their labels. Clearly, a system that can make accurate predictions will be in a position to maximize its goals.

The reason people form categories to maximize prediction is because of the nature of objects in the external world. Formally, the following is the characterization that I will assume in my rational derivations. I will assume that the world seen so far has consisted of n objects which are partitioned into s disjoint sets or categories. Each object can be classified according to some r dimensions (for simplicity I will only consider cardinal dimensions) where each dimension i has some $m_i$ values. The members of a category belong in that category by virtue of possessing theoretical probabilities $p_{ij}$ that they will display value j on dimension i. These probabilities provide the intensional definition of a category in contrast to its extensional definition which can be gotten simply by listing the category members.

These assumptions are intended as descriptions of the external world not just of the perception of the world in the human head. One can ask why the objects in the world should partition themselves in disjoint partitions defined by conjunctions of features. I cannot say I know the total answer but there are some obvious things to point at. For instance there is the genetic phenomenon of species that enforces a disjoint (no crossbreeding) partitioning of conjunctively defined categories (the common genetic code within a species). Other types of objects like physical elements and tools tend to produce similar disjoint partitionings of conjunctively defined categories. One can also question the probabilistic definition of category membership since this is in contradiction to the tradition in the artificial intelligence work on categories. However, I think it is indisputable that category members do display their features with only certain probabilities. Most labradors are black and have four legs but neither feature is displayed universally.

## An Ideal Algorithm for Categorization

Given the aforementioned formalization, we can go to characterizing what the ideal algorithm would be for categorization ignoring computational costs. Our basic situation is that the system has observed n objects and their features and is presented with a n + 1st object with at least one feature missing and must predict the probability that it will display value j on dimension i. The following equation is the obvious one for that prediction:

$$Pred_{ij} = \sum_{X} P(X|F)P(ij|X) \qquad (6)$$

where the summation is over all partitions X of the n + 1 objects into categories. $P(X|F)$ is the probability of that partition given the observed features of the n + 1 objects, and $P(ij|X)$ is the probability that the n + 1st object will display value j on dimension i if X is the partitioning.

The problem with this ideal solution is the number of partitions grows exponentially with n. I have not been able to find the closed form expression but the number of partitions is approximately $(n + 2)!/(3*2^n)$. Thus, for instance, there are the following 15 partitions of the 4 objects abcd: (abcd) (a,bcd) (b,acd) (c,abd) (d,abc) (ab,cd) (ac,bd) (ad,bc) (a,b,cd) (ab,c,d) (a,c,bd) (ac,b,d) (a,d,bc) (ad,b,c) (a,b,c,d).

It is entirely unreasonable to suppose that the human system could correspond with the prescriptions of this algorithm if that meant computing the value exactly. The human system may have some way of approximating the ideal algorithm. I have no proof that computing the quantity in Equation 6 is np-complete. For all I know there is an equivalent calculation which is computationally tractible.

## An Iterative Algorithm for Categorization

Despite the lingering possibility that the ideal algorithm may have a tractible form, research in machine learning has failed to find such an algorithm and the new trend is for iterative algorithms (e.g., Fisher, 1987; Lebowitz, 1987). I have worked with the following iterative algorithm:

1. Initialize the partitioning to be the empty set.
2. Given a partitioning of the first m objects, calculate for each category K the probability $P_K$ that the m + 1st object comes from category K. (Let $P_0$ be the probability that the object comes from a new category.)
3. Create a partitioning of the first m + 1st objects with the object assigned to the category with the maximum probability.
4. To predict value j on dimension i for the n + 1st object

$$Pred_{ij} = \sum_K P_K P(ij|K) \qquad (7)$$

To apply this algorithm, we need to derive rational formulas for $P_K$ and $P(ij|K)$. The latter is involved in the former so I will simply present a rational analysis of $P_K$. Again, we can derive a Bayesian analysis of this quantity:

$$P_K = P(K|F_{m+1}) = \frac{P(K)P(F_{m+1}|K)}{\sum_I P(I)P(F_{m+1}|I)} \qquad (8)$$

where $P(K|F_{m+1})$    is the probability that the m + 1st object belongs to category K given that it has feature structure $F_{m+1}$,

where $P(K)$    is the prior probability that the object comes from category K

$P(F_{m+1}|K)$    is the probability of feature structure $F_{m+1}$ given the object comes from category K

In deriving $P(K)$ we are interested in the prior probability that two objects will be in the same category in advance of information about their features. A reasonable constraint to place on any formula for P(K) is that the probability that two objects find themselves in the same category be independent of the the total number of objects to be categorized. Let this be the *coupling probability,* which we will call c. It can be shown that there is only one formula satisfying this constraint and this is

$$P(K) = \frac{cn_K}{(1 - c) + cm} \tag{9}$$

where c is a coupling probability
$n_K$ is the number of objects in category K
m is the total number of objects

In addition, we need the following formula for $P(\emptyset)$, the probability that the m + 1st object comes from an entirely new category

$$P(\emptyset) = \frac{1 - c}{(1 - c) + cm} \tag{10}$$

The remaining quantity to specify is the conditional probability $P(F_{m+1}|K)$ that the m + 1st object will display its feature structure given that it comes from category K. In developing an analysis of this quantity, we will assume as an approximation that the probability of displaying a value on one dimension is independent of the probability on another dimension. If so, we can have the following mathematical development:

$$P(F_{m+1}|K) = \prod_i P(ij|K) \tag{11}$$

where $P(ij|K)$ is the probability of displaying value j on dimension i. This turns on our assumptions about the joint density function $f_i(x_1, x_2, \ldots, x_m)$ which is the probability density that $p_{i1} = x_1, p_{i2} = x_2, \ldots, p_{im} = x_m$.

Recall that $p_{ij}$ is the theoretical probability that an item in a category will display value j on dimension i. If we assume a uniform density for $F_i$ then it can be shown (Anderson, 1990) that $P(ij|K)$ has the following form:

$$P(ij|K) = \frac{c_{ij} + 1}{n_K + m_i} \tag{12}$$

where $n_K$ is the number of objects in category K
$c_{ij}$ is the number of objects in category K with
the same value as the object to be classified
$m_i$ are the number of dimensions on dimension i

It turns out the iterative algorithm so defined does a very credible job of categorization. It does a good job of classifying the 630 soybeans diseases of Michalski and Chilausky (1980) which have been a standard test case in artificial intelligence. Table 1.2 illustrates a simpler example structure which it has been

TABLE 1.2
Features I

| Animals | Hair | Light | Color | Lays eggs | Mammal | Flies | Big | Aggressive | Beak | Gives milk |
|---|---|---|---|---|---|---|---|---|---|---|
| WHALES | 0 | 1 | 0 | 1 | 0 | 0 | 1 | 0 | 0 | 1 |
| SEALS | 0 | 1 | 0 | 1 | 0 | 0 | 1 | 0 | 0 | 1 |
| DOGS | 1 | 0 | 0 | 1 | 1 | 0 | 1 | 1 | 0 | 1 |
| CATS | 1 | 0 | 0 | 1 | 1 | 0 | 0 | 1 | 0 | 1 |
| HORSES | 1 | 0 | 0 | 1 | 1 | 0 | 1 | 0 | 0 | 1 |
| BEARS | 1 | 0 | 0 | 1 | 1 | 0 | 1 | 1 | 0 | 1 |
| BATS | 1 | 0 | 0 | 1 | 0 | 1 | 0 | 0 | 0 | 1 |
| HUMANS | 0 | 1 | 0 | 1 | 0 | 0 | 1 | 0 | 0 | 1 |
| MICE | 1 | 1 | 0 | 1 | 1 | 0 | 0 | 0 | 0 | 1 |
| PLATYPUS | 1 | 0 | 1 | 1 | 1 | 0 | 0 | 0 | 1 | 1 |
| CHICKENS | 0 | 1 | 1 | 0 | 0 | 0 | 0 | 0 | 1 | 0 |
| PENGUINS | 0 | 0 | 1 | 0 | 0 | 0 | 1 | 0 | 1 | 0 |
| ROBINS | 0 | 0 | 1 | 0 | 0 | 1 | 0 | 0 | 1 | 0 |
| OSTRICHES | 0 | 1 | 1 | 0 | 0 | 0 | 1 | 0 | 1 | 0 |
| CROWS | 0 | 0 | 1 | 0 | 0 | 1 | 0 | 0 | 1 | 0 |
| PARROTS | 0 | 0 | 1 | 0 | 0 | 1 | 0 | 0 | 1 | 0 |
| SPARROWS | 0 | 1 | 1 | 0 | 0 | 1 | 0 | 0 | 1 | 0 |
| EAGLES | 0 | 1 | 1 | 0 | 0 | 1 | 1 | 1 | 1 | 0 |
| HAWKS | 0 | 1 | 1 | 0 | 0 | 1 | 0 | 1 | 1 | 0 |
| SEAGULLS | 0 | 1 | 1 | 0 | 0 | 1 | 0 | 0 | 1 | 0 |

applied to. Here we have 20 animals classified according to 10 binary dimensions. The values were made up by me and in retrospect they have some errors. Nonetheless, depending on the values set for c it merges all 20 into one category, breaks the 20 into two sets of the 10 mammals and 10 birds, further subdivides whales, humans, and seals as a subcategory of animals (by accident and mistake I gave these three mammals the same binary feature description), or divides the objects into 20 separate categories.

## Psychological Accuracy

Of more interest than how this does as an artificial intelligence algorithm is the question of how well it does as a model of human categorization behavior. I have applied it to the now classic data of Medin and Schaffer (1978) where it did better than their original model using only a single parameter, c, rather than their many.

I have also applied it to the long series of experiments involving the Posner and Keele (1968) stimuli using an encoding of these materials developed by Hintzman. It accounts for all the phenomena that Hintzman lists for these materials. I have also successfully predicted the results of a complicated experiment of Elio and Anderson (1981), which no model before Hintzman's was able to account for.

Rather than discussing the specific experiments in detail, it is worthwhile listing some of the major phenomena that are known about human categorization and explaining how the model accounts for each:

1. Clearly the research indicates that, to a degree, people extract the central tendency of a set of instances in that their behavior is a function of the distance from that central tendency. This simply reflects a sensitivity to the statistical correlation between features and category identity which amounts to using conditional probabilities in a Bayesian analysis.

2. In addition to distance from a central tendency, the literature has found an effect of distance from specific examples (e.g., Medin & Schaffer, 1978). This is produced by the tendency of the model to break diverse categories into subcategories where the features cluster together. The reason for this is that predictive power is gained by such decomposition.

3. It has shown that when a category has multiple central tendencies subjects can pick this up (Neumann, 1977). As with point (2) this is produced by the tendency to break a large diverse category into smaller categories that increase predictability.

4. Research such as that of Medin and Schaffer has shown that categorization is a non-linear function of similarity—that the increase in performance as we go from two to three matching features is greater than the increase in going from one to two. This can be traced back to equation (11) where probabilities (measuring similarity) multiply rather than add.

5. There is an effect of category size in many experiments including the Posner and Keele task. This is simply a sensitivity to base rates.

6. Rosch, Mervis, Gray, Johnson, and Boyes-Braem (1976) documented the many circumstances in which there appear to be basic level categories. The existence of such categories in our framework is simply a consequence of the fact that these categories maximize the predictability of the world—which is basically Rosch's original point.

7. It is not necessary for feedback on category membership to be given in order for categories to emerge (Fried & Holyoak, 1984). Categories will emerge any time they increase the predictability of the universe. However, by applying category labels we increase the amount of structure that can be predicted and so enhance the value of category membership. So, labels should enhance categorization but are not essential.

8. The more things that can be predicted from category membership the more likely a category is to be formed even though this means one has to learn more about a category (Billman, 1983).

Thus, it seems that categorization phenomena can be again explained from a rational perspective assuming that the controlling factor is the structure of the world and not the structure in the human head. Note again this analysis does not deny that PDP mechanisms may be the way that the mind implements this rational analysis. However, it denies that PDP models provide an adequate explanation of the phenomena.

## CONCLUSIONS

In summary, we have looked at three cognitive architectures. For each we have taken a signature phenomenon and developed a reasonable model of the world in which that phenomenon occurs and the goals of humans operating in that world. We have made a few assumptions about computational costs that are not at all mechanism specific. We have derived the signature phenomena as solutions to the optimization problems we defined. In each case this rational analysis led to an account that was as accurate or more accurate than the original mechanistic account.

Now we come to the hard question of what the implications are of these demonstrations. I am not really sure what the implications are but I will hazard two guesses. However before I do, I want to forestall misunderstanding by disavowing two possible interpretations of the point of this chapter.

One possible reaction to the relative good showing of the rational analysis might be renewed effort to develop a better cognitive architecture. There is a tendency to view this rational analysis as a first-order approximation which any self-respecting architecture ought to do better than. These results might be thus be taken as damning the three architectures we considered rather than praising rational analysis. However, I think simply looking for a better architecture really misses the point. First, it does not deal· with the fundamental identifiability problems that haunt our search for such mental mechanisms. More important it looses the essential insight that it is no accident that architectures that correspond to human behavior compute in the way they do. They do so because this is in fact what is optimal given the world in which they reside.

A second reaction might be to take this as an indictment of mechanistic accounts of mind and a call for a retreat to behaviorism. After all, the argument might go, we have shown that human behavior can be predicted by reference to the environment without reference to what is in the head. However, to retreat back to behaviorism would be to leave us with the same computationally inadequate models of mind that we abandoned 30 years ago. The simple fact is that the optimal behavior is often going to be computationally complex and mechanistic accounts give us a way of expressing that complexity and simple stimulus-response associations do not.

While I am confident that the aforementioned two are the wrong reactions, I am less certain about the positive proposals I have to make, but here they are: My first guess is that cognitive architectures should be viewed as notations for expressing the behavioral functions that emerge as the solutions to the optimization problems in a rational analysis. The real theory lies in the assumptions made in the statement of the optimization problem—that is, the assumptions about the goals, the world, and the computational limitations. These assumptions do not have the same identifiability problems that the mechanistic models do and lead to a much deeper explanation of the phenomena at hand. However, something computationally powerful like a Turing-equivalent architecture is necessary if we are going to be able to express the solution to these optimization problems.

Thus, the theory is in the framing of the information processing problem and the architectures provide notation for expressing the solutions to the optimization problems. I see a one-to-many mapping between framings and architectures. That is, one can take a single framing and for every architecture find some configuration of its mechanisms that enable the optimal behavior to be computed. Choice among architectures is then not to be determined by veracity of empirical predictions. Rather it is to be determined by how easy it is to work out the optimal behavior in that architecture. Ease of use is the classic criterion for selecting among notations. Empirical veracity is reserved for theories.

My second guess (which is a variation on the first guess) is that architectures in some form may play a role in actually framing the optimization problem. Recall earlier that step (3) in developing a rational analysis was to make some assumptions about computational cost. In the case of memory, the assumption was that there was a retrieval cost. In the case of categorization, the assumption was that a certain function was not computable and another was. These were relatively bland assumptions but they do reflect the architecture. It is possible in other applications of a rational analysis, the computational assumptions might be richer. On this view, much of the detail we associate with an architecture might be just theoretical notation, but there may be some core, contentful assumptions. This view would encourage us to sift the notation from the content in our architectures, using relevance to rational analysis as a basis for making that discrimination. Basically, architecture would define the bounds on optimization in a rational analysis or, in Simon's hillclimbing metaphor, define the contours of the surface on which the local optimization takes place.

## ACKNOWLEDGMENTS

This research was supported by the Computer Sciences Division, Office of Naval Research and DARPA under Contract Number N00014-86-K-0678. Reproduction in whole or in part is permitted for purposes of the United States Government. Approved for public release; distribution unlimited.

# REFERENCES

Anderson, J. R. (1976). *Language, memory, and thought*. Hillsdale, NJ: Lawrence Erlbaum Associates.

Anderson, J. R. (1982). Acquisition of Cognitive Skill. *Psychological Review, 89*, 369–406.

Anderson, J. R. (1983). *The Architecture of Cognition*. Cambridge, MA: Harvard University Press.

Anderson, J. R. (1983). Retrieval of information from long-term memory. *Science, 220*, 25–30.

Anderson, J. R. (1987). Methodologies for studying human knowledge. *The Behavioral and Brain Sciences, 10*, 467–505.

Anderson, J. R. (1990). *The Adaptive Character of Thought*. Hillsdale, NJ: Lawrence Erlbaum Associates.

Billman, D. (1983). *Inductive learning of syntactic categories*. Unpublished doctoral dissertation, University of Michigan.

Burrell, Q. L. (1980). A simple stochastic model for library loans. *Journal of Documentation, 36*, 115–132.

Burrell, Q. L. (1985). A note on aging on a library circulation model. *Journal of Documentation, 41*, 100–115.

Burrell, Q. L., & Cane, V. R. (1982). The analysis of library data. *Journal of the Royal Statistical Society, Series A*(145), 439–471.

Dupre, J. (1987). *The latest on the best*. Cambridge, MA: MIT Press.

Elio, R., & Anderson, J. R. (1981). The effects of category generalizations and instance similarity on schema abstraction. *Journal of Experimental Psychology: Human Learning and Memory, 7*, 397–417.

Fisher, D. H. (1987). Knowledge acquisition via incremental conceptual clustering. *Machine Learning, 2*, 139–172.

Fried, L. S., & Holyoak, K. J. (1984). Induction of category distributions: A framework for classification learning. *Journal of Experimental Psychology: Learning, Memory, and Cognition, 10*, 234–257.

Glenberg, A. M. (1976). Monotonic and nonmonotonic lag effects in paired-associate and recognition memory paradigms. *Journal of Verbal Learning and Verbal Behavior, 15*(1), 1–16.

Laird, J. E., Newell, A., & Rosenbloom, P. S. (1987). Soar: An architecture for general intelligence. *Artificial Intelligence, 33*, 1–64.

Lebowitz, M. (1987). Experiments with incremental concept formation: UNIMEM. *Machine Learning, 2*, 103–138.

Marr, D. (1982). *Vision*. San Francisco: Freeman.

McClelland, J. L., Rumelhart, D. E., & Hinton, G. E. (1986). *The appeal of parallel distributed processing*. In D. E. Rumelhart & J. L. McClelland, and the PDP Research Group, *Parallel Distributed Processing*. (Vol. 1.)

Medin, D. L., & Schaffer, M. M. (1978). Context theory of classification learning. *Psychological Review, 85*, 207–238.

Michalski, R. S., & Chilausky, R. L. (1980). Learning by being told and learning from examples: An experimental comparison of the two methods of knowledge acquisition in the context of developing an expert system for soybean disease diagnosis. *International Journal of Policy Analysis and Information Systems, 4*, 125–161.

Neumann, P. G. (1977). Visual prototype information with discontinuous representation of dimensions of variability. *Memory & Cognition, 5*, 187–197.

Newell, A., & Rosenbloom, P. (1981). Mechanisms of skill acquisition and the law of practice. In J. R. Anderson (Ed.), *Cognitive skills and their acquisition*, pp. 1–55. Hillsdale, NJ: Lawrence Erlbaum Associates.

Posner, M. I., & Keele, S. W. (1968). On the genesis of abstract ideas. *Journal of Experimental Psychology, 77*, 353–363.

Rosch, E., Mervis, C. B., Gray, W., Johnson, D., & Boyes-Braem, P. (1976). Basic objects in natural categories. *Cognitive Psychology, 7*, 573–605.

Rosenbloom, P. S., Laird, J. E., & Newell, A. (1988). *The chunking of skill in knowledge*. In H. Buoma & B. A. G. Elsendoorn (Eds.). *Working models of human perception*. London: Academic Press.

Rumelhart, D. E., McClelland, J. L., and the PDP research group. (1986). *Parallel distributed processing: Explorations in the microstructure of cognition*. Cambridge, MA: Bradford Books.

Salton, G., & McGill, M. J. (1983). *Introduction to modern information retrieval*. New York: McGraw-Hill.

Siebel, R. (1963). Discrimination reaction time for 1023—alternative task. *Journal of Experimental Psychology, 66*, 215–226.

Simon, H. A. (1972). *Theories of bounded rationality*. In C. B. Rander & R. Radner (Eds.), *Decision and organization*. Amsterdam: North-Holland.

Stritter, E. P. (1977). *File migration*. Doctoral dissertation, Stanford University, Stanford: Stanford Linear Accelerator Center.

Vining, D. R. (1986). Social versus reproductive success: The central theoretical problem of human sociobiology. *The Behavioral and Brain Sciences, 9*, 167–216.

# 2 Cognitive Architectures and Rational Analysis: Comment

Herbert A. Simon
*Department of Psychology, Carnegie Mellon University*

John Anderson has written a provocative chapter whose thesis may be over-simplified to read:

To understand the behavior of an adaptive organism, don't study the organism; study its environment.

When we are served a gelatin desert shaped like an exotic animal, and want to know why it takes that form, we are well advised to look for the mold in which it was made. We need to know nothing about gelatin except that, in liquid form it adapts its shape to the shape of whatever vessel receives it, and retains that shape when it sets. The adaptive principle of gelatin (its "goal") when in liquid form is to minimize the level of its center of gravity.

Anderson invites us to view the human mind, when confronted with a new kind of task, as a bowl of gelatin that fits itself optimally to the demands of the task, acquiring the strategy that is most appropriate for performing it efficiently. If we accept his invitation, then we are relieved of the tedium (if that is the right word) of comparing cognitive architectures and experimenting to determine which one best describes human task behavior. We are even excused from the tedium of inventing the architectures in the first place: what goes on in the mind doesn't matter (much).

## THE OPTIMAL ADAPTATION HYPOTHESIS

The hypothesis that adaptive systems are to be understood by computing their optima from the structure of their environments has played a central role in several domains of science: most notably in economics and evolutionary theory. As we shall see, it has not been absent from psychology. It may be instructive, and useful for evaluating Anderson's proposal, to see how it has fared in these various domains. I begin with economics.

## Optimization in Economics

The foundation stone of contemporary neo-classical economics is the hypothesis that economic actors are rational (i.e., perfectly adaptive), and that their rationality takes the form of maximizing expected subjective utility. The term "maximizes" is clear enough. "Expected" is meant in its technical sense in probability theory—that is, as in the phrase "expected value." "Subjective" means in terms of the actor's estimates of the relevant probabilities of events. "Utility" means the actor's own ordering of preferences among outcomes, assumed to be consistent, but otherwise wholly arbitrary.

Now how can we use this formula to predict behavior? Let us, for example, suppose that a businessman is faced with a demand schedule for the product of his firm (which tells him the amount he can sell at any given price) and a cost schedule (which tells how much it will cost him to produce any given amount). As yet we can conclude nothing about his behavior unless we know what he is trying to accomplish—what his utility function is. *If* we make the additional assumption that his utility is measured by his net profit, then we can instantly predict the quantity he will produce (the quantity that maximizes the difference between total revenue and total cost).[1]

## Difficulties with Economic Optimization

That sounds rather powerful and convenient. A description of the environment (the demand and cost schedules), and an innocent assumption about motives (utility = profit) is all we need to know to predict behavior. No tiresome inquiries into the businessman's mental states or processes.

*Defining Goals.* Complications only begin to arise when we try to apply this model to the real world. How do we know the real businessperson wants to maximize profit? Perhaps he or she wants to maximize the respect received from the community, or the friendliness of workers or of customers. That would lead to very different behavior.

If we think that profit really is the criterion of choice, it cannot be because of any requirement imposed by the task, but because of something stored in the businessperson's head. The content and shape of the utility function can only be determined by empirical study of what goes on in that head. No amount of study of the task environment will help.

We may wish to dismiss this objection as not very fundamental. After all, if we are talking about cognitive tasks, isn't it reasonable to assume, without a

---

[1] I have made this businessman masculine because he is just a caricature of a real human being, neither his sex nor his thought processes affecting his behavior.

great deal of fuss about empirical verification, that people want to perform such tasks as quickly, accurately, and efficiently as possible? For many purposes of experimentation and explanation that's a good enough assumption (though we may have to worry a bit about the speed/accuracy tradeoff), and we make it all the time in our laboratory work.

*Incomplete Information.*   But there are other difficulties, even if we ignore this one. Does the businessperson really know the cost and demand schedules, and know them accurately? When we observe the actual operation of businesses, we find that a great deal of time and effort is devoted to finding out just what these schedules are—how much it will cost to produce the product and how much of it can be sold at different prices. And seldom do businesspeople imagine that they really know the answers to these questions with any accuracy. The real world is filled with large quantities of uncertainty.

At this point the estimates of expected utilities come into play. Where do the subjective probabilities come from? Can we infer these from the task environments, or must we enter the heads of the actors to see how they estimate them (or whether, in fact, they do or don't use anything resembling subjective probabilities in their deliberations)? So in a world where the givens are not really given but must be inferred by the adaptive organism, there is in fact no way in which behavior can be predicted from the external environment without consideration of how that environment is apprehended (and with what accuracies and errors) by the intendedly adaptive actors.

*Generation of Representations and Alternatives.*   Other limitations of the theory of maximization of subjective expected utility are equally important. The theory also assumes the formulation of the problem to be given to the actors, as well as a complete inventory of possible alternatives of action. There is no place in such a theory for a focus of attention or for a search for new alternatives (e.g., for new products, for new markets). The problem representation and the alternatives, like the cost and demand schedules, are assumed to be given as an objective part of the external environment. These heroic assumptions create a further gulf between the optimization theory and the conditions under which real world economic decisions are made.

I have made all of these points elsewhere at much greater length (Simon, 1982, Vol. 2, Secs. VII and VIII), and many others have made them also. Economists today are conscious of a crisis in their discipline that derives directly from these difficulties, but this is not the place to make the case against neo-classical economics, nor to prescribe for its ills.

*Auxiliary Assumptions.*   Before leaving the economic example, however, one other point should be made. In order to restore at least a modicum of realism to their models, and to fit them to the observed phenomena, economists are accustomed to introducing into their reasoning various qualifying assumptions that amount to departures from the model of perfect adaptation. For example, the Keynesian explanation of unemployment hinges essentially on the assumption that labor is "sort of" rational, but not wholly rational. Labor wants higher wages—but fails to distinguish accurately between increases in money wages and increases in real wages. Since it is real wages that buy bread and meat, and not money wages, this failure in discrimination is a genuine irrationality, or imperfect adaptation. Yet it is precisely such grains of irrationality in the economic oyster that produce the pearls of the real-world phenomena—in this case unemployment.

The plain fact is that the conclusions that economists draw from their optimizing models seldom depend critically upon the optimizing assumptions, but they do depend critically upon the auxiliary assumptions of departures from rationality—that is, assumptions of imperfect adaptation. It is these qualifying auxiliary assumptions that do the greatest part of the work in leading economic theories to their conclusions. Change the assumptions, while retaining the postulate of optimization, and you change the conclusions.

Once a behavior has been observed, it is usually rather easy to find some auxiliary assumptions describing circumstances under which the observed behavior is the optimal response. It is especially easy to find such assumptions if we do not require that they be supported by any direct empirical evidence of their presence. And it is even easier if we may introduce new auxiliary assumptions for each new phenomenon we wish to explain. Precautions need to be taken against this kind of adhokery not only in the behavioral sciences, but in the natural sciences as well. As Poincare put it, when discussing some experimental anomalies that arose in physics at the turn of the century: "An explanation was necessary, and was forthcoming; they always are; hypotheses are what we lack the least."

In economics, then, the apparent escape from the study of the psychology of economic actors is illusory. It is not, in fact, possible to predict their behavior solely, or even mainly, from a study of their task environments. Economists have avoided this unpleasant conclusion because they have been willing to make their auxiliary assumptions—their assumptions about human thought processes—from the armchair without requirements of empirical verification. That this kind of "casual empiricism" (the economists' name for it) is rampant in economics is easily verified by examining the professional literature. It is hardly a model for the study of human rationality by other disciplines.

Explanation by means of optimization assumptions is sometimes extolled as a method of great parsimony. But when it is combined with the lavish use of auxiliary assumptions it is far from parsimonious. Unless the phenomena that are explained are numerous and complex, the degrees of freedom provided by the ad hoc assumptions can easily outnumber the data points to be explained.

## Adaptation by Natural Selection

Economics is not the only discipline in which optimization theory plays a central role. In the Darwinian theory of evolution by natural selection, appeal is often made to arguments of optimization. It is sometimes asserted that, by the terms of the theory, only systems that optimize will survive. This assertion has also often been borrowed by neoclassical economists to explain why they need not be concerned with the processes of decision: whatever the processes, only the firms that maximize profits will survive.

When we examine the logic of natural selection more closely, we see that it does not imply optimization at all. All it implies is that if there are two or more organisms competing for the same resources (occupying the same ecological niche), the one that uses the resources most efficiently, in terms of multiplying its numbers (fitness) will replace the others. It does not have to be best in any absolute sense; it need only be better than its competitors.

To use evolutionary theory to predict behavior, we must first know what behaviors are available, for the theory makes no claim that all the relevant behaviors have been discovered or are known to the actors. Before it was opened to European settlement, the biota of Australia had perhaps reached some sort of evolutionary equilibrium. That this equilibrium was not in any sense a global optimum was revealed as soon as rabbits were introduced and showed by multiplying that they were "fitter" than some of the indigenous organisms.

The theory of natural selection is not an optimizing theory for two reasons. First, it can, at best, produce only local optima, because it works by hill-climbing up the nearest slope. It has no mechanism for jumping from peak to peak, hence is likely to be trapped repeatedly on knolls well below the highest summit. Second, it selects only among the alternatives that are available to it, and has no way of guaranteeing that new, and better, alternatives, will not appear from time to time. Indeed, the whole story of biological evolution is a tale of just such successive appearances. So evolution deals with systems that never reach an optimum, and whose definition of the optimum is continually changing.

It is not surprising, therefore, that we see very little prediction in the literature of evolution. What we see are explanations, post hoc, of the observed facts. If the facts were different, we would have no great difficulty in finding another evolutionary explanation for them. There are many adaptive paths to the fitness goal.

For a further elaboration of these arguments, see my *The Sciences of the Artificial*, (1978), "The Evolutionary Model," pages 52–60, which also discusses the myopia of evolution and why it doesn't produce optimization. There is a related discussion in the chapter on "Rationality and Teleology" in my book *Reason in Human Affairs,* (1986) Chapter 2, especially on pages 66–72, where myopia is discussed again.

For our present purposes, the central point—both with respect to evolutionary theory and economic theory that uses auxiliary assumptions—is that "optimization" theories of these kinds do not determine unique solutions or make unique predictions. They lend themselves, therefore, to after-the-fact explanations of what we already know, but provide no convincing evidence that these explanations bear any relation to the real causal mechanisms of processes. To demonstrate causality and to understand process, we cannot limit ourselves to analyzing the environment of behavior, but must study the behaving system, and specifically the limits on its powers of adaption.

## Optimization in Psychology

The idea that adaptive behavior is to be explained by the shape of the environment also has a long history in psychology. Egon Brunswik was an early exponent of this idea (see his [1956] work on the role of the distal stimulus), and it is central to Gibson's (1979) view of perception as it is of Marr's (1982). Anderson has already quoted Marr's view on this point:

> An algorithm is likely to be understood more readily by understanding the nature of the problem being solved than by examining the mechanism (and the hardware) in which it is embodied.

The evolutionary version of the optimization hypothesis, essentially identical with that set forth in standard Darwinian theory, has been espoused by Donald Campbell (1974), and another version of it is to be found in the work of Lumsden and Wilson (1981). In application to psychology, however, the argument for optimization does not have to rely on natural selection among behaviors to produce adaptation. The organism's capabilities for learning and for solving problems provide direct means for adaptation. Of course Campbell points out that learning and problem solving processes, insofar as they employ trial and error, are themselves evolutionary mechanisms that depend on natural selection for their efficacy. An important difference, however, is that in this case the trial and error can take place in mental problem spaces, and does not necessarily rely on experimentation in the real world.

The same objections that have been raised against evolutionary explanations in biology and economics can be raised against their employment in psychology. Evolution (and learning and problem solving) do not guarantee uniqueness of the adapted behavior, much less its optimality. At best they only predict improvement over previous behavior. In no way do they provide adequate explanations of the behavior that actually occurs. Any one of many alternative local optima could be equally well explained, if they occurred, by reference to the environment variables.

## WHAT DOES RATIONALITY IMPLY ABOUT BEHAVIOR?

In my paper, "The Functional Equivalence of Problem Solving Skills," reprinted in Simon (1979), Chapter 4.5, I described four strategies for solving the Tower of Hanoi problem. All four strategies are "rational," in Anderson's sense, since all four produce a solution path, from the usual starting point, of minimum length. From our knowledge of the task environment, therefore, we can predict the solution path that efficient subjects will follow, independent of their strategies and their architectures.

But what *can't* we predict, without additional information about the subject? We can't predict which strategy the subject has learned, although with the help of thinking-aloud protocols, this is ascertainable. We can't predict whether the subject, if interrupted for fifteen seconds, will be able to continue toward the solution without error—that depends on the strategy being used. We can't predict whether the subject will be able to solve the problem efficiently if the number of disks is increased—that also depends upon the strategy, since different amounts of short term memory (an architectural variable, not an environmental one) are needed with different strategies.

Empirically, we find that a plurality of subjects under usual experimental conditions learn the move-pattern strategy. There is nothing in the task environment that implies that this is the strategy that will be learned. Its prevalence seems to derive from the readiness with which subjects notice sequential patterns (1-2-1-3-1-2-1-4-1-2-1-3-etc.) and remember them. This is a function of mental architecture, not of the demands of the task environment.

So while we may agree with Anderson that in this task a "signature," the solution path, can be inferred from the demands of the environment, this signature by no means exhausts our interest in the subjects' behavior. If we are interested in learning and in transfer, we need to know what strategies they adopt. Strategies are aspects of behavior that can be observed empirically without too much trouble. And the learning of strategies, as well as the consequences of employing one strategy rather than another, are functions of cognitive architecture. Since they vary with the architecture, they can be used to infer properties of the architecture.

### Some Counterexamples?

Up to this point, I have been proceeding mainly on the high road of theory, trying to show why it is impossible in principle to explain adaptive behavior simply by examining the structure of the task environment. But John Anderson has provided us with three actual, and ingenious, examples of such explanation. The empiricism I have been espousing would argue that hypothetical reasoning must yield to valid counterexamples.

What are the facts? Do Anderson's models explain the phenomena he describes as optimal responses to the task requirements? Or is the real work in his models being done by auxiliary assumptions? And even if it turns out that certain "signature" data can be predicted without much reference to architecture, do we wish to limit ourselves to these data, and are there other ways of inferring what the underlying architecture and strategies really are? Let us examine the models one by one.

## The Power Law in Learning

In the first example, an optimization model is built to predict the relation between practice and speed of performance in the Seibel task, the relation being linear on a logarithmic scale. Anderson postulates a memory of independent items that are accessed through a key word index. (We see that a number of architectural assumptions, although rather general ones, have to be made at the outset. The model does not by any means derive its power solely from knowledge of the requirements of the task.) It is further assumed that there is a cost associated with retrieving each successive item, and a cost associated with failing to retrieve the desired item. Finally there is associated with each item a probability that the item is a desired one, and it is assumed that this probability is known, at least ordinally, by the processor. (In fact, the derivation of the log-linear relation assumes that the cardinal values of the probabilities are known.)

*Probability of Retrieval.*    The optimization principle is to retrieve items in order of decreasing probability until the expected gain from retrieving the next item is less than the cost of retrieving it. From this principle, and using a number of auxiliary assumptions that I will mention in a moment, Anderson shows that this probability will be a linear function of the number of times the item has been used in the past.

*Practice and Latency.*    But we still do not have a prediction of the observed relation between practice and latency. This is then obtained by the additional derivational step that "under the transformation from need probability to latency proposed in Anderson (1990) the power function relationship remains." In the source cited, Anderson derives the transformation from the assumption that the need probabilities of items are distributed according to Zipf's law, a law that has been found empirically to fit a wide range of not unrelated phenomena. The Zipf's law assumption is quite plausible, but it is an empirical assumption, not an optimization assumption. Zipf's law is clearly doing as much of the work as is the optimization assumption.

The structure of the argument, then, is this. By use of the optimization principle with numerous auxiliary assumptions, we infer a linear relation between practice and probability of retrieval. Then, with another assumption, we derive a monotonic relation of appropriate shape between probability and latency. From this it follows that latency and practice are connected by a power law. Would it not be simpler, and more parsimonious, simply to postulate the latter law without deriving it? But whether that law holds or not is a matter of how the memory functions, and not a simple consequence of optimization.

*The Auxiliary Assumptions.*    I must return briefly to the other auxiliary assumptions that are made in the course of the optimization argument. There appear to be about four of these. The first is embedded in Anderson's equation (2), and determines how the need probabilities change in the course of repeated memory searches—a very specific Bayesian assumption, describing one of a large number of possible inductive rules. The second is that items are distributed by desirability according to the gamma function—a very specific assumption, buttressed by some evidence from library systems. The third is that usage of items decays exponentially. The fourth is that repeated retrievals of items are distributed according to the Poisson process. These last three are assumptions about the structure of the task environment, and are empirically testable.

The conclusion that need probability varies linearly with number of uses is primarily due to the first and fourth assumptions, and is probably not very sensitive to the others. The two critical assumptions, rather than the optimization criterion, are doing most of the work of the derivation, and the first assumption is a specification of architecture or strategy, not of environment.

Notice that in the Seibel task, all needed items are actually retrieved. Hence, there is no question of stopping the search when the cost of retrieving an item is too large. It seems odd to base the derivation of the relation between frequency of past use and latency on the optimization of this inoperative mechanism.

*Further Predictions of the Model.*    But Anderson makes additional claims of parsimony for his derivation. From it he obtains two other empirically observed effects: a forgetting function, and familiar effects of massed and distributed practice. The forgetting effect derives directly from inserting an exponential decay function among the auxiliary assumptions, and is surely derivable from the latter without any optimization. But the decay function is motivated by our knowledge that, empirically, there is memory decay, and is an assumption about architecture, not about task requirements. No parsimony here.

Likewise, the derivation of effects of spacing of practice requires two additional auxiliary assumptions—that memory for some items decays faster than memory for others, and that the relevance of items is revived periodically. The first of these assumptions is architectural. Anderson does not show in detail how the spacing effect is derived from these assumptions, but it may be inferred that the opportunity for items to be revived over longer time intervals is at the root of it.

The explanation of the data in the Seibel task, and the others that are discussed in connection with the model, provides something less than a convincing demonstration of the power of the model, or its parsimony. Its ability to postdict some empirical phenomena is not at all independent of architectural assumptions, and no more independent of the numerous auxiliary assumptions that have to be introduced along the way. It would appear that equally convincing post hoc characterizations of the data can be derived from these auxiliary assumptions without the aid of the optimization procedure. But these characterizations are not explanations in any deep sense. They are simply summaries of the empirically observed phenomena.

## The Fan Effect

In his second example of the prediction of "signatures" from optimization in a specified task environment, Anderson uses the same model as before of the effects of practice on the need probability of items in memory. He now employs the model to show that "the fan effect is a consequence of memory using the correlation between cues and a memory's relevance to predict when the memory is needed." That is to say, people "optimize" by keeping better access to memories that are likely to be relevant.

What is notable about this example is that the prediction is quite bland, and certainly does not require anything as strong as an optimization assumption to derive it. Anderson is correct in asserting that little can be inferred from it about architecture—*Any* architecture that kept items close at hand on the basis of recent or frequent use would do the trick. Any such architecture would exhibit the *Einstellung* effect as well!

The conclusion to be drawn is not that we can substitute optimization procedures for an understanding of architecture. Rather, it is that we need to look at more subtle phenomena—for example, detailed thinking-aloud protocols of individual subjects—if we want to learn about architecture and to discriminate among different architectures. We need to detect architecture, not with a few "signatures," but with a wide range of converging phenomena. Feigenbaum and I (1984) have used just such a strategy to examine the validity of the EPAM model, which we have proposed as a (partial) architecture for human memory.

## Categorization

The structure of the argument for Anderson's third example is very similar to that for the fan effect. Human beings, given repeated learning trials, gradually acquire skill in categorizing objects. If the learning time is long enough, and the set of objects not too complex, they may even learn to categorize them "optimally" by some external criterion. (The fact that many biologists since Linnaeus have spent their professional careers modifying and improving plant and animal taxonomies is perhaps evidence that in the real world optimality of systems of categories doesn't come quickly or easily.)

Anderson now shows that he can define an algorithm (a search procedure that optimizes, if at all, only asymptotically) that will improve its categorizations much as people do. Undoubtedly there are many such algorithms. What we really wish to know is which of these are actually used by people in learning to categorize. We are not interested in what categories they will ultimately learn: That is not psychology but botany or entomology or whatever science the phenomena belong to. Our interest is in the learning process itself—not a hypothetical one or an optimal one, but the one that people use. We want a learning theory precisely because people do not arrive at optimal classifications immediately or costlessly. We wish to understand what sly tricks they use to arrive at classifications at all, and what prospects there are for improvement of the process.

The example illustrates once again that the interesting and important issues for psychology are not to demonstrate that people are motivated to behave rationally when the circumstances are simple enough to make such behavior possible. The interesting issues are precisely to determine what internal limits (computational or other) prevent people from attaining optimality, or attaining it rapidly and costlessly, and to understand how people use the computational capabilities they have in order to cope with these limits.

## OPTIMIZATION OR BOUNDED RATIONALITY?

Bounded rationality is what cognitive psychology is all about. And the study of bounded rationality is not the study of optimization in relation to task environments. It is the study of how people acquire strategies for coping with those environments, how those strategies emerge out of problem space definitions, and how built-in physiological limits shape and constrain the acquisition of problem spaces and strategies. At each of these steps there is room for alternative processes, any of which would meet satisfactorily (not optimally) the requirements of the task environment. The environment cannot predict which of these alternatives will govern the adaptive behavior.

I would repeat for cognitive psychology what I said, more than forty years ago about organization theory (*Administrative Behavior,* p. 240):

> . . . if there were no limits to human rationality, administrative theory [read: cognitive theory] would be barren. It would consist of the single precept: Always select the alternative, among those available, which will lead to the most complete achievement of your goals. The need for an administrative theory [cognitive theory] resides in the fact that there *are* practical limits to human rationality, and that these limits are not static, but depend upon the . . . environment in which the individual's decision takes place.

## The Two-Bladed Scissors

The moral to be drawn from our discussion is not that the task environment is unimportant in explaining the behavior of an adaptive system, but that one must consider both the task environment and the limits upon the adaptive powers of the system. Only in the simplest cases will the system behavior be predictable from an optimization argument. Almost always, structure and limits to adaptation will, to some degree, "show through," and hence will have to be taken into account. The outer environment and the inner structure are the two blades of the scissors, and both blades must be present and operative for a satisfactory dissection of what is going on.

In writing the final, theoretical, chapter of *Human Problem Solving,* Allen Newell and I were confronted with the same problem of defining the *laws* of the behavior of adaptive, thinking, organisms. How could there be such laws if problem solvers were adaptive? Our proposed resolution of the problem can be found on pages 788 to 789 of our book. I will give its flavor by quoting a couple of passages, adding comments in square brackets.

> . . . The task environment (plus the intelligence of the problem solver) determines to a large extent the behavior of the problem solver, independently of the detailed internal structure of his information processing system. [So far we are in agreement with Anderson.]
>
> . . . A few, and only a few, gross characteristics of the human IPS are invariant over task and problem solver.
>
> These characteristics are sufficient to determine that a task environment is represented (in the IPS) as a problem space, and that problem solving takes place in a problem space. [problem space = representation.]
>
> The structure of the task environment determines the possible structures of the problem space. [The representation is not uniquely determined, but only constrained by the task environment.]
>
> The structure of the problem space determines the possible programs [strategies] that can be used for problem solving. [The strategy is not uniquely determined, but only constrained by task environment and problem space.]

The two blades of the scissors, in this formulation, are (a) the task environment and (b) the problem space conjoined with the strategy used for searching it. It is the organism that constructs a problem space and strategy to deal with the task environment. The problem space and strategy are usually adapted to the task, but in a much weaker sense than optimization.

Among the computational limits that are important in shaping behavior are limits on the capacity of short-term memory, the presence or absence of external memory aids, the failure of human subjects to use best-first search (primarily because of short-term memory limits), and the general absence of any optimization processes for selecting problem representations.

Moreover, representations and strategies are not usually given, but have to be discovered by the problem solver. Nor are they unique; in a particular task domain, many satisfactory (not optimal) alternatives may be potentially available. Which particular representations and strategies will be discovered by particular subjects and under what circumstances cannot be predicted from a knowledge of the task structure, but depends on the other blade of the scissors as well.

The evidence that has been gathered over the past decade or more on differences in difficulty of problems that have isomorphic task domains (Kotovsky, Hayes, & Simon, 1986; Kotovsky & Simon, 1990) provides a striking example of the inadequacy of a one-bladed scissors for explaining problem-solving performance. The fact that one form of a problem can require, on average, sixteen times as much effort to solve as another isomorph of the same problem cannot be readily explained with principles of optimization. We have to discover what limitations of the problem solver prevent him or her, in the more difficult case, from proceeding in exactly the same manner as in the easier one, the two being fully isomorphic.

In those situations where behavior that is optimal can be learned and where the behavior of the expert can properly be described as optimal, it may still be of great interest to understand how someone progresses from novice to expert performance—that is, how learning takes place. But the very notion of "optimal" learning is ambiguous. Presumably optimal learning would be instant learning, and since very little human learning takes place instantly, we need to understand the internal limitations to adaptation that constrain its speed.

## Detecting Architectures and Strategies

I am more sanguine than is Anderson that empirical evidence can discriminate among cognitive strategies and among cognitive architectures, and can show some to be more acceptable than others as models of human information processing. But to accomplish this we have to confront the adaptive systems we are studying with complex tasks that will stretch their abilities to behave "optimally," and will reveal the structural limits on their adaptation.

It may well be that in many cases where adaptation to the external environment is reasonably effective, "signature data" will be predictable from the requirements of the situation. If people are adding up columns of figures (under circumstances where they usually get the right answers), then the sums they write down will be predictable in the manner that Anderson describes. The conclusion I would draw, however, is not that the process or the architecture of the system reaching the result is inscrutable. My conclusion would be that we need data other than these "signature data" to discover what the process and architecture are.

To identify mechanisms, strategic and structural, we cannot be satisfied with aggregated data of total performance (speed of performance, aggregate accuracy or success), but have to observe as many details of the ongoing processes as we can. Classical static experimental designs have to give way to studies of dynamic processes, observed through the recording of protocols, eye movements, the details of errors, and such other means as our ingenuity may suggest. It is along this route that we can solve the difficult problems of identifiability that always confront us in trying to understand the mechanisms that adaptive systems employ in achieving their ends.

### Final Comment: Mind and Brain

My discussion, as well as Anderson's, has been carried on wholly at the level of symbolic information processes. Neither of us has mentioned, though we surely both believe, that thinking is implemented by a biological organ called the brain. Architecture is simply a high-level description of the brain in terms of its information-processing properties. To claim that architecture is more notation than substance is to make the same claim for the brain—the fact that it supports adaptive behavior makes unnecessary any curiosity about how it operates.

Now such a claim is not wholly outrageous. In fact, a weaker form of the same claim is at the root of the idea that human thinking can be simulated (its processes as well as its outcomes) by computer. The exact ways in which neurons accomplish their functions is not important—only their functional capabilities and the organization of these. Nothing else will show through to "behavior."

But what does show through is precisely what we have been calling "architecture." And for that reason architecture is by no means all notation; it has real substance in its effects on behavior. In my view, Anderson assigns too little weight to architecture (and by implication to strategies) as determinants of adaptive behavior.

## ACKNOWLEDGMENTS

This research was supported by the Personnel and Training Programs. Psychological Sciences Division, Office of Naval Research, under Contract No. N00014-86-K-0768; and by the Defense Advanced Research Projects Agency, Department of Defense, ARPA Order 3597, monitored by the Air Force Avionics Laboratory under contract F33615-81-K-1539. Reproduction in whole or in part is permitted for any purpose of the United States Government. Approved for public release; distribution unlimited.

## REFERENCES

Anderson, J. R. (1990). *The adaptive character of thought*. Hillsdale, NJ: Lawrence Erlbaum Associates.
Brunswik, E. (1956). *Perception and the representative design of psychological experiments*. Berkeley, CA: University of California Press.

Campbell, D. T. (1974). Evolutionary epistemology. In P. A. Schilpp (Ed.), *The philosophy of Karl Popper*. La Salle, IL: Open Court.

Feigenbaum, E. A., & Simon, H. A. (1984). EPAM-like models of recognition and learning. *Cognitive Science, 8,* 305–336.

Gibson, J. J. (1979). *The ecological approach to visual perception*. Boston MA: Houghton-Mifflin.

Kotovsky, K., Hayes, J. R., & Simon, H. A. (1985). Why are some problems hard? *Cognitive Psychology, 17,* 248–292.

Kotovsky, K., & Simon, H. A. (1990). What makes some problems really hard: Explorations in the problem space of difficulty. *Cognitive Psychology, 22,* 143–183.

Lumsden, C. J., & Wilson, E. O. (1981). *Genes, mind and culture*. Cambridge, MA: Harvard University Press.

Marr, D. (1982). *Vision*. San Francisco, CA: W. H. Freeman.

Newell, A., & Simon, H. A. (1972). *Human problem solving*. Englewood Cliffs, NJ: Prentice-Hall.

Simon, H. A. (1947). *Administrative behavior*. New York: Macmillan.

Simon, H. A. (1978). *The sciences of the artificial* (2nd ed.). Cambridge, MA: MIT Press.

Simon, H. A. (1979). *Models of thought*. New Haven, CT: Yale University Press.

Simon, H. A. (1982). *Models of bounded rationality* (Vol. 2). Cambridge, MA: MIT Press.

Simon, H. A. (1986). *Reason in human affairs*. Stanford, CA: Stanford University Press.

# 3

# Nature, Nurture, and Connections: Implications of Connectionist Models for Cognitive Development

James L. McClelland
Eric Jenkins
*Carnegie Mellon University*

When it comes to selecting an architecture for modeling cognition, we have a choice. We can start with a symbolic architecture, in which the putative constituents of abstract cognition (symbols) are taken as modeling primitives; or we may adopt an alternative view, that symbolic *behavior* emerges from the operation of a system of simple, sub-symbolic processing units. Connectionist models take this latter tack. In these models, processing occurs through the propagation of activation among a number of simple processing units. The knowledge that governs processing is stored in the strengths of the connections among the units. And learning occurs through the gradual adjustment of the strengths of these connections. At first glance it may seem that such mechanisms are far removed from symbolic thought. Yet we will argue in this chapter that they may form the basis of the acquisition of a number of cognitive abilities, and that they may help us answer basic questions about the process of cognitive development. Several different kinds of answers have been given to these questions. We will see how the connectionist framework opens them anew and suggests what may be different answers in many cases.

## THE PHENOMENA

The field of cognitive development is replete with examples of dramatic changes in children's thinking as they grow older. Here we give three examples: (a) Failures of conservation and compensation, (b) Progressive differentiation of knowledge about different kinds of things, (c) U-shaped learning curves in language acquisition.

## Failures of Conservation and Compensation

Perhaps the best known phenomena in cognitive development are the dramatic failures of conservation that Piaget has reported in a wide range of different domains. One domain is the domain of liquid quantity. A child of 3 is shown two glasses of water. The glasses are the same, and each contains the same amount of water, and the child sees that the amount is the same. But when the contents of one of the glasses is poured into a wider container, the child will say that there is less liquid in the wider container.

It is typical to say that this answer that the young child gives reflects a failure to recognize two things: (a) That quantity is conserved under the transformation of pouring from one container to another; and (b) that greater width can compensate for less height. Many tasks are specifically designed to tap into the child's ability to cope with these kinds of compensation relations between variables.

One such task developed by Inhelder and Piaget (1958), the so-called *balance-scale task,* is illustrated in Fig. 3.1. In this task, the child is shown a balance scale with pegs at evenly spaced intervals to the left and right of a fulcrum. On one peg on the left are several weights; on one peg on the right are several weights. The scale is immobilized, and the child is asked to judge which side will go down, or whether they will balance. We will have occasion to examine performance in this task at length below; for now it suffices to note that young children (up to about 6 or 7 in this case) typically respond as if the distance from the fulcrum was completely irrelevant. They will say the scale should balance if the weight is the same on both sides, regardless of distance. Otherwise they say the side with the greater weight will go down. These children, then, appear to miss the fact that lesser weight can be compensated for by greater distance. Typically by the age of 11 or so children have some appreciation for this trade off; the details of the developmental progression are quite interesting, as we shall see below.

## Progressive Differentiation of Ontological Categories

Other researchers, studying different domains, have noticed other kinds of developmental progressions. Keil (1979) studied children's judgements about whether you could say things like "A rabbit is an hour long." He supposed such judgments tapped children's knowledge about different kinds of things. In these

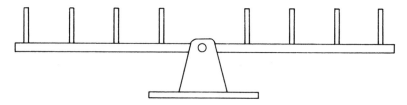

FIG. 3.1.   Balance scale of the kind first used by Inhelder and Piaget (1958), and later used extensively by Siegler (1976; 1981; Siegler & Klahr, 1982). Reprinted from Siegler, 1976, Fig. 1, with permission.

judgments, Keil was interested not in whether the child saw a sentence as true or false, but in whether the child felt that one could make certain kinds of predications (e.g., that something is an hour long) when the something is a member of a certain "ontological category" (e.g., living thing). Keil found that children were much more permissive in their acceptance of statements than adults were, but their permissiveness was not simply random. Rather, they would accept statements that over-extended predicates to categories near the ones they typically apply to, but would not extend them further. Thus some children will accept predications like "The rock is asleep," but not "The rock is an hour long." It was as though children's knowledge of what predicates apply to particular categories becomes progressively more and more differentiated, as illustrated in Fig. 3.2.

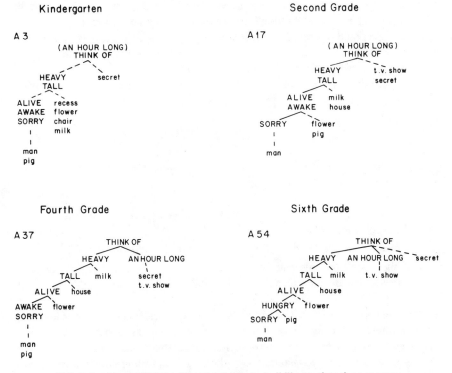

FIG. 3.2. Four different "predictability trees" illustrating the progressive differentiation of concepts as a function of age. Terms in capitals at internal nodes in the trees represent predicates, and terms in lower case at terminal nodes in the trees represent concepts that are spanned by all the predicates written on nodes that dominate the terminal. A predicate spans a concept if the child reports that it is not silly to apply either the predicate or its negation or both to the concept. Thus the first tree indicates that the child will accept "The girl is (not) alive," and "The chair is (not) tall" but will not accept "The chair is (not) alive." Parentheses indicate uncertainty about the application of a predicate. Redrawn from Keil, 1979, Appendix C, with permission.

## U-Shaped Learning Curves in Language Development

Early on children often get certain kinds of linguistic constructions correct which they later get wrong; only later do they recover their former correct performance. One example is the passive construction, applied to semantically biased materials, such as "The man was bitten by the dog." (See Bever, 1970, for a discussion of the development of the use of the passive construction.) Early in development, children correctly interpret such sentences; they appear to be using information about what roles the different nouns typically play in the action described by the verb, since they tend to be correct only when the correct interpretation assigns the nouns to their typical roles. At an older age, children respond differently to such sentences, treating the first noun-phrase as the subject; semantic constraints are over-ridden, and there is a tendency to interpret "The man was bitten by the dog" as meaning "The man bit the dog." Finally, children interpret the sentence correctly again, but for a different reason. It would appear that they now know how to understand passives in general, since at this stage they can also interpret semantically neutral and even reverse-biased sentences (such as "the dog was bitten by the man") correctly.

## THE QUESTIONS

The phenomena reviewed above raise basic questions about cognitive development. Three of these questions are:

- Are these different phenomena simply unrelated facts about development in different domains?
- Are there principles that all of these phenomena exemplify?
- If there are principles, are they domain specific, or are they general principles about development?

Different kinds of developmental theorists have answered such questions in very different ways. To Piaget, each failure of compensation or conservation reflected a single common developmental stage; the phenomena were intrinsically related by the characteristics of the stage, and these characteristics provided the basis for explanation.

Others have taken a very different approach. Keil (1979), following Chomsky's analogous argument for language, argued for *domain specific principles* of development. His view is that each cognitive domain has its own laws that provide constraints on what can be learned. These constraints limit the hypotheses that the child can entertain, thereby making it dramatically easier for the child to acquire adult abilities in the face of the impoverished information that is provided by experience with the world.

The main thrust of the remainder of this chapter is to argue that recent developments in connectionist learning procedures suggest a dramatic alternative to these kinds of views. The alternative is simply the hypothesis that these diverse developmental phenomena all reflect the operation of a single basic learning principle, operating in different tasks and different parts of the cognitive system.

## THE LEARNING PRINCIPLE

The principle can be stated in fairly abstract terms as follows:

> Adjust the parameters of the mind in proportion to the extent to which their adjustment can produce a reduction in the discrepancy between expected and observed events.

This principle is not new. It might well be seen as capturing the residue of Piaget's accommodation process, in that accommodation involves an adjustment of mental structures in response to discrepancies. (See Flavell, 1963, for a discussion of Piaget's theory.) It is also very similar to the principle that governs learning in the Rescorla-Wagner model of classical conditioning (Rescorla & Wagner, 1972). What is new is that there exists a learning procedure for multi-layer connectionist networks that implements this principle. Here, the parameters of the mind are the connections among the units in the network, and the procedure is the back propagation procedure of Rumelhart, Hinton, and Williams (1986).

The learning principle lies at the heart of a number of connectionist models that learn how to do various different kinds of information processing tasks, and that have applications to phenomena in cognitive and/or language development. Perhaps the simplest such model is the past-tense model of Rumelhart and McClelland (1986). The development of that model predated the discovery of the back propagation learning procedure, thereby forcing certain simplifications for the sake of developing an illustration of the basic point that lawful behavior might emerge from the application of a simple principle of learning to a connectionist network. Subsequent models have used back propagation to overcome some of these limitations. Included in this class are NETtalk (Sejnowski & Rosenberg, 1987) and a more recent model of word reading (Patterson, Seidenberg, & McClelland, 1989). The present effort grew out of two observations of similarities between the developmental courses seen in models embodying this principle, and the courses of development seen in children: First, the course of learning in a recent model of concept learning by Rumelhart (1990) is similar to aspects of the progressive differentiation of concepts reflected in Keil's (1979) studies of predictability. Second, the course of learning in a recent model of sentence comprehension by McClelland, St. John, and Taraban (1989) mirrors aspects of the progression from reliance on semantic constraints, to reliance on word order, to, finally, reliance on complex syntactic patterning such as the passive voice. We do not mean to claim that the models in question are fully adequate models of the developmental progression in either case; we only mean to claim that they seemed suggestive: They raised the possibility that part of the explanation of these and other developmental phenomena might be found in the operation of the learning principle as it adjusts connection strengths in a network subjected to patterns arising in its environment.

The remainder of this chapter presents two experiments assessing the applicability of this conjecture to another developmental phenomenon, namely the acquisition of the ability to take both weight and distance into account in the balance scale task described above. The task has been studied extensively by Siegler and his colleagues (Siegler, 1976, 1981; Siegler & Klahr, 1982), and quite a bit is known about it. We will first review the developmental findings. Then we will describe a connectionist model that captures these phenomena by applying the learning principle stated above (McClelland, 1989). As a follow-up, we will describe a second model that captures effects of specific experience on developmental change (Jenkins, 1986).

## DEVELOPMENT OF JUDGMENTS OF BALANCE

In an important monograph, Siegler (1981) studied children's performance in the balance scale task and three other tasks in which two cues had to be taken into account for correct performance. In all cases, as in the balance scale task, the correct procedure requires multiplication. For example, in the balance scale task, to determine which side will go down, one must multiply the amount of weight on a given side of the beam times the distance of that weight from the fulcrum. The side with the greater product will go down; when the products are the same, the beam will balance.

Siegler studied children in several age groups, as well as young adults. Each child was asked to judge 24 balance problems. In each case, the scale was immobilized so that there was no feedback. The 24 problems could be divided into four of each six types:

- Balance. In this class of problem, the weight is the same on both sides of the scale and the weight is the same distance from the fulcrum on both sides.

- Weight. In these problems, the weights differ but distance from the fulcrum is the same on both sides.

- Distance. Here the weight is the same on both sides, but the distance from the fulcrum differs.

- Conflict. Here both weight and distance differ and are in conflict, in that the weight is greater on one side but the distance from the fulcrum is greater on the other. There are three types of conflict problems:
  - Conflict–weight. In these cases, the side with the greater weight has the greater torque (that is, the greater value of the product of weight times distance).
  - Conflict–distance. In these cases, the side with the greater distance has the greater torque.
  - Conflict–balance. Here the torques are the same on both sides.

Siegler's analysis of children's performance assumed that children use rule-governed procedures. Four such procedures or *rules* as Siegler called them are shown in Fig. 3.3. Each of these rules corresponds to a distinct pattern of performance over the six problem types. For example, children using Rule 1 should say the side with the greater weight will go down in weight problems and in all three types of conflict problems. They should think the scale will balance on balance problems and distance problems. In general, the mapping from the rules to expected performance is extremely straightforward. The only point that needs explication is the instruction *muddle through* when weight and distance conflict in Rule 3. In practice it is assumed to mean "guess randomly among the alternatives," so that 1/3 of the responses would be left-side-down; 1/3 right-side-down, and 1/3 balance.

Siegler compared the performance of each child tested with each rule, and counted discrepancies from predicted performance based on the rule. Children who scored less than four discrepancies from a given rule were scored as using that rule.

For our purposes, there are four basic findings that emerge from Siegler's analysis:

1.  Lawful behavior. In general, performance of children over the age of 5 is extremely regular in the balance scale task. Overall about 90% of children tested conform to one of the four rules.

2.  Developmental progression. As children get older, they appear to progress through the use of the different rules. The progression from Rule 1 to Rule 3 can be thought of as a progression in which at first the weight cue is relied on exclusively, while at the end distance and weight are both taken into account. In between (Rule 2), distance is taken into account only if it does not conflict with the weight cue. Children aged 5 to 7 typically use Rule 1, and college students typically use rules 3 or 4. Many college students do not have explicit knowledge of the torque principle. Children younger than age 5 tend not to be scorable strictly in terms of one of the rules; however, they appear to show an increasing tendency to behave in accordance with Rule 1.

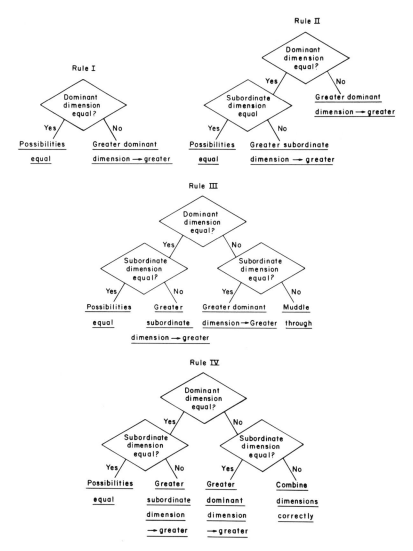

FIG. 3.3. Siegler's (1976, 1981) four "rules" for answering balance scale problems. Each Rule is in fact a full procedure, rather than a single rule. Reprinted with permission from Siegler (1981), Fig. 1.

3. Generality. The same four rules appear to be adequate to characterize performance in all three of the domains that Siegler studied. Though the developmental progression was not identical across domains, there was in all cases a trend from simpler to more complex rules with development.

4. Lack of correlation between domains. Even though children seem to progress through the same rules in different domains, they do not do so in lock-step; the correlation across domains is low, particularly in terms of the higher-num-

bered rules, so that children who are showing Rule 3 behavior in one task may be showing Rule 1 behavior in another and Rule 4 in a third.

## MODEL OF THE BASIC PHENOMENA

The model we describe here was developed by McClelland (1989). It is based on earlier work by Jenkins (1986) relevant to other aspects of Siegler's data (Siegler, 1976; Siegler & Klahr, 1982) to which we will turn our attention below.

The model is sketched in Fig. 3.4. Of course, the model is a drastic over-simplification of the human mind and of the task; but as we shall see it allows us to capture the essence of Siegler's findings, and to see them emerge from the operation of the learning principle described above.

The model consists of a set of input units, to which balance problems can be presented as patterns of inputs; a set of output units over which the answer to

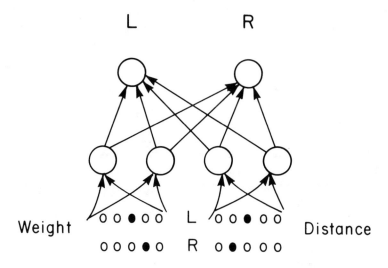

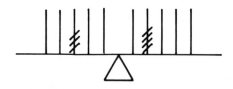

FIG. 3.4.  The network used in the simulation of the development of performance in the balance scale task.

each problem can be represented; and a set of hidden units, between the input and the output. Connections run from input units to hidden units and from hidden units to output units.

The input units can be divided into two groups of 10. One group is used to represent information about weight and the other is used to represent information about distance. In each case the input representation imposes as little structure as possible on the input patterns. Each possible value of weight or distance from the fulcrum is assigned a separate unit. The ordering of values from low to high is not given in this representation; the network will have to learn this ordering. For the convenience of the reader, the units are arranged in rows according to which side of the beam they are from, and within each row they are arranged from left to right in order of increasing weight or distance from the fulcrum; but this ordering is unknown to the model before it is trained, as we shall see.

Though the two dimensions are not intrinsically structured for the model, the design of the network does impose a separate analysis of each dimension. This separation turns out to be critical; we will consider the implications of this architectural simplification below. The separation is implemented as follows: there are separate pairs of hidden units for each dimension. Two hidden units receive input from the weight input units and two receive input from the distance input units.

Each of the four hidden units projects to each of the two output units. The left output unit can be thought of as a "left side down" unit, and the right one as a "right side down unit." Thus a correct network for the task would turn on the output unit corresponding to the side with the greater torque, and would turn off the unit for the other side. For balance problems, we assume that the network should turn both units on half-way. Note that this coding of the output patterns does tell the network that balance is between left side down and right side-down.

*Processing.*   Balance problems of the kind studied by Siegler can be processed by the network by simply turning on (i.e., setting to 1) the input units corresponding to a particular problem and turning off (i.e., setting to 0) all other input units. The input from the problem illustrated in Figure 3.7 is shown by using black to indicate those input units whose activations are 1.0, and white for the units whose activations are 0.

The inputs are propagated forward to the hidden units. Each hidden unit simply computes a net input:

$$net_i = \sum_j w_{ij}a_j + bias_i.$$

Here $j$ ranges over the input units. Each hidden unit then sets its activation according to the logistic function:

$$a_i = \frac{1}{1 + e^{-net_i}}$$

In these equations, $w_{ij}$ is the strength of the connection to hidden unit $i$ from input unit $j$, $a_j$ is the activation of input unit $j$, and $bias_i$ is the modifiable bias of hidden unit $i$. This bias is equivalent to a weight to unit $i$ from a special unit that is always on.

Once activations of the hidden units are determined, the activations of the output units are determined by the same procedure. That is, the net input to each output unit is determined based on the activations of the hidden units, the weights from the hidden units to the output units, and the biases of the output units. Then the activations of the output units are determined using the logistic function.

*Responses.*    The activations of the output units are real numbers between 0 and 1; to relate its performance to the balance scale task, these real-valued outputs must be translated into discrete responses. If the activation of one output unit exceeded the activation of the other by .333, the answer was taken to be "more active side down." Otherwise, the answer was assumed to be "both sides equal."

*Learning.*    Before training begins, the strengths of these connections from input to hidden units and from hidden to output units are initialized to random values uniformly distributed between $+.5$ and $-.5$. In this state, inputs lead to random patterns of activity over both the hidden and output units. The activations of the output units fluctuate approximately randomly between about .4 and .6 for different input patterns. The network comes to respond correctly only as a result of training. Conceptually, training is thought of as occurring as a result of a series of experiences in which the network is shown a balance problem as input; computes activations of output patterns based on its existing connection weights; and is then shown the correct answer. The signal that drives learning is the difference between the obtained activation of each output unit and the correct or target activation for that unit. The back-propagation procedure of Rumelhart, Hinton, and Williams (1986) is then used to determine how each connection strength in the network should be adjusted to reduce these differences. Since the procedure is quite well-known, suffice it to say that it exactly implements the learning principle stated above, and restated here in network terminology:

> Adjust each weight in the network in proportion to the extent to which its adjustment can produce a reduction in the discrepancy between the expected event and the observed event, in the present context.

Here the "expected event" is the pattern of activation over the output units that is computed by the network, the observed event is the pattern of activation the environment indicates these units have, and the present context is the pattern of activation over the input units. Note that the direction of change to a connection (positive or negative) is simply the direction than tends to reduce the discrepancy between computed output and the correct or target output.

*Environment.* The environment in which a network learns plays a very strong role in determining what it learns, and particularly the developmental course of learning. The simulations reported here were based on the assumption that the environment for learning about balance problems consists of experiences that vary more frequently on the weight dimension than they do on the distance dimension. Of course, we do not mean to suggest that all the learning that children do that is relevant to their understanding of balance takes the form of explicit balance problems of the kind our network sees. Rather, our assumption that the experience on balance problems is dominated by problems in which there is no variability in weight is meant as a proxy for the more general assumption that children generally have more experiences with weight than with distance as a factor in determining the relative heaviness of something.[1]

The specific assumptions about the sequence of learning experiences were as follows. The environment consisted of a list of training examples containing the full set of 625 possible problems involving 25 combinations of possible weights (1 to 5 on the left crossed with 1 to 5 on the right) crossed with 25 combinations of possible distances (1 to 5 steps from the fulcrum on the left crossed with 1 to 5 steps from the fulcrum on the right). Two corpora were set up. Problems in which the distance from the fulcrum was the same on both sides were listed 5 times each in one corpus, and 10 times each in the other corpus. Other problems were listed only once in each corpus.

*Training and testing regime.* Four simulation runs were carried out, two with each of the two corpora just described. In each run, training consisted of a series of epochs. In each epoch, 100 patterns were chosen randomly from the full list of patterns in the corpus. In each epoch, weight increments were accumulated over the 100 training trials and then added into the weights at the end of the epoch, according to the momentum method described in Rumelhart, Hinton, and Williams (1986 p. 330); parameters were $\eta = 0.075$, $\alpha = .9$).

After weight updating at the end of each epoch, the network was given a 24 item test, containing four problems of each of the six types described above, taken from an experiment of Siegler's. (A few of the examples had to be modified since Siegler's experiment had used up to six pegs.)

## A Comment on the Simulation Model

The model described above obviously simplifies the task that the learner faces and structures it for him to some degree. In particular, it embodies two principal assumptions which are crucial to the successful simulations we will consider below:

---

[1]An alternative assumption which might account for the developmental data just as well is the assumption that the weight dimension is pre-structured before the child comes to consider balance problems, while the distance dimension is not. The assumption that distance varies less frequently than weight but that neither dimension is initially structured allows us to observe the structuring process for both dimensions.

*Environment Assumption.*    The model assumes that the environment is biased, so that one dimension—in this case weight—is more frequently available as a basis for predicting outcome than the other.

*Architecture Assumption.*    The model assumes that the weight and distance dimensions are analyzed separately, before information about the two dimensions is combined.

Both of these assumptions are crucial to the success of the model. In an unbiased environment, both cues would be learned equally rapidly. Effects of combining the cues from the start as prescribed by the architecture assumption are more complex, but suffice it to say for now that the apparent stagelike character of performance is much less clear unless this assumption is adopted.

An important topic for further research will be to examine what variants of these assumptions might still allow the model to be successful. For example, regarding the environment, differences in salience (i.e., strength of input activations) and structuredness of the dimensions might also produce similar results.

The issue of structuredness of the dimensions is a key point that needs to be considered as it relates to the present simulation. For both dimensions, the input representations encode different weights and distances from the fulcrum using distinct units. This means that different values are distinguishable by the model, but they are not structured for it; for example the input itself provides no indication that a distance or weight of 3 is between 2 and 4. The network must learn to represent the weights and distances in structured ways in order to solve the balance problem. We will see that it does this later.

## Results

In general performance of the model conformed to one of the four rules described by Siegler. Over the four runs, the model fit the criteria of one of Siegler's four rules on 85% of the occasions, not counting an initial pre–Rule 1 period (In Siegler, 1981, the conformity figure is about 90%). Of course, the model was not consulting these rules or following the step-by-step procedures indicated in them; rather its behavior was simply scorable by Siegler's criteria as consistent with the succession of rules. Excluding the initial period, failures to fit the rules were of three types: Cases in which a rule fit except for a position bias that gave difficulty on balance problems, cases in which performance was borderline between Rules I and II, and combinations of these two problems. (Siegler [personal communication] does find some borderline cases between Rule 1 and Rule 2, but the position bias cases are not typical of children's performance.)

*Overall Developmental Trends.*    Epoch by epoch performance in each of the four runs is shown in Figs. 3.5 and 3.6. One generally observes the expected developmental progression. Each simulation run is slightly different, due to differences in the random starting weights and the sequence of actual training

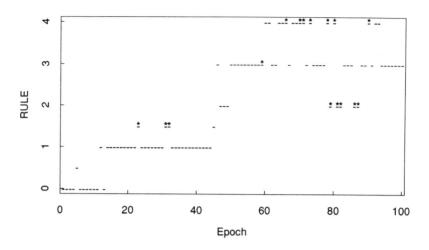

## RULES BY EPOCH: RUN 1

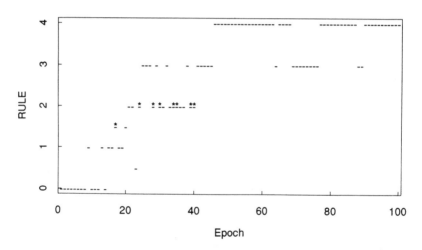

## RULES BY EPOCH: RUN 2

FIG. 3.5. Epoch by epoch performance of the simulation model in the two runs with a 5 to 1 bias favoring problems in which distance did not vary. Performance is scored by Rule. Cases marked by * missed a rule due to position bias. Rule 0 corresponds to always saying "balance," and occurs at the beginning of training. Rule 1.5 corresponds to performance on the borderline between Rules 1 and 2.

experiences, but there are clear common trends. Over the first 10 epochs or so, the output of the model was close to .5 on all test patterns; by our scoring criteria, all of these outputs count as "balance" responses, but of course they really represent a stage in which neither weight nor distance governs performance. The next few epochs represent a transition to Rule 1, in that in this phase the model is showing some tendency to activate the output unit on the side with the greater weight, but this tendency is variable across patterns and the discrepancy between the activations of the output units is not reliably greater than .33 when the weights differ.

After this brief transition, performance of the model has generally reached the point where it was responding consistently to the weight cue while systematically ignoring the distance dimension. This pattern continued for several more epochs. There was a brief transitional period, in which the model behave inconsistently on the *distance* problems crucial to distinguishing between Rule 1 and Rule 2 behavior. After several epochs in this phase, use of the distance cue reached the point where performance on all types of conflict problems became variable. The model generally continued in this phase indefinitely, sometimes reaching the point where its performance was generally scorable as fitting Rule 4 and sometimes not.

The variability in the model's performance from epoch to epoch is actually quite consistent with test-retest data reported in Siegler (1981). Rule 2 behavior is highly unstable, and there is some instability of behavior in other rules as well.

*Performance in each phase.*    Siegler's criteria for conformity to his rules allow for some deviations from perfect conformity; in fact only 83% of test problems must be scorable as consistent with the rule. Given this, it is interesting to see whether the discrepancies from the rules that are exhibited by the model are consistent with human subject's performance. In general, they seem to be quite consistent, as Fig. 3.7 indicates. Each panel shows percent correct performance by the model averaged over the tests on which the model scored in accordance with one of the four rules. Also shown are data from two groups of human subjects as well as the pattern of performance that would be expected from a perfect rule user.

For Rule 1, the model differs very little from humans. For Rule 2, again the correspondence to human data is very close. Both the model and the humans show some slight tendency to get *conflict–distance* problems correct, and to occasionally miss *distance* and *balance* problems. For both Rule 1 and Rule 2, the tendency to miss *balance* problems is slightly greater in the model than in the children's data. For Rule 3, the model exaggerates a tendency seen in the human data to be correct on *conflict–weight* problems more often than on *conflict–distance* problems. The major discrepancy from the data is that the model is too accurate on conflict-balance problems. For Rule 4, the model again exaggerates a tendency seen in the human data to have residual difficulties with conflict problems.

## RULES BY EPOCH: RUN 3

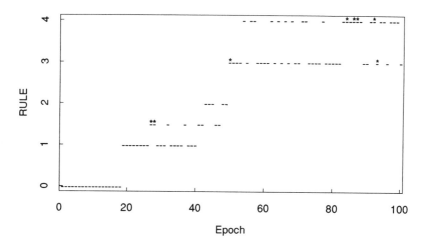

## RULES BY EPOCH: RUN 4

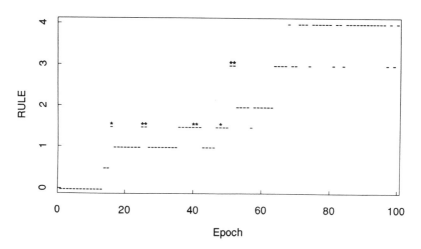

FIG. 3.6. Epoch by epoch performance of the simulation model in the two runs with a 10 to 1 bias favoring problems in which distance did not vary. Performance is scored by Rule, as in Fig. 3.8.

With the exception of the *conflict-balance* problems in Rule 3, the human data seem to fall about half-way between the model and perfect correspondence to the rules. It is tempting to speculate that some human subjects—particularly Rule 4 subjects—may in fact use explicit rules like the torque rule some of the time. It is, indeed, easy for the adult subjects who contribute to the Rule 4 results to

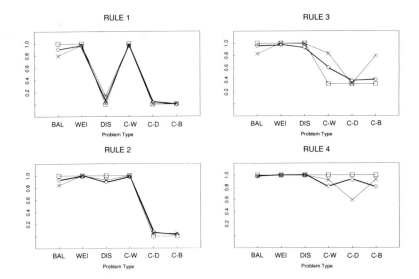

FIG. 3.7. Children's performance by problem type on the balance scale task, together with the performance of the simulation model and expected performance based on each rule. The heavy line with diamonds indicates children's performance. The model's performance is given by the light line with x's, whereas performance predicted from the rule is given by the light line with squares. For each child and each test of the simulation, performance was precategorized according to the best fitting rule. Then, percent correct responses by problem type were calculated averaging over children or simulation tests falling into each rule.

follow the torque rule if instructed specifically in this rule. However, it is evident that the subjects who fall under the Rule 4 scoring criteria do not in fact adhere exactly to the rule. Perhaps this group includes some individuals performing on the basis of implicit knowledge of the trade-off of weight and distance as well as some who explicitly use the torque rule, and perhaps some individuals use a mixture of the two strategies.

*Further correspondences between the model and child development.* So far we have seen that the balance scale model captures the pattern of development seen in the studies of Siegler (1976, 1981). There are two further aspects of the developmental data which are consistent with the gradual buildup of strength on the distance dimension that we see in the model:

1. Wilkening and Anderson (in press) present subjects with one side of a balance beam, and allow them to adjust the weight on the other side at a fixed distance from the fulcrum to make the scale balance. Over the age range of 9 to

20, in which children are generally progressing from late Rule 1 or Rule 2 to Rule 3 or Rule 4 according to Siegler's methods, they find an increasing sensitivity to the distance cue. Unfortunately it is difficult to be sure whether this reflects different numbers of subjects relying on the distance cue, or (as we see in the model) differences in degree of reliance among those who show some sensitivity to the distance cue.

2. For children who exhibit Rule 3 on Siegler's 24-item test, careful assessment with a larger number of conflict problems indicates the use of cue compensation strategies, rather than random guessing (Ferretti, Butterfield, Cahn, & Kerkman, 1985). Thus children are not simply totally confused about conflict problems during this stage but have some sensitivity of relative magnitudes of cues, as does the model. The exact degree of correspondence of the model's performance and human performance on these larger tests remains to be explored.

*The mechanism for developmental change.*    Given the generally close correspondence between model and data, it is important to understand just how the model performs, and how its performance changes. To do this, it is helpful to examine the connections in the network at several different points in the learning process. Figure 3.8 displays the connections from the run that produced the results shown in the top panel of Fig. 3.6, at 4 different points during learning: At epoch 0, before any learning; at epoch 20, early in the Rule 1 phase; at epoch 40, at the end of the Rule 1 phase; and at epoch 100, when the simulation was terminated. Each of the four large rectangles in each panel shows the weights coming into and out of one of the four hidden units. The two on the left receive input from the weight dimension, and the two on the right receive input from the distance dimension.

In the first panel, before learning begins, all the connection strengths have small random values. In this situation, the output of the hidden units is not systematically related to magnitudes of the weights or distances, and is therefore of no use in predicting the correct output. At this point, the hidden units are not encoding either relative weight or relative distance, and are therefore providing no information that would be useful for predicting whether the left or right side should go down.

The first phase of learning consists of the gradual organization of the connections that process the amount of weight on each side of the balance scale. Recall that the network receives problems in which the distance cue varies much less frequently than problems in which the weight cue varies. Learning to rely on the weight cue proceeds more quickly than learning to rely on the distance cue as a simple result of this fact. The rate of learning with respect to each type of cue is relatively gradual at first, but then speeds up, for reasons that we will explore below. The relatively rapid transition from virtually unresponsive output to fairly strong reliance on the weight cue represents the brief transition to Rule 1 respond-

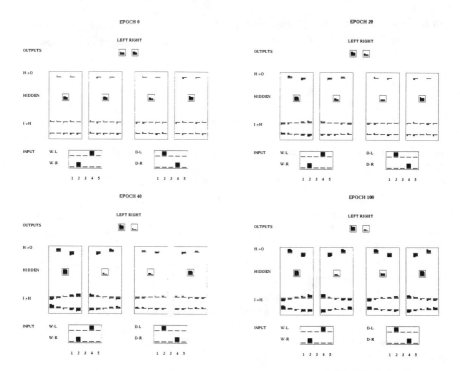

FIG. 3.8.   Connection strengths into (I→H) and out of (H→O) each of the hidden units, at each of four different points during training. Activations of input, hidden, and output units are also shown, for a conflict balance problem, in which there are 2 weights on peg 4 on the left and 4 weights on peg 2 on the right. Magnitude of each connection is given by the size of the blackened area. Sign is indicated by whether the blackened area extends above or below the horizontal baseline. Note that activations are all positive, and range from 0 to 1. The connection strengths range between +6 and −6. See text for further explanation.

ing. The result of this phase, in the second panel of the figure, is a set of connections that allow the hidden units on the left to reflect the relative amount of weight on the left vs. the right side of the balance scale. The leftmost hidden unit is most strongly excited by large weights on the left and small weights on the right, and most strongly inhibited by large weights on the right and small weights on the left. The activation of this unit, then, ranges from near 0 to near 1 as the relative magnitude of weight ranges from much more on the right to much more on the left. Correspondingly, this unit has an excitatory connection to the left-side-down output unit, and an inhibitory connection to the right-side-down output unit. The second hidden unit mirrors these relationships in reverse. At this point, then, the hidden units can be said to have learned to represent something they were not representing before, namely the relative magnitude of the inputs. Note that this information is not explicitly contained in the input, which simply distinguishes but does not order the different possible values of weight on the two sides of the balance scale.

At this point, the connection strengths in the distance part of the network remain virtually unchanged; thus, at the hidden unit level, the network has not yet learned to encode the distance dimension.

Over the next 20 epochs, connections get much stronger on the weight dimension, and we begin to see some organization of the distance dimension. While this is going on, the overt behavior of the network remains Rule 1 behavior. The network is getting ready for the relatively rapid transition to Rule 2 and then to Rule 3 which occurs over the next several epochs of training (as shown in the top panel of Fig. 3.6), but at epoch 40, the end of the Rule 1 phase, the distance connections are still not quite strong enough that they can yet push activations of the output units out of the balance range. With further learning, the distance cue becomes stronger and stronger; this first causes the distance cue to govern performance when the weights are in balance, giving rise to Rule 2 behavior. Further strengthening causes the distance cue to win out in some conflict problems, giving rise to behavior consistent with Rules 3 and 4. At epoch 100 of this particular run, the weight dimension maintains a slight ascendancy, so that with the particular *conflict–balance* problem illustrated, the model activates the left-side down unit, corresponding to the side with the greater weight, more than it activates the right-side down unit.

A couple of aspects of the developmental progression deserve comment. As Fig. 3.9 illustrates, the connection strengths are largely insensitive to differences early on, then go through a fairly rapid transition in sensitivity and then level off again. The acceleration seen in learning is a result of an inherent characteristic of the gradient descent learning procedure coupled with the architecture of the network. The procedure adjusts each connection in proportion to the magnitude of the effect that adjusting it will have on the discrepancy between correct and actual output. But the effect of a given connection depends on the strengths of other connections. Consider the connection coming into a hidden unit from one of the input units. An adjustment of the strength of this input connection will have a small effect on the output if the connections from the hidden unit to the output units are weak. In this case, the input connection will only receive a small adjustment. If however, the connections from the hidden units to the output units are strong, an adjustment of the strength of the input connection will have a much larger effect; consequently the learning procedure makes a much larger adjustment in this case. A slightly different story applies to the connections from the hidden units to the output units. When the connections from the input to the hidden units are weak and random, the activations of the hidden units are only weakly related to the correct output. Under these circumstances, the adjustments

## Hidden to Output

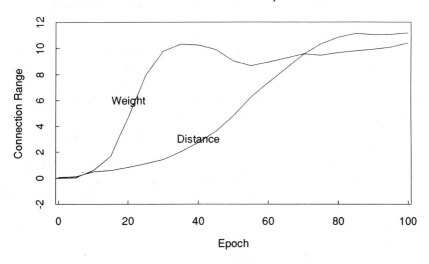

## Input to Hidden

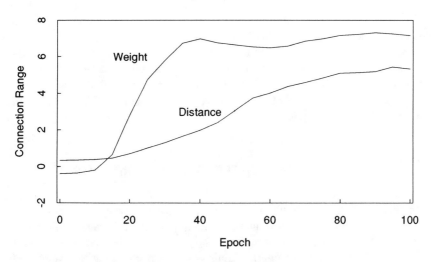

FIG. 3.9. Relative magnitude of connection strengths encoding weight and distance, as a function of training. Magnitude is given by the range of connection strengths (most positive minus most negative) coming into one weight or distance hidden unit (lower panel) and coming out of weight or distance unit (upper panel).

made to the output weights tend to cancel each other out, and progress of learning is very slow. It is only after the input weights become organized that learning can proceed efficiently on the output side of the hidden units.

The story we are telling would be a very sad one, were it not for the fact that it is not all or none. It is not that there is no learning at all at first. In that case, there would be no gradual change to the point where learning becomes more rapid. Rather, it is simply that initially learning is simply *very* gradual; so gradual that it does not show up in overt behavior. Gradually though this initially slow learning accelerates, producing an increasing readiness to learn.

The differential readiness to learn allows the model to account for the results of an experiment described by Siegler (1976), on the effects of training for young vs. old Rule 1 children. Siegler showed 5- and 8-year-old Rule 1 children a series of distance problems or a series of conflict problems. The children were allowed to try to predict which side would go down, and were then shown what actually happens. The results were striking. Of the children who saw the outcomes for distance problems, both age groups were very likely to exhibit Rule 2 behavior on a post-test. However, of the children who saw the outcomes for conflict training, the younger children either continued to behave in accordance with Rule 1 or became inconsistent in their responding. The older children, on the other hand, benefitted from the conflict training. On a post test, the older children were very likely to exhibit Rule 2 or Rule 3 behavior. In further experiments on early Rule 1 children, Siegler reported that these children do not represent the distance correctly: When asked to reproduce a balance beam configuration, they could usually get the number of weights correct, but could rarely place them on the correct pegs. Younger Rule 1 children who were then trained to represent the distance correctly were able to learn from experience with conflict problems like the older Rule 1 children.

## SIMULATIONS OF FEEDBACK EXPERIMENTS

This general pattern of results fits closely with what we would expect based on what we have already learned about the model. Particularly interesting are the effects of feedback on conflict trails on early and late Rule 1 performance. The model was shown a set of conflict trials with feedback, using the weights obtained early in the Rule 1 phase (epoch 20) and later (epoch 40). In the former case, performance gradually reverted to random. In the latter case, it shifts after only one exposure to the set of conflict trials to the rule 2 level. The reason for the deterioration in the first case is simply that early in Rule 1, the weights in the network do not encode distance information at all. As a result the conflict trials appear to involve a pattern of very inconsistent feedback concerning the correct predictions to make based on the weights alone. Later in Rule 1, the distance cue is weakly encoded. While it is still too weak to actually cause the output to be strongly enough affected by the distance cue to actually affect performance, it is strong enough for a small amount of experience to cause a further increase in strength to the point where the distance cue is strong enough to influence performance.

## Feedback Simulation Trials

The general approach taken here can be extended to cover the full range of training experiments carried out by Siegler (1976). Simulations more closely matching the design of these experiments were carried out by the second author. For these simulations, a similar architecture was used. One major difference was the addition of 2 more output units. These additional output units received input from the hidden units on the distance dimension. In general, these additional output units, from now on to be referred to as distance encoding units, were not involved in the simulations except where outlined below.

The purpose of these simulations was to model the training experiences from Siegler's second and third experiments. The issue at this point was whether the model could simulate the effects of training with distance problems versus training with conflict problems.

To simulate the stability of the system's knowledge about the weight dimension, the learning mechanism's proportion of change with respect to error for the connections from the weight units and the weight internal units and from the weight internal units to the balance scale output units (their learning rates) were, respectively, .00 and .025, while the proportion of change with respect to error for all of the distance dimension connections was .05.

To begin the simulation of Siegler's second experiment, the model was initialized by training only the connections between the weight input units and the weight-hidden units, and between the weight-hidden units and the balance scale output units. This training was performed by presenting the model with 50 epochs of input and feedback for each possible configuration of weight and balance problems with no distance information provided to the model. On the balance scale prediction task, this system produced perfect Rule 1 behavior. From this base performance level, the model received two types of training in separate sessions. In one session, the model received feedback training similar to the distance feedback training in Siegler's second experiment. That is, the model was trained with 16 different patterns and their associated correct responses; 12 patterns with equal weight input to the two sides of the weight input units and different distance inputs to the two sides of the distance input units (Distance problems), 2 patterns with equal weight and distance inputs (Balance problems), and 2 patterns with different weight inputs to the two sides of the weight input units and equal distance input to the two sides of the distance input units (Weight problems).

In the second session, after reinitialization of the system to the base performance level, the model received feedback training similar to the conflict training in Siegler's second experiment. That is, the model was trained with 16 different patterns and their associated correct responses; 12 patterns with greater weight input to one side of the weight input units and greater distance input to one side of the distance input units (Conflict problems), and 2 patterns with equal weight and distance inputs (Balance problems), and 2 patterns with different weight inputs to the two sides of the weight input units and equal distance input to the two sides of the distance input units (Weight problems).

In both of these sessions, the model received 40 epochs (640 trials) of training. A measure of the effectiveness of the training trials was plotted over the course of the forty training epochs. The effectiveness measure, called the sum of squares error term (SSERROR), measures the difference between the activations of the prediction responses of the model over the training set of patterns and the activations of correct responses for the set of patterns. Therefore, a large error term represents an inability of the model to produce correct predictions, while a small term represents a close match between the predictions of the model and the correct responses.

Figures 3.10a and 3.10b show SSERROR plotted over training epochs during distance training and conflict training, respectively. In Fig. 3.10a, we can see that distance training causes the model's predictive performance over the training problem set to improve dramatically. In contrast, Fig. 3.10b shows that conflict training did not increase the model's predictive performance over the training problem set. These graphs indicate that, in the 40 epoch time frame, the model learned from the distance training but did not learn from the conflict training.

A more dramatic demonstration of this difference in learning was exhibited in the model's performance on the prediction task following the feedback training. Like many of Siegler's five year old subjects, the model learned to perform as a rule 2 user after distance training; in addition to getting balance, weight and conflict-weight problems correct, the model was able to correctly predict distance problems as well. After conflict training, however, the model did not learn to perform at all different from rule 1 behavior. Hence, the model closely simulated the behavior of the 5-year-olds.

The next step in the evaluation of the model was to give distance encoding training to the base performance model. The model's encoding training was not the same as the training that Siegler presented to his subjects; instead, this training was only meant to get the model to categorize the distance input into one of the three relative values. Thus, this training involved modification of only the connections between the distance input units, the hidden units of the distance dimension, and the distance encoding units at the output level. This encoding training set included every configuration of distance as input to the network (36 patterns) paired with the corresponding relative distance value (more distance left, more distance right, or equal distance) as the target feedback for the distance encoding units.

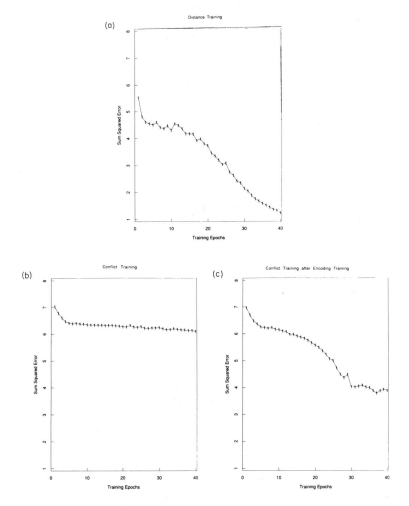

FIG. 3.10.    Network error over training for (a) distance training, (b) conflict training, and (c) conflict training after encoding training.

For example, the model was presented at the input level with the activation pattern for three right and two left, and trained to produce the pattern of activation for more distance right across the distance encoding units. The model received 25 epochs of training with this training corpus. This training allowed the distance hidden units to discriminate distance input patterns as greater distance left, greater distance right or equal distance. No training occurred between any of the other units of the model during the distance encoding training phase. Following this encoding training, the model was again tested on the prediction task. The model, like Siegler's subjects, did not exhibit a change in behavior. Finally, the model was provided with the same conflict training as had been provided in the earlier conflict training session. In contrast to Fig. 3.10b, the plot of the effectiveness of conflict training after encoding training (Fig. 3.10c) shows that conflict training dramatically increases the model's predictive performance over the training problem set. This graph indicates that the model was able to learn from the conflict training after encoding training. Following this training, the model was again tested on the prediction task.

This time, the model was able to correctly use the distance information to predict distance problems. It also learned, like the children, not to rely strictly on the weight cues to predict the conflict problems and thus its performance went down on the conflict weight problems (from 100% correct to 75% correct) and up on the conflict distance and conflict balance problems (both from 0% correct to 50% correct).

In essence, the model learned to perform as a rule 3 user after the conflict training following the encoding training. Hence, the model simulated the learning abilities of many of the 5- and 8-year-olds on the conflict training task after receiving distance encoding training.

To understand how this model works, it is important to understand the internal structure that develops during training. So, before distance training, after distance training, after conflict training, and after encoding training followed by conflict training, the model was presented with 15 different distance configurations (patterns of activation) across the distance input units. There were five configurations each; of more distance right, more distance left, and equal distance (balance). After each presentation of a distance configuration, the average activation of the two sets of units of the distance internal group were measured and plotted against each other. The two sets of units were chosen by examining the activation values and attempting to determine which, if any, of the units tended to have correlated activation values. Units with correlated activation values were considered members of a common set for the purposes of this analysis. Units could not be chosen *a priori* due to fact that the learning mechanism recruits units to code similar functions only during the course of training.

To display these activations in response to different inputs, two-dimensional graphs were constructed with each axis specifying the average activation level of one set of units. For each graph, five points are plotted which mark the activations of the two sets of internal units when the five configurations of more distance right were presented—these are marked with an 'R'. Likewise, each of the five points for the internal activations for the configurations of more distance left and balanced distance are marked with an 'L' and a 'B', respectively. Upon examining these activation values before training, it was discovered that these sets of input patterns were not discriminated in any way in the distance internal group. Because the connection strengths of the connections to these units were not trained, every input pattern produced almost the same activation pattern at the internal level and thus all of the points ended up on top of each other. Thus, this graph is not shown. However, when this same procedure was performed after distance training, the activations shown in Fig. 3.11a were produced. Here, we see that the network has learned to internally represent similar distance input similarly (all of the R's, L's, and B's are clustered together), and, more importantly, to represent different distance inputs differently (the R, L, and B clusters are separated away from each other). What is claimed, then, is that during training, the model restructured the internal representations for each problem association in such a way that the concept of relative distance—more distance left, right, and equal distance—emerged from the representations.

This analysis was also performed after conflict training and the results are shown in Fig. 3.11b. In this case, the training did not allow for the formation of the relative distance concept within 40 epochs of training. The internal representations for the different distance configurations did not differentiate into the three

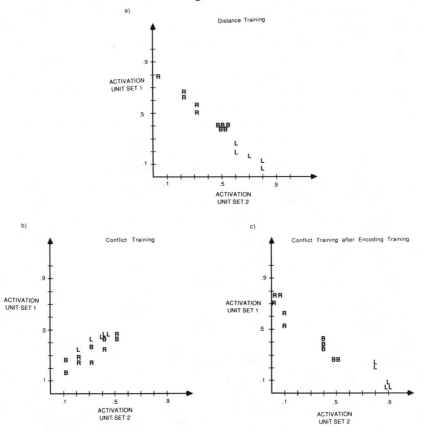

FIG. 3.11.   Activations of the units of the internal distance group for (a) distance training, (b) conflict training, and (c) conflict training after encoding training.

clusters of their distance relative relationships. Without this abstract relationship, the model was unable to generalize to new configurations and thus, in the prediction task, did not change its behavior. However, when this analysis was performed after encoding training, (which produced the relative distance representations at the internal level as shown in Fig. 3.11c), the model was able to learn to use relative distance cues on the prediction task.

## Shortcomings of the Model

Taken together, the two versions of the simple network model of the balance beam task that we have described above exhibit a striking correspondence with many aspects of the developmental facts. These correspondences have, we think, important implications for theories of cognitive development. Before we turn to these correspondences, we first consider a few shortcomings of the model. Three failures of the first version to fit aspects of Siegler's data must be acknowledged: First, the model can never actually master Rule 4, though some subjects clearly do. Second, it's behavior during Rule 3 is slightly different from humans (though it should be noted that the "human" Rule 3 pattern is actually a mixture of different strategies according to Klahr and Siegler, 1978). Third, it can exhibit position biases that are uncharacteristic of humans, who seem (at least, from the age of 5 on) to "know" that there is no reason to prefer left over right.

There are other shortcomings at well. Perhaps the most serious is in the input representations, which use distinct units to represent different amounts of weight and distance. This representation was chosen because it does not inherently encode the structure of each dimension, thereby forcing the network to discover the ordering of each dimension. But it has the drawback that it prevents the network from extrapolating or even interpolating beyond the range of the discrete values that it has experienced.

Finally, Siegler has reported protocol data that indicates that subjects are often able to describe what they are doing verbally in ways that correspond fairly well to their actual performance. It is not true that all subject's verbalizations correctly characterize the Rule they are using, but it is true, for example, that subjects who are sensitive to the distance cue mention that they are using this cue and those who are not tend not to mention it. The model is of course completely mute.

What are we to make of these shortcomings in light of the overall success of the model? Obviously, we cannot take it as the final word on development of ability to perform the balance scale task. We would suggest that the model's shortcomings may lie in two places: First, in details of the encoding of inputs and of the network architecture; and second, in the fact that the model only deals with acquisition of implicit knowledge.

Regarding the first point, it would be reasonable to allow the input to encode similarity on each dimension by using input representations in which each unit responded to a range of similar values so that neighboring weights and distances produced overlapping input representations; furthermore, the inputs could well make use of a relative code of magnitude to keep values within a fixed range. This would probably overcome the interpolation and extrapolation problems (we have no stand on whether such codings are learned or pre-wired).

These kinds of fixes would not allow the model to truly master Rule 4 and perhaps rightly so, since it seems likely that Rule 4 (unlike the other rules) can only be adhered to strictly as an explicit (arithmetic) rule. Indeed, it must be acknowledged that there is a conscious, verbally accessible component to the problem solving activity that children and adults engage in when they confront a problem like the balance scale problem. The model does not address this activity itself. However, it is tempting to suggest that the model captures the gradual acquisition mechanisms which establish the possible contents of these conscious processes. One can view the model as making available representations of differing salience as a function of experience; these representations might serve as the raw material used by the more explicit reasoning processes that appear to play a role. This is of course sheer speculation at this point. It will be an important part of the business of the ongoing connectionist exploration of cognitive development to make these speculations explicit and testable.

## IMPLICATIONS OF THE BALANCE SIMULATIONS

The model captures several of the more intriguing aspects of cognitive development. It captures its stage-like character, while at the same time exhibiting an underlying continuity which accounts for gradual change in readiness to move on to the next stage. It captures that fact that behavior can often seem very much to be under the control of very simple and narrow rules (e.g., Rule 1), yet exhibit symptoms of gradeness and continuity when tested in different ways. It captures the fact that development, in a large number of different domains, progresses from an initial over-focussing on the most salient dimension of a task or problem—to the point where other dimensions are not even encoded—followed by a sequence of further steps in which the reliance on the initially unattended dimension gradually increases.

As mentioned previously, the model can be seen as implementing the accommodation process that lies at the heart of Piaget's theory of developmental change. Accommodation essentially amounts to adjusting mental structures to reduce the discrepancy between observed events and expectations derived from the existing mental structures. According to Flavell (1963), Piaget stressed the continuity of the accommodation process, in spite of the overtly stage-like character of development, though he never gave a particularly clear account of how stages arise from continuous learning (see Flavell, 1963, pp. 244–249 for a description of one attempt). The model provides such a description: it shows clearly how a continuous accommodation-like process can lead to a stage-like progression in development.

*Changes in representation and attention through the course of develop-ment.* When a balance scale problem is presented to the model, it sees it in different ways, depending on its developmental state. At all times, information is in some sense present in the input for determining what is the correct response. However, at first this information produces no real impression; weak, random activations occur at the hidden level and these make weak, random impressions at the output level. At the beginning of the Rule 1 behavioral phase, the model has learned to represent relative amount of weight. The pattern of activation over the hidden units captures relative weight, since one unit will be more activated if there is more weight to the right, and the other will be more activated if there is more weight to the left; both units take on intermediate activations when the weights balance. At this point, we can see the model as encoding weight, but not distance information. Indeed, as we have seen at this point the network could be said to be ignoring the distance cue; it makes little impact on activation, and learning about distance is very slow at this point. At the end of the Rule 1 phase, in spite of its lack of impact on overt behavior, the network has learned to represent relative distances; at this point it is extremely sensitive to feedback about distance; it is ready to slip over the fairly sharp boundary in performance between Rule 1 and Rule 2. Thus, we can see the Rule 1 stage as one in which overt behavior fails to mirror a gradual developmental progression that carries the model from extreme unreadiness to learn about distance at the beginning of this phase to a high degree of readiness at the end.

This developmental progression seems to resolve the apparent paradoxical relation between observed stage-like behavioral development and assumed con-tinuity of learning. To us this is the most impressive achievement of the model; it provides a simple, explicit alternative to maturational accounts of stage-like progression in development.

It must be noted, however, that the success of the model depends crucially on its structure. In fact the results are less compelling if either of the following changes are made: (a) if balance is treated as a separate category, rather than being treated as the intermediate case between left-side-down and right-side-down; (b) if the connections from input to hidden units are not restricted as they are here so that weight is processed separately from distance before the two are combined.

More generally, it is becoming clear that architectural restrictions on connec-tionist networks are crucial if they are to discover the regularities we humans discover from a limited range of experiences (Denker et al., 1987; Rumelhart, in preparation). This observation underscores that fact that the learning principle, in itself, is not the only principle that needs to be taken into account. There proba-bly are additional principles that are exploited by the brain to facilitate learning and generalization. Just what these additional principles are and the extent to which they are domain specific remains to be understood in more detail.

Extending this observation a step further, we can see the connectionist frame-work as a new paradigm in which to explore basic questions about the relations of nature and nurture. We may find that successful simulation of developmental processes depends on building in domain specific constraints in considerable detail; if so this would support a more nativist view of the basis of domain–specific skills. On the other hand, it may turn out that a few other general principles in addition to the learning principle are sufficient to allow us to capture a wide range of developmental phenomena. In this case we would be led toward a much more experience-based description of development. In either case, it seems very likely that connectionist models will help us take a new look at these important basic questions.

## CONCLUSIONS

The exploration of connectionist models of human cognition and development is still at an early stage. Yet already these models have begun to capture a new way of thinking about processing, about learning and, we hope the present chapter shows, about development. Several further challenges lie ahead. One of these is to build stronger bridges between what might be called cognitive–level models and our evolving understanding of the details of neuronal computation. Another will be to develop more fully the application of cognitive models to higher-level aspects of cognition. The hope is that the attempt to meet these and other challenges will continue to lead to new discoveries about the mechanisms of human thought and the principles that govern their operation and adaptation to experience.

## ACKNOWLEDGMENTS

The text of this article overlaps substantially with the text of an earlier article by McClelland (1989) and contains excerpts from an article by Jenkins (1986). The work reported here was supported by ONR and DARPA Under Contract Number N00014-86-K-0349, by an NIMH Career Development Award MH00385 to the first author, by ONR Contract N00014-82-C-0374, and by NSF Grant BNS 88-12048.

## REFERENCES

Bever, T. G. (1970). The cognitive basis for linguistic structures. In J. R. Hayes (Ed.), *Cognition and the development of language* (pp. 279–362). New York: Wiley.

Denker, J., Schwartz, D., Wittner, B., Solla, S., Hopfield, J., Howard, R., & Jackel,

L. (1987). *Automatic learning, rule extraction, and generalization* (AT&T Bell Labs Technical Report). Holmdel, NJ: AT&T Bell Labs.

Feldman, J. A. (1988). Connectionist representation of concepts. In D. Waltz & J. A. Feldman (Eds.), *Connectionist models and their implications: Readings from cognitive science* (pp. 341–363). Norwood, NJ: Ablex.

Ferretti, R. P., Butterfield, E. C., Cahn, A., & Kerkman, D. (1985). The classification of children's knowledge: Development on the balance scale and inclined plane tasks. *Journal of Experimental Child Psychology, 39,* 131–160.

Flavell, J. H. (1963). *The developmental psychology of Jean Piaget.* Princeton, NJ: D. Van Nostrand.

Grossberg, S. (1978). A theory of visual coding, memory, and development. In E. L. J. Leeuwenberg & H. F. J. M. Buffart (Eds.), *Formal theories of visual perception.* New York: Wiley.

Hinton, G. E. (1989). Learning distributed representations of concepts. In R. G. M. Morris (Ed.), *Parallel distributed processing: Implications for psychology and neurobiology* (pp. 46–61). New York: Oxford University Press.

Hinton, G. E. (in press). Connectionist learning procedures. *Artificial Intelligence.*

Hinton, G. E., McClelland, J. L., & Rumelhart, D. E. (1986). Distributed Representations. In D. E. Rumelhart, J. L. McClelland, & the PDP research group (Eds.), *Parallel distributed processing: Explorations in the microstructure of cognition. Volume I.* Cambridge, MA: Bradford Books.

Inhelder, B., & Piaget, J. (1958). *The growth of logical thinking from childhood to adolescence.* New York: Basic Books.

Jenkins, E. A., Jr. (1986). Readiness and learning: A parallel distributed processing model of child performance. Pittsburgh, PA: Carnegie-Mellon University, Psychology Department.

Keil, F. C. (1979). *Semantic and conceptual development: An ontological perspective.* Cambridge, MA: Harvard University Press.

Klahr, D., & Siegler, R. S. (1978). The representation of children's knowledge. In H. W. Reese & L. P. Lipsitt (Eds.), *Advances in child development and behavior* (pp. 61–116). New York: Academic Press.

McClelland, J. L. (1985). Putting knowledge in its place: A scheme for programming parallel processing structures on the fly. *Cognitive Science, 9,* 113–146.

McClelland, J. L. (1989). Parallel distributed processing: Implications for cognition and development. In R. G. M. Morris (Ed.), *Parallel distributed processing: Implications for psychology and neurobiology* (pp. 8–45). New York: Oxford University Press.

McClelland, J. L., & Rumelhart, D. E. (1981). An interactive activation model of context effects in letter perception: Part 1. An account of basic findings. *Psychological Review, 88,* 375–407.

McClelland, J. L., & Rumelhart, D. E. (1985). Distributed memory and the representation of general and specific information. *Journal of Experimental Psychology: General, 114,* 159–188.

McClelland, J. L., Rumelhart, D. E., and the PDP research group. (1986). *Parallel distributed processing: Explorations in the microstructure of cognition. Volume II.* Cambridge, MA: Bradford Books.

McClelland, J. L., St. John. M., & Taraban, R. (1989). Sentence comprehension: A parallel distributed processing approach. *Language and Cognitive Processes, 4,* 287–335.

Patterson, K., Seidenberg, M. S., & McClelland, J. L. (1989). Connections and disconnections: Acquired dyslexia in a computational model of reading processes. In R. G. M. Morris (Ed.), *Parallel distributed processing: Implications for psychology and neurobiology* (pp. 131–181). New York: Oxford University Press.

Rescorla, R. A., & Wagner, A. R. (1972). A theory of Pavlovian conditioning: Variations in the effectiveness of reinforcement and non-reinforcement. In A. H. Black & W. F. Prokasy (Eds.), *Classical conditioning II: Current research and theory.* New York: Appleton-Century-Crofts.

Rumelhart, D. E. (in preparation). *Generalization and the learning of minimal networks by back propagation.*

Rumelhart, D. E. (1990). Brain style computation: Learning and generalization. In S. Zornetzer, J.

Davis, & C. Lau (Eds.), *An introduction to neural and electronic networks* (pp. 405–420). New York: Academic Press.

Rumelhart, D. E., & McClelland, J. L. (1986). On learning the past tenses of English verbs. In J. L. McClelland, D. E. Rumelhart, & the PDP research group (Eds.), *Parallel distributed processing: Explorations in the microstructure of cognition. Volume II*. Cambridge, MA: Bradford Books.

Rumelhart, D. E., & Norman, D. A. (1982). Simulating a skilled typist: A study of skilled cognitive-motor performance. *Cognitive Science, 6,* 1–36.

Rumelhart, D. E., Hinton, G. E., & McClelland, J. L. (1986). A framework for parallel distributed processing. In D. E. Rumelhart, J. L. McClelland, & the PDP research group (Eds.), *Parallel distributed processing: Explorations in the microstructure of cognition. Volume I*. Cambridge, MA: Bradford Books.

Rumelhart, D. E., Hinton, G. E., & Williams, R. J. (1986). Learning internal representations by error propagation. In D. E. Rumelhart, J. L. McClelland, & the PDP research group (Eds.), *Parallel distributed processing: Explorations in the microstructure of cognition. Volume I*. Cambridge, MA: Bradford Books.

Rumelhart, D. E., McClelland, J. L., & the PDP research group. (1986). *Parallel distributed processing: Explorations in the microstructure of cognition. Volume I*. Cambridge, MA: Bradford Books.

St. John, M. F., & McClelland, J. L. (1988). *Learning and applying contextual constraints in sentence comprehension*. (AIP Technical Report). Pittsburgh, PA: Carnegie Mellon University, Departments of Computer Science and Psychology, and University of Pittsburgh, Learning Research and Development Center.

Sejnowski, T. J., & Rosenberg, C. R. (1987). Parallel networks that learn to pronounce English text. *Complex Systems, 1,* 145–168.

Siegler, R. S. (1976). Three aspects of cognitive development. *Cognitive Psychology, 8,* 481–520.

Siegler, R. S. (1981). Developmental sequences within and between concepts. *Monographs of the Society for Research in Child Development, 46* (No. 189, pp. 1–74).

Siegler, R. S., & Klahr, D. (1982). When do children learn? The relationship between existing knowledge and the acquisition of new knowledge. In R. Glaser (Ed.), *Advances in instructional psychology, Vol. 2* (pp. 121–211). Hillsdale, NJ: Lawrence Erlbaum Associates.

Wilkening, F., & Anderson, N. H. (in press). Representation and diagnosis of knowledge structures. In N. H. Anderson (Ed.), *Contributions to information integration theory*.

Williams, R. J. (1986). The logic of activation functions. In D. E. Rumelhart, J. L. McClelland, & the PDP research group (Eds.), *Parallel distributed processing: Explorations in the microstructure of cognition. Volume I*. Cambridge, MA: Bradford Books.

# 4

# Toward the Knowledge Level in Soar: The Role of the Architecture in the Use of Knowledge

Paul S. Rosenbloom
*Information Sciences Institute, University of Southern California*

Allen Newell
*School of Computer Science, Carnegie Mellon University*

John E. Laird
*Department of Electrical Engineering and Computer Science, University of Michigan*

Soar has been described as an architecture for a system that is to be capable of general intelligence (Laird, Newell, & Rosenbloom, 1987). One way to specify what this might mean is to enumerate the set of capabilities that, based on the field's cumulative experience, appear to be required for general intelligence: to be able to work on the full range of tasks, to be able to use the full range of problem-solving methods and varieties of knowledge, to be able to interact with the outside world in real time, and to learn about the world and the system's own performance. Progress can then be evaluated by determining the degree to which the architecture supports such capabilities. For Soar, such an evaluation reveals significant progress in the areas of tasks (Laird, Newell, & Rosenbloom, 1987), problem-solving methods (Laird & Newell, 1983, Laird, 1983) and learning (Steier et al., 1987); some progress in the area of outside interaction (Laird, Hucka, Yager & Tuck, in press); and an unclear situation in the area of knowledge.

The problem with such an approach to specifying (and evaluating progress towards) general intelligence is the lack of theoretical justifications for the set of capabilities included. Without such justifications it is unclear, for example, whether some new form of learning that is developed is necessary for general intelligence, or just an interesting oddity. In addition, whole categories of critical capabilities may be unknowingly omitted. What is needed is a more fundamental definition of general intelligence from which the required capabilities can be derived (or at least justified).

One idea that shows promise towards providing such a definition is the *knowledge level* (Newell, 1982). The idea of the knowledge level is based on earlier developments in the area of computer systems levels (Bell & Newell, 1971). A computer systems level consists of a *medium* that is processed, *components* that provide primitive processing, *laws of composition* that permit components to be assembled into *systems,* and *laws of behavior* that determine how system behavior depends on the component behavior and the structure of the system. Existing levels (and their media) include the device level (electrons), the circuit level (current), the logic level (bits), the register-transfer level (bit-vectors), and the program (or symbol) level (symbols, expressions). In terms of these levels, an *architecture* is a register-transfer level system that defines a symbol level.

The knowledge level is a distinct computer systems level that lies immediately above the symbol level. The medium processed at the knowledge level is knowledge. An agent—a system at the knowledge level—consists of a physical body that can interact with an environment, knowledge, and a set of goals. The law of behavior is the *Principle of Rationality:* "If an agent has knowledge that one of its actions will lead to one of its goals, then the agent will select that action" (Newell, 1982, p. 102). Once knowledge is acquired, it is available for all future goals. There are no capacity limitations on the amount of knowledge that can be available or on the agent's ability to bring it to bear in the selection of actions that achieve its goals. An essential feature of the knowledge level is that the agent's behavior is determined by the content of its knowledge, not by any aspects of its internal structure. It abstracts away from the processing and representation of the lower levels. This lack of significant internal structure implies that there are no laws of composition at the knowledge level.

The knowledge level provides a straightforward, though not uncontroversial, definition for intelligence. A system is intelligent to the degree that it approximates a knowledge-level system (Newell, In press). Perfect intelligence requires a complete lack of internal resource limitations. However, this ideal is unreachable in physically realizable systems that are required to make decisions using bounded resources over a sufficiently wide range of goals using large bodies of knowledge. Such systems can at best only approximate a knowledge-level system, and thus achieve some level of intelligence that is less than perfect. The ideal of perfect intelligence also does not entail the generality of that intelligence. A system's behavior is characterized both by its intelligence and by its generality. Generality for a knowledge-level system is the range of interactions that it can have with the environment, the range of goals it can have, and the range of knowledge that it can acquire and use. Intelligence is how well the system applies its knowledge to the tasks within its scope.

Assuming this knowledge-level definition of general intelligence, the key question for the architecture is how it supports the knowledge level for a sufficiently broad set of goals and knowledge. How does it approximate rationality with bounded resources? How does it support the acquisition and use of knowledge? A complete answer to the key question requires answering a number of such subquestions. In (Newell, in press), a beginning was made at answering the first subquestion. In this chapter we provide the beginnings of an answer to the second subquestion. We examine how the Soar architecture supports and constrains the representation, storage, retrieval, use and acquisition of three pervasive forms of knowledge.

The first form of knowledge to be examined is *procedural* knowledge. Procedural knowledge is knowledge about the agent's actions. It includes knowledge about which actions can be performed, which actions should be performed when (control knowledge), and how actions are performed. The second form of knowledge to be examined is *episodic* knowledge. Episodic knowledge is knowledge about what objects, actions, and action sequences have occurred in the agent's past. It allows answering such questions as "Did this object, action, or action sequence occur (in this context)?" and "What objects, actions, or action sequences occurred (in this context)?" The third and final form of knowledge to be examined is *declarative knowledge*. Declarative knowledge is knowledge about what is true in the world. These final two forms of knowledge have often been referred to collectively as propositional knowledge, with the term "semantic knowledge" used in place of declarative knowledge (Tulving, 1983).

The plan for this chapter is to start with a brief conventional description of the Soar architecture, followed by its redescription in terms of the direct support it provides for knowledge. The core of the chapter then consists of in-depth analyses of how procedural, episodic, and declarative knowledge are represented, stored, retrieved, used, and acquired in Soar. Special emphasis is placed on how the architecture supports and constrains these abilities. The chapter is concluded with a summary of key points and important directions for future work.

## SOAR[1]

Research on Soar to date has focused on the development (and application) of an architecture for intelligence that is based on formulating all symbolic goal–oriented behavior as search in problem spaces. The problem space determines the set of states and operators that can be used during the processing to attain a goal. The states represent situations. There is an initial state, representing the initial situation, and a set of desired states that represent the goal. An operator, when applied to a state in the problem space, yields another state in the problem space. The goal is achieved when a desired state is reached as the result of a sequence of operator applications starting from the initial state. Each goal defines a problem-solving context ("context" for short) that contains, in addition to a goal, roles for a problem space, a state, and an operator.

---

[1]This section describes Soar 4.5 (Laird et al., 1989), which is the basis for the analyses in this chapter.

Problem solving for a goal is driven by decisions that result in the selection of problem spaces, states, and operators for the appropriate roles in the context. Decisions are made by the retrieval and integration of preferences—special architecturally interpretable elements that describe the acceptability, desirability, and necessity of selecting particular problem spaces, states, and operators. The context in which a preference is applicable is specified by its goal, problem-space, state, and operator attributes. When present, they specify the objects that must already be selected in the context for the preference to be valid. For example, the following is a desirability preference stating that operator *o1* is at least as good as any other operator—that is, it is *best*—for state *s1*, problem space *p1*, and goal *g1*.

(preference *o1* ^role operator ^value best
^goal *g1* ^problem-space *p1* ^state *s1*)

There are two types of acceptability preferences—acceptable and reject—to rule an operator into and out of consideration for selection. A reject preference overrides an acceptable preference. There are five types of desirability preferences—worst, worse, indifferent, better, and best—to determine the relative desirability of considered objects. Worst and best are unary preferences. Worse and better are binary preferences. Indifferent can be binary or unary, in which case the object is indifferent to all other competing objects with indifferent preferences. There are two types of necessity preferences—require and prohibit—for asserting that an object must or must not be selected for a goal to be achieved. Details on the semantics of preferences can be found in Laird et al., 1987.

All long-term knowledge is stored in a recognition-based memory—a production system. Each production is a cued-retrieval unit that retrieves the contents of its actions when the pattern in its conditions is successfully matched. By sharing variables between conditions and actions, productions can retrieve information that is a function of what was matched. By having variables in actions that are not in conditions, new objects can be generated/retrieved.

Transient process state is contained in a working memory. This includes information retrieved from long-term memory, results of decisions made by the architecture, information currently perceived from the external environment, and motor commands. It should be clear that this process state is much more than just a single state in a problem space. The process state is the entire transient state of the system, which includes as components, states in problem spaces, and in fact whole problem-solving contexts. It provides the cues for retrieving additional information from long-term memory.

Structurally, working memory consists of a set of objects and preferences about objects. Each object in working memory has a class name, a unique identifier, and a set of attributes with associated values, which may be constants or identifiers (allowing a graph structure of objects). For example, a particular box could be represented by the following object.

(box *b1* ^name box1 ^height 10 ^width 4 ^depth 2)

The class is "box," the identifier is "*b1,*" the name of the box is "box1," and the box has a height of 10 a width of 4 and a depth of 2.

For each problem-solving decision, the contents of working memory is elaborated by parallel access of long-term memory to exhaustion. All productions that match the current working memory are fired in parallel, and this repeats until no productions match. This elaboration process retrieves into working memory new objects, new information about existing objects, and new preferences. When quiescence is reached—that is, when no more productions can fire—an architectural decision procedure interprets the preferences in working memory according to their fixed semantics. If the preferences uniquely specify an object to be selected for a role in a context, such as selecting the current operator for a state, then a decision can be made, and the specified object becomes the current value of the role. The whole process, an elaboration phase followed by a decision, then repeats.

If the decision procedure is ever unable to make a selection—because the preferences in working memory are either incomplete or inconsistent—an *impasse* occurs in problem solving because the system does not know how to proceed. When an impasse occurs, a subgoal with an associated problem-solving context is automatically generated for the task of resolving the impasse. The impasses, and thus their subgoals, vary from problems of selection (of problem spaces, states, and operators) to problems of generation (e.g., operator application). Given a subgoal, Soar can bring its full problem-solving capability and knowledge to bear on resolving the impasse that caused the subgoal. For example, if an operator-tie impasse occurs because multiple operators are competing for selection with insufficiently distinguishing preferences, then a subgoal is created in which Soar can (among other things) execute operators to evaluate the competing alternatives. Productions can then create preferences based on these evaluations, allowing the decision to be made.

When impasses occur within impasses—if, for example, there is insufficient knowledge about how to evaluate a competing alternative—then subgoals occur within subgoals, and a goal hierarchy results (which therefore defines a hierarchy of contexts). The top problem space consists of task operators; such as, to recognize an item. The subgoals are generated as the result of impasses in problem solving. A subgoal terminates when the impasse is resolved.

Soar learns by acquiring new productions that summarize the processing that leads to the results of subgoals, a process called *chunking*. The actions of the new productions are based on the results of the subgoal. The conditions are based on those working memory elements in supergoals that were relevant to the determination of the results. Relevance is determined by using the traces of the productions that fired during the subgoal. Starting from the production trace that generated the subgoal's result, those production traces that generated the working-memory elements in the conditions of the trace are found, and then the traces that generated their condition elements are found, and so on until elements are reached that are in supergoals. Productions that only generate desirability preferences do not participate in this backtracing process—desirability preferences only affect the efficiency with which a goal is achieved, and not the correctness of the goal's results.

Soar's perceptual–motor behavior is driven by a set of asynchronous modules, and mediated through the state in the top context. Each perceptual and motor modality (module) has its own state attribute to which perceptual information is added and/or motor commands are taken. New sensory information arrives in working memory whenever it is available, and motor commands are sent to the appropriate motor modules as soon as they are added to working memory. Sensory information can be retained by explicitly attaching it to other existing structures. Otherwise, it will be displaced when new information arrives.

Figure 4.1 summarizes the major functional and structural components of the Soar architecture—its memories, basic computational cycle, learning, and interfaces.

- Purpose of Research: Architecture for general intelligence.
- Organizing Framework: Goals and problem spaces.
- Long-term Memory: Recognition–based productions.
- Short-term Memory: Objects and attributes.
- Basic Computation Cycle: Elaboration (access LTM until quiescence) and decision.
- Decisions: Preference–based for problem spaces, states, and operators.
- Subgoal Creation: Impasses in decision scheme.
- Learning: Chunking—summarize processing of subgoal as a production.
- Interface to External Environment: Asynchronous through top state.

FIG. 4.1.   Summary of Soar.

## ARCHITECTURAL SUPPORT FOR KNOWLEDGE

The conventional description of Soar provided in the previous section does not always make clear the ways in which the architecture directly supports knowledge. That is the task for this section—to make explicit the ways the architecture directly supports knowledge in general, and procedural, episodic, and declarative knowledge in particular. The question of indirect architectural support is left to the later sections, which examine each of these three types of knowledge in detail.

General support is provided by productions, the elaboration phase, impasses, subgoals, problem space search, working memory, and chunking. Productions provide for the explicit storage of knowledge. The knowledge is stored in the actions of productions, while the conditions act as access paths to the knowledge. The process of retrieving knowledge by the matching and firing of a production comprises a search of the system's explicitly stored long-term knowledge. It is thus termed *knowledge search* (or *k–search*). Knowledge retrievable by k-search—that is, by the firing of a production—is termed *k–retrievable knowledge*. K-search is efficient, but relatively limited in its capabilities.

Knowledge that is not retrievable by the firing of a single production may still be retrievable by the firing of multiple productions in a single elaboration phase. This happens when information retrieved early in an elaboration phase provides the cues that allow the desired information to be retrieved by a later production firing. It also happens when the desired information is distributed among the actions of multiple productions, which retrieve it by firing jointly within the same elaboration phase. This is termed *k\*–search,* and knowledge retrievable through elaboration is termed *k\*–retrievable knowledge*. k\*–search is exhaustive but efficient, allowing the system to use a significant body of knowledge in its decisions even under relatively stringent time constraints.

The creation of impasses provides a means for determining when the k\*–retrievable knowledge is an inadequate basis for making a decision. The decision procedure can detect incompleteness and inconsistency in the set of k\*–retrievable preferences, but cannot directly detect incorrect or suboptimal knowledge.

Subgoals provide contexts in which knowledge that is not k\*-retrievable can be retrieved by *problem–space search* (or *ps-search*). Knowledge that is retrievable by ps–search is termed *ps–retrievable knowledge*. Because problem-space search (ps–search) is always eventually grounded in production firings (k\*–search), there is a fairly direct relationship between ps–retrievable knowledge and k\*-retrievable knowledge.[2] Knowledge that is ps–retrievable in the current context is constructed from pieces of knowledge which are independently k\*–retrievable in other contexts, but not jointly k\*–retrievable in the current context. Ps–search allows for the consideration of alternatives and the deliberate construction of information, whereas k\*–search provides for only the monotonic accumulation of knowledge. Problem–space search is selective and slow, but can with sufficient resources retrieve any knowledge in the system's knowledge level.

---

[2]Here, and in the remainder of this chapter the terms k\*-search and k\*-retrievable knowledge will be assumed to subsume the terms k-search and k-retrievable knowledge, respectively, except where the distinction is particularly crucial.

Working memory provides a locus where retrieved knowledge can be examined and used. It also provides a locus where new knowledge can reside temporarily before it is stored into long-term memory by chunking. Chunking provides a means of creating new productions, thus directly augmenting the system's store of k*–retrievable knowledge, and indirectly augmenting its store of ps–retrievable knowledge. Chunking is the mechanism for converting ps–search to k*-search.

Procedural knowledge is specifically supported by the architecture in four ways. First, production execution is a primitive form of controlled action. Executing a production performs a form of retrieval in which the retrieved information is adapted to the current situation before being retrieved. The nature of the adaptation is determined by the production's variables. Variables that are shared between conditions and actions result in the retrieved information being instantiated to be about existing objects. Variables that exist only in actions result in the creation of new objects. Control is exerted on production execution by the match. Production conditions specify situations that must hold in working memory in order for the retrieval actions to be executed (Newell, Rosenbloom, & Laird, 1989). Unlike traditional production systems, there is no additional conflict resolution process that participates in the control of production execution.

Second, the selection of an object for a context slot is also a primitive form of controlled action. Selections are actions performed by the architecture that change the focus of problem solving in working memory. For example, the selection of a new operator changes what the system is attempting to accomplish. Preferences represent architecturally interpretable control information for the selection process.

Third, the concept of a problem-solving operator is partially supported by the architecture. The architecture provides an operator role in contexts and the decision procedure that enables the selection of operators for operator roles. It also provides for the generation of impasses when there is insufficient knowledge about how to select or execute an operator. An important form of support not provided is an architecturally interpretable operator language. Instead, operator execution always eventually grounds out in memory retrieval (and motor behavior). How this happens may be quite complicated, involving numerous subgoals, or the interpretation by productions—that is, by further memory retrieval—of an arbitrary operator language.

Fourth, the architecture provides motor commands that perform primitive actions in the external environment. There is not yet a complete and standard set of motor commands in Soar. Instead, what exists is a text-output module, providing basic text-output commands, and a flexible mechanism for adding new modules to, for example, control robot arms (Laird et al., in press) and mobile robots. Selection of motor commands is not provided directly by the architecture. It is under the control of the knowledge (productions) which retrieve the motor commands into working memory, usually under the aegis of operator execution.

Episodic knowledge is specifically supported by the chunking and execution of new productions. Chunking acquires new productions based on problem-solving episodes. The actions of a chunk correspond to information that was generated as the result of an episode. When the chunk executes it retrieves information that is similar to that generated during the episode—though, as mentioned above, the retrieved information is generally adapted to the current situation rather than being a verbatim record of the earlier episode's results. The conditions of the chunk ensure that the adapted results are only retrieved in similar situations. Not provided by the architecture is a mechanism that creates verbatim records of the system's experiences for later examination.

Declarative knowledge is specifically supported by the working and production memories. Working memory is a transient memory of objects, with associated attributes and values. These objects are declarative in that they are examinable (by productions), but they need not have a fixed semantics. Production memory provides for long-term storage of declarative structures—in the actions of productions—which can be retrieved (and adapted) by production execution.

## PROCEDURAL KNOWLEDGE

As mentioned in the introduction, procedural knowledge is knowledge about the agent's actions, which includes knowledge about which actions can be performed, which actions should be performed when (control knowledge), and how actions are performed. Procedural knowledge is already one of the most well developed and understood parts of Soar. Soar was, after all, originally developed as a general problem-solving architecture. Thus this section primarily serves as a review, but it also serves to develop a number of the basic concepts used in the subsequent sections on episodic and declarative knowledge. The discussion is divided into subsections covering the three subdomains mentioned above: performable actions, action control, and action performance. For each of these subdomains we discuss how the knowledge is represented, stored, retrieved, used, and acquired. This same suborganization will be followed in later sections on episodic and declarative knowledge.

### Performable Actions

Performable actions are represented as operators, along with acceptable preferences that can cause the operators to be considered in some set of situations. Each operator is represented in working memory as an object—a declarative structure—rather than a production. For example, an operator in the Eight Puzzle that slides a tile from one cell on the board to an adjacent one could be represented as (operator $o1$ ^name slide). When augmented with parameters specifying the source and destination cells for the tile, the operator can be represented as (operator $o1$ ^name slide ^source $c1$ ^destination $c2$), where the symbols $c1$ and $c2$ are the identifiers of the two cells.

The declarative structure for operators, and their acceptable preferences, are stored in the actions of productions. The entire object can be stored in the actions of a single production (k–retrievable); it can be distributed across the actions of a group of productions that all fire within a single decision cycle (k*–retrievable); or it can be distributed across multiple productions that fire in a subgoal that constructs the operator, bit by bit (ps–retrievable).

Problem spaces are a major source of context for operator retrieval. The production in which the above Eight Puzzle operator is stored will have a condition which tests that the Eight Puzzle problem space is the one currently selected in a context before retrieving the operator for the context. It is also often useful to utilize the operator's preconditions as a source of retrieval context. If this is done, then the operator is only retrieved in situations for which it is applicable. An alternative is to retrieve the operator according to means–ends analysis, that is, when the operator will reduce the difference between the current state and the desired state. With means-ends analysis, an operator may be retrieved even when its preconditions are not satisfied by the current state.

Operators by themselves do nothing. The architecture does not understand the language(s) in which operators are written, and therefore does not know how, based just on the operators themselves, to either select among them or to perform them. The best the architecture can do without additional knowledge is to perform various default actions based on its understanding of their acceptable preferences. It can select an operator if it is the only candidate available, and generate an impasse if there is more than one operator, or if the selected one cannot be executed.

Operators, and their acceptable preferences, are cues for retrieving a variety of additional knowledge. The operator structure can trigger knowledge about how to select and perform operators. The acceptable preferences can trigger knowledge in both prospective and retrospective fashions. Prospectively, acceptable preferences for operators determine what operators are being considered for the next selection. Retrospectively, acceptable preferences for operators act as episodic knowledge about what operators were considered for what states.

Operators, and their acceptable preferences, are acquired by the chunking of problem-solving episodes that generate them as results. Chunking does not by itself generate new operators, but it can convert ps–retrievable operators into k*–retrievable ones, as well as store away in production memory new operators that are generated. The conversion of operator knowledge from ps–retrievable to k*–retrievable is the obvious caching effect produced by chunking. Storage of newly generated operators factors into two cases. If the new operators are generated internally, then they must have already been ps–retrievable—that is, retrievable by problem space search—thus reducing this case to the previous caching situation. If the new operators are based on external information, chunking can turn unretrievable operators into k*-retrievable operators. This is a more subtle consequence of chunking that is worth looking at in some detail.

Yost and Newell (1988) demonstrated how new operators could be acquired from external information, in the context of a system called TAQ (Yost, 1987) that acquires new tasks (i.e., problem spaces) from external descriptions. In more recent work, this approach has been extended to take simple English instructions for a range of immediate-reasoning tasks, such as categorical syllogisms and sentence verification (Lewis, Newell, & Polk, 1989). Figure 4.2 shows the two basic steps. The first step in task acquisition is to comprehend an externally provided description of the task to be acquired. This description can conceptually take a variety of forms—versions of TAQ have accepted descriptions in simple English sentences and in a formal problem space notation. The outcome of the comprehension process is the presence in working memory of a declarative description of a problem space for the task. The second step is to solve the problem using the declarative description interpretively. That is, at each point in task performance, if the next required activity—such as the generation of an operator—is not directly performable by k*-search, then a subgoal occurs. Within the subgoal, the declarative task description is examined and interpreted by a set of pre-existing problem spaces that search through the declarative task description for information about what to do in the current situation.

The chunks acquired for these interpretation subgoals directly implement the required activity. Chunking the comprehension process converts unretrievable operators into ps-retrievable operators—using memorization techniques described later—and chunking of the interpretation process makes the ps–retrievable knowledge k*-retrievable.

## Action Control

Control knowledge—that is, knowledge about how to select among performable actions—is represented to the architecture by operator preferences. The three types of preferences described previously in this chapter—acceptability, desir-

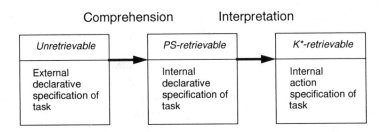

FIG. 4.2.   The two stages of acquiring operator knowledge.

ability, and necessity—are used to represent three qualitatively different types of control knowledge. Acceptability preferences represent knowledge about whether an operator is to be considered for execution. Unconsidered operators have no effect on the decision procedure; they cannot be selected, nor can they cause an impasse to occur. Desirability preferences represent heuristic information that can be brought to bear in determining what operator is likely to lead towards goal satisfaction. Necessity preferences represent constraints derived from the goal. They can be used to guarantee that certain conditions are always (or never true) during the search, thus eliminating the need to explicitly test them at the end. In the extreme, necessity preferences can be used to explicitly represent the entire sequence of steps in a procedure that achieves some goal, eliminating the need for an explicit goal test at the end.

Preferences are stored in the actions of productions. In any particular situation an arbitrary preference can be k–retrievable, k*–retrievable, ps-retrievable, or unretrievable. The primary context for preference retrieval is the object being considered and the objects already selected as part of the problem solving context. For example, the retrieval context for operator preferences in the Eight Puzzle includes the operator being considered (to slide a tile from cell $c1$ into cell $c2$), the goal to be achieved (a solution to the Eight Puzzle), the problem space (Eight Puzzle), and the state to which the operator is to be applied. For binary preferences, such as better worse and indifferent preferences, the retrieval context includes multiple contending objects.

Preferences are used both by the architecture—the decision procedure—and by other knowledge. The architecture uses preferences to determine what selection to make, or what type of subgoal to generate if no selection can be made. As mentioned previously in this chapter, preferences can act as cues about what the decision procedure is going to do, and to reconstruct what it did in the past.

Preferences are acquired by the chunking of problem-solving episodes that generate preferences as their results. Most of our experience in acquiring preferences involves the acquisition of desirability preferences and that is all that will be discussed here, though the acquisition of acceptable preferences is covered under the discussion of operator acquisition.

As with knowledge about performable actions, chunking can turn ps–retrievable preferences into k*–retrievable preferences, and convert unretrievable preferences into ps-retrievable and k*–retrievable preferences. The most common way to turn ps-retrievable preferences into k*–retrievable ones involves a look-ahead search. This process has been described in detail elsewhere (Laird, Newell, & Rosenbloom, 1987), but the essence is to use Soar's basic search capability along with knowledge—about how to evaluate states, how to back up evaluations to earlier operators and states, and how to generate preferences from evaluations—to generate, and thus learn via chunking, preferences about operators that have tied for selection.

As demonstrated in (Golding, Rosenbloom, & Laird, 1987), it is possible to use external advice to assist in the process of converting ps–retrievable knowledge into k*–retrievable knowledge. If advice is given about what alternatives are good (or bad, for that matter), the advice can be turned into preferences which guide the look-ahead search. This can reduce the amount of search required without changing the chunks that are learned for the search. Externally provided knowledge can also be used to shift a piece of control knowledge from unretrievable to k*–retrievable using the techniques described in the section on "Performable Actions." (Yost & Newell, 1988).

## Action Performance

As mentioned previously, Soar does not have a single, architecturally interpretable language for action performance. Instead, there are several distinct ways of representing action performance. One way to represent action performance, at least for external actions, is as some combination of motor commands. Retrieval of motor commands into working memory causes the associated motor systems to behave in appropriate fashions. There is a fixed language of motor commands, as determined by the available motor systems.

A second way to represent action performance is as a subprocedure that performs the action when executed. In Soar terms, the subprocedure is the processing in a subgoal that arises when the results of performing the action are not k*–retrievable. Within the subprocedure, the types of procedural knowledge described in this section would be applied recursively.

A third way to represent action performance is as the state that results from applying the operator representing the action. As with operators, the entire state can be stored in the actions of a single production (k–retrievable), it can be distributed across the actions of a group of productions that all fire within a single decision cycle (k*–retrievable), or it can be distributed across multiple productions that fire under different circumstances (ps–retrievable). The ps-retrievable case corresponds to the representation of action performance as subprocedures that is described above. Such a procedural representation—that is, representation as a subprocedure, rather than representation of a procedure—can actually be used for any piece of knowledge, whether the knowledge is itself about procedures or not.

The primary context for the retrieval of a result state is the conjunction of relevant features of the previous state and the operator. The result state is used as the basis for further problem solving, by serving as part of the retrieval context for goal testing, result generation, state and operator evaluation, and operator generation, selection, and application. The result state's acceptable preference is used by the decision procedure to select the state as the current state. As mentioned in the previous subsections, other knowledge may also use the preference prospectively to determine what state is going to be selected, and retrospectively to determine what state was selected, and what operator and state preceded it.

Acquisition of result states occurs by the chunking of problem-solving episodes that generate such states. One of the most common ways to acquire a k*– retrievable result state is to chunk over the process of executing a procedure that represents an action. As with the acquisition of knowledge about control, external advice can be utilized to speed up the process of acquiring knowledge about action performance. In one version, demonstrated for subtraction, Tic-Tac-Toe, and simple block manipulation, the system starts out with a set of primitive operators that are sufficient to implement the individual tests and modifications made by any operator. Advice is then used to determine which elements the action should test and generate for the specific operator being acquired. Given the primitive operators, this approach allows arbitrary operators to be acquired from advice.

Another way to acquire knowledge about action performance is to chunk over the process of interpreting an externally provided description of the action, as in (Yost & Newell, 1988). The process proceeds much as did the corresponding one in the earlier section on "Performable Actions," where in this case, one or more chunks are learned that can retrieve the result state in the future.

## Summary

Procedural knowledge appears to be adequately supported by the current architecture. This should not be too surprising as it was originally designed for this; or at least for representing problem-solving knowledge. One aspect that might come as a surprise is that productions, though they are a primitive form of action, are not the model for action—operators are. Another possibly surprising aspect is that there is no single architecturally interpreted operator language. The fixed operator language common to most systems is replaced by the ability to perform operators by memory retrieval—either k*–retrieval or ps-retrieval—in conjunction with motor commands. The flexibility of this approach allows performance knowledge to be represented either directly in action form or as declarative structures that are interpreted. In fact, with the aid of software interpreters it should be possible to construct arbitrary operator languages. One example of such an approach is the language and interpreter used in the task acquisition work.

Learning has an important place in the use of procedural knowledge. By converting ps-retrievable knowledge into k*–retrievable knowledge, it can improve the system's ability to retrieve relevant knowledge under real-time constraints, and thus improve the system's approximation to the principle of rationality. It can convert interpreted behavior into direct action. It can also acquire new knowledge from the outside world, allowing the system to expand the tasks it can work on and the knowledge that it can use on those tasks.

# EPISODIC KNOWLEDGE

Episodic knowledge is knowledge about what has occurred. In general, the individual elements of episodic knowledge can be viewed as instances of a binary predicate, Occurred($x$, $y$), where $x$ is an object, action, or sequence of actions that has occurred—for simplicity we will refer to all such members of the class of things that can occur as *events*—and $y$ is a context in which the event occurred. Two loose but illustrative examples are Occurred("gaf," "List 1 of Experiment 2"), which denotes that a particular object (the nonsense trigram "gaf") occurred in a particular context (during the first list of experiment 2), and Occurred("pull-knob then turn-knob," "setting time on watch"), which denotes that a particular sequence of actions (pulling out of the watch's knob followed by turning of it) occurred in a particular context (the setting of the watch).

There are two notable features about the role or episodic knowledge in Soar. First, episodic knowledge can be represented at many different levels of explicitness. Second, although the representation, storage, retrieval, and use of episodic knowledge is rather straightforward, the acquisition of some forms of episodic knowledge is quite challenging. It leads us to posit the existence of comparatively complex strategies for acquiring these forms of episodic knowledge.

## Representation

One way to represent episodic knowledge is completely as declarative structures; that is, as objects with attributes and values. In such a representation, the above two examples might appear as follows.

> (occurred $e1$ ^event $o1$ ^context $c1$)
> (object $o1$ ^name gaf)
> (context $c1$ ^experiment 2 ^list 1)
>
> (occurred $e2$ ^event $s1$ ^context $c2$)
> (sequence $s1$ ^action1 $a1$ ^action2 $a2$)
> (action $a1$ ^name pull–knob)
> (action $a2$ ^name turn–knob)
> (context $c2$ ^name setting–time–on–watch)

However, not all of this knowledge need be represented directly as declarative structures. The alternative is to omit some of the components from the explicit representation, and assume them implicitly by default. The key to making this work is an understanding of the episodic nature of chunking; that is, that chunks are acquired as the result of problem-solving episodes, and execute in contexts that are similar to the ones in which they were learned. Spinning out the consequences of this understanding leads to a sequence of ways of omitting and modifying components of the representation.

The first component that can be omitted is the context. The conditions of a chunk represent both the context in which the information was learned and the contexts in which it should be retrieved. Therefore, when information is retrieved from long-term memory it can be assumed that it was learned in a situation that was similar to the retrieval situation. Eliminating the explicit context from the example above leaves the following explicit structures.

> (occurred $e1$ ^event $o1$)
> (object $o1$ ^name gaf)
>
> (occurred $e2$ ^event $s1$)
> (sequence $s1$ ^action1 $a1$ ^action2 $a2$)
> (action $a1$ ^name pull-knob)
> (action $a2$ ^name turn-knob)

The next component that can be omitted is the occurred predicate, which, now that the context is removed, just states that its event occurred. If it is assumed that all knowledge that is retrieved from long-term memory got there via chunking— even if the system starts out with a number of productions, after sufficient time nearly all of its productions should have been acquired by chunking—then it can be assumed that any structures retrieved from long-term memory must have been seen before. Therefore, the explicit predicate can be eliminated in favor of the assumption that anything that is retrieved has occurred. Eliminating the occurred predicate from the example leaves the following explicit structures.

> (object $o1$ ^name gaf)
>
> (sequence $s1$ ^action1 $a1$ ^action2 $a2$)
> (action $a1$ ^name pull–knob)
> (action $a2$ ^name turn–knob)

The episodic knowledge about the gaf event is now represented quite simply as a typical Soar object—all structures that were introduced solely for their role in representing episodic knowledge have been deleted. This is thus its final form. However, for the watch event, two additional steps are needed to convert its action sequence into its final form. The first step involves a change in nomenclature to replace actions with operators. Operators are intended to represent actions that can be performed rather than actions that were performed, but the assumptions made so far imply that if an operator is retrieved in a context then it must have been learned in a similar context. Operators can therefore stand in for actions that have occurred. Making this change eliminates the need for creating new structures to explicitly represent actions that have occurred, using the existing operator structures instead.

> (sequence $s1$ ^operator1 $a1$ ^operator2 $a2$)
> (operator $a1$ ^name pull-knob)
> (operator $a2$ ^name turn-knob)

The second, and final, step is to replace the explicit representation of operator sequences with preferences. As mentioned previously, preferences can be used retrospectively to determine what objects were selected. Through their context fields—the goal, problem-space, state, and operator fields—they can also be used to determine what objects were current in the context at the time the object was selected. The following recoding of the example represents that operator $a1$ was acceptable in the situation characterized by $g1$, $p1$, and $s1$; that state $s2$ was acceptable in the situation where operator $a1$ was additionally selected (it is $a1$'s result); and that operator $a2$ was acceptable in the situation where state $s1$ has been replaced by state $s2$.

(preference $a1$ ^value acceptable ^role operator
  ^goal $g1$ problem–space $p1$ ^state $s1$)
(operator $a1$ ^name pull-knob)
(preference $s2$ ^value acceptable ^role state
  ^goal $g1$ problem–space $p1$ ^state $s1$ ^operator $a1$)
(preference $a2$ ^value acceptable ^role operator
  ^goal $g1$ problem–space $p1$ ^state $s2$)
(operator $a2$ ^name turn-knob)

As was true of the gaf event earlier, the watch event is now represented without the use of any structures introduced solely for their role in representing episodic knowledge. The explicit structures that are left may actually be larger than some of the previous (this is not true of the gaf example), but they are structures that are already available because of their role in problem solving. This is thus Soar's native form of episodic knowledge. The significance of this is three-fold. First, this is the form of episodic knowledge which is available without positing additional semantics (or apparatus). Second, this form of episodic knowledge will always be around anyway, so it needs to be taken into consideration. Third, because it posits no additional apparatus, it should automatically compose well with the other capabilities in the system.

## Storage

The manner of storage of episodic knowledge is a function of the representation that is used. Components that are directly represented as declarative structures are stored in the actions of productions. The "gaf" example might be stored in a production like the following (or across multiple productions).[3]

→
(occurred $<e1>$ ^event $<o1>$ ^context $<c1>$)
(object $<o1>$ ^name gaf)
(context $<c1>$ ^experiment 2 ^list 1)

---

[3]Symbols enclosed in angle brackets, such as $<e1>$, are variables.

Though this production is shown without conditions, as described later in this chapter, it is necessary (and possible) to add additional conditions to restrict the situations in which such declarative structures are retrieved.

Assumed parts are simply omitted from the actions. However, for the context assumption to work, a representation of the context must appear in the conditions of the production. This doesn't allow the context to be retrieved as an explicit structure, but does constrain the explicit structures to be retrieved only in contexts similar to the ones in which they were learned. The "gaf" example above would be stored as a production like the following one.

$$(\text{context } <c1> \text{ }^\text{experiment 2 } ^\text{list 1})$$
$$\rightarrow (\text{object } <o1> \text{ }^\text{name gaf})$$

## Retrieval

Explicit episodic knowledge is retrieved in the same way as are other declarative structures; that is, by a combination of k*–search and ps-search. Omitted components are retrieved by assumption. If the context of occurrence is omitted, then it is assumed to share critical features with the retrieval context. If the predicate is omitted, occurrence is assumed for retrieved information. If actions are omitted, operator retrieval is assumed to denote an action that was executed. If sequence information is omitted, preferences are assumed to denote sequences of operators and states that occurred.

## Use

There has not yet been a great need for episodic knowledge in the tasks that have so far been implemented in Soar. Nonetheless, it has been used in several distinct ways. One way is the use of preferences as the basis for a form of chronological backtracking—a short-term episodic use in which the preferences remain in working memory throughout. Soar normally backtracks in look-ahead search by terminating subgoals that lead to failure. However, there are times when Soar thinks it knows what it is doing—so no look-ahead search is being performed— yet failure still occurs. Backtracking under these circumstances involves examining the acceptable preference for the state at which failure occurred to find out which state was current when the failed state was selected. This prior state is then reselected, and problem solving is continued.

A second use is as the basis for recognition and recall tasks (Rosenbloom, Laird, & Newell, 1987, 1988a). In a recognition task the system is presented with a list of items to be memorized. It is then prompted with an item which may or may not be in the list. Its task is to say *yes* if the item was in the list and *no* if it wasn't. A recall task is similar, but instead of being prompted with an item, the system must produce as many of the items in the list as it can, without producing items not in the list. These tasks require episodic knowledge because they ask questions about what happened in the system's past.

A third use is as the basis for the transfer of procedural knowledge. The procedural knowledge that Soar learns can be viewed as really being episodic knowledge about the past behavior of the system. To use this episodic knowledge as procedural knowledge, there is an implicit assumption that what is descriptive of the past is normative for the future. This assumption is maintained until it leads to an error, at which point the system attempts to recover by doing something other than what is directly dictated by its past experience (Laird, 1988).

The issue of errors is actually a key one when native episodic knowledge is used, because, whenever an assumption is made, the possibility for error creeps in. There are four classes of situations that can lead to errors. Some of these are intrinsic in the nature of the world, while others arise because of specific architectural commitments in Soar. The first class of errors arises because of mistakes in credit assignment. Soar cannot examine the conditions of productions, so when knowledge is retrieved it can only guess as to which aspects of the retrieval context were shared with the context in which the knowledge was learned. This can lead to both errors of commission and omission. Suppose, for example, that the system is winding a watch at the same time it is trying to recall the elements that occurred in list 1 of experiment 2. It will retrieve both "gaf" and "pull-knob then turn-knob." The problem is that there is no a priori reason to assume that one of these events is in the list and that the other is not. In this particular case it might be able to use background or other contextual knowledge to reason that the watch events were not part of the list, but in other cases it may not be so lucky.

The second class of situations arises because of mistakes in context generalization. There is a trade-off between the scope of applicability of knowledge and its utility as episodic knowledge. The more general is the context, the more situations in which the knowledge can be retrieved, and thus be available for use. However, increasing the generality also decreases the ability to discriminate the situations in which the knowledge was originally learned from related situations. This can be seen clearly in the acquisition and use of control knowledge. The more general is the control knowledge, the more search is eliminated, assuming the generalization is correct. However, generality also implies that the knowledge will be retrieved in a variety of contexts, many of which are only remotely like the one in which the knowledge was learned.

The third class of situations arises because of mistakes in memory attribution. The only examinable structures in Soar are those in its working memory. Such structures could arise from memory retrieval, from intervention by the architecture (the decision procedure), or from perception. Only those that arise from memory retrieval embody episodic knowledge. Normally this shouldn't be a problem because the decision procedure and perceptual systems each create structures in a characteristic fashion: the decision procedure only modifies certain special attributes of goals; perception always adds its structures to special attributes of the state in the top context. However, the possibility remains.

The fourth, and final class of situations can be caused by any of the first three. It occurs because of mistakes in co-occurrence attribution. Such failures occur when the system mistakenly thinks it has previously experienced an event because it has experienced all of its individual pieces, though never all as part of a single event. Suppose, for example, that in one context the system sees a large ball, and in a similar context it sees a green ball. A co-occurrence error occurs if the system thinks that it saw both in the same context, or worse, that it has seen a single large green ball. In the recognition and recall tasks this problem is partially dealt with by assuming that $k*$–retrievable objects have been experienced, while ps-retrievable and unretrievable objects have not. The rationale is that $k*$–retrieval, being a limited computational mechanism, has a limited ability to put things together in novel ways, while ps-retrieval allows arbitrary structures to be created.

## Acquisition

Episodic knowledge is acquired by chunking problem-solving episodes. Though this is somewhat of a tautology for Soar, it is not always as simple as it sounds. The simple case is the acquisition of episodic knowledge about objects generated in subgoals. If such objects are returned as results of their subgoals, then chunks are created which can later be used as episodic knowledge about the objects. The variety of subgoal results—objects, operators, preferences, and so on—leads directly to variety in the episodic knowledge that can be learned.

Under normal circumstances this episodic knowledge is represented in what we have referred to as native form; that is, predicates, contexts, actions, and sequences are represented respectively by chunk existence, production conditions, operators, and preferences. However, if the system monitors its own performance, and creates declarative structures representing what has transpired, then the chunks created for such structures can be used as explicit declarative-form episodic knowledge about what has transpired. In addition, such chunks can be used as native episodic knowledge about the monitoring process itself.

One form of episodic knowledge that cannot be handled this easily is knowledge about what has happened to the system; that is, knowledge about what the system has perceived rather than knowledge about what the system has generated. The "gaf" example presented above is a typical perceptual event. The episodic knowledge to be acquired is about the perception of "gaf" in a particular context (experiment 2, list 1). As described previously, Soar's input mechanism attaches perceptual information to the state in the top problem–solving context. In order for information about the event to be stored into long-term memory by chunking, an internal episode must be generated in which this perceptual information is used.

For perceptual events it is relatively easy to acquire a form of episodic knowledge akin to a familiarity test. The system must simply chunk over a subgoal in which it examines a representation of the perceptual event and the context, and generates as a subgoal result an occurred predicate covering them (Rosenbloom Laird, & Newell, 1987). A familiarity chunk for this example might look like one of the following two productions, depending on whether the context is explicit or not.

$$(object <ol> \char"5E name gaf)$$
$$(context <cl> \char"5E experiment 2 \char"5E list 1)$$
$$\rightarrow$$
$$(occurred <el> \char"5E event <ol> \char"5E context <cl>)$$

$$(object <ol> \char"5E name gaf)$$
$$(context <cl> \char"5E experiment 2 \char"5E list 1)$$
$$\rightarrow$$
$$(occurred <el> \char"5E event <ol>)$$

In the systems so far implemented, context is actually ignored in the learning of episodic knowledge. By having no explicit representation of context in either the conditions or the actions of the chunks, the context is effectively the entire history of the system. In this form, the "gaf" familiarity chunk looks like the following:

$$(object <ol> \char"5E name gaf)$$
$$\rightarrow$$
$$(occurred <el> \char"5E event <ol>)$$

Familiarity chunks allow the determination of whether an event has occurred before in a particular context. Whenever a representation of the event appears in working memory along with a representation of the context, an occurred predicate will be retrieved for them. Familiarity chunks can thus support performance in recognition tasks, where the task is to determine whether a presented object has been seen before.

What familiarity chunks do not directly support is the retrieval of events that occurred in a particular context. For an event to be retrieved by the execution of a chunk, the event must be stored in the actions of the chunk, and not tested in its conditions. A retrieval chunk for the "gaf" example should look something like the following (with an assumed context and predicate):

$$(context <cl> \char"5E experiment 2 \char"5E list 1)$$
$$\rightarrow$$
$$(object <ol> \char"5E name gaf)$$

For such productions to be learned by Soar, they must be created by chunking over some form of problem solving. But chunking is not an indefinitely flexible mechanism. A chunk's actions are always based on the results of a subgoal, and its conditions are always based on a dependency analysis of the results. This immediately imposes two constraints on the nature of the problem solving that can underly the acquisition of retrieval chunks.

1. For the event to appear in the actions of a chunk, it must be generated as a result of a subgoal.
2. For the event to not appear in the conditions of the chunk, the subgoal results must not depend on an examination of the event.

The first constraint is relatively easy to meet; for example, by creating a copy of the perceptual event in a subgoal, and returning the copy as a result. However, attempting to meet both constraints at once leads to the *data chunking problem:* if the result is based on examining the object to be learned, then the conditions of the chunk will also test the object, allowing it to only be retrieved when it is already available. For example, using the copying strategy for the "gaf" example would lead to a chunk like the following:

$$\text{(context} <c1> \ \hat{}\,\text{experiment 2} \ \hat{}\,\text{list 1)}$$
$$\text{(object} <o1> \ \hat{}\,\text{name gaf)}$$
$$\rightarrow$$
$$\text{(object} <o1> \ \hat{}\,\text{name gaf)}$$

In contrast to the desired retrieval chunk, this one tests that "gaf" is already in working memory before it will retrieve it. So it doesn't do the job.

The solution to the data chunking problem is to separate the result generation process from the use of the perceptual event. Result generation must be based on what the system already knows, rather than on the perceptual event. One approach involves assembling the result from components that the system can already retrieve (Rosenbloom, Laird, & Newell, 1987). For example, if the letters "g," "a," and "f" are retrievable, then "gaf" can be generated by retrieving and assembling them. This is a syntactic compositional process which may or may not respect any specific semantic rules in performing the assembly. Another approach is to start with the context and to chain through a sequence of productions which form a pre-existing, though possibly indirect, link between the context and the event (Rosenbloom, 1988). For example, (object o1 ˆname gaf) can be generated if (context c1 ˆexperiment 2 ˆlist 1) is already in working memory, and if the following two retrieval chunks exist.

$$\text{(context} <c1> \ \hat{}\,\text{experiment 2} \ \hat{}\,\text{list 1)}$$
$$\rightarrow$$
$$\text{(object} <o1> \ \hat{}\,\text{name fem)}$$
$$\text{(object} <o1> \ \hat{}\,\text{name fem)}$$
$$\rightarrow$$
$$\text{(object} <o1> \ \hat{}\,\text{name gaf)}$$

Either approach requires the system to start out with a set of primitive elements that can be generated. Other more complex structures can then be built up out of compositions of these primitive elements. For the work on recognition and recall, the system was initialized with the ability to generate the 26 letters. Conceivably, Soar could have been initialized with an even lower level of primitives, such as simple lines, curves, and points, from which it would construct the letters. It could also have been initialized with more meaningful primitives, such as the primitive ACTs in Conceptual Dependency Theory (Schank, 1975) or the epistemological primitives in KL-ONE (Brachman, 1979).

Though the perceptual event cannot be used directly in the generation process, it is still used in two critical ways. The first is as the basis of a goal test for the generation process. The generation process can conceivably return any event that it can either assemble or chain to, so a goal test is necessary to determine when the desired event has been generated. The straightforward approach of comparing the perceptual and generated events does not work. Instead, it leads to a secondary version of the data chunking problem in which the comparison causes tests of the perceptual event to appear in the conditions of the chunk.

To avoid this secondary data chunking problem, the goal test is based on a familiarity chunk for the perceptual event rather than directly on the event. Given a familiarity chunk for the perceptual event, the generation goal test is satisfied when a familiar but unretrieved event is generated. The test of familiarity guarantees that the event has been seen in the current context (or a similar one). If the event is unretrieved, it is one that the system has not previously learned to generate. This test is somewhat overgeneral in that it can't guarantee that the generated event is a copy of the current perceptual event. However, at worst it will only generate a different event that is familiar in the same context. If this happens, it is always possible to try again to generate an event that corresponds to the input event. The use of a familiarity chunk as the goal test for the generation process makes this is a generate-recognize approach to recall (see, for example, Watkins & Gardiner, 1979), though focused on the acquisition phase rather than the retrieval phase.

The second way that the perceptual event is used is as the basis for controlling the search through the space of events that can be generated. The goal test determines the correctness of the result, but does not affect the efficiency of the search. Using the perceptual event as control knowledge makes the search tractable, potentially removing all backtracking, without affecting the correctness of the result. Thus the result technically does not depend on such control knowledge. The bottom line is that the use of search control knowledge can speed up performance without introducing additional conditions into chunks (recall from earlier in this chapter that chunking does not backtrace through the use of desirability preferences by the decision procedure). Of secondary importance is that the use of the perceptual event as search control increases the likelihood that the first event generated will correspond to the perceptual event rather than to another familiar but unretrieved event.

When the generation, goal testing, and control processes are all put together, a retrieval chunk can be learned that is identical to the one that was desired. Context can be treated in the same ways that it is for familiarity chunks. It can be explicit (in the actions), assumed (in the conditions), or completely ignored (nowhere). The systems so far implemented have ignored context.

One consequence of this approach to the acquisition of retrieval chunks is that it forces information storage to be based on an understanding process. The understanding may be only of syntax (surface structure), or it may be of a deeper semantic (deep structure) nature, but without it, learning will not occur. There is no simple assignment operation—such as the SETQ operation in Lisp—that allows an unanalyzed structure to be stored in long-term memory. A second consequence is that the understanding process must be a reconstructive—or analysis-by-synthesis—process (Bartlett, 1982; Neisser, 1967), in which events are reconstructed in terms of known structures. A third consequence is that the storage process is semantically penetrable. Other knowledge can potentially alter the reconstruction process, and thus what is stored, leading to generalization and other forms of bias in the memory structures that are stored.

## Summary

Soar can represent, store, retrieve, use, and acquire episodic knowledge. However, the situation is nowhere near as clean and simple as it was for procedural knowledge. In fact, if we were to sit down to design a capability for episodic knowledge from scratch, with no constraints, we would be unlikely to design it as currently embodied by Soar. What the architecture most directly supports is native episodic knowledge about structures generated by the system itself. Such knowledge is represented, stored, retrieved, and acquired without requiring additional cognitive effort. However, the assumptions required to use such knowledge can lead to errors. By increasing cognitive effort, more explicit forms of episodic knowledge can be acquired that require fewer assumptions for use, and thus hopefully lead to fewer errors. Such structures are not terribly dissimilar to the structures used in other episodic memory proposals, such as Scripts (Schank & Ableson, 1977) and E-Mops (Kolodner, 1985).

The situation is even more complicated for episodic knowledge about perceptual events. Three features of the architecture yield strong constraints on how the knowledge is acquired.

1. Chunk actions are based on subgoal results.
2. Chunk conditions are based on the supergoal structures upon which the results depend.
3. Perceptual information arrives in the top goal.

Together these features force a reconstructive approach to knowledge acquisition. Though this approach is considerably more complicated than simple verbatim storage of what has transpired, it does have a number of promising properties.

Given the overall picture of episodic knowledge, as relatively complicated and messy, it is important to ask whether this signals a need for modification of the architecture. One key question is the appropriateness of the levels of support and constraint that are provided by the architecture. For psychology, this is a matter of the extent to which the level of support models human capabilities, and the level of constraint models human limitations. For AI, this is a matter of whether the system achieves an appropriate level of episodic functionality. A second key question is whether there are more appropriate mechanisms—for either definition of "appropriate"—for the support of episodic knowledge which could be integrated cleanly into the architecture. Providing detailed answers to these two key questions remains for future work.

## DECLARATIVE KNOWLEDGE

Declarative knowledge is knowledge about what is true in the world. Examples include the facts that dogs have four legs and that Fido is a dog. Declarative representation comes in many forms, such as natural language, diagrams, maps, charts, tables, and graphs. This is also the area with which logic is classically concerned. A logic has a syntax specifying the form that statements take, and a semantics which relates logical statements to an abstract conceptualization of the world. For first order predicate calculus (FOPC) the syntax is based on constants, variables, predicates, connectives ($\land$, $\lor$, $\lnot$, and $\supset$), and quantifiers ($\forall$ and $\exists$). The mapping between the syntax and the semantics, called the interpretation, is used to determine the truth of statements expressed in the syntax of the logic.

In this section we are primarily concerned with the syntactic side of declarative knowledge, taking advantage of logic's privileged role in AI as a language for representing declarative knowledge. We examine how declarative knowledge is represented (its syntax), stored, retrieved, used, and acquired. On the issue of semantics, we assume that the meaning of a structures is determined by a combination of two factors: its relationship to the outside world, as mediated by the perceptual and motor systems, and how it is used by internal processes.

As with episodic knowledge, the main challenge is in the acquisition of declarative knowledge. The data chunking techniques described earlier are extended to handle declarative representations.

### Representation

As with episodic and procedural knowledge, there are several different ways that declarative knowledge can be represented in Soar.[4] The most flexible and general approach is to represent each syntactic component—whether it be a constant,

---

[4]In this section we focus on derivation-based representations for logic. Other representations are possible, such as validity-based techniques—see, for example, (Polk & Newell, 1988) and (Polk, Newell, & Lewis, 1989) for research on mental models in Soar. These have somewhat different properties, but much of the discussion would remain the same.

variable, predicate, connective, or quantifier—as an object. The details of exactly how this is done are not crucial, but the general flavor should be clear from the following example which shows a statement in FOPC and how it could be translated into a set of objects in Soar.

$$\forall \ x \ [P(x) \supset Q(x)]$$

(quantifier $q1$ ˆname forall ˆvariable $v1$ ˆbody $b1$)
(variable $v1$ ˆname x)
(connective $b1$ ˆname implies ˆantecedent $a1$ ˆconsequent $c1$)
(predicate $a1$ ˆname p ˆargument $v1$)
(predicate $c1$ ˆname q ˆargument $v1$)

For simple statements containing no quantifiers or variables, no predicates with more than two arguments, and no connectives except for $\wedge$, there is a simpler native representation that takes direct advantage of Soar's object structure. Constants are represented as objects, predicates as attributes, and conjunction as simultaneous occurrence. Here's a simple example about Fido.

$$\text{Category(Fido, Dog)} \wedge \text{Alive(Fido)}$$

(object $o1$ ˆname fido ˆcategory $o2$ ˆalive)
(object $o2$ ˆname dog)

This native representation is more succinct than the previous one, but in exchange it lacks expressibility.

Another variation is to use productions as a representation for a subclass of implications. A production can represent a universally quantified implication in which the antecedent is a conjunction of predicates, and the consequent is an existentially quantified conjunction of predicates.

$$\forall(x_1,...,x_n)[C_1(x_1,...,x_n) \wedge ... \wedge C_j \ (x_1,...,x_n) \supset$$
$$\exists(y_1,...,y_m) \ [A_1(x_1,...,x_n,y_1,...,y_m) \wedge ... \wedge A_k(x_1,...,x_n,y_1,...,y_m)]]$$

The existential quantifier in the consequent arises from the ability to create new objects when variables appear in actions that are not in conditions. A form of negation as failure is also available in the antecedent which allows a predicate to be assumed false unless it is explicitly known to be true (that is, available in working memory).

Implications encoded as productions are non-examinable and can only be used to forward chain. We do not discuss them further here. Instead we focus on examinable structures of either of the first two types.

## Storage

Storage of declarative knowledge is straightforward. As with declaratively represented procedural and episodic knowledge, declarative knowledge is stored in the actions of productions.

## Retrieval

Declarative knowledge is retrieved by k*–search and ps-search. If the knowledge is stored directly in productions, k*–search can retrieve it, otherwise ps-search is required. Hopefully, by this point, this is obvious. However, less obvious is what the context should be for retrieval of declarative knowledge. The retrieval contexts for both procedural and episodic knowledge are straightforward. An element of procedural knowledge is retrieved when it may be needed to produce behavior. An element of episodic knowledge is retrieved when a context is established that is similar to the one in which the episode occurred (at least if the context is tested in production conditions rather than stored in production actions). In contrast, declarative knowledge is by its essence not associated with a particular context. The knowledge is true, independent of context, and should be usable in any context requiring it.

On the other hand, if declarative knowledge is stored with no context—that is, with a null set of production conditions—the knowledge will not only be retrievable in all contexts, it will in fact be retrieved in all contexts, swamping the system with true but irrelevant information. One approach to controlling the retrieval of declarative knowledge is to use the connectedness among facts as a co-relevance heuristic. This is often implemented by the mechanism of spreading activation, which retrieves facts close to those that are already retrieved (Anderson, 1983; Collins & Loftus, 1975). Another approach is to control the retrieval of declarative knowledge by providing a partial description of the knowledge to be retrieved (Norman & Bobrow, 1979). The partial description then delineates the set of things which appear to be relevant.

The approach that we have taken is to store declarative knowledge in a discrimination network that allows retrieval of objects by partial description (Rosenbloom, Laird, & Newell, 1988a). Given any partial description, a single object is retrieved along with the facts about it. The construction of this discrimination network is discussed below, under acquisition.

One last important aspect of the retrieval of declarative knowledge concerns the basis for believing that structures retrieved from long-term memory represent true facts about the world. This belief must be based on the implicit assumption that the system knew what it was doing during the episode in which the structures were acquired. In other words, the system must trust its past behavior. This is one form of assumption that cannot be completely avoided by adding more explicit structure. Even if explicit true-in-world annotations are added to all structures representing true facts about the world, the system must still trust that in the past it only added such annotations when the facts were true. It might be more "careful" about adding such annotations than it is about adding structures to working memory in general, but since there is no oracle for truth, it is still assuming that these annotations were added correctly. This assumption that the annotations are true is of the same type as the original one. It may localize the assignment of trust, but can not completely eliminate it.

## Use

Declarative knowledge has a multitude of uses. It can be used to describe procedures so that they can be reasoned about, or followed interpretively (from which native procedures can be compiled). It can be used to explicitly describe episodes. It can be used to describe knowledge whose function is not yet clear. It can be used as the basis for memorization tasks. A complete list would go on considerably longer, but this gives a sampling of typical uses.

## Acquisition

The acquisition of declarative knowledge has much in common with the acquisition of episodic knowledge. Declarative knowledge that is generated as the result of a problem solving episode is directly acquired by chunking, with a retrieval context that corresponds to those elements of the situation on which creation of the knowledge depended. Likewise, the acquisition of perceptually originating declarative knowledge utilizes the data chunking solution described previously in this chapter. Though, to go beyond the types of structures acquired in the research on episodic knowledge, Soar was initialized with primitive elements for the 26 letters, plus a set of primitive attributes (isa, has, color, response, letter1, letter2, letter3, letter4, letter5, letter6, letter7, letter8, letter9, letter10).[5] Using these primitives, facts are represented by attributes relating named objects. For example Isa(Fido, Dog) is represented by the following structures.

```
(object <f> ˆletter1 <f1> ˆletter2 <f2> ˆletter3 <f3>
    ˆletter4 <f4> ˆisa <d>)
(letter <f1> ˆname f)
(letter <f2> ˆname i)
(letter <f3> ˆname d)
(letter <f4> ˆname o)
(object <d> ˆletter1 <d1> ˆletter2 <d2> ˆletter3 <d3>)
(letter <d1> ˆname d)
(letter <d2> ˆname o)
(letter <d3> ˆname g)
```

This is a variation on the native representation described previously in this chapter. The primary difference is that names, which were unanalyzable atoms in the earlier representation, have been expanded out to where their internal structure is open for examination and creation.

There are a number of ways in which the acquisition of declarative knowledge is more complicated than the acquisition of episodic knowledge in Soar. We have

---

[5]In future work we will be examining how to loosen up the requirement that attributes be pre-existing primitives as well as investigating different levels of primitive elements.

so far isolated three additional issues that must be resolved in the acquisition of perceptually originating declarative knowledge. (a) How is a discrimination network to be acquired that can control the retrieval of declarative knowledge? (b) How is knowledge about objects acquired incrementally? (c) How do chunks store the components of an object?

As mentioned earlier, utilizing the data chunking solution alone results in the acquisition of context-free declarative knowledge.[6] Acquiring a discrimination network thus requires an augmentation of the basic data chunking solution. Abstractly, the approach is to modify the simple memorization strategy underlying data chunking so that the acquisition of new knowledge involves relating the new knowledge to what is already known. If in the process of establishing relations, an explanation is created as to why the new knowledge is different from similar existing knowledge, this should lead to discrimination. Similar processing could lead to generalization, or other alterations of the new knowledge prior to its being stored (Anderson, 1986; Rosenbloom 1988).

The current implementation in Soar uses such a strategy to perform object-centered discrimination. Given a new fact, such as Isa(Fido, Dog), the system uses the features of Fido to see what object is retrieved from the discrimination network. If Fido is retrieved, no discrimination is necessary. If some other object, such as Fred, is retrieved, Fido's features are compared with Fred's to find a difference, such as the letter "d" in the third position of the name.[7] This difference is then used as the justification for generating a new symbol representing Fido, and for rejecting Fred as the object to be retrieved. If there is more than one difference, one is picked indifferently.

By thus loosening the prohibition against examining perceptual knowledge during result generation, discriminating conditions are added to retrieval chunks which control when the acquired knowledge is retrieved. Schematically, the production resulting from this process looks like the following.

$$\text{Retrieved}(g35) \wedge \neg \text{ Rejected}(g35) \wedge \text{letter3}(g35, e)$$
$$\wedge \text{ Perceived}(p) \wedge \text{letter3}(p, d) \rightarrow \text{Reject}(g35) \wedge \text{Retrieve}(g37) \quad (1)$$

This production says that if there is a retrieved, but not yet rejected, object with symbol g35 and an "e" as its third letter, and the perceived object's third letter is "d," then reject the retrieved object and create a new symbol (g37) for the perceived object. Each such retrieval production forms one link in the discrimination network that is constructed as new objects are perceived. This discrimination network supports k*–retrievability—that is, retrievability by a combination

---

[6]There is a corresponding, but not identical, issue for perceptually originating episodic knowledge which has not yet been addressed: how the situational context is incorporated into chunk conditions.

[7]In the current implementation, discrimination is always based on features of object names, rather than on other facts known about the object.

of production firings within a single elaboration phase—rather than the k–retrievability that is possible for knowledge stored with no context.

Consider what happens when the following three facts are learned in sequence, ignoring for now all of the learning except for the creation of the discrimination network.

$$Isa(Fred, Cat)$$
$$Isa(Fido, Dog)$$
$$Isa(Carl, Dog)$$

First, Fred is processed. Because no object has been learned previously, no discrimination is necessary, and the only action to be taken is the creation of a new symbol for Fred. This results in the acquisition of a production which generates the symbol for Fred if no object has already been retrieved.

$$\neg \ Retrieved() \rightarrow Retrieve(g35) \tag{2}$$

Second, Cat is processed. Given the features of Cat, the symbol for Fred (g35) is retrieved by production 2. As described, the information about Fred is cued off of Fred's symbol, so the retrieval of g35 leads to the retrieval of what is known about Fred. Once this knowledge is retrieved, Cat is discriminated from Fred. The system chooses indifferently one of the discriminating letters of the objects' names—in this case the second letter—yielding the following production.

$$Retrieved(g35) \ \wedge \ \neg \ Rejected(g35) \ \wedge \ letter2(g35, r)$$
$$\wedge \ Perceived(p) \ \wedge \ letter2(p, \ a) \rightarrow Reject(g35) \ \wedge \ Retrieve(g36) \tag{3}$$

Third, Fido is processed. Fred is retrieved and discriminated from Fido by the third letter, yielding production 1. Fourth, Dog is processed, Once again, Fred is retrieved, and the discrimination is again based on the third letter, yielding the following production:

$$Retrieved(g35) \ \wedge \ \neg \ Rejected(g35) \ \wedge \ letter3(g35, e)$$
$$\wedge \ Perceived(p) \ \wedge \ letter3(p, \ g) \rightarrow Reject(g35) \ \wedge \ Retrieve(g38) \tag{4}$$

Fifth, Carl is processed. This time Fred is retrieved and then immediately rejected by production 3, which also retrieves Cat. Carl is then discriminated from Cat by the third letter, yielding the following production:

$$Retrieved(g36) \ \wedge \ \neg \ Rejected(g36) \ \wedge \ letter3(g35, t)$$
$$\wedge \ Perceived(p) \ \wedge \ letter3(p, \ r) \rightarrow Reject(g36) \ \wedge \ Retrieve(g39) \tag{5}$$

Sixth, Dog is processed. Fred is retrieved, and then immediately rejected by production 4, which also retrieves the symbol for Dog. Because there is no mismatch between the perceived and retrieved objects, no discrimination is necessary, no new symbol is generated, and no new production is created. At this point the discrimination network has the shape shown in Figure 4.3.

Given a partial specification of an object name, the symbol for the object whose name matches most closely—according to the structure of the discrimina-

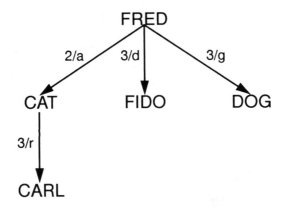

FIG. 4.3. Discrimination network acquired from sequence of facts.

tion network—is retrieved. The knowledge associated with the object is acquired with a retrieval context consisting of the object's symbol. As with episodic knowledge, this occurs by first acquiring a familiarity chunk for the new knowledge, and then acquiring a retrieval chunk which depends on the object's symbol.

Unfortunately, this approach depends on having all of the knowledge about the object available at once, which raises the second issue: How to incrementally acquire knowledge about objects. If the familiarity chunk must recognize the entire object, as it does in the previously published approaches, no learning can occur about an object until all of the knowledge about it is available. Conceptually, the solution to this problem is straightforward. Data chunking is applied to each fragment of an object individually. The processes of familiarization and generation are performed independently for each letter of the object's name, and for each fact about the object. As an example, the individual familiarity and retrieval productions for the first letter of Fred's name look like the following:

$$\text{letter1}(g35, f) \rightarrow \text{Familiar[letter1}(g35, f)] \qquad (6)$$

$$\text{Retrieved}(g35) \land \neg \text{ Rejected}(g35) \rightarrow \text{letter1}(g35, f) \qquad (7)$$

The implementation of this solution allows new facts to be acquired about known objects, for example, that Color(Fido, Red). However, what is given up in going with this solution is the ability to use familiarity chunks to directly perform recognition tasks. Object recognition must now be based on multiple productions. The obvious way to do this is to sort the object through the discrimination network. If the new object is the same as the one stored in the node at which discrimination ends, then it is recognized.

The third issue is how references to learned objects should be stored in retrieval chunks. For primitive objects, such as the letters, the answer is simple. The value is stored directly in the actions of the retrieval chunk, as shown in production 7. However, for values that are objects, the situation is more complicated and leads to a sequenced pair of discriminations, similar to the approach taken by EPAM (Feigenbaum & Simon, 1984).

Suppose the system has already learned about the object bej, a nonsense trigram, and that the retrieval cue associated with bej is its first letter (b). Then suppose that the system is presented with a paired associate (a stimulus–response pair) in which bej is the response, for example Response(gaf, bej). This pair would be represented as follows:

(object $s$ ^letter1 $s1$ ^letter2 $s2$ ^letter3 $s3$ ^response $r$)
(letter $s1$ ^name g)
(letter $s2$ ^name a)
(letter $s3$ ^name f)
(object $r$ ^letter1 $r1$ ^letter2 $r2$ ^letter3 $r3$)
(letter $r1$ ^name b)
(letter $r2$ ^name e)
(letter $r3$ ^name j)

If g41 is the symbol for gaf and g42 is the symbol for bej, the obvious retrieval production to create for this pair (ignoring for now the retrieval productions for the objects' names) is the following.

$$\text{Retrieved(g41)} \land \neg \text{ Rejected(g41)} \rightarrow \text{Response(g41, g42)} \qquad (8)$$

However, the rule that is actually created will have an additional condition which tests bej's retrieval cue (b).

$$\text{Retrieved(g41)} \land \neg \text{ Rejected(g41)} \land \text{Letter1(g42, b)}$$
$$\rightarrow \text{Response(g41, g42)} \qquad (9)$$

This happens because the retrieval cue is examined in order to retrieve g42 from the discrimination network. Therefore, the appearance of g42 in the chunk's actions leads to the cue appearing in the chunk's conditions. Such a retrieval production cannot support performance in paired–associate tasks, where after studying a list of stimulus–response pairs, the subject must generate responses when given just the corresponding stimuli.

One solution to this problem is to include a (partial) description of the value object in the retrieval production rather than the object itself. If the description is created anew, by data chunking, from the information provided in the paired associate, no additional retrieval cues get incorporated. With this change, the following chunk is learned.

$$\text{Retrieved(g41)} \land \neg \text{ Rejected(g41)} \rightarrow \text{response(g41, letter1}(-, \text{b))} \quad (10)$$

Given such a chunk (or set of chunks), the paired associate task can be performed by using the stimulus features to retrieve its symbol (g41), using the stimulus symbol to retrieve a (possibly partial) description of the response (letter1$(-, b)$), using the description of the response to retrieve the response symbol (g42), and then using the response symbol to retrieve the information about the response (bej).

Using this strategy the task now requires two independent retrievals from the discrimination network—one to retrieve the stimulus symbol and one to retrieve the response symbol. This is similar to the double discrimination performed by EPAM during paired associate tasks (Feigenbaum & Simon, 1984). However, it occurs in Soar not because of a need to match the data, but as a means of enabling responses to be retrieved from stimuli in the absence of any additional response cues.

## Summary

The representation, storage and use of declarative knowledge are relatively straightforward in Soar. The architecture provides some support for these capabilities through the primitive attribute–value representation, the ability to store declarative structure in productions, and the ability to examine declarative structures in working memory. The architecture does not enforce a fixed semantics for declarative knowledge, nor does it provide default inference mechanisms that automatically generate structures representing knowledge that is implied by its existing structures. Both of these, if part of the architecture, would imply excessive rigidity in how the system could behave. To the extent they are needed, provision should be made by adding knowledge and problem spaces on top of the fixed architecture.

The acquisition and retrieval of declarative knowledge is considerably less straightforward. Chunking is provided as a means for acquiring declarative knowledge, but the problem solver must be put through a number of contortions for the system to acquire the appropriate chunks from externally provided knowledge. In addition to the constraint imposed by the data chunking problem, a related architectural constraint restricts how known objects can be used in the acquisition of new knowledge. The solution to the problem posed by this constraint leads to an approach which is increasingly like the discrimination network structure of the EPAM model of memory.

Retrieval of declarative knowledge is supported by production firing, but considerable additional complexity arises from the need to constrain retrieval to what might be relevant. The discrimination network we have employed provides one approach to this. Though the approach currently seems somewhat ad hoc, the abstract characterization of the process as relating the new knowledge to existing knowledge, leads to the hope that it will eventually be placed on a principled footing.

Further work is clearly called for in developing and evaluating the acquisition and retrieval mechanisms that have been proposed (and implemented).

# CONCLUSIONS

Taking an architecture seriously means living within its constraints and using what support it provides, at least until it is clear that the architecture must be modified. In this chapter we have taken a step towards evaluating the level of support and constraint which the Soar architecture provides for the knowledge level, a concept that is closely related to the idea of general intelligence. This helps us to understand the extent to which the architecture's current levels of support and constraint are adequate for achieving general intelligence. It also provides an alternative way of viewing Soar in which its architectural mechanisms are subjugated to their role in supporting knowledge. This complements other efforts that view Soar as a set of mechanisms (Laird, Newell, & Rosenbloom, 1987), a hierarchy of meta-levels (Rosenbloom, Laird, & Newell, 1988b), a hierarchy of cognitive levels at different time scales (Newell, in press; Rosenbloom, Laird, Newell, & McCarl, in press), a physical symbol system (Newell, Rosenbloom, & Laird, 1989), and a general goal–oriented system (Rosenbloom, 1989).

Our particular focus in this step has been on how the Soar architecture supports and constrains the representation, storage, retrieval, use, and acquisition of three pervasive forms of knowledge: procedural, episodic, and declarative. The analysis reveals that Soar adequately supports procedural knowledge—to some extent it was designed for this—but that there are still significant questions about episodic and declarative knowledge. These questions arise primarily because of consequences of the principle source of constraint in Soar, the fact that all learning occurs via chunking. Chunking can support the acquisition of episodic and declarative knowledge, but in so doing it imposes significant requirements on how the problem solving underlying this acquisition proceeds. These requirements amount to architecturally-derived hypotheses about how learning occurs. We have reported here some new results that elaborate on these hypotheses in the acquisition of declarative knowledge, but considerable future work is still called for in both the development and testing of these hypotheses.

One obvious question at this point is why not just add new architectural mechanisms that directly support the acquisition of episodic and declarative knowledge? Assuming that appropriate mechanisms could be developed, there are still at least two critical reasons not to rush into adding them to the architecture. The first reason is that the integration of new mechanisms into an existing architecture can have major consequences. An integrated architecture is more than just a collection of useful mechanisms. It must be constructed so that its mechanisms compose appropriately with each other. The number of potential interactions that need to be worried about increases rapidly—exponentially, if there can be interactions among all possible subsets—with the number of mechanisms. Frequently, the addition of a perfectly reasonable new mechanism will cause strongly dysfunctional behavior in others of the existing mechanisms.

Though there are times when an architectural addition is absolutely required, and a research effort must be engendered to get the interactions right (as recently occurred for perceptual–motor behavior in Soar (Wiesmeyer, 1988)), almost always a conservative strategy is what is required.

The second reason is that rushing to add new mechanisms discourages learning about the limits of the existing mechanisms, and their combinations. This is essential to understanding the scope and limits of the architecture. It is also essential to discovering the deeper, nonobvious consequences of the architecture. If we had jumped to add new learning mechanisms to Soar, we would never have discovered how the current mechanisms inherently imply a reconstructive learning strategy. The discovery of such nonobvious consequences is some of the most interesting research that can be done with architectures.

This being said, much additional work is still needed. One issue to be addressed is the origins of the bootstrap knowledge that allows new procedural, episodic, and declarative knowledge to be acquired. The acquisition of perceived procedural knowledge requires the existence of an interpreter for the knowledge. The acquisition of perceived episodic and declarative knowledge requires a set of pre-existing primitive elements plus the knowledge about how to familiarize, discriminate, and construct object representations. It appears necessary to add some of this to the architecture, such as the ability to generate a set of primitive elements. Other parts may just be specific instances of more general capabilities, which of course must themselves be either innate or learned. For example, the interpreter for procedural knowledge may be just an instantiation of a more general comprehension process. The same may also be true of the discrimination and construction processes for declarative and episodic knowledge. The current implementation does not quite look like this, and architectural changes may be required before it does, but this is one promising path to pursue.

Finally, a number of additional steps must still be taken before the relationship of the Soar architecture to the knowledge level is completely tied down. The most important missing aspect is the relationship between Soar's mechanisms and the principle of rationality. The key issue is how its architectural mechanisms, such as its decision procedure and subgoal generator, allow Soar to approximate rationality even under the constraints of its being a physical system with time and space bounds. We have commented briefly on how chunking increases Soar's ability to bring knowledge to bear under real-time constraints, but much more is left to be done.

## ACKNOWLEDGMENTS

This research was sponsored by the Defense Advanced Research Projects Agency (DOD) under contract numbers N00039-86C-0033 (via subcontract from the Knowledge Systems Laboratory, Stanford University), and F33615-87-C-1499

(ARPA Order No. 4976, monitored by the Air Force Avionics Laboratory), by the National Aeronautics and Space Administration under cooperative agreement numbers NCC 2-538 and NCC 2-517, and the Office of Naval Research under contract numbers N00014-86-K-0678 (Information Sciences Division) and N00014-88-K-0554 (Computer Science Division). The views and conclusions contained in this document are those of the authors and should not be interpreted as representing the official policies, either expressed or implied, of the Defense Advanced Research Projects Agency, the National Aeronautics and Space Administration, the Office of Naval Research or the US Government.

## REFERENCES

Anderson, J. R. (1983). A spreading-activation theory of memory. *Journal of Verbal Learning and Verbal Behavior, 22,* 261–295.

Anderson, J. R. (1986). Knowledge compilation: The general learning mechanism. In R. S. Michalski, J. G. Carbonell, & T. M. Mitchell (Eds.), *Machine learning: An artificial intelligence approach* (Vol. II). Los Altos, CA: Morgan Kaufmann.

Bartlett, F. C. (1932). *Remembering: A study in experimental and social psychology.* Cambridge, England: Cambridge University Press.

Bell, C. G. & Newell, A. (1971). *Computer structures: Readings and examples.* New York: McGraw-Hill.

Brachman, R. J. (1979). On the epistemological status of semantic nets. In N. V. Findler (Ed.), *Associative networks.* New York: Academic Press.

Collins, A. M., & Loftus, E. F. (1975). A spreading-activation theory of semantic processing. *Psychological Review, 82,* 407–428.

Feigenbaum, E. A., & Simon, H. A. (1984). EPAM-like models of recognition and learning. *Cognitive Science, 8,* 305–336.

Golding, A., Rosenbloom, P. S., & Laird, J. E. (1987). Learning general search control from outside guidance. *Proceedings of IJCAI-87.* Milan. Los Altos, CA: Morgan Kaufman.

Kolodner, J. L. (1985). Memory for experience. In G. Bower (Ed.), *Psychology of learning and motivation* (Vol. 19). New York: Academic Press.

Laird, J. E. (1983). *Universal subgoaling.* Doctoral dissertation, Carnegie-Mellon University. (Available in Laird, J. E., Rosenbloom, P. S., & Newell, A. (1986). *Universal subgoaling and chunking: The automatic generation and learning of goal hierarchies,* Hingham, MA: Kluwer.

Laird, J. E. (1988). Recovery from incorrect knowledge in Soar. *Proceedings of AAAI-88.* St. Paul. Los Altos, CA: Morgan Kaufman.

Laird, J. E., Hucka, M., Yager, E. S., & Tuck, C. M. (in press). Robo-Soar: An integration of external interaction, planning and learning using Soar. *Robotics and autonomous systems.*

Laird, J. E., & Newell, A. (1983). A universal weak method: Summary of results. *Proceedings of IJCAI-83.* Karlsruhe. Los Altos, CA: William Kaufman.

Laird, J. E., Swedlow, K. R., Altmann, E., Congdon, C. B., & Wiesmeyer, M. (1989). *Soar User's Manual: Version 4.5.* (Unpublished).

Laird, J. E., Newell, A., & Rosenbloom, P. S. (1987). Soar: An architecture for general intelligence. *Artificial Intelligence, 33,* 1–64.

Lewis, R. L., Newell, A., & Polk, T. A. (1989). Toward a Soar theory of taking instructions for immediate reasoning tasks. *Proceedings of the 11th Annual Conference of the Cognitive Science Society.* Ann Arbor, MI. Hillsdale, NJ: Lawrence Erlbaum Associates.

Neisser, U. (1967). *Cognitive Psychology.* New York: Appleton-Century-Crofts.

Newell, A. (1981). The knowledge level. *Artificial Intelligence 18*, 18–127.

Newell, A. (in press). *Unified theories of cognition*. Cambridge, MA: Harvard University Press.

Newell, A., Rosenbloom, P. S., & Laird, J. E. (1989). Symbolic architectures for cognition. In M. I. Posner (Ed.), *Foundations of cognitive science* (pp. 93–131). Cambridge, MA: MIT Press.

Norman, D. A., & Bobrow, D. G. (1979). Descriptions: An intermediate stage in memory retrieval. *Cognitive Psychology, 11*, 107–123.

Polk, T. A. & Newell, A. (1988). Modeling human syllogistic reasoning in Soar. *Proceedings of the 10th Annual Conference of the Cognitive Science Society*. Montreal. Hillsdale, NJ: Lawrence Erlbaum Associates.

Polk, T. A., Newell, A., & Lewis, R. L. (1989). Toward a unified theory of immediate reasoning in Soar. *Proceedings of the 11th Annual Conference of the Cognitive Science Society*. Ann Arbor, MI. Hillsdale, NJ: Lawrence Erlbaum Associates.

Rosenbloom, P. S. (1988). Beyond generalization as search: Towards a unified framework for the acquisition of new knowledge. In G. F. DeJong (Ed.), *Proceedings of the AAAI Symposium on Explanation-Based Learning*. Stanford, CA: AAAI.

Rosenbloom, P. S. (1989). A symbolic goal-oriented perspective on connectionism and Soar. In R. Pfeifer, Z. Schreter, F. Fogelman-Soulie, & L. Steels (Eds.), *Connectionism in perspective*, (pp. 245–263). Amsterdam: Elsevier.

Rosenbloom, P. S., Laird, J. E., & Newell, A. (1987). Knowledge level learning in Soar. *Proceedings of AAAI-87*. Seattle. Los Altos, CA: Morgan Kaufmann.

Rosenbloom, P. S., Laird, J. E., & Newell, A. (1988). The chunking of skill and knowledge. In B. A. G. Elsendoorn & H. Bouma (Eds.), *Working models of human perception*. London: Academic Press.

Rosenbloom, P. S., Laird, J. E., & Newell, A. (1988). Meta-levels in Soar. In P. Maes & D. Nardi (Eds.), *Meta-level architectures and reflection*. Amsterdam: North Holland.

Rosenbloom, P. S., Laird, J. E., Newell, A., & McCarl, R. (in press). A preliminary analysis of the foundations of the Soar architecture as a basis for general intelligence. *Artificial Intelligence*.

Schank, R. C. (1975). *Conceptual information processing*. Amsterdam: North Holland.

Schank, R., & Ableson, R. (1977). *Scripts, plans, goals and understanding*. Hillsdale, NJ: Lawrence Erlbaum Associates.

Steier, D. M., Laird, J. E., Newell, A., Rosenbloom, P. S., Flynn, R., Golding, A., Polk, T. A., Shivers, O. G., Unruh, A., & Yost, G. R. (1987). Varieties of Learning in Soar: 1987. P. Langley (Ed.), *Proceedings of the Fourth International Workshop on Machine Learning*. Los Altos, CA, Morgan Kaufmann.

Tulving, E. (1983). *Elements of episodic memory*. New York: Oxford University Press.

Watkins, M. J., & Gardiner, J. M. (1979). An appreciation of generate-recognize theory of recall. *Journal of Verbal Learning and Verbal Behavior, 18*, 687–704.

Wiesmeyer, M. (1988). *Soar I/O Reference Manual, Version 2*. Unpublished manual.

Yost, G. R. (1987). *TAQ: Soar Task Acquisition System, Version 2*.

Yost, G. R., & Newell, A. (1988). *Learning new tasks in Soar*. Unpublished manual.

# An Instructable Connectionist/Control Architecture: Using Rule-Based Instructions to Accomplish Connectionist Learning in a Human Time Scale

5

Walter Schneider and William L. Oliver
*University of Pittsburgh, Learning Research and Development Center*

Building an architecture for human cognition is a complex task requiring the incorporation of multiple mechanisms in a smoothly functioning system. There are two major cognitive architectural approaches to processing. Both approaches are well represented by other contributors to this volume. The symbolic processing approach (e.g., SOAR, Laird, Newell, & Rosenbloom, 1987; ACT*, Anderson, 1983) represents processing as the manipulation of symbols via rules or productions. Connectionist processing involves the association of input and output patterns via association matrices (see Rumelhart & McClelland, 1986; Schneider, 1987). These two approaches are often viewed as competing alternatives for cognitive processing (see Smolensky, 1988).

Our research treats these two approaches as complementary. We believe that human cognition involves connectionist-like, associative best-match processing combined with an attentional system that allows rule-like processing. In this chapter we describe a hybrid architecture in which both kinds of processing occurs.

This chapter uses a hybrid connectionist rule processing architecture. A specific computer simulation, CAP2 (described in detail later in the chapter), implements the hybrid processing. CAP2 has both a modular data network and a control network. The data network is a two dimensional lattice of connectionist networks (see Fig. 5.6). Each module in the data network is a standard connectionist net with a single layer of hidden units (see Fig. 5.5). There are three control lines for each module that control whether the module receives and holds messages, transmits messages, or reports its activity to the control network. The controller is a recurrent connectionist implementation of a finite state machine (see Fig. 5.7). The output sequence of messages produced by the controller depends on the initial task vector and reports from the data network. The output of the control network sets control signals and can provide input vectors to the data network (see Fig. 5.8). The control network can quickly learn control sequences to reconfigure and modulate the data network to perform novel tasks in a small number of training trials. As the data network is exercised, it captures input–output associations in the data network connections. With extended practice of consistent tasks, the data network can perform complex operations in the absence of control network input.

This hybrid architecture is used to address three major issues in learning that are typically neglected in connectionist learning. First, the control network allows the system to use task decomposition and instructions to learn much more effectively than the nondecompositional (whole) learning typical of connectionist learning. Second it allows a single modular network to be dynamically reconfigured for specialized problems. Generally, unique connectionist models (in terms of layers, vector sizes, etc.) are created for each psychological task (e.g., McClelland & Rumelhart, 1988). The alternative approach of physically reconfiguring a network for each problem by changing gross connection patterns is neurally implausible. In CAP2, the data network is dynamically reconfigured by altering the control settings to the modules in the data network. Third, the architecture addresses the problem of sequencing control signals to guide sequential behavior. The CAP2 control processor can learn "rules," which in turn specify the control settings to perform complex tasks within the data network. The rule learning system can memorize single presentations of the correct output states and temporary intermediate states to allow learning to occur in the absence of an external trainer after a small number of training trials.

The present hybrid approach is related to previous work on human *controlled processing* (see Schneider, 1985; Schneider & Detweiler, 1987, 1988; Shiffrin & Schneider, 1977). Humans perform most novel tasks in a serial, effortful, attentional form of processing. With practice a second form of processing, *automatic processing,* develops. In our architecture, automatic processing involves the categorization, associative retrieval, and transmission of messages within a modular connectionist network. The controlled processing occurs through the sequential execution of rules that control the flow of information within the modular network. The architecture simulates the transition from controlled to automatic processing as behavior becomes less guided by rules and more directly elicited by associative retrieval. The modular design of the architecture allows cognitive processing to occur in stages so that tasks can be broken down into subtasks that are executed in sequence during controlled processing. In addition, task decomposition permits the connectionist learning to occur much faster than would otherwise occur.

In this chapter we examine how the hybrid approach can deal with two central issues in human learning. The first issue concerns developing an architecture that scales well so that it can learn complex tasks in a reasonable time scale. A model is said to scale badly if its learning times grows unreasonably long as the complexity of the learning task is increased. Minsky and Papert (1988) comment that the scaling problem is the crucial problem facing any system that learns complex tasks. They criticize connectionist learning for scaling much worse than human learning.

The second central issue concerns how an architecture learns from instruction. There is effectively no role for instruction in standard connectionist models. A connectionist model is trained by presenting it with a training set of input-output patterns.[1] The model adjusts its connection weights so that it can produce the desired responses to each input. Learning is determined only by the set of patterns presented and the ordering of the presentations. Humans may also learn through a simple process of mapping inputs to outputs as is demonstrated in concept learning experiments (Gluck & Bower, 1988). On each trial, subjects are presented a stimulus and then told the desired response. The subjects are provided no other information and the experiments are often designed to discourage the use of self-generated verbal rules. Learning of this kind can be very slow. For example, Biederman and Shiffrar (1987) review studies and present new results indicating that "chicken sexers" in the poultry business learn their trade gradually. These specialists are trained by being presented input–output patterns. They are trained by experts who first present them with example chicks and then tell them the correct diagnoses. Learning required several years. In contrast, by instructing students on what relationships to look for, Biederman and Shiffrar were able to train the students to perform as well as experts on a test of chicken-sexing in a matter of minutes. When instructed, the students learned the rules needed to perform components of a perceptual task that the experts had apparently taken months or years to learn.

Some of the enthusiasm about connectionist processing is perhaps based on the false belief that humans can learn complex categories by presenting them with input–output patterns. In the absence of instructions, humans are not very impressive learners. For example humans have a great deal of difficulty learning concepts that require the integration of more than four dimensions (e.g., Estes, 1986). However, humans can learn very complex concepts when given instructions. For example, with instruction bright high school students can learn calculus, although a few would discover it on their own.

## TASK DECOMPOSITION TO IMPROVE SCALING

As task complexity increases, the learning time of both connectionist and symbolic processing systems can dramatically increase (e.g., see Minsky & Papert,

---

[1]So-called "unsupervised" learning procedures do not map input patterns to output patterns, but these learning procedures cannot learn complex cognitive tasks unless they are embedded in a complex architecture. Unsupervised learning plays an important role in Grossberg's (1987) cognitive architecture.

1988). Although many different methods can be used to learn complex tasks, these methods will dramatically differ in how fast they learn and how capable they are at carrying out the task. For example, medical diagnosis could be learned as a one stage process, in which sets of symptoms would be directly associated with the best treatments. On the other hand, medical diagnosis could be learned as a multistage process. In the first stage the disease would be identified, and in the second stage the best treatment would be selected by taking into account the disease and the severity of symptoms. If the mappings between symptoms and treatments involve complex interactions, learning in two stages may be much faster than learning in one stage.

Production system models of learning assume that subjects use task decompositions to carry out complex tasks (e.g., Anderson, 1983; Klahr, Langley, & Neches, 1987). The learning that occurs in these models often involves modifying task decompositions to make them more efficient (e.g., via composition, Lewis, 1987). Similarly, much research in cognitive psychology has been aimed at understanding how human subjects consciously decompose problems (e.g., Newell & Simon, 1972) and how even the performance of basic cognitive processes are decomposed into stages of processing (e.g., Sternberg, 1969). The recent successful use of connectionist procedures to model complex tasks have invariably depended on the use of task decomposition. For example, recent connectionist models of basic visual processes (Koch & Ullman, 1985; Rueckl, Cave, & Kosslyn, 1989), speech recognition (Waibel, 1989), language comprehension (Miikkulainen & Dyer, 1989), and backgammon playing (Tesauro & Sejnowski, 1988) have assumed explicit task decompositions. The CAP2 architecture is designed with the aim of providing psychologically plausible methods for decomposing tasks. The same basic methods involving structurally similar components can be used to model many different tasks so that ad hoc methods need not be developed as new problems are encountered.

Some traditional connectionist models have indirectly made use of task decompositions. Networks of units in these models have been structured to reflect the different levels of representations that the investigator knows exists in the training sets. The networks consist of multiple levels of hidden units with each level corresponding to a different level of representation. By limiting the number of hidden units at each level, some networks have been shown to discover hierarchical relationships among stimuli (e.g, Hinton, 1986). This decomposition of representations does not lead to faster learning. Generally, networks with more than three levels learn extremely slowly (see Ballard, 1987).

With an appropriate decomposition, a complex task can be divided into smaller subtasks. An immediate consequence of a good decomposition is that the number of problem states that must be considered to solve a problem is greatly reduced. For instance, to carry out addition with the normal paper and pencil algorithms, people must only memorize 100 addition facts and an algorithm for adding one column at a time. In contrast to connectionist models that rely on the random presentation of training stimuli (McCloskey & Cohen, 1989), people learn arithmetic procedures from instructions and structured sequences of example problems that augment the instructions (VanLehn, 1987). By using arithmetic procedures people can solve addition problems of arbitrary size. Without a task decomposition, a learning system would be faced with learning to map $10^{10}$ different addend combinations in order to solve all possible five-column addition problems!

## Simulating Digital Logic Gate Learning with Connectionist Networks

A task involving digital logic provides an example of problem solving with various degrees of task decomposition. In studies of electronic troubleshooting skills, subjects learn to predict the outputs of digital logic gates like those appearing in Fig. 5.1. The different gate symbols are presented at random to the subjects with inputs of 0s and 1s, and the subjects learn to respond with the correct 0 or 1 responses. The number of inputs to the gates can be varied in an

**Logic Gates**

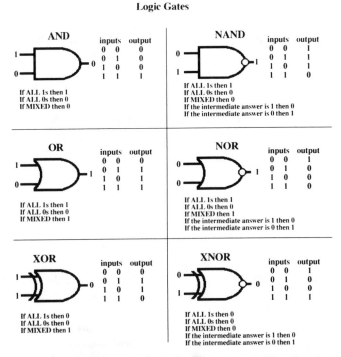

FIG. 5.1. The digital logic gates learned by the simulations. The tables show the mapping of inputs to outputs. The verbal rules also provide the solutions.

experiment because the rules apply to arbitrary numbers of inputs (e.g., for an AND gate to yield an input of 1, all of its inputs must be 1). The gates are presented on a computer screen and the speed and accuracy of each response is recorded. The subjects are instructed on the rules for each gate and told to respond as quickly as possible without making errors. Initially, the subjects take about 2 seconds to respond correctly to each gate, and after several thousands of practice trials they respond in about 0.7 seconds (Carlson, Sullivan, & Schneider, 1989). The gate task would seem suited for connectionist modelling, because many have argued that connectionist models are most appropriate for tasks that yield responses in under a second (e.g., Rumelhart & McClelland, 1986).

Subjects decompose the prediction of gate outputs into three subproblems (see Carlson, Sullivan, & Schneider, 1989). The first stage, input recoding, codes the inputs as all 1s, all 0s or mixed. The second stage, gate mapping, takes the output from the first stage and the gate type (AND, OR, or XOR) and predicts the output of 1 or 0. The third stage, negation, takes the negation symbol and the output from the gate mapping stage and predicts the final output. A model could associate all the input combinations (inputs, gate type, and negation) directly to the output in one step or perform the task in three decomposed stages as is typical of the human performance.

In the gate task the number of states to be learned increases exponentially with task complexity. The overall number of states to be learned when task decomposition does not occur is equal to $2^i \times g \times n$ where where $i$ equals the number of gate inputs, $g$ equals the number of gate types, and $n$ equals the number of negation states. For the six-input gates, there are 384 states to be learned ($2^6 \times 3 \times 2$). With task decomposition, the number of states is equal to $2^i + (g \times r) + (n \times o)$ where $g$ is the number of recoding states (e.g., ALL 1s) and $o$ is the number of output states of the gate mapping stage. For the six-input gates, there are 77 states to learn ($2^6 + (3 \times 3) + (2 \times 2)$). Note that the task decomposition reduces the growth of states from a multiplicative to an additive function. More generally, if a task is decomposed into three stages, the following equations give the number of states to be learned.

| Without Task Decomposition | With Task Decomposition |
|---|---|
| $A^{B(X+Y+Z)}$ | $A^{BX} + A^{B(X'+Y)} + A^{B(Y'+Z)}$ |

Where $A$ and $B$ are constants, $X$, $Y$, and $Z$ are the complexity of the component tasks, and the $X'$ and $Y'$ are the complexity of the output of the component tasks.

We explored the effects of task decomposition on learning time in connectionist simulations of the gate task using the backpropagation learning algorithm (Rumelhart, Hinton, & Williams, 1986). Networks learned the gate task (see Fig. 5.1) for 2, 4, and 6 input gates with the AND, OR, and XOR functions for normal and negated gates. The first set of simulations looked at gate learning without task decomposition. The network architecture for these simulations is shown in the left panel of Fig. 5.2. All of the inputs were connected to a hidden layer that was in turn connected to an output layer resulting in a fully interconnected feedforward network. Networks of this kind are frequently used in connectionist modeling (e.g., NETtalk, Sejnowski & Rosenberg, 1987). The second set of simulations looked at gate learning with task decomposition. The task was decomposed into the three stages of processing that the human subjects were instructed to use to perform the task. The network architecture for this second series of simulations is shown in the right panel of Fig. 5.2. The inputs representing information about the gates and their inputs were connected to hidden layers that combined information corresponding to the different stages of processing. The first stage carried out recoding, the second stage carried out gate mapping, and the third stage carried out negation. In the following sections of this chapter we will describe the simulation methods and the extent to which gate learning was sped up by task decomposition.

*Gate Learning without Task Decomposition.*    A simple network architecture can simulate one stage learning that maps stimulus features directly to output responses. A number of well known simulations of cognitive architectures have used these simple network architectures (e.g., Sejnowski & Rosenberg, 1987). As we noted previously, these models often take a long time to learn, suggesting that the same modeling approach for the gate learning task might learn unacceptably slowly as the problem is scaled up.

The left panel of Fig. 5.2 shows how inputs were connected to a hidden layer

**Network Architectures**

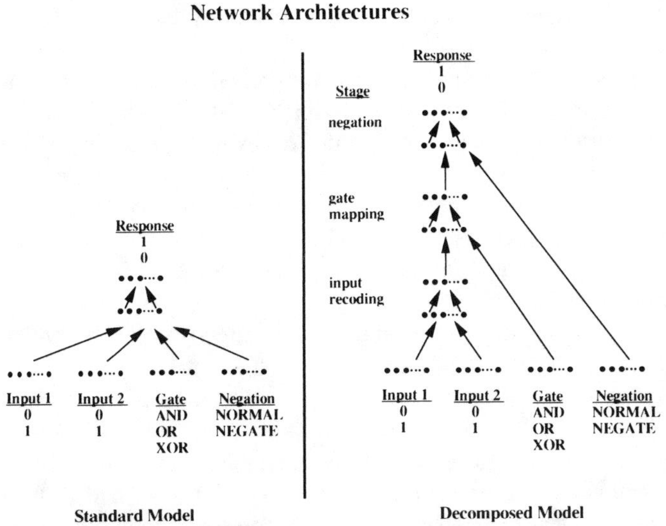

FIG. 5.2.   The network architectures for the gate simulations without (left panel) and with (right panel) task decomposition.

of 50 units that in turn projected to an output layer of 50 units. The network was trained over trials to output the correct responses to its inputs. The input layer of the network was segmented into vectors or sets of units that represented gross features of the stimuli (e.g., gate type). Each vector consisted of 50 units. Each code for a particular state (e.g., 0, 1, AND, OR, XOR, NEGATION) was a random vector with on the average half of its elements in the 1 state and half in the 0 state. Specific input patterns were presented to the network on each training trial. This loading of activations occurred by clamping the input units to values specified by the input patterns.

Different networks were used to simulate the gate task with two–, four–, and six–input gates. These networks differed only in their numbers of input vectors—as additional 50 unit vectors were needed to represent the additional gate inputs. The numbers of input units that were mapped to the output units for the two-, four-, and six-input gate simulations were 200, 300, and 400, respectively. These input units included the 50 units that encoded the presence or absence of negation, the 50 units that encoded the gate type and an additional 50 units for each gate input. Thus, the largest network was made up of 400 input units, 50 hidden units at the input layer of the response module, and 50 units encoding the response.

Our previous simulations of gate learning that we have reported elsewhere (Oliver & Schneider, 1988) used small numbers of units (6 to 10 input units and 1 output unit) to encode stimulus features and responses. This parsimonious method of encoding information resulted in relatively small networks that lacked the computational benefits of networks with large numbers of units. We have found, for instance, that networks that use vector encodings learn much faster (in terms of number of trials) and result in learning that is more resistant to retroactive interference than networks that use small numbers of units. This model uses a vector coding in which many stimuli can be coded in the same units (a 50–element vector) rather than unit–specific codes that are more characteristic of connectionist models (see McClelland & Rumelhart, 1988). The vector coding allows simplified control processing and allows the model to store many possible codes. Ideally the vector lengths in these models would be on the order of hundreds or even thousands of units to approximate the kinds of vector encodings that may occur in the human nervous system, however vectors of this size lead to prohibitively long learning times on serial computers. Vectors of size 50 are large enough to show the statistical behavior we expect of large vectors.

At the beginning of each simulation, vectors of 0s and 1s were randomly generated to encode information associated with each vector. Each of the 50 units in the vectors took on values of 0 and 1 with equal probabilities. Three different random vectors were generated to encode the AND, OR, and XOR gates; two random vectors were generated to encode the presence and absence of negation; and two random vectors were generated for each of the vectors representing the gate-inputs. The target responses of 0s and 1s were also encoded as 50 unit random vectors. Once these vectors were generated, they were used consistently throughout the simulation.

The patterns presented to the network on each trial were made up of vector combinations specifying the gate type, the presence or absence of negation, and the inputs of 1s and 0s. For a given simulation, there were 3 (gate types) X 2 (negation/no negation) X $2^n$ patterns to learn, where n equals the number of gate inputs. Thus, the networks with 2, 4 and 6 gate inputs were required to learn 24, 96, and 384 unique patterns, respectively. The network was trained by repeatedly cycling through a set of patterns. For each cycle or epoch, as it is commonly called, the network was presented a random sequence of all possible patterns for the gates and their inputs. For the networks with four and six gate-inputs, particular gate-input combinations (e.g., all 1s) were resampled within an epoch to achieve the same frequency of 0 and 1 responses that occurred in the two-input gate simulations. For example, gate inputs of all 1s occurred on 25% of the AND gate trials in the two–input gate simulation. The all 1s pattern would occur only 2% of the time in the six-input gate simulation, allowing the network to become biased towards always responding 0. By increasing the occurrence of all 1s for AND gates such biases could be prevented. The method used to permute patterns across trials resulted in 24, 136, and 584 patterns per epoch for the two-, four- and six-input gate networks, respectively. The order in which the stimuli were presented to the network was randomly determined before each epoch.

A response to an input pattern was scored correct if it matched the correct target vector better than the incorrect target vector. The degree of match between the output and the target vectors was measured by computing the sum of their element-by-element squared deviations. This squared error of the network is the error measure that back propagation minimizes through the weight adjustments and is hence the appropriate similarity metric for computing response accuracy (McCloskey & Cohen, 1989).

At the beginning of a simulation, the connection weights and biases were set to small random values. Because a network's learning speed (in trials) depends partly on its starting random weights, it is necessary to aggregate across several simulation runs to obtain stable estimates of learning times. The random generation of vectors introduced an additional source of stochastic variation for the learning times. The learning times reported in this chapter were based on 20 simulation runs.

The networks were trained to a criteria of 100 percent accuracy. Because a network's responses are completely determined by its inputs and weights, its errors are systematic. These systematic errors, no matter how few, indicate that the network has not learned the classification rules for the training set. In contrast, the errors human subjects make on the gate task are unsystematic, and, as long as their error rates are low, it is possible to determine that they have learned the classification rules. The requirement that the networks learn to a high accuracy criterion meant that the response values of the output units closely matched the target values. The average error pure unit was usually close to zero (.006) when the accuracy criterion was reached.

On each trial, vectors representing the gates, negation and inputs were loaded into the input layer. Activation propagated forward in the network to produce a response. The response was compared with the target response to compute an error measure and accuracy. The connection weights were then adjusted with the backpropagation network learning procedure. The methods for propagating response and adjusting weights followed the methods described in McClelland and Rumelhart (1988). These methods included the use of momentum and the clipping of the target values to prevent saturation of the network. If the network responded correctly to all patterns on an epoch, learning was halted. The trial of the last error served as the dependent measure of learning time for a simulation.

Simulations were carried out to find the learning parameters that yielded the fastest learning times for the three simulations. An additional requirement of the parameters was that they yielded stable learning times. Parameter settings which resulted in any of the 20 runs learning in numbers of trials exceeding three times the standard deviation of mean were considered unacceptable. An exhaustive search for these parameter settings was not carried out because of the size of the parameter space and the time required to run the simulations. Initially, several of the learning parameters were fixed to commonly used values and the learning rate was varied to find the fastest learning times. These values were .5 for wrange (the range around 0 of the initial random weights), .9 for momentum (a parameter influencing the extent to which the weight adjustments were time averaged), and .9 for tmax (the adjustment of the target values, so that output units were trained to respond .1 and .9 instead of 0 and 1). The reader should see McClelland and Rumelhart (1988) for technical details concerning these parameters.

The recommendations of several researchers for finding the best parameters were followed. For instance, Tesauro and Janssens (1988) found that simultaneously reducing the learning rate and raising momentum led to faster learning of a parity problem. This relationship seemed to hold true for the gate problem as well. On the recommendation of Plaut, Nowlan, and Hinton (1986) the weights for the different levels of the network were adjusted with different learning rates. Because there is a large fan in of connections to the hidden layer, or input layer of the response module, units can become locked on extreme values thereby slowing learning. The learning rate for the weights between the response module input layer (the hidden layer) and the response module output layer was larger by a factor equal to the degree of fan in of connections to the response module input layer. This adjustment allows the effective learning rate for all units to be equal throughout the network and results in faster learning times for some problems. Thus, for the six–input gate simulation, the learning rate parameter for the weights at the second level was 8 times larger than the learning rate parameter for the weights at the first level. This value is arrived at because the fan for the first level is 400 units to 50 units versus 50 units to 50 units at the second level.

Figure 5.3 shows the mean trials to criterion for the two, four-, and six-input gate networks. The plotted values represent the best learning times (in trials) that we obtained. The learning rate parameters were .02, .005, .001 for the two–, four–, and six–input simulations, respectively. The momentum parameters were .9, .92, and .95 for the two–, four–, and six–input simulations, respectively. The number of trials needed to train the networks to perform the gate task grew dramatically as the number of gate inputs was increased. This growth in trials reflected the exponential increase in the numbers of patterns that had to be learned. The number of epochs needed to train the network actually dropped with increasing problem complexity ( perhaps reflecting greater efforts to optimize the learning parameters). The two–, four–, and six–input gate networks required averages of 39, 24, and 19 epochs of training, respectively.

The number of epochs to criterion may have decreased with the increasing network size because of generalization of learning among the patterns. Such generalization has been observed in a few studies (e.g., Sejnowski & Rosenberg, 1987), but other studies found that the number of epochs to criterion increased with increasing number of patterns to be learned to further compound the scaling problem. Tesauro (1987) found that epochs scaled as a 4/3 power of increasing network size for a parity problem; and Tesauro and Sejnowski (1988) found exponential scaling of training epochs in a backpropagation network that learned to play backgammon. Sublinear scaling of epochs is needed to counteract the

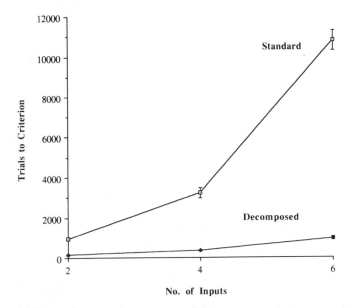

FIG. 5.3.   Trials to criterion for the standard and decomposed models as a function of the number of gate inputs. The error bars indicate standard errors of the mean. Bars do not appear for points where the error bars were too small to draw.

exponential growth of input patterns that results from increasing problem complexity. Without sublinear scaling of epochs, the numbers of trials required to learn problems will often grow exponentially.

The long learning times (10,835 trials) for the six-input gates far exceeds human learning times for the task which is on the order of 300 trials (Oliver & Schneider, 1988). Nor could such learning account very well for gradual speed up on the task, since human subjects essentially asymptote on the task after only a few thousand trials.

A faster connectionist learning procedure could possibly learn the task in reasonable numbers of trials. There are already many variants of backpropagation (e.g., Durbin & Rumelhart, 1989; Fahlman, 1988; Hinton, 1987; Jacobs, 1988) and other learning procedures (e.g., Gallant & Smith, 1987) that have been shown to learn problems faster than backpropagation. Faster learning procedures, however, do not always generalize as well as backpropagation because they depend on memorization of patterns.

*Gate Learning with Task Decomposition.*    The benefits of task decomposition in the gate learning task were explored in simulations that used the same task decomposition used by human subjects. Identical simulation methods were used as in the previous simulations except that the decomposed models used additional modules that were separately trained on each trial. Although task decomposition provides a means for reducing the numbers of input patterns that must be learned to master a problem, it is not entirely clear how to exploit this benefit within a connectionist architecture. The simulations described in this section demonstrate how modular networks can be configured to match psychologically plausible task decompositions.

A hierarchically organized feedforward network was configured to carry out the gate task in three stages (see Fig. 5.2, right panel). The first stage involved the input recoding stage described earlier. The inputs of 1s and 0s were recoded as all 1s, all 0s, or mixed. The second stage took these representations of the inputs and combined them with representations of the gate type to yield a 1 or 0 answer. A final stage used the 1 or 0 answer along with the code representing the presence or absence of negation to generate the final answer. For example, the following stages generated an answer of 0 for an XNOR gate with inputs of 0 1 0 1 0 0: In the recoding stage the inputs were recoded as MIXED, in the gate mapping stage the MIXED inputs and the XOR gate type combined to yield an answer of 1, and in the negation stage the answer of 1 and the presence of negation combined to yield the final answer of 0.

It is important to note that the rules specified the stages used to carry out the task as well as how the states that occurred at each stage were mapped to intermediate representations. We assume that subjects begin performing the task by executing these rules sequentially and then gradually switch to associative responding in which state information at each stage of processing evokes intermediate representations to be used by the next stage (see the section on Rule Learning, later in this chapter). The declarative knowledge encoded in the rules provided the state information needed to carry out connectionist learning at each stage during the sequential performance of the task.

The network architecture used in the simulations is shown in the right panel of Fig. 5.2. The encodings of the inputs were identical to the encodings used in the previous simulations. There were separate vectors to encode the gate type, negation, and the different gate inputs. Separate networks were used to learn the two-, four-, and six-input gates. The vectors for the gate inputs were connected to a 3–layer network that solved the recoding task. The vector encoding the gate type was connected to a network that also received inputs from the recoding module. This network was trained to give the correct 0 or 1 response (gate mapping). The vector encoding the presence or absence of negation was connected to a network that also received inputs from the output of the gate mapping network lower in the hierarchy. All layers of units were fully interconnected. Each layer within a module was made up of 50 units.

The methods for coding the inputs to the networks were the same as in the simulations that we described previously. In addition to the input vectors, vectors coded state information for the each network. Separate random vectors coded the ALL 1s, ALL 0s, and MIXED states for the recoding network, the 1 and 0 states for the gate mapping network, and the 1 and 0 states for the negation network. All of these additional vectors served as the target patterns for their associated networks. For example, when the gate–inputs were 0 0 0 0, the recoding network would be trained to output the ALL 0s vector. The methods for presenting patterns to the networks were identical to the methods used in the previous simulations.

The recoding, gate mapping, and the negation networks were trained to respond with the appropriate state vectors when patterns were loaded into the input modules. There was no adjustment for the amount of fan in of connections, which varied from one module to another. No extensive search was carried out to find the optimal learning parameters. The momentum, tmax, and wrange parameters were set to .9, .9, and .5, respectively. Simulations were carried out to identify values for the learning rate parameters that could learn the task with the other parameters fixed to the above values. Learning times were averaged over 20 runs at each setting of the learning parameters.

The training occurred sequentially for each of the three stages on every trial. The recoding network was the first network to be trained after responding to the input vectors representing the gate inputs. Forward propagation activated a response pattern in the network's output layer. This activated pattern was then matched with the correct target response to assess response accuracy and to compute error. This error was then back propagated through the recoding network according to the usual procedure to adjust the weights. The correct target pattern (e.g., ALL 1s, ALL 0s, or MIXED), not the actual output from the input coding module, was then used to activate the next network in the hierarchy. A rule was used to load the correct output even if an incorrect or weak response had been generated in response to the inputs. The gate mapping network received the output of the recoding network as well as the vector that coded the gate type. The gate mapping network then responded with an output pattern that was matched against the correct intermediate vector code and then trained to a 1 or 0 answer. The correct output vector for the gate mapping network then served as the input to the negation network along with the input vector that coded the presence or absence of the negation symbol. A final response for the modular network was generated at the output layer of the negation network. This response was also matched to the correct vectors that coded the response of 0 or 1. The negation network was trained by adjusting its weights with backpropagation.

Accuracy of each network's response was assessed with the best match procedure. A response was scored correct if the sum of the squared deviations between the response pattern and the correct target pattern was smaller than the sum of the squared deviations between all of the network's other target patterns. Response accuracy was assessed on each trial for the recoding, gate mapping and negation networks. If all three networks responded correctly to all patterns in an epoch, learning was halted. The trials of last errors for the different learning stages served as the dependent measures of learning time.

Figure 5.4 shows the mean numbers of trials to criterion for each stage for the

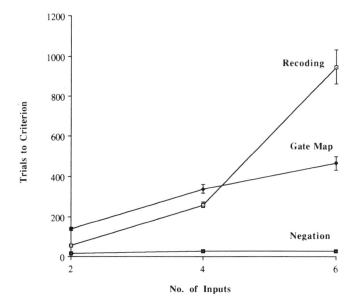

FIG. 5.4.   Trials to criterion for the recoding, gate mapping, and negation stages as a function of the number of inputs.

two–, four–, and six–input gate networks. The learning rates were .06, .02, and .02 for the two-, four-, and six–input gate networks, respectively. The number of trials required for recoding the inputs increased as the number of gate inputs increased. Once the slowest learning network had reached criterion, the modular network as a whole had effectively learned the task. These times to learn the task for the three modular networks are plotted in Fig. 5.3.

Task decomposition greatly speeded learning. The six-input gate network with decomposed learning required 948 trials to learn the task, whereas the network that did not use task decomposition required 10,835 trials. This speed up in learning was achieved without extensive parameter search, suggesting that decomposition provides a general method within the architecture to deal with the scaling problem. Learning parameters may not need to be tuned specifically for each new problem that is modelled. Furthermore, the speed up occurred even though the cycling of patterns was not optimal for training the decomposed network. The network that learned negation, for instance, was not systematically cycled through the four input combinations it had to map, as would occur if the network was trained in isolation.

## CAP2 ARCHITECTURE

CAP2 is a computer simulation program for creating connectionist architectures in which controlled processing and task decomposition occurs. CAP2 is an abbreviation for Controlled Automatic Processing model 2.[2] CAP2 is designed for exploring architectural issues that arise when connectionist and controlled processing are combined. The architecture is modular and is defined at multiple levels of detail. At the macro level, it includes a system of modules that pass vector and scalar messages. Scalar messages are used to control the activity in the modules. Vector messages encode perceptual and conceptual information. CAP2 has two kinds of modules: control modules and data modules. Data modules will be described first.

A data module in CAP2 transforms and transmits vector messages. It takes one or more vectors as input and produces a single output vector. For instance, a data module might take three vectors as inputs corresponding to "C," "O," and "W" and produce an output vector standing for the word "COW". The data module (see Fig. 5.5) is a three layer connectionist network. The output layer from a module provides the input for modules at the next level. The input is transformed through a set of connection weights that change with learning. The

---

[2]CAP2 is an extension of CAP1 (Schneider, 1985; Schneider & Detweiler, 1987) which is a processing model with single layer modules. CAP2 allows simulating a wider class of structures including multiple layer modules and is structured to facilitate exploration of modular vector processing networks.

Module Microstructure

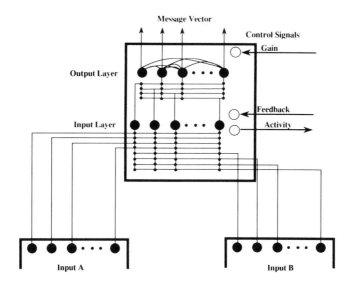

FIG. 5.5.   The microstructure of a module in CAP2. Inputs to the module are collected at the *input layer* after passing through connection matrices of weights that reflect prior learning. Activation then flows through a second connection matrix to the *output layer.* Backpropagation learning allows specific input patterns to reliably evoke specific output patterns. Autoassociative learning, which is controlled by the *feedback* control signal, occurs at the output layer to categorize and latch patterns of output activations. A *message vector* is transmitted to other modules. The strength of the message is controlled by a *gain signal.* When two input vectors flow into a module an *activity report* signal is generated that indicates how well they match.

*input layer* for a module collects input from multiple incoming vectors. The input layer projects to the *output layer*. In terms of a typical three layer back propagation network, there is an input layer (the output from the previous stage), a hidden layer (the input layer for the module) and an output layer (the output layer for the module). In some versions of the model (see Shedden & Schneider, 1990) there are connections within the module's input layer or output layer. These connections provide an autoassociative input that categorizes patterns, reduces noise effects, and allows pattern completion of partial vectors (see Anderson, 1983). Each of the layers in a module is assumed to be a vector of many units (e.g. 50 units in the present model). Each unit sums up its inputs and applies a logistic function to that sum to determine the activation. Learning occurs for each module through backpropagation (Rumelhart, Hinton, & Williams, 1986) so that output layers learn to respond consistently to patterns of inputs from other modules.

This architecture contrasts with traditional connectionist architectures by including control operations. In addition to data vectors that transmit between levels, there are *control signals* that control the activity of modules (see Fig. 5.5). The *activity report* is a scalar that is the sum of the squared activity of all the units in the input layer. It codes whether a data module is active and has a vector to transmit. The activity report can also provide information on whether two incoming vectors additively evoke similar vectors. This provides a mechanism for determining whether a vector is associated with other vectors stored in a different module. For instance, the activity report could quantify the degree of semantic match between the vectors evoked by visual and lexical vectors.

The *gain control* determines how strongly the output of a module activates the other modules to which it is connected. The gain of a message vector is modified in the model by multiplying each of its elements by a scalar. If the gain is low, no vector is transmitted. If it is high (1.0), the vector is transmitted at full strength.

The third control signal is the *feedback*. This signal controls the strength of the autoassociative feedback within the module. When the feedback is low, the module will accept new input. If the feedback is high, the module latches the current input and is insensitive to new input (see Schneider & Detweiler, 1987, pp. 79–81; Shedden & Schneider, 1990).

It is important to note that the control signals encode only a small amount of the information available in a data module. For example, a data vector might code the specific visual shape of a letter, whereas an activity report might encode only how well the stimulus matches a memory representation stored in a different module. The activity information indicates which modules are active and have messages to send. Control processes can then determine which modules should have the highest priority to transmit and how well incoming information matches stored memory representations.

The modules in the data network are organized into a two-dimensional lattice (see Fig. 5.6) with multiple levels and multiple modules in each level. Each module in one level connects to multiple modules at the next level. The network can be dynamically reconfigured to perform different tasks. Altering the control parameters provides a rapid software–type switch that temporarily activates and deactivates modules without changing connection weights. Because the connection weights change slowly and store all the knowledge in the network, they cannot be drastically altered for a temporary reorganization of the network. By reducing the gain, a module's output is blocked and effectively removed from processing. By altering the feedback, the input to a module can be latched, decayed, or blocked. By controlling the feedback and gain parameters, a large lattice of modules could be reconfigured for many tasks (e.g., a 6 by 6 lattice could be reduced to 4 levels of modules: 6 modules at the first level and one at each successive layer).

The design of the data modules is consistent with our current limited understanding of cortical neurophysiology (see Schneider & Detweiler, 1987, pp. 57–61). Cortical processing appears to be modular (see Mountcastle, 1979) involv-

## Data Modules

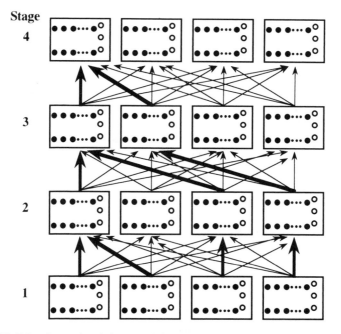

FIG. 5.6.   A matrix of data modules that can be used to solve tasks requiring stages of processing. The dark arrows indicate possible paths through which information could flow to perform the logic gate task to be discussed later in the paper. Inputs to the first stage of processing evoke stable patterns of activation at later stages after activations cascade through intervening modules.

ing interconnected modules at multiple levels (see Van Essen, 1985). The modules devoted to visual processing at stages beyond the first cortical stage (beyond V1 or striate cortex) appear to consist of two layer networks of excitatory pyramidal cells (see Lund, Hendrickson, Ogren, & Tobin, 1981). The outputs of these module appear to be modulated by a set of inhibitory neurons called chandelier cells that contact the pyramidal cells that project to the next cortical modules. The chandelier cells make contact to the initial segment of the pyramidal cell axons. These connections may enable a chandelier cell to gate or attenuate the output of the population of output neurons. Feedback within a module may occur through the connections that exist between the input layer of pyramidal cells (layer 4 cells) and the output layer of pyramidal cells (layer 2-3 cells). This feedback may also be modulated by the chandelier cells. In addition there are pyramidal cells within layers 5 and 6 that receive input from the input layer cells and project to subcortical structures that may provide the basis for attentional control. Currently, physiological data suggest that the structural principles represented in the current connectionist/control architecture are likely to be present in human cortical processing.

The control signals connect to the *controller,* which is a connectionist module with specialized connections (see Fig. 5.7). The controller is a sequential net (see Elman, 1988) that can learn to respond with sequences of output vectors with complex list structures. The sequential net, like other modules, has three layers. The first layer includes two subvectors. The first is the *task* subvector. The task subvector encodes the task that is to be performed with controlled processing. Sample tasks include searching the visual field for a match, comparing inputs to a particular code, and executing a series of logical rules. The second subvector is the *compare result.* It encodes activity reports from the data network that result from match operations. A third subvector, the *context* subvector (Fig. 5.7), encodes the activations of the hidden layer on the previous processing cycle.

The output layer of the sequential net has subvectors that encode operations

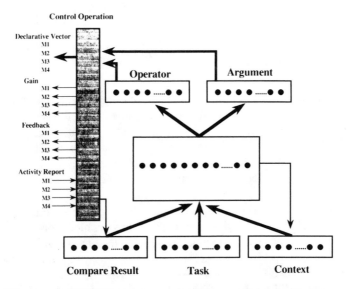

FIG. 5.7. The sequential rule network. The network is trained to output sequences of operations to perform cognitive tasks. Vectors encode the *current task, context* information in the form of prior activations of hidden units, and the *comparison* result of immediately preceding vector comparisons. Information about comparisons are encoded by incoming activity reports. The sequential network outputs on each processing cycle a control operation specified by an operator and an operator argument. The operations control processing in the data network by specifying the gains and feedbacks of specific modules.

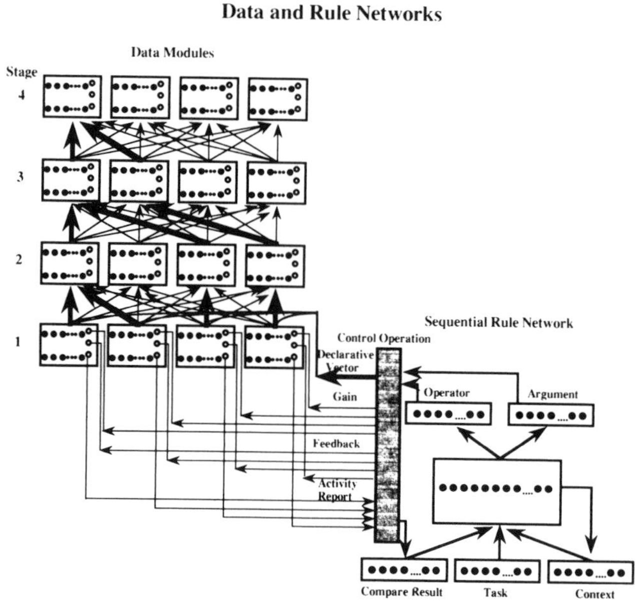

**Data and Rule Networks**

FIG. 5.8. The control signals between the sequential data networks. Only the connections between the sequential network and the first layer of data modules appear in the figure.

and arguments for those operations. In the current implementation, the network only generates one operation and argument at a time. The output of the network specifies the *control operation* to be performed. The current operations include: *attend* to a module, *compare* vectors from different modules, enable a module to *receive* a vector, and indicate that a task is *done*. For example, the receive operation decreases the feedback for a particular module so that it can receive the input from another module. The attend operation sets the data network report to monitor the activity report of a particular module. The second output subvector, the *argument subvector,* encodes arguments of the operations. For example, the arguments can reference specific modules (e.g., attend to module level 1 upper left visual field) or specific vectors for comparison (e.g., transmit vector CAT). The sequential network is assumed to interact with the data network via the control signals as illustrated in Fig. 5.8. This implementation of operations assumes that the operation and argument subvectors of the control network connect directly to all of the data modules, so that the control operations can influence the data network's activities.[3] The execution of the control network's operations is not currently implemented with a connectionist network but rather in C code.

---

[3]We assume that basic subroutines, such as how to search the set of active modules for a match, either come prewired or develop through early experience with one's environment.

The middle layer of the sequential net is a traditional backpropagation hidden layer. It has in addition, however, recurrent connections from the hidden layer back to the inputs. The activity of the hidden units is copied back to an additional subvector in the input layer to serve as input on the next trial. Elman (1988) has shown that these recurrent connections give the network memory for contexts permitting it to learn sequential dependencies among input patterns. The network is able to learn complex sequences of steps needed to carry out tasks.

In order to have a functioning architecture, all of its processing components must be fully specified. This requirement to fully specify an architecture is, of course, one of the strengths of the computational approach to modelling. By using the architecture to model human learning and performance, the plausibility of the general approach can be assessed. In designing the architecture, we are not committed to many of the specific details. For instance, the backpropagation learning procedure that is used in CAP2 to associate patterns is only an approximation of the learning that might occur in the human cognitive architecture. We are more committed to the structural assumptions of the architecture. These assumptions include: (a) An assumption that there is a processing substrate in the human cognitive architecture akin to a data network that carries out and stores memories of cognitive processing and that can be acted upon by control processes; (b) An assumption that modular network structures serve as functional units of processing; (c) An assumption that the information that passes between modules is represented as vectors; and (d) An assumption that memory associations among vectors develop through learning that is similar to the learning that occurs in connectionist models. Ideally, as the architecture is developed and modified, these basic structural properties will remain.

## Mechanisms for Instructable Decomposition

CAP2 provides two mechanisms for task decomposition. The first involves *configuring the data network* with a number of stages and number of modules in each stage. By altering the control signals, a subset of the modules can be made active for a given problem. For the gate task, three intermediate modules could be active to perform the input coding, gate mapping, and negation stages of processing.

The second decomposition mechanism in CAP2 involves *specifying the number of states in each stage*. For example, in the input coding task, all inputs are encoded into one of three states 1s, 0s, or mixed. A given input is mapped to one of three vectors. Instead of requiring the network to discover the appropriate responses for the intermediate stages, the network is directly trained on these appropriate responses. Information of this kind is usually provided to people when they are instructed on a procedural task. For instance, students are told stages and states necessary to perform multiple column addition. In CAP2 each state is represented as a random vector. The modules at each stage of processing learn to associate outputs with the appropriate inputs.

CAP2 captures knowledge that is initially specified in rules and the task environment into connection weights stored in the data network. For example, in the gate coding problem, the initial rule might be "compare all the inputs to the code 'one'; if they all match, the output of the input coding stage is the 'all ones' code." The sequential network is separately trained so that it can execute these rules. On each trial the controller attends to a series of inputs that are compared to a given vector and then evokes an output for each stage. Associative learning changes the connection weights so that the inputs can eventually evoke the output in the absence of controlled processing.

It is important to note that the data network is not simply learning the rules stored in the controller. The rules are often poor specifications of the problem that must be tuned by interaction with the specific stimuli that the data network encounters during learning. The data network will encode statistical regularities inherent in a training set even though these regularities are not reflected by the rule set. For example, in the model for the gate task, the strength of the module's responses will in part reflect the frequency of particular gate and gate input combinations in the training set.

The interaction of the data network with the environment as coded in the stimulus vectors also provides greater specificity of the associations to be learned. Learning to drive a stick shift provides an example of the kind of learning that the architecture would ideally simulate. The rules that an instructor gives a novice driver specify the stages to carry out and the relevant states for those stages (e.g., when you reach 15 mph release the gas pedal, push in the clutch, and move the gear shift lever to the upper right). After the learner has practiced the task, it is not the rule that is eventually learned but rather the appropriate responses to stimulus conditions that occurred whenever a shift operation occurred (e.g., the sound of the engine, the visual flow, and the pressure of acceleration on one's back). The complex set of inputs, most of which are not present in the rule description, become the triggering condition for the response. The rule is important for identifying the basic operations and a subset of the conditions that would allow that student to perform the basic task. But practice on the task builds up the rich set of associations needed to perform the task at a high level of expertise. The expert's performance is not brittle and does not degrade in many related conditions (e.g., if the speedometer is broken).

The association of input to output vectors that occurs in CAP2 is related to the chunking operation in SOAR (Laird, Newell, & Rosenbloom, 1987) and the compilation process in ACT* (Anderson, 1983), but differs in that it encodes subsymbolic information not specified in the rules. Sensitive tuning of responses is possible partly because stimulus information can be represented with a fine grain size in the vector representations. Many different features encoded in the vectors can be weighed together to influence responding. To achieve the same tuning of responses in a production system would require building up productions with highly complex condition sides and then having to select among a huge set of such productions.

## Combined Symbolic and Connectionist Processing

The CAP2 architecture can perform symbolic processing. Vectors can be stored in modules and manipulated like symbols represented as bit vectors are manipulated by conventional computers. Manipulation of symbols in CAP2 occurs through interactions with the control network, which can configure the data network to be a standard symbol processing system by storing and transferring bits as single units. For example, CAP2 could model how people identify palindromes (e.g., that the sequence XTUQ is the reverse of QUTX). Palindromes could be identified by loading the initial sequence of letters into four modules which then would be compared to the second sequence of letters for matches. Comparisons would occur sequentially. It is important to note that humans easily detect palindromes and can perform the task with arbitrary stimuli (e.g., words, sentences, or pictures). In standard connectionist models, detecting novel palindromes typically requires a huge amount of training with the specific stimuli. To detect any four-word palindrome would require recognizing about $10^{20}$ patterns, assuming a human word vocabulary.

The data network in CAP2 can perform symbolic expansion and compression or chunking operations (see Schneider & Detweiler, 1987, pp. 101–106, for a review of chunking in CAP2). A vector in one module can activate a series of vectors at later stages. Thus, expanding information from a chunk occurs when a single vector evokes several vectors at the next level. For example, the cue "Gettysburg Address" could evoke a phrase that could evoke a sentence and then, in turn, evoke a series of sentences. Compressing information into a chunk involves having several vectors in modules at one level evoke a single vector at the next level (e.g., the letter string "C," "A," "T," at one level is compressed into a single new vector representing "CAT") at the next level.

The data network can report to the control network the results of symbolic-like comparisons. Perhaps the most basic symbolic operation is determining the degree of match of comparisons. In CAP2, control operations are performed on entire vectors not on individual units. When two vectors input to a module, their additive effect evokes a third vector. The degree to which two vectors evoke the same code in a module is reflected by the length of the vector that results from the summed response they produce at the module's input layer. Because the two input vectors connect to the input layer through separate connections (see Fig. 5.5), they can individually produce the same response due to prior learning. The activity report of the two vectors quantifies the similarity in the responses produced by the two incoming vectors. A geometric interpretation of the activity report is shown in Fig. 5.9 with vectors of two units. The activity report would be the squared lengths of the vectors that appear at the bottom of the figure. In general, if the separate evoked responses of two vectors are $x_i$ and $y_i$, their activity report is given by

$$\text{activity report} = \sum_{i=1}^{n} (x_i + y_i)^2$$

# Vector Matching

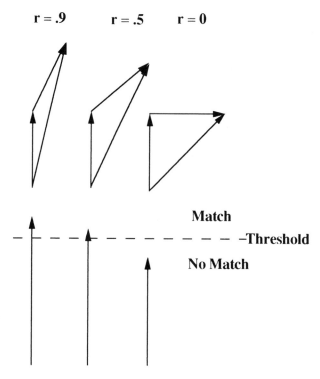

FIG. 5.9.   A geometric representation of vector matching. The addition of highly correlated vectors results in longer vectors than the addition of less correlated normalized vectors. A match occurs when a preset threshold is exceeded.

which is equivalent to

$$\text{activity report} = \sum_{i=1}^{n} x_i^2 + \sum_{i=1}^{n} y_i^2 + 2|x|\,|y|\,\cos\theta$$

where $n$ is the number of units in the vectors, $\theta$ is the angle between the vectors, and $|x|$ is the Euclidian length of $x$. If the vector lengths are normalized to 1, the average activity report is $1 + 1 + 2\cos\theta$. If the two vectors evoke the same code ($\cos\theta=1$), the activity level is 4. If they evoke uncorrelated codes ($\cos\theta=0$), the activity level is 2. If the match criterion is set to 4 only perfect matches are allowed. If the match criterion is set to 3, the two vectors must correlate greater than .5 to provide a match. In practice, the additive response of the two vectors pass through the logistic function resulting in more complex mathematics than appears above. The magnitude of the activity report will nonetheless reflect the correlations of the evoked activities when compared to a baseline activity report that would result from the transmission of unrelated vectors. Note that this match comparison permits both symbolic matching (e.g., there was a match) and partial matching, which is characteristic of subsymbolic processing (see Smolensky 1988).

The connectionist processing within each module allows learning to generalize so that matching operations are less brittle than symbolic matching operations. The output activation that a vector evokes is a function of its similarity to related vectors stored in a module. The autoassociative feedback categorizes an evoked output to its closest match. The connectionist learning in CAP2 can also associate input to output patterns that are not specified by symbolic rules. The statistical pattern recognition that occurs in connectionist processing enables the system to make complex non-linear categorization decisions that were not explicitly encoded in the input. A well-known model that exemplifies connectionist categorization is NETtalk (Sejnowski & Rosenberg, 1987), which maps letter string to word pronunciation in the absence of explicit rules.

## CAP2 RULE LEARNING

The sequential net in the controller allows CAP2 to learn rules that interact with the data network to perform the decomposed task. The rules specify the sequential algorithms subjects either decide to use on their own or are told to use when instructed on the task. We have implemented initial versions of the sequential net and have found that it can learn the rule sets to carry out the gate learning task. In this chapter we will provide only an overview of how the rule learning works. The nature of rule learning will be detailed in later papers (Schneider & Oliver, in preparation).

To be useful, rule learning must be achieved in a small number of trials. The controller can be thought of as a teacher of the data network. If teaching the controller required as many trials as teaching the data network (e.g., 10,835 trials for the six input case), little would be gained by having a controller. In our empirical work on electronic troubleshooting we have found college subjects learn rules for all six gates in 216 trials or 36 trials per gate (Oliver & Schneider, 1988). This was the point at which subjects made few errors.[4] Our goal for the sequential rule learning was to acquire the task in 50 trials per gate.

Rules were learned by associating a sequence of operations (and associated

---

[4]Several thousand trials were required before the subjects would be able to respond to the gates within .75 seconds (Carlson, Sullivan, & Schneider, 1989). However, a criterion of thousands of trials is more appropriate for the learning of the data network than the learning of the rule network, which should be functional much sooner.

arguments) with the task to be performed along with the information needed to coordinate the operations. Table 1 shows the rules to execute a NAND gate. In the simulation, the vectors coding the task, data network report, hidden layer, operation and argument were all 50 unit vectors. Each state of the input and output vectors was assigned a random code of 0s and 1s. The sequential net was instructed by presenting the sequence of operations in the order that they would be executed on individual sample trials. This instruction is analogous to having a teacher verbalize the rules to perform the task for a specific example. For example, to respond to the NAND gate with inputs of all 1s, the sequence of rules performed would be: "perform the recoding task first; attend to the gate inputs; check if they are all 1s; if so, remember that the inputs are all 1s; next perform the mapping task for the AND gate; look at the gate's symbol; check to see if it has an AND shape (i.e., a flat back); if so, recall the gate mapping state; if it is all 1s the intermediate answer is 1; now perform the negation task; look for the visual negation symbol; if it is present, recall the intermediate answer; if it is 1, the final answer is a 0." If any of the rule's conditions is not met, a branch to a different set of rules must occur. For instance, if the intermediate answer is 0 instead of 1, a different a set of rules would apply negation to produce the final answer of 1. The sequence of operations in Table 5.1 carries out the rules described above, but at a finer level of detail. Note that separate operations indicate when a subtask is done. Also a module must be attended to before a vector can be compared or received.

TABLE 5.1
Control Network Operations for the NAND Gate

| Cycle | Task | Compare Result | Operator | Argument |
|---|---|---|---|---|
| 1 | recode all 1's | — | Attend | Visual Input Modules |
| 2–8 | recode all 1's | — | Compare | All 1s |
| 9 | recode all 1's | match | Attend | Recoding Module |
| 10 | recode all 1's | match | Receive | All 1s |
| 11 | recode all 1's | match | Done | — |
| 12 | map AND | — | Attend | Gate Module |
| 13 | map AND | — | Compare | And |
| 14 | map AND | match | Attend | Recoding Module |
| 15 | map AND | match | Compare | All 1s |
| 16 | map AND | match | Attend | Gate Mapping Module |
| 17 | map AND | match | Receive | 1 |
| 18 | map AND | match | Done | — |
| 19 | negate 1 | — | Attend | Negation Module |
| 20 | negate 1 | — | Compare | Negate |
| 21 | negate 1 | match | Attend | Recoding Module |
| 22 | negate 1 | match | Compare | 1 |
| 23 | negate 1 | match | Attend | Negation Module |
| 24 | negate 1 | match | Receive | 0 |
| 25 | negate 1 | match | Done | — |

**Input Recoding Rule**

Compare the inputs to one. If all match the input state is ALL 1s
none match the input state is ALL 0s
otherwise the input state is MIXED

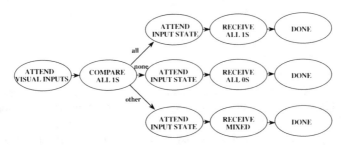

FIG. 5.10.   The control operations that are needed to recode the inputs. Different branches are followed depending on the result of the
COMPARE ALL 1s match.

The simulation learned to perform the task by executing the rules one step at a
time. On each step of the rule set, the model was presented the task subvector
and the network report and trained to respond with the correct operation and the
operation's correct argument. Backpropagation learning was used to change the
weights from the input to the output for that step. The activations of the hidden
layer were copied back to the input layer to serve as inputs for the next input
presentation. These "context units" were fully interconnected with the hidden
layer. The additional units and connections allows the system to maintain sequential information to learn such tasks as finite state grammars (see Elman,
1988; Cleeremans, Servan-Schreiber, & McClelland, 1989). The simulation was
considered to have learned the task when it could produce the sequence of output
operations and operation arguments. If the output matched the correct target
vector better than the other target vectors, the output was considered correct.[5]

The sequential network could learn the rule sets relatively quickly, (in about
120 trials). This learning time is faster than the learning times for humans, (216
trials), the decomposed model (932 trials for the six input case) and much faster
than the learning time for the single stage model (10,835 trials for the six input
case).

When learning the rule set for the gate task, the sequential rule network must
learn to perform rule structures that branch. The sequential net learned an "if-
else" structure by learning single cases for each branch of the "if-else" rule (see
Fig. 5.10). The branching is determined by the data network report. For example, when performing gate mapping, the rule network would specify that the

---

[5]In later versions of the model we will add an autoassociative output layer which will implement
the best match operation in a connectionist network.

AND gate symbol should be searched for at a particular visual location. In the event of a nonmatch, the rules encoded in the rule network would branch to look for the OR gate. Further branching would occur depending on whether matches or nonmatches occur. In this way a set of rules can deal with the different contingencies that arise when a task is to be performed. After training, the sequential network takes the correct branches based on the output from the data network. Even more complex control structures can be developed. For example, if the sequential network stores and monitors vectors in the data modules, looping structures can be learned.

It should be noted that the rule knowledge is brittle and performs much as novices perform during the early stage of rule learning. The rules must be presented in exactly the same form to speed learning. If the network is presented two logically equivalent rules sets for the same problem across trials, learning is slowed (e.g., an AND can be solved by "If all 1s respond 1, else 0"; or If any 0s, respond 0, else 1"). Similarly, when students learn in classroom settings, they often ask that the rules presented to them retain a rote, rigid form throughout instruction. They are often frustrated when an instructor fails to repeat definitions of concepts with the same verbatim wording used previously. Note that, although the rule knowledge is brittle, once the knowledge is captured in the data network, the knowledge is no longer dependent on the specific form of the rules used to initially learn the task.

## GENERAL DISCUSSION

The present hybrid connectionist/control architecture illustrates the complementary nature of symbolic and connectionist processing. The architecture provides mechanisms for using rule-based instructions so that complex tasks can be learned in reasonable numbers of trials. The simple one module connectionist solution required 10,835 trials to learn a problem that humans learn in 216 trials. By decomposing the task into three stages, learning time was reduced by a factor of ten. Such reductions in learning times will be especially necessary to model more complex tasks. To accomplish task decomposition, the network had to be configured into stages of processing. There also had to be a method for evoking the appropriate states at each stage for each instance of the problem. This required the availability of a sequential rule processor to modulate the data network to determine the appropriate states for each module for each instance. We demonstrated that the sequential network could learn the sequence of rules by being presented verbal-like listing of the rule sets.

The resulting hybrid model performs a task differently at early and later phases of its learning. In the first phase, the sequential network learns the rules to perform the task. During initial acquisition many errors are made and performance is slow as each step of the rule set is executed. This is similar to *controlled processing* (Shiffrin & Schneider, 1977) or interpretive execution of declarative productions (Anderson, 1983). Once the rule set is acquired, the sequential net can perform the task reliably. The processing is slow and brittle. During rule execution, the sequential network monitors the activity reports from the data network and sends signals to carry out control operations. As the controller executes the rules, the data network associates the attended states at each stage of processing to the responses at the next stage. The rule execution provides a task decomposition and specification of intermediate states for each stage. The knowledge that is captured in connection weights in the data network reflects associations between particular instances and the response of the next stage that is specified by the rule being executed. These associations can include information not directly coded in the rules. At a later phase of learning, associative retrieval in the data network directly evokes a sequence of states at different stages of processing. The data network can categorize the modules's inputs to the best matching states and its performance is not as brittle as the performance of the sequential network. Once the data network reliably responds to inputs, performance is fast and does not require guidance from the sequential rule network. This type of processing is characteristic of *automatic processing* (see Shiffrin & Schneider 1977) or procedural knowledge (Anderson, 1983).

As a model of human cognition, the hybrid architecture we are developing should provide benefits over standard connectionist learning. Ideally, the architecture will benefit from instructions, quickly encode new rule sets, exploit task decompositions, execute sequential behaviors, and perform tasks requiring variable binding (e.g., palindrome detection).

The hybrid architecture should also provide benefits over symbolic processing. Ideally, the capturing of knowledge in the connection weights in the data network will model fast parallel processing, reduce the brittleness in accessing knowledge, and permit the acquisition of knowledge not specified by rules.

## Hybrid Architecture and Human Processing

The hybrid architecture provides a better match to human processing than either symbolic or connectionist processing alone. Human controlled processing acquires rules quickly, as would be expected of symbolic learning systems. However, the development of automatic processing in humans typically requires hundreds to thousands of trials which is more representative of connectionist learning of decomposed tasks. Human learning benefits immensely from instruction. As humans practice they acquire knowledge that is not specified in the instructions. Humans can forget rule knowledge but still perform the task after extensive practice (e.g., with what finger does one type the letter "c" on a typewriter?). Humans can perform symbolic processing but there are clear limits to such processing. For example, chess experts and novices use sequential search to look for best moves, but the extent of this search is severely limited because of memory constraints (deGroot, 1965). Human attentional processing supports the presence of both controlled rule processing and automatic associative processing (see Shiffrin, 1988). Physiological evidence suggests the presence of control structures (Schneider & Detweiler, 1987).

Pylyshyn (chap. 7 this volume) questioned whether the connectionist/control architecture we have described is a mere implementation of a symbolic architecture with connectionist components. According to his view, the computational power of such a system depends more on its formal properties as a symbolic processing system than on the properties of the connectionist hardware. While the formal properties of an architecture determines what could in principle be computed by an architecture without bounds (e.g., a Turing machine with an infinite tape), they do not necessarily determine what can be computed in a constrained system implementation. Matters of implementation are likely to play a crucial role in determining what gets computed and how long it takes. An architecture for human cognition may use rulelike behavior that has the drawback of being slow and brittle and also use connectionist, associative retrieval to replace the rule–based processing. Understanding more about the implementation of cognitive algorithms may help us understand why people learn quickly in some situations and slowly in other situations. In addition, much research in psychology is concerned with why people have trouble using optimal algorithms to solve problems or why they do not reason consistently. People may have these problems partly because of inherent limitations on processing, such as memory and attentional limitations. These limitations may be traced to the implementation of the cognitive architecture.

## CONCLUSION

The present connectionist/control architecture illustrates the complementary interaction of symbolic and connectionist processing. The architecture involves a data network of modules that transmit vector messages. A control network modulates the data network. The resulting hybrid architecture allows learning from instruction and faster learning through task decomposition. The connectionist processing enables less brittle comparison and faster processing than symbolic rule processing. The learning times for different task decompositions for a task were compared. The use of task decomposition allowed for an almost ten–fold improvement in the learning times. Traditional single module connectionist learning learned too slowly compared to human learning. A combination of task decompostion and rule learning provides a good match to the human data. Hybrid connectionist/control models have significant computational advantages over purely connectionist or purely symbolic systems.

# REFERENCES

Anderson, J. A. (1983). Cognitive and psychological computation with neural models. *IEEE Transactions on Systems, Man, and Cybernetics, 13,* 799–815.

Ballard, D. H. (1987). Modular learning in neural networks. *Proceedings of the Ninth Annual Conference of the Cognitive Science Society* (pp. 279–284). Hillsdale, NJ: Lawrence Erlbaum Associates.

Biederman, I., & Shiffrar, M. M. (1987). Sexing day-old chicks: A case study and expert systems analysis of a difficult perceptual-learning task. *Journal of Experimental Psychology: Learning, Memory, and Cognition, 13,* 640–645.

Carlson, R. A., Sullivan, M. A., & Schneider, W. (1989). Practice and working memory effects in building procedural skill. *Journal of Experimental Psychology: Learning, Memory, and Cognition, 15,* 517–526.

Cleeremans, A., Servan-Schreiber, D., & McClelland, J. L. (1989). *Encoding sequential structure in simple recurrent networks.* Technical report CMU-CS-88-183, Computer Science Department, Carnegie Mellon University, Pittsburgh, PA.

deGroot, A. D. (1965). *Thought and choice in chess.* The Hague: Mouton.

Durbin, R. E., & Rumelhart, D. E. (1989). Product units: A computationally powerful and biologically plausible extension to backpropagation networks. *Neural Networks, 1,* 133–142.

Elman, J. L. (1990). Finding structure in time. *Cognitive Science, 14,* 179–212.

Estes, W. K. (1986). Memory storage and retrieval processes in category learning. *Journal of Experimental Psychology, 115,* 155–174.

Fahlman, S. E. (1988). *An empirical study of learning speed in back-propagation networks.* Technical Report CMU-CS-88-162, Carnegie-Mellon, Computer Science Department, Pittsburgh, PA.

Gallant, S. I., & Smith, D. (1987, June). *Random cells: An idea whose time has come and gone . . . And come again?* Paper presented at the IEEE International Conference on Neural Networks, San Diego.

Gluck, M. A., & Bower, G. H. (1988). Evaluating an adaptive network model of human learning. *Journal of Memory and Language, 27,* 166–195.

Grossberg, S. (1987). Competitive learning from interactive activation to adaptive resonance. *Cognitive Science, 11,* 23–63.

Hinton, G. E. (1986). Learning distributed representations of concepts. *Proceedings of the Eighth Annual Conference of the Cognitive Science Society* (pp. 1–12). Hillsdale, NJ: Lawrence Erlbaum Associates.

Hinton, G. E. (1987). Connectionist learning procedures. Technical report CMU-CS-87-115. Computer Science Dept., Carnegie Mellon University, Pittsburgh, PA.

Jacobs, R. A. (1988). Increased rates of convergence through learning rate adaptation. *Neural Networks, 1,* 295–307.

Johnson-Laird, P. N. (1983). *Mental models.* Cambridge, MA: Harvard University Press.

Klahr, D., Langley, P., & Neches, R. (Eds.) (1987). *Production system models of learning and development.* Cambridge, MA: MIT Press.

Koch, C., & Ullman, S. (1985). Shifts in selective visual attention: towards the underlying neural circuitry. *Human Neurobiology, 4,* 219–227.

Laird, J. E., Newell, A., & Rosenbloom, P. S. (1987). Soar: An architecture for general intelligence. *Artificial Intelligence, 33,* 1–64.

Lewis, C. (1987). Composition of productions. In D. Klahr, P. Langley, & R. Neches (Eds.), *Production system models of learning and development* (pp. 329–358), Cambridge, MA: MIT Press.

Lund, J. S., Hendrickson, Ogren, M. P., & Tobin, E. A. (1981). Anatomical organization of primate visual cortex area VII. *The Journal of Comparative Neurology, 202*, 19–45.

McClelland, J. L., & Rumelhart, D. E. (1988). *Explorations in parallel distributed processing: A handbook of models, programs, and exercises.* Cambridge, MA: MIT Press.

McCloskey, M., & Cohen, N. J. (1989). Catastrophic interference in connectionist networks: The sequential learning problem. In G. H. Bower (Ed.) *The psychology of learning and motivation* (Vol. 24, pp. 109–166).

Miikkulainen, R., & Dyer, M. G. (1989). *A modular neural network architecture for sequential paraphrasing of script-based stories.* Technical Report UCLA-AI-89-02, Computer Science Department, University of California, Los Angeles.

Minsky, M., & Papert, S. (1988). *Perceptrons (Expanded Edition).* Cambridge, MA: MIT Press.

Mountcastle, V. B. (1979). An organizing principle for cerebral function: The unit module and the distributed system. In F. O. Schmitt, & F. G. Worden (Eds.), *The neurosciences.* Cambridge, MA: MIT Press.

Newell, A., & Simon, H. A. (1972). *Human problem solving.* Englewood Cliffs, NJ: Prentice-Hall.

Oliver, W. L., & Schneider, W. (1988). Using rules and task division to augment connectionist learning. *Proceedings of the Tenth Annual Conference of the Cognitive Science Society* (pp. 55–61). Hillsdale, NJ: Lawrence Erlbaum Associates.

Plaut, D. C., Nowlan, S. J., & Hinton (1986). *Experiments on learning by back-propagation.* Technical Report CMU-CS-86-126, Carnegie-Mellon, Computer Science Department, Pittsburgh, PA.

Rueckl, J. G., Cave, K. R., & Kosslyn, S. M. (1989). Why are "what" and "where" processed by separate cortical visual systems? A computational investigation. *Journal of Cognitive Neuroscience, 2*, 171–186.

Rumelhart, D. E., Hinton, G. E., & Williams, R. J. (1986). Learning internal representations by error propagation. In D. E. Rumelhart & J. L. McClelland (Eds.), *Parallel distributed processing* (pp. 318–364). Cambridge, MA: MIT Press.

Rumelhart, D. E., & McClelland, J. L. (Eds.). (1986). *Parallel distributed processing: Explorations in the microstructure of cognition. Volume 2: Psychological and biological models.* Cambridge, MA: MIT Press.

Schneider, W. (1987). Connectionism: Is it a paradigm shift for psychology? *Behavior Research Methods, Instruments, & Computers, 19*, 73–83.

Schneider, W., & Detweiler, M. (1987). A connectionist/control architecture for working memory. In G. H. Bower (Ed.), *The psychology of learning and motivation* (Vol. 21, pp. 54–119). New York: Academic Press.

Schneider, W., & Oliver, W. L. (in preparation). *Connectionist implementations of rule learning.*

Sejnowski, T. J., Rosenberg, C. R. (1987). Parallel networks that learn to pronounce English text. *Complex Systems, 1*, 145–168.

Shedden, J. M., & Schneider, W. (1990). A connectionist model of attentional enhancement and signal buffering. *Proceedings of the Twelfth Annual Conference of the Cognitive Science Society.* Hillsdale, NJ. Lawrence Erlbaum Associates.

Shiffrin, R. M. (1988). Attention. In R. C. Atkinson, R. J. Herrnstein, G. Lindzey, & R. D. Luce (Eds.), *Steven's handbook of experimental psychology* (pp. 739–811). New York: Wiley.

Shiffrin, R. M., & Schneider, W. (1977). Controlled and automatic human information processing: II: Perceptual learning, automatic attending, and general theory. *Psychological Review, 84*, 127–190.

Smolensky, P. (1988). On the proper treatment of connectionism. *Behavioral and Brain Sciences, 11*, 1–74.

Sternberg, S. (1969). The discovery of processing stages: Extensions of Donders' method. *Acta Psychologica, 30*, 276–315.

Tesauro, G. (1987). Scaling relationships in back-propagation learning: Dependence on training set size. *Complex Systems, 1,* 367–372.

Tesauro, G., & Janssens, B. (1988). Scaling relationships in back-propagation learning. *Complex Systems, 2,* 39–44.

Tesauro, G., & Sejnowski, T. J. (1988). *A parallel network that learns to play backgammon.* Technical Report CCSR-88-2, Center for Complex Systems Research, University of Illinois at Urbana-Champaign.

Van Essen, D. C. (1985). Functional organization of primate visual cortex. In A. Peters & E. G. Jones (Eds.), *The cerebral cortex, (Vol. 3).* New York: Plenum.

VanLehn, K. (1987). Learning one subprocedure per lesson. *Artificial Intelligence, 31,* 1–40.

Waibel, A. (1989). Modular construction of time-delay neural networks for speech recognition. *Neural Computation, 1,* 39–46.

# 6

## Goal Reconstruction: How Teton Blends Situated Action and Planned Action

Kurt VanLehn
William Ball
*Learning Research and Development Center and Computer Science Department, University of Pittsburgh*

When you purchase a programming language, what you actually receive is a program (an interpreter or a compiler) that causes text written in the programming language to control the actions of the computer. When you buy an expert system shell or an AI programming environment, you get not only an interpreter but a variety of other programs as well. For instance, you often receive inference engines, data base management tools, graphics packages and libraries of utility programs. When you obtain a symbolic architecture, you receive an interpreter and some extra capabilities, most of which are not found even in the most advanced expert system shells. For instance, in the Pittsburgh architectures— Soar (Rosenbloom, Newell, & Laird, chap. 4 in this volume), Prodigy (Carbonell, Knoblock, & Minton, chap. 9 in this volume) and Theo (Mitchell et al., chap. 12 in this volume)—the extra capabilities include a kind of dynamic optimization. Programs automatically get faster as they run. From a purely pragmatic view, a symbolic architecture is just an expert system shell with some novel features added. Even architectures that are intended to model human cognition resemble augmented expert system shells. If one removed the automatic learning from ACT* (Anderson, 1983), it would be indistinguishable from many expert system shells on the market, because they too have a semantic net database and a production system programming language. On the other hand, the current state of the art is merely a stage in the development of much more powerful architectures. Architectures may evolve to the point where they are no longer programmed but instead acquire expertise through training and experience in much the same way that humans do. However, it is fair to say that we do not yet have such general problem solvers. Currently, an architecture is a programming language with some powerful, unusual extra capabilities.

147

This chapter discusses an extra capability that few architectures have, even though it is both useful from a programming point of view and arguably a good approximation to a human capabilities. People can reconstruct goal structures and other aspects of their internal state that have been forgotten. For instance, suppose one is interrupted in the middle of solving a difficult problem by a long involved phone call. When the phone call is over, one can eventually pick up the problem solving where one left off. This capability is called *goal reconstruction.* Because goal reconstruction requires no special training to acquire it and it does not have to be acquired separately for each a new problem solving procedure one learns, goal reconstruction is arguably a fundamental, task-general capability of human problem solvers. Goal reconstruction is also a useful capability even for an artificial problem solver. It permits recovery from interruptions of the problem solving by processes that modify the body of procedural knowledge, such as an inferential learning process or a programmer debugging the procedural knowledge. In short, goal reconstruction is both a fundamental human capability and a useful capability for AI architectures.

Goal reconstruction is part of the larger process of maintaining a goal structure. Our analysis of goal reconstruction is based on the insight that goal maintenance is a special case of the notorious frame problem in AI. The frame problem is to keep a model of the world up to date as actions take place in the world. Sometimes actions have unexpected and wide-ranging effects, which may make it difficult to calculate how much of the model needs changing in order to reflect the change wrought by the action on the real world. Of course, if the agent can see the world, then perceptual processing can be partially substituted for the cognitive processing that calculate updates to the model. At first glance, the frame problem has nothing to do with goal maintenance. Goals are not usually though of as being a part of the real world, so literally speaking, maintenance of goals is not maintenance of an internal model of the external world. However, the agent's knowledge, when viewed as a disembodied logical system, can be applied to the external world in order to generate a virtual or ideal goal structure. For the sake of the analogy, we can pretend that this Platonic goal structure is "in the real world".[1] Now it is clear that maintaining the agent's internal goal structures is exactly a frame problem: it must manipulate its internal goal structures so that they accurately reflect changes in the external, Platonic goal structures. As always in the frame problem, perceptual processing can be substituted, at least in principle, for internal calculations. This chapter discusses computa-

---

[1]Many AI problem solvers assume that high level descriptions, such as "block-1 supports block-2," are part of the real world. In fact, a robot would have to infer such relationships with the aid of a sophisticated vision system. Goals are also produced by inferences. So it is not such a great leap to consider goals as well as "block-1 supports block-2" relationships as being "in the real world".

tional mechanisms for implementing this "in principle" tradeoff between perceptual and cognitive maintenance of goals.

## THREE PROBLEMS TO BE SOLVED BY GOAL RECONSTRUCTION

Goal reconstruction is a solution to three problems in cognitive theory. Two of the problems stem from inadequacies in current accounts of human working memory for goals. The third problem is that current accounts of problem solving overemphasize planning and plan-following, because much of human behavior is *situated* as opposed to being *planned*. This section contains a discussion of each problem in turn.

The first problem has to do with working memory capacity for goals. People cannot remember arbitrarily large goal structures for arbitrarily long times. For instance, a telephone call often causes one to forget one's place in a problem. An early approach to modeling this human trait was to assume that goals were held in a capacity limited memory, called STM or working memory. For instance, Newell and Simon (1972, p. 808) claimed that "STM holds about five to seven symbols, but only about two can be retained for one task while another unrelated task is performed." Because working memory holds both goals and intermediate results, and these can accumulate quickly while problem solving, it is difficult to perform significant computations when working memory is strongly capacity limited. Thus, it was assumed that people use the external world as a storage place for temporary results while problem solving, and this makes it just like a working memory. For instance, Newell and Simon say (p. 801) that the operative "STM should be defined, not as internal memory, but as the combination of (a) the internal STM (as measured by the usual psychological tests) and (b) the part of the visual display that is in the subject's foveal view." Thus, instead of trying to remember an intermediate result, such as $T = 0$, the person writes it down on a worksheet. Things are not so simple for goals, however, because people do not usually write goals on their worksheets. Anderson (1983, p. 161) showed how to reconstruct Tower of Hanoi goals using task-specific knowledge about the puzzle, but he did not present a general capability. Thus, goal reconstruction has been thought for some time to be important as a way of increasing the effective capacity of working memory, although a general model of goal reconstruction was never developed.

Another problem in cognitive theory involves the access characteristics of goal memory. In most models of human goal storage, goals are held in a last-in-first-out goal stack (Laird, Newell, & Rosenbloom, 1987; Newell & Simon, 1972; VanLehn, 1990). That is, when a person is done with a goal and needs to select a new goal to work on, the only goals that can be selected are those that were most recently created and are not yet accomplished. This restriction is called the LIFO (last–in–first–out) convention. Consider, for instance, a cognitive procedure with the following goal structure:

*Top goal*
  *Subgoal 1*
    *Sub-subgoal A*
    *Sub-subgoal B*
  *Subgoal 2*
    *Sub-subgoal C*
    *Sub-subgoal D*

Suppose all these goals are conjunctively related, so that achieving the top goal means that all the subgoals must be achieved. Suppose further that the lowest goals, the ones with letters as their names, correspond to physical actions that an experimenter could observe the subject doing. Let us see what kinds of goal selection orders are allowed by the LIFO restriction. Suppose the top goal constructs subgoals 1 and 2 at the same time. Subgoal 2 is selected, and constructs goals C and D at the same time. Goal C is selected. After it is finished by performing some physical action, the subject must choose either goal 1 or goal D, as these two have been constructed but not yet executed. The LIFO restriction implies that goal D must be chosen, as it is younger. Thus, in a LIFO architecture, the experimenter would never see actions in the sequence CADB, as this interleaves subgoals of goals 1 and 2. Of the 24 possible permutations of the four primitive goals, only 8 can be generated by a LIFO architecture.

Intuitively, the LIFO restriction is quite implausible. It essentially says that there are some subgoals that one can recall but cannot select. In the example above, one can recall subgoal 1 (since it will be selected later) and yet one cannot select it because subgoal D is younger. For instance, suppose the top goal is "do evening chores" and subgoals 1 and 2 are, respectively, "clean breakfast dishes" and "prepare dinner." A LIFO restriction would mean that one would have to clean all the breakfast dishes before starting the dinner preparation, or vice-versa. On this analysis, many people violate the LIFO restriction nightly.

The problem with the evening–chores example is that we do not really know what the goal structures of the subjects are. There are other goal structures than the one above that would allow a LIFO architecture to interleave dish–cleaning actions with dinner-preparing actions.

There are, however, good examples of the LIFO constraint being violated. We discovered eight elementary school students (from a sample of 26) who executed subtraction procedures in a non-LIFO order (VanLehn, Ball, & Kowalski, 1989). The goal structure of subtraction procedures is quite well understood (VanLehn, 1990), and there is no reason to believe that these students' goal structures were any different from their peers'. If the eight students did have one of the standard goal structures, then the sequence of physical actions they made could only be accomplished by violating the LIFO constraint.

Moreover, there were strong regularities in the 8 students' actions that make it highly unlikely that their behavior is due to working memory failures wherein a basically LIFO goal storage mechanism "accidentally" marks the wrong goal as most recent. This source of non-LIFO execution should appear as random "point" mutations to the standard execution sequence and it should also be fairly infrequent. This was not what the eight students did. They generally had two or more stable execution orders, some of which could only be generated by a non–LIFO architecture. For instance, one student had three stable orders:

1. The standard order. Columns are processed right-to-left, and the borrowing for one column is finished before the next column is begun.
2. Horizontal order. All the borrowing in the problem is done on a right-to-left horizontal pass across the columns. Then the columns are answered on a second horizontal pass, which may be either right-to-left or left-to-right.
3. Vertical order. Columns are processed in right-to-left order. However, borrows are not completed before moving on to the next column. Instead, all marks in column, including any marks caused borrows from earlier columns, are done together.

The student used the standard order on four problems, the horizontal order on four problems, the vertical order on three problems, and a blend of the horizontal and vertical orders on two problems. The systematicity of her behavior makes it implausible that her non-LIFO orderings are based on working memory failure.[2]

These eight students provide clear examples of violations of the LIFO constraint. They allow us to conclude what was intuitively obvious all along: people can select any goal for execution that they can recall. Whether or not it is sensible to make a non–LIFO choice is, of course, task specific. The reason the LIFO constraint has survived as long as it has in models of the architecture is due to the structures of the task domains, which generally require or encourage a LIFO selection of goals. Subtraction, which is not one the task domains typically studied in the architecture literature, does not have this LIFO property.

This work shows that the *operative* working memory is non–LIFO, but as Newell, Simon, Anderson, and others have pointed out, the operative working memory is implemented in part by visual perception. It could still be the case that

---

[2]One might think that this subject has three distinct subtraction procedures, one for each order. However, this would not explain her ability to blend the horizontal and vertical orders, as she does on two problems. For more discussion of this and other challenges to the conclusions, see VanLehn, Ball, and Kowalski (1989).

*internal* working memory is LIFO and that the non–LIFO aspects of the subtraction subjects' behavior is due to the way they infer or reconstruct goals from what they see. This led us to investigate the process of goal reconstruction.

A third problem in cognitive theory comes from recent work in robotics and ethnomethodology. Several investigators have worried that real-time, adaptive control of behavior does not allow for interleaving planning and plan following. Instead, people just act. As Agre and Chapman (1987, p. 268) put it, "Rather than relying on reasoning to intervene between perception and action, we believe activity mostly derives from very simple sorts of machinery interacting with the immediate situation. This machinery exploits regularities in its interaction with the world to engage in complex, apparently planful activity without requiring explicit models of the world." This belief that action is derived by cursory examination of the situation rather than reasoning is often called the situated action paradigm (Suchman, 1987).

It would be wrong to think that the proponents of situated action claim people's mental apparatus makes it impossible for them to plan their actions. As Agre and Chapman (1987, p. 272) put it, "We do *not* believe that the human central system has no state. Our point is simply that state is less necessary and less important than is often assumed." Currently developed computational models of situated action (Agre & Chapman, 1987; Brooks, chap. 8 in this volume) are claimed to be interesting architectures *for robotics* and not literal models of human cognitive capabilities. These architectures have so little internal state that they cannot model simple tasks, such as counting or mental multiplication, that humans can easily perform. Even mundane tasks, which are intended to be the forte of these architectures, sometimes cannot be done in a purely situated way. For instance, one of us once had a job washing glassware in a medical laboratory. The procedure was to wash the glassware 6 times in tap water then 6 times in distilled water. Since one cannot tell by looking at a piece of glassware how many times it has been washed, the Pengi architecture (Agre & Chapman, 1987) cannot solve this task.

Suchman (1987) does take situated action as an account of human behavior, so her position is more complex than her robotics colleagues. Suchman points out that people *do* plan, as for example, when they study a river rapids in order to plot a course for their canoe. However, these plans "are constituent as an artifact of our *reasoning about* action, not as the generative *mechanism of action.*" (Suchman, 1987, p. 39, emphasis original) Suchman is mostly concerned with plans derived as post-hoc explanations of behavior, so her book does not contain a clear statement about the causal entailments of plans made in advance of an action. Her choice of a canoeing example suggests that she does believe that advance planning can effect actions, albeit indirectly: planning to paddle to the left around a boulder in the rapids is one factor involved in causing the ultimate action of paddling to the left of the boulder. Suchman's major point, however, is that advance planning is rare, and even when it does occur, "plans are best viewed as a weak resource for what is primarily *ad hoc* activity" (bid, p. ix).

The situated action position is certainly partially right, because current models of the human problem solving have emphasized planned action rather than situated action. In part this is due to their historical roots, which lie in studies of people working with puzzles, mathematical problems and other tasks where planned actions are probably more common than situated actions. The problem for cognitive modeling is to develop an architecture that can easily and seamlessly oscillate between planned action and situated action, since both occur in human behavior and we are often not even aware, even in retrospection, of the transitions between them (Suchman, 1987).

We believe that goal reconstruction is exactly what is needed for this seamless oscillation between situated and planned action. We describe an architecture that can operate with almost no internal state by rapidly reconstructing whatever goals are necessary in the current situation. We demonstrate that these goal reconstruction processes are formally identical to processes for perceptual parsing of the situation, so goal reconstruction can be thought of as high-level perception. This nicely captures the principal intuition of the situated action paradigm, which is that much action is guided by perception. On the other hand, when goals can be recalled or when they *must* be recalled, the architecture can do that as well. So it can develop plans in memory and follow them. Moreover, this sort of planned activity blends seamlessly into situated activity.

In short, goal reconstruction is claimed to be a solution to these three problems in cognitive modeling: How do people access more goals than they can reliably store in memory? How do people implement a non-LIFO goal store? How do people blend situated and planned action?

## RECONSTRUCTION IN SEVERAL PROBLEM-SPACE ARCHITECTURES

Goal reconstruction depends strongly on interpretation of visual scenes, so it would seem that any model of goal reconstruction should include at least a rudimentary model of perception. However, it is convenient to start the discussion by ducking the question of perception entirely. In this section, an initial mechanism for goal reconstruction is developed. In the next section, the initial model is augmented with a rudimentary model of perceptual processing.

A standard way to avoid modeling perception (and motor control as well—but that is irrelevant to this paper) is to use a problem space. In order to model a given task, the theorist specifies a set of primitive predicates and a way of composing them into descriptions of a problem state. In the model, the *current problem state,* which is one of these compositions of primitive predicates, represents that which the person infers from perceiving the real problem state. Thus, the problem space technique avoids the perception issue by postulating the output from the perceptual interpretation processes without describing the processes themselves.

There are many ways to implement a problem space. This section argues that goal reconstruction is simple to implement in any of the implementations of problem spaces. However, in order to make the argument easier to follow, an implementation of goal reconstruction will be described for a particular implementation of problem spaces. This implementation depends crucially on a Truth Maintenance System or TMS. Although this is a standard piece of technology in AI, it was developed fairly recently (deKleer, 1986; Doyle, 1979), so not all readers may be familiar with it. The first subsection describes a TMS-based implementation of problem spaces and how a TMS works. The second subsection presents a simple implementation of goal reconstruction. The third subsection argues that goal reconstruction is simple to add to other implementations of problem spaces.

## Modeling State Changes with a TMS

The implementation of problem spaces presented here is the one pioneered by Strips (Fikes, Hart, & Nilsson, 1972). The TMS-based implementation of Strips problem spaces was developed more recently and is used by Prodigy (Carbonell et al., chap. 9 in this volume) and other problem solvers.

A state is represented by a set of literals in a first order logic. A literal is just a single predicate which may or may not be negated. Thus, *on (block56,block2)* and *not (clear(top(block2)))* are both literals. Literals that are used to represent states have no variables in them. They have only constants, such as *block56,* and functions of constants, such as *top(block2).* We use the Prolog convention of capitalizing variables. Constants, functions and predicates are written in lower case.

Perception (reading the state) is modeled by matching expressions against the set of literals that represents the current problem state. To find out what block is on *block2,* the expression on *(X,block2)* is compared to all the literals in the current state until one is found that matches (unifies) with it. Matching causes the variable x to be matched to a constant, say *block56,* thus answering the question of which block is on *block2.*

Action is represented by adding and deleting literals from the current state, thus creating a new state. A generic action is called an operator, and its generic effects are represented by a list of literals to be added to the current state (the add-list) and a list of literals to be deleted (the del-list).

In order to allow this economical description of actions to model complicated state changes, rules are used to maintain logical relationships that hold in all states. For instance, suppose the problem space uses a literal *indirectly-on (X,Y)* that means that X is directly on top of Y (i.e., *on (X,Y))* or X is on top of something that is indirectly-on Y. Two rules can be used to provide a formal recursive definition of *indirectly-on:*

1. *If on (X,Y) then indirectly-on (X,Y).*
2. *If there is a Z such that on (X,Z) and indirectly-on (Z,Y), then indirectly-on (X,Y).*

Given these rules, the operators need only mention their effects on the on literals. They do not have to mention *indirectly–on* literals in their add–lists and del–lists since the effects on those can be calculated with the two rules above. For the sake of discussion, let us distinguish *primitive* literals from *derived* literals. A primitive literal is one that is added directly to the problem space by an operator's execution because a generic version of it appeared in the operator's add–list. A derived literal is one that is added by the execution of a rule.

Although it is clear that the rules provide the knowledge that is required for omitting derived literals from add-list and del-lists, it is not as simple as it might seem to get the system to use this knowledge effectively. There are two basic methods. The simpler one, which was used by Strips, is to create a new empty state, add all the primitive literals specified by the operator's add-list and copy all the primitive literals from the old state that are not mentioned by the operator's del–list. Now the new state has all the primitive literals that it should have. The derived literals are added by repeatedly firing the rules until no new derived literals are inferred. Many of these derived literals will be equal to ones in the preceding state. For instance, if block A is on block B in the old state, and the action does not effect that, then *indirectly–on (A,B)* is true in both the old state and the new state. Thus, this method of modeling action amounts to *reconstructing* problem states.[3]

The other method of modeling, which is used by Prodigy (Carbonell et al., chap. 9 in this volume), achieves exactly the same result, but is more efficient because it substitutes cheap copying and removal operations for expensive rederivation operations. The copying and removal operations use a TMS. The basic idea is to copy all the literals in the old state, including the derived ones, then remove all the literals that should be removed and add all the literals that should be added. The trick is to remove only the right literals. This happens in two stages. First, all the primitive literals that are explicitly mentioned in the operator's del–list are retracted. Second, the TMS retracts derived literals whose derivations depend on retracted primitive literals. In order to do this, the derivations of the literals have to be remembered.[4] If any of the primitive literals in the

---

[3]Although this description uses forward chaining, most problem solvers use backwards chaining. Instead of drawing all possible inferences as soon as the state is created, backward chaining makes inferences only when the problem solver poses a query, such as *indirectly-on (X,block2)*. The important point is that in the reconstruction method, only the primitive literals are copied from the old state to the new state. Exactly when the derived literals are inferred does not matter.

[4]A derivation is a proof tree whose leaves are primitive literals. Thus, if rule 1 is used to derive C from A and B, and rule 2 is used to derive E from C and D, then the derivation for E is the tree (E(C(AB))D).

derivation are retracted, then the derived literal is also retracted. This retraction process is guaranteed to retract all and only the appropriate derived literals.

Next, the TMS–based system adds the literals from the operator's add-list and runs rules until quiescence. There is a trick that is used to speed this part of the process up. It is often the case that one of the derived literals that was retracted during the first phase is rederived during the second phase. Since the system has to remember derivations anyway, it is can save work by looking up the derivations that depended on this literal and calculate which ones can now be reinstated because the literal has been reasserted. Reinstating old retracted literals can be computationally cheaper than reinferring them. This trick is called *un–outing* (de Kleer, 1968; Doyle, 1979).

An example of a TMS–based state maintenance may be helpful. Suppose that whenever a block is supported directly or indirectly by the table, then X is stable. This is expressed by the following rule

*If indirectly–on(X,table) then stable (X).*

Suppose that in the old state, block56 is indirectly on the table and stable because it is on block2, which is directly on the table. That is, *on (block56,block2)* and *on(block2,table)* imply that *indirectly–on (block56,table)* by the rules listed earlier, and this implies *stable (block56)*. Suppose that an operator applies, and moves block56 off block2 and onto the table. The del-list of the operator will retract *on(block56,block2)* and the TMS will thus retract *indirectly–on (block56,table)* and *stable (block56)* because their derivations depended on the retracted literal. Eventually, all the appropriate literals will be removed from the state. Now the TMS adds literals from the add-list, including *on (block56,table)*. The rules are run, and they infer *indirectly–on (block56,table)*. The TMS notices that this literal is identical to one in the old state. It uses the un–outing mechanism to reinstate *stable (block56)* immediately without referring to the inference rule. It knows that this is appropriate because the derivation of *stable (block56)*, which has to be saved anyway for retraction to work correctly, indicates that *stable (block56)* depends only on *indirectly–on (block56,table)*.

## Goal Reconstruction in a Problem-Space Architecture

Although both the reconstruction and TMS methods of implementing state change are widely used in AI (see Charniak and McDermott's (1986) textbook, section 7.3), it is rarely recognized that they can also be used for maintaining the problem solver's goal structures. This section sketches a problem solver, similar to Amord (de Kleer, Doyle, Steele, & Sussman, 1977), that uses a TMS to maintain its goal structures.

A goal is usually defined to be a description (i.e., logical expression) of a state that is desired. A goal is satisfied if the current state matches the description. A pending goal is a logical expression that does not match the current state. Suppose problem solving starts with an initial state that contains a pending goal, which is represented by wrapping the pseudo-connective *pending–goal* around a logical expression. Thus, the goal of holding block37 in one's hand can be represented by *pending–goal (holding(block37))*.

When pending goals are represented this way, the rule mechanism mentioned above can be used to calculate what kinds of actions are appropriate for the given goals. This is most easily demonstrated with an example. The following rules indicate how to achieve a *holding(X)* goal given that the hand can only hold one block at a time.

> *If pending-goal (holding(X)) and not (holding(Y)),*
> *then executable (pick-up(X)).*

> *If pending-goal (holding(X)) and holding (Y) and not (X=Y),*
> *then pending-goal (not(holding(Y))).*

> *If pending-goal (not(holding(Z))) and holding (Z)*
> *then executable (put-down(Z)).*

These rules use pseudo-literals of the form executable (Op), where Op is an operator, in order to indicate that the specified operator is an appropriate action. In this case, if the initial state is the literals

> *holding (block6)*
> *pending-goal (holding(block37))*
> *not (block37=block6)*

then the second and third rules will add the following derived literals:

> *pending-goal (not(holding(block6)))*
> *executable (put-down(block6))*

This represents the process of deciding that putting down the block being held is a good idea given the current goal and the current situation. Much more complicated reasoning can also be represented.

When an action is finally taken, some or all of the *pending–goal* literals must be retracted because their predicates will now be true and only unsatisfied goals are represented with *pending–goal* literals. Both the reconstruction methods and the TMS method work just fine for updating *pending–goal* literals. Let us consider reconstruction first. In order to model the state change caused by executing the operation *put–down (block6)*, reconstruction adds the literal *not (holding(block6))* to the new state because that literal is mentioned in the operator's add-list. Then it copies over primitive literals from the old state that are not mentioned in the del-list. This adds *pending–goal (holding(block37))* and *not (block37=block6)* to the new state. Notice that the old derived literal, *pending-goal (not(holding(block6)))*, is not copied over. Now the reconstruction method runs the rules, which adds to the state the literal *executable (pick-up(block37))*.

This demonstrates how the reconstruction method works to maintain goal structures. Essentially, it starts over from the top level goal, which is the only one that is a primitive literal, and rederives as much of the goal structure as is still relevant. In this very simple illustration, no old goals were reconstructed. Usually, many old goals will be reconstructed.

The TMS method can be used in order to avoid some of the computation of reconstruction. In order to use it, the derivation of a goal must be stored with the goal. For instance, with *executable(put–down(block6))* the system associates the tree

> *executable (put-down(block6))*
> *pending-goal (not(holding(block6)))*
> *pending-goal (holding(block37))*
> *holding (block6)*
> *not (block37=block6)*
> *holding (block6)*

which records its derivation via the rules listed earlier. In order to update the state, the TMS method first retracts *holding(block6)* because it is mentioned in the operator's del-list. Since this literal occurs in the derivations of both *pending–goal (not(holding(block6)))* and *executable (put–down(block6)),* those two literals are retracted as well. Next the system adds *not (holding(block6))* because that literal is mentioned by the operator's add-list. The rules run, and the literal *executable (pick-up(block37))* is derived. This demonstrates how the TMS method can maintain goal structures.

The TMS method is more memory intensive than the reconstruction method. It requires that the problem solver remember all the derived literals from the old state and moreover, it should remember the derivations of each literal as well. What would happen if memory failed? If a literal was completely forgotten and the literal was going to be retracted anyway, then it does not matter that it was forgotten. On the other hand, if the literal was not going to be retracted, then it must still be derivable from literals in the new state, so the rules will end up deriving it. So forgetting a literal does no harm. What if the literal is not forgotten, but its derivation is, or worse yet, only part of its derivation is forgotten? The problem solver must somehow detect this and treat the whole literal as if it were forgotten. If it can do that, then the literal and its derivation will be reconstructed if necessary and retracted (via forgetting) otherwise. Although the TMS-based method requires memory storage for the derivations, it is quite robust because it can easily reconstruct forgotten derivations.

From this perspective, the TMS method and the reconstruction methods are just two ends of a continuum. If all the derived literals can be recalled, then the faster TMS method is used. If none of the derived literals can be recalled, then the slower reconstruction method is used. If only some of the derived literals are recalled, then TMS-based retraction and reconstruction are used jointly to produce the appropriate goal structure. This is a seamless combination of reconstruction and recall.

Notice that the primitive literals cannot be forgotten. If they are, then the whole scheme falls apart, since there are no rules for deriving them from other literals.[5] However, problem spaces are usually designed so that the primitive literals model unforgettable information. For instance, the literals that describe the current state are usually chosen to correspond to perceptually available information (e.g., which block is my hand holding?), and are thus unforgettable. The top level goals are assumed to be either perceptually available (e.g., from instructions written on a card handed to the subject) or very familiar. Literals that reside unchanged in all states (e.g., *not (block37=block6)*) correspond to common sense or well-learned facts.

The next step in the argument is to show that this mechanism for maintaining goals solves the three problems mentioned in the introduction: capacity limitations on goal storage, non–LIFO access to goals, and blending situated and planned action.

The capacity problem is that many computations seem to require more goals than the human short-term memory system has room to store. At first glance, it seems that this mechanism completely solves the capacity problem. As long as the top level goal is held in long term memory, any other goals that are forgotten can be reconstructed. However, if we take an extremely simple model of the short–term store, such as a buffer with seven cells, then it is possible for the goal reconstruction mechanism to fail. As goals are reconstructed, the rules generate literals that may be needed a few moments later by other rules. If more than 7 of these literals are generated, then some may be lost from memory before being used. It is important to note, however, that although the number of literals requiring storage in STM may be large, they do not have to be stored there for very long. It is well known that the number of chunks that can be recalled from STM varies inversely with the delay between storage and recall. The simple buffer model does not reflect this, although more complex buffer models could.

A standard model with the appropriate decay properties is based on spreading activation. In this model, gaining access to a goal requires that the goal exist in memory and that its activation level be above some threshold. In order to recall an old goal, activation can be spread up through the derivation trees starting with the literals that stand for perceptual chunks (which are presumably highly active as they are the current focus of visual attention) and the top–level goal. This corresponds to normal retrieval of an old goal. If the goal is inaccessible via spreading activation, then it can be reconstructed. Some elements of its derivation tree will be accessible (in the worst case, only the leaves can be retrieved).

---

[5]Actually, some literals can be both primitive and derived because they appear in both the add-list of operators and the conclusions of rules. These literals could be reconstructed if forgotten, at least in principle. They will continue to be ignored in order to simplify the discussion.

These trigger rules whose execution creates new literals that are copies of the forgotten ones. In most spreading activation theories (e.g., ACT*—Anderson, 1983), newly created elements are given high activation. Although activation decays rather rapidly at first, as long as the goal reconstruction process occurs rapidly and without interruption, it should be possible to reconstruct large numbers of goals. Thus, the initial impression that a TMS-based mechanism solves the goal capacity problem is actually correct, although there appear to be some subtle interactions with the operation of the underlying memory system.

The second problem mentioned in the introduction is that people sometimes execute goals that are not the most recently created pending goal. In LIFO architectures, this is not possible. The architecture sketched in this section is not necessarily a LIFO architecture. If the rules are run to quiescence, then they will find all pending goals whose preconditions are met and mark them as executable. The problem solver is free to choose any of them for execution.

The last problem mentioned in the introduction is to find a way to blend situated action and planned action. In a single-agent world, the above mechanism suffices. If all goals are forgotten during a state change, then the agent can be said to have no state, so it is a situated-action agent. The calculations that are performed by goal reconstruction would have to be performed by any agent possessing the same knowledge, and the above mechanism makes it seem that the intermediate results of these calculations must be stored as literals. However, one can replace the rules by gates in a combinatorial logic and the literals by wires connecting gates. Seen this way, the goal reconstruction calculation requires no more state than Agre and Chapman's (1987) Pengi or Brook's (chap. 8 in this volume) subsumption architecture. So in a world where the only source of state change is the agent itself, the TMS–based goal maintenance mechanism seamlessly blends situated and planned action.

If the world has multiple sources of state changes, then the agent must supplement the add-list and del-list with perceptual operations. These have the same effects as the lists do, in that they cause addition and retraction of literals. The TMS propagates these through the goal structure in the usual way. Thus if another agent helps our agent by satisfying one of our agent's pending goals, then perception will add a literal to the state, and the TMS will ultimately retract that goal. Similarly, if a hostile agent undoes a goal that our agent previously accomplished, then the un-outing mechanism of the TMS will quickly reinstate the goal.[6] Thus, the agent will behave adaptively in a changing world where not all of the changes are under its control. The TMS-based mechanism is adequate for blending situated and planned action even in a multiple agent world.

---

[6]This TMS-based goal maintenance mechanism does not model the process of deciding which executable action to execute. This is called *action arbitration* by Agre and Chapman (1987) and Brooks (chap. 8 in this volume). Their systems seem to use some ad hoc priority-based system to do action arbitration. Presumably, such a system could be used here as well, or a more complex system, like the goal preferences of Prodigy (Carbonell et al., chap. 9 in this volume), could be used instead.

In addition to solving the three problems mentioned in the introduction, the TMS-based goal maintenance system bears striking similarities to the overall human memory system. As noted earlier, when people are distracted from a task by a long telephone call, they have the ability to reconstruct the goals and other internal state that they have forgotten. On the other hand, if they are not distracted, then they do not require similarly extended periods of time for reconstructing their state after each action. Moreover, there seems to be no sharp boundary between human retrieval and reconstruction. The seamless combination of TMS and reconstruction methods also has the same lack of a sharp boundary. It is well known that human recall is facilitated by making the perceptual environment at recall similar to the perceptual environment at storage. This is consistent with the TMS/reconstruction combination, where the accuracy and availability of the whole state depends strongly on the accuracy and availability of the primitive literals. In short, the combined TMS-reconstruction method of state updating is qualitatively similar to human memory, at least as far as problem solving is concerned.

## Goal Reconstruction in Precondition-Based Problem Solvers

The simplicity of the TMS-based goal maintenance system is due to its use of rules for reasoning about goals. Although this is elegant and allows certain issues to be presented clearly, rule–based representations of planning knowledge can be awkward and redundant, especially for conjunctive goals. A more widely used technique represents that knowledge in the operators themselves as a set of *preconditions* on the operator. This is the representation used by Strips (Fikes, Hart, & Nilsson, 1972) and its many descendants. The goal reconstruction capability of the Amord–style problem solver can also be implemented in a Strips-style problem solver. The next few paragraphs demonstrate this.

An example will help in comparing Amord–style and Strips–style problem solvers. In a Strips–style problem solver, the *pick–up* operator could be represented as:

> *Name: pick–up*
> *Arguments: X*
> *Preconditions: not(holding(Y))*
> *Add–list: holding(X)*
> *Del–list: on(X,Z)*

This representation replaces the rules listed earlier for the Amord-style reasoning about goals. For instance, one of the rules mentioned earlier says

> *If pending–goal (holding(X)) and holding(Y) and not(X=Y),*
> *then pending–goal (not(holding(Y))).*

Let us use the Strips representation to do the example mentioned earlier, where the goal is *holding(block37)*. The system searches for an operator whose add–list matches the goal. In this case, *pick–up* is found. Next, the preconditions are checked. In this case, the precondition is false, because *holding(block6)* is true. Whenever a precondition is not satisfied, the system makes it into a subgoal. Thus, the system makes *not(holding(block6))* a goal. Clearly, this Strips–style reasoning has achieved the same effect as the inference rule from the Amord-style problem solver. The knowledge representation, however, is more parsimonious.

Most Strips-style problem solvers do not use a TMS for maintaining their goal structures. In fact, we do not know of any that use a TMS. Instead, they use a *goal tree,* or more frequently, just a part of the tree arranged in a *goal stack.* Although less elegant than the TMS-based method, goal maintenance with a goal tree has all the same properties. The next few paragraphs are a point–by–point comparison of the goal tree and TMS methods of maintaining goals.

In TMS-based maintenance of goals, the derivation of each goal must be stored so that retraction and un-outing can function correctly. Instead of a derivation, a tree-based goal maintainer uses the goal tree itself. Instead of a TMS data structure indicating that *pending–goal (not(holding(block6)))* was derived from *pending–goal (holding(block37))* and other literals, the goal tree has a data structure indicating that *pending–goal (not(holding(block6)))* is a subgoal of *pending–goal (holding(block37))* caused by an unsatisfied precondition.

In TMS-based maintenance of goals, executing an operator first causes all satisfied goals to be retracted. In tree-based maintenance, the exact process of finding satisfied goals seems to vary from one problem solver to the next. However, the gist of the method is to check goals in the tree and see if the goal's literal is now in the current state. If it is, then that goal is satisfied and all its subgoals are now irrelevant. These goals are marked appropriately or removed from the tree. If a goal stack is used instead of a goal tree, this phase can be accomplished by popping the stack.

After the satisfied goals have been dealt with, the TMS method infers new goals using its inference rules, whereas the tree–based method infers new goals using the operators' preconditions.

One of the advantages of the TMS–based method of goal maintenance for modeling humans is the seamless integration of reconstruction and recall. The same advantage can be obtained with a goal tree. If parts of the goal tree are forgotten, they can be reconstructed by starting at an ancestor goal and using the usual precondition-based subgoal creation method. If subgoals are created that are equal to ones that have not been forgotten, then the new tree can be attached at this point to the tree rooted at the recalled subgoal. The goal indexing mechanism used in GPS (Ernst & Newell, 1969) and most of its successors will cause this reattachment (which is equivalent to un-outing) to happen automatically. Thus, in most cases no new mechanisms need to be added to the system in order to achieve a qualitative similarity to human behavior.

This section has shown that goal reconstruction is a capability that can be easily added to a problem–solving architecture. Moreover, the goal maintenance mechanism shifts seamlessly from recall to reconstruction of goals, which makes its performance qualitatively similar to human behavior.

## Goal Reconstruction in Procedure-Following Systems

In our vocabulary, a goal serves two purposes. It is both a description of a desired state of the world, and it is a part of the control structure of the problem solver. For some tasks, the description of desired states mention features that cannot be detected by unaided perception. If a person has already washed a piece of medical glassware 6 times in tap water, then washing it 6 times in distilled water will achieve a state of cleanliness that is not distinguishably different from its current state. The only simple description of the goal to be achieved is just the procedure for achieving it: wash the glassware 6 times in distilled water. A large number of tasks have this property. After a house is built or a tax form is filled out, the results look to the visible eye like a house or a tax form. But the quality of the house or the tax accounting can vary widely depending on which procedures were followed in achieving it. Properly cured concrete looks exactly the same as an improperly cured concrete. The only way to know if the properly–cured–concrete goal has been met is destructive testing (which partly undoes the goal of having properly cured concrete) or checking that the proper curing procedure has been followed. Many goals in human culture have the property that they are partly specified by the visible state to be achieved and partly specified by the procedures that should be followed in achieving them.

Although most problem–solving architectures can only accept goals that are specified by descriptions of the desired state, Sierra is one that is specifically designed to follow procedures (VanLehn, 1987, 1990). Recently, it has been augmented with the ability to accept goals specified as desired states. The resulting architecture, called Teton, is documented in an appendix to this chapter.

When goals are specified by procedures, reconstruction of goals becomes more complicated. Teton can handle some cases (but not all) with a fairly simple mechanism. Teton uses a Strips–like operator representation for procedural knowledge. In addition to the usual slots for preconditions and so forth, operators can have a *shortcut condition*. This condition is checked just before executing an operator. If it is true, then the operator is not executed but its goal is marked "satisfied" anyway. For example, in order to reconstruct the goals of the following partially completed multiplication problem,

$$
\begin{array}{r}
336 \\
\times\ 208 \\
\hline
2682 \\
7200
\end{array}
$$

Teton would run the multiplication procedure which causes an operator, call it *Single–digit–multiply,* to be instantiated for each of the three digits in the multiplier, 208. Suppose the operator has a shortcut condition that is true if the partial product row to be filled already has some digits in it and there is something written underneath that row (i.e., another partial product row or a bar). In the case of the units digit instantiation of *Single–digit–multiply,* the shortcut condition is true, so the operation is marked completed. However, the shortcut conditions are false in the case of the tens digit, so execution resumes with that operation. Thus, Teton reconstructs goals then judiciously takes "shortcuts" instead of executing some of them.

As a quick check on the plausibility of this type of processing, we took a protocol from a subject who was asked to complete the partially solved problem shown above. She said:

> Alright. Since there are two columns done [referring to the partial product rows], I know that the first digit on the right hand side of the bottom number has been multiplied. Um. I would start the, um, since the second column is a zero, somebody has filled in the zero. I would now go to the third digit on the bottom column and do all the multiplication involved there. Two times six is twelve, two times three is six plus one is seven, two times three is six and then I would do the addition starting from the right hand side, and get the answer.

The first sentence corresponds to taking the shortcut on the *Single–digit–multiply* of the units digits of the multiplier. The second sentence corresponds to the execution of the *Single–digit–multiply* of the tens digit. The rest of the protocol corresponds to execution of *Single–digit–multiply* for the hundreds digit. This protocol corresponds quite well with the type of goal reconstruction used by Teton.

Shortcut conditions are task-specific knowledge about how to reconstruct specific goal trees. Sometimes people may have to learn shortcut conditions, and sometimes they may be able to deduce them from general principles in the midst of reconstructing a goal.

There is another type of task–specific knowledge about goal reconstruction that people sometimes use. If one can anticipate forgetting some goals, say because the phone is ringing and one intends to answer it, then one can take steps now that will make reconstruction much easier to do later. For instance, if one is interrupted by a ringing phone in the middle of adding up a long column of figures, one can write the subtotal down and mark the last number added in. This will enable reconstruction later. Teton does not handle this sort of knowledge. It would be a fascinating behavior to simulate, because the agent must have a crude model of forgetting in order to plan ways to prevent forgetting from happening. It also must be able to tell what aspects of its state are worth saving, so it must understand its capabilities for goal reconstruction.

As usual in cognitive modeling, we can model the most common cases but the other cases are orders of magnitude harder to model. Goal reconstruction is easily modeled when goals are descriptions of visible aspects of the state, as in the case of the Amord–style problem solvers and the Strips–style problem solvers. When goals are partially procedures, then the shortcut conditions of Teton can handle some of the cases. However, the remaining cases of goal reconstruction present tricky problems that are likely to resist modeling for some time.

## ARITHMETIC LEARNING: AN APPLICATION
## REQUIRING PERCEPTION

The preceding account of goal reconstruction ignored perceptual processes and assumed that their output was available in the form of literals in the current problem state. Part of the novelty of situated action is the claim that perceptual processing handles most of the load in guiding activity. In this chapter we discuss how to integrate perception and problem solving in such a way that goal reconstruction retains all the good properties that it had when problem solving was based on problem spaces.

This investigation grew out of a study of how people learn arithmetic, algebra equation solving and other written procedures. There is fairly good evidence that students pay close attention to the visual syntax of the written expressions and may even induce visual features into their procedures that the teacher did not intend them to learn (VanLehn, 1986, 1990). This reliance of visual features is the key to explaining many otherwise mysterious phenomena, as the following example illustrates. When students are introduced to borrowing, teachers usually use the simplest subtraction problems they can—ones with just two columns. Here is a borrowing problem that has been solved in the manner taught in many American textbooks:

$$
\begin{array}{r}
2\ 14 \\
\cancel{3}\ \cancel{4} \\
-\ 1\ 8 \\
\hline
1\ 6
\end{array}
$$

Some students notice that the decrement action takes place in the leftmost column of the problem, and induce that all such actions should take place in the leftmost column. This leads them to make errors like the following one:

$$
\begin{array}{r}
1 \\
\cancel{2}\ \ \ 18 \\
\cancel{3}\ 2\ \cancel{8} \\
-\ \ \ 1\ 9 \\
\hline
2\ 1\ 9
\end{array}
$$

Early versions of Sierra simply postulated a problem space that includes leftmost and other relations that students induce. It would leave out relations that did not seem to play any role in their learning. Thus, the initial state would contain the literal *leftmost (column3)* but it would not contain the literals *rightmost (column1)* or *hundreds (column3)*. Although this allowed Sierra to explain the systematic errors of thousands of students, it also pushed the mystery of learning back one more level. Sierra explained how procedures are learned, but what explains how the problem spaces are learned? This comment is not meant to denigrate the accomplishment—all models of learning bottom out on some kind of assumptions about prior knowledge, and most models of procedure acquisition bottom out on the problem space, just as early versions of Sierra did.

In the case of mathematics, it is particularly important to explain problem spaces rather than assume them. The problem space embeds knowledge of mathematical notation, which is something that students learn (and mislearn!) in school. Whereas someone might naturally think of a column of 3 wooden blocks as something that is important enough to see and record in the problem space as a composite structure, such as *stack(block37, block6, block13)*, the habit of seeing a subtraction problem as columns instead of rows is something that has to be learned in school.

As a first step in determining how people acquire mathematical problem spaces, and knowledge of notational syntax in particular, it is wise to determine what the representation of that knowledge is like. This makes it easier to formulate learning models for notational knowledge.

Pursuit of these goals led us to the problem of devising a representation of notational knowledge that could be nicely integrated with mathematical problem solving. The first part of this section discuss some constraints on the representation of notational/perceptual knowledge. These were uncovered by trying simple approaches and discovering that they were inadequate. The second part of the section presents a system that seems to meet all the constraints. Moreover, its structure sheds some light on the distinction between situated and planned activity.

## The Need for Global Parsing

The first attempt at representing notational/perceptual knowledge was to assume that task–specific terms in the problem space were defined by task-general terms using standard first-order logic. Thus, *column (X)* is defined to be a sequence of three vertically aligned cells, and *cell (Y)* is defined to be a digit, a blank or a digit that has been scratched out and written over. The *column (X)* definition might be represented formally as:

*column (X) ::= part-of(X,C1) & part-of(X,C2) & part-of (X,C3) &
cell (C1) & cell (C2) & cell (C3) &
sequence (X) & first (X, C1) & last (X,C3) & middle (X, C2) &*

*ordered (X,C1,C2) & ordered (X,C2,C3) & ordered
(X,C1,C3) &
adjacent (C1,C2) & adjacent (C2,C3)*

Learning mathematical notation is assumed to consist of learning definitions like this one. There are a variety of machine learning algorithms sufficient for learning such concepts from examples and a given set of primitive concepts (e.g., VanLehn, 1987; Vere, 1975; Winston, 1975). In this case, the given concepts are perceptual primitives, such as *adjacent (X,Y)*. This is not the large loophole that one might imagine because the set of perceptual primitives needed for mathematical symbol manipulation is surprisingly small. For instance, one vocabulary sufficient for arithmetic and algebra required only ten predicates (see p. 183, VanLehn, 1983). A much more complex vocabulary would be needed for, say, high school geometry or mechanical drafting.

It might seem that the major difficulty in this approach to explaining the acquisition of mathematical problem spaces would be determining how people acquire concepts such as *column*. In fact, this approach failed utterly before even getting to that stage. Even when definitions are constructed by hand, it proved impossible to find definitions that would perform like people do. For Sierra, the visual world was represented as a Cartesian plane with characters centered at particular x-y coordinates. One problem was to get a definition of "algebraic formula" that is true of "2 + 3" when it stands alone in the plane, but to be false of "2 + 3" when it is embedded in "2 + 3x." Another problem is that adjacent (3,x) should be true of (a) below and false of (b) despite the fact that the two symbols are closer in (b) than in (a):

a.  $3 \; x \; = \; y$

b.  $3 \; y \; = \; x$
$x \; = \; y/3$

The problem here is that an interpretation of a subset of some mathematical symbols is acceptable only if it participates in a global interpretation which includes all the symbols. This is analogous to many English words, such as "run," which can be interpreted either as a noun or a verb depending on the global interpretation of the sentence it is a part of. Compare "I'm not going to run today" with "I had a good run today." In the analysis of both English and mathematical syntax, better techniques are based on context–free grammars or something like context–free grammars.

## Grammatical Definitions of Task-Specific Problem Representations

In order to use context-free grammars as a representation for knowledge of mathematical notation, a few augmentations to the standard formalisms were

TABLE 6.1
A Simplified Grammar for Arithmetic Notation

| | | | |
|---|---|---|---|
| 1. Problem | ← | Sign ColumnS | ; horizontal |
| 2. Sign | ← | + | |
| 3. Sign | ← | − | |
| 4. Sign | ← | × | |
| 5. ColumnS | ← | Column ColumnS | ; horizontal |
| 6. ColumnS | ← | Column | |
| 7. Column | ← | Cell Cell Cell | ; vertical |
| 8. Cell | ← | Digit | |
| 9. Cell | ← | Blank | |
| 10. Digit | ← | 1 | |
| 11. Digit | ← | 2 | |
| . . . | | | |

needed. For instance, because mathematical notation is two-dimensional, rules need to indicate whether their constituents are arranged horizontally, vertically or diagonally. Table 6.1 shows a simplified grammar for arithmetic problems.

This grammatical formalism accomplishes what the first-order logical definitions of terms could not. It can properly parse arithmetic and algebraic expressionse. Unfortunately, a very nasty problem was encountered when Sierra's problem space machinery was replaced with a parser for this formalism.

The problem occurs when states change. For Sierra, state changes are always due to writing a new symbol on the visual page. When this happens, there is usually not much change in the parse tree.[7] Filling a column's answer in a subtraction problem only affects one small part of the parse tree—that which concerns the particular blank cell that is filled by the new symbol. Sometimes, however, writing a single symbol has effects on other parts of the tree. Writing

---

[7]A parse tree is a record of the derivation or parsing of a particular sentence, or in this case, of a particular mathematical expression. A parse tree for the vertical form of 2 + 1 when parsed by the grammar of table 6.1 would be:

*Problem—Derived via rule 1 from:*
 *Sign—Derived via rule 2 from:*
  *+ (perceived)*
 *ColumnS—Derived via rule 6 from:*
  *Column—Derived via rule 7 from:*
   *Cell—Derived via rule 8 from:*
    *Digit—Derived via rule 11 from:*
     *2 (perceived)*
   *Cell—Derived via rule 8 from:*
    *Digit—Derived via rule 10 from:*
     *1 (perceived)*
   *Cell—Derived via rule 9 from:*
    *Blank (perceived)*
where indenting represents the hierarchical relationships in the tree.

one symbol changes "2 + 3" into "2 + 3x," which changes the interpretation of the 3. In order to allow for arbitrary changes in the state, Sierra ignores the old state's parse tree and constructs a new one for the current state. This has the unfortunate side-effect of making obsolete most of the goals held in Sierra's working memory because most goals have arguments that mention nodes in the parse tree. When the visual scene is parsed anew, a whole new parse tree is produced, but the goals continue to mention nodes from the old parse tree. By parsing the current state, Sierra makes obsolete all the goals with objects as arguments.

Several years ago, this seemed like a nasty technical problem with no important theoretical implication. It was circumvented with some subtraction-specific hacks and banished to appendix 8 of the first author's dissertation (VanLehn, 1983).

## Annotated Grammars: Another Version of Situated Action

In the intervening years, the situated action paradigm has begun exploring the idea that people rarely plan by building up stacks or trees of pending goals. Instead, they parse the situation so as to "see" possibilities for actions. Thus, goals are not held in memory, but perceived in the situation.

In order to better understand the implications of the situated action view, we implemented an architecture, called *Rocky*. Instead of a procedure, Rocky has a grammar that is just like the one used by Sierra to represent knowledge of mathematical notation except that it has a few extra annotations. For instance, the rule for parsing a column, rule 7 in table 3-1, is annotated to indicate the numerical relationship among its the cells in the column:

7. *Sub-column* → *Digit$_1$ Digit$_2$ Digit$_3$*   *; vertical*
   *where: Digit$_3$ = Digit$_1$ − Digit$_2$*

We call this kind of knowledge representation an *annotated grammar*. With proper interpretation, it seems quite likely that an annotated grammar can generate actions and solve problems just as well as a procedure.

By getting rid of goals, the annotated grammars approach solves the problem of goals becoming obsolete. Each time the state changes, a new parse tree is constructed and nodes that are capable of having actions taken on them are marked as executable. The resulting parse tree quite literally wears the possibilities for action on its sleeve. Thus, an annotated grammar not only parses the visual plane, it also does all the reasoning that would normally be done by the rules mentioned earlier that compute with literals named *goal* and *executable*.

Annotated grammars seem to implement what Suchman (1987) had in mind when she said, "We generally do not anticipate alternative courses of action, or their consequences, until *some* course of action is already under way. It is frequently only on acting in a present situation that its possibilities become clear." (Suchman, 1987, p. 52, original emphasis)

Unfortunately, the annotated grammars approach ran into grave difficulties when we tried to implement some of the less visually oriented mathematical procedures. For instance, consider a common procedure for solving multiplication problems, which involves skipping zeros in the multiplier, as in the following problem:

$$
\begin{array}{r}
2345 \\
\times\ 1204 \\
\hline
9380 \\
469000 \\
+2345000 \\
\hline
2823380
\end{array}
$$

There are four multiplier digits, but only three partial products. In order to properly pair off the multiplier digits and the partial products, an annotated grammar must encode what amounts to a right–to–left traversal of the multiplier digits. Similarly, it is difficult to differentiate the zeros that are inserted in order to vertically align the partial procedures from the zeros produced by multiplications (see the second partial product above). Counting or some other kind of iteration is needed in order to determine these mapping from the visual plane. This cannot be done in the representation for grammars used by Rocky. Although the representation could perhaps be augmented, this would go against the situated action paradigm, which tries to obtain action without explicit execution of procedural knowledge, such as an iteration across a string of digits.

The underlying problem is that the only way to properly understand some problem states is to know how they were derived, and this historical information is sometimes not present in the perceptual information. In the task of washing medical glassware, one cannot tell by looking at a piece of glassware how many times it has been washed. An annotated grammar cannot perform this task.

In retrospect, it appears that Rocky's version of situated action is too extreme. It tries to keep *no* historical information about the problem solving and instead work only with what it can infer from the current situation. This is a rather implausible hypothesis, for surely a person in the middle of a problem would recall and use information about immediately preceding actions and decisions if such historical information were useful. As argued earlier, most architectures based on problem spaces have this property (or could have it given a few simple augmentations). They recall goals when they can and reconstruct them otherwise. Their reconstruction proceeds from primitive literals, which often represent outputs from perceptual processing. Somehow this useful and psychologically plausible property has been lost in the attempt to deepen the model of perception so as to allow for task-specific knowledge about mathematical notation.

## A TMS–Based Parser

Let us temporarily abandon the parsimony of unifying procedures and grammars and return to the old assumption that procedures and grammars are two distinct bodies of knowledge. This means that there are two types of internal state, a parse tree and a goal structure. The parse tree nodes correspond to the objects that would exist in the current problem state if a problem space approach were being used.

This means we must solve the updating problem wherein all goals that refer to parse nodes become obsolete with each state change because the parse trees for different states share no nodes. What we would like is an updating technique that will allow parse trees from consecutive states to share as many nodes as possible. Only parse nodes for parts of the visual plane that are "really new" would be built. However, the definition of "really new" depends on the task.

A solution that we think will work (it has only been partially implemented) is based on the same TMS-reconstruction method that was used successfully with regular problem spaces. The key idea is to note that parsing a visual scene is a special kind of inference, where grammar rules correspond to inference rules and parse nodes correspond to literals. A TMS is used to retract only those literals (parse nodes) that are changed, directly or indirectly, by the writing of a new symbol on the visual plane. In order to make this idea work for mathematical notation, however, we must be very careful about the representation of blank space in the visual plane.

As a running example, consider the change from "2 + 3" to "2 + 3x." The status of the 3 should be changed, but the parse node for the whole formula should stay the same. Suppose that the grammar is just

$$
\begin{array}{ll}
sum \rightarrow term + term & ; \ horizontal \\
term \rightarrow term \ term & ; \ horizontal \\
term \rightarrow 2 & \\
term \rightarrow 3 & \\
term \rightarrow x &
\end{array}
$$

Let parse nodes be represented by unary ground literals. The predicate is the category of the constituent and the argument is a region. For concreteness, let a region be represented by four numbers in square brackets, corresponding to the left, top, right and bottom boundaries of the region. Thus, term ([5,23,25,13]) represents a term occupying a certain region. With these definitions, the first grammar rule becomes the following inference rule.

*If there are three regions, R1, R2 and R3 such that*
   *term(R1) & plus(R2) & term(R3) &*
   *right-boundary(R1) = left-boundary(R2) &*
   *right-boundary(R2) = left-boundary(R3) &*
   *region C is the union of regions R1, R2 and R3,*
*then sum(C).*

The visual plane is represented by primitive literals and the grammar (inference) rules create derived literals.

In order to make the TMS–reconstruction method work, literals that mean the same thing, relative to the task, should be syntactically equal. Recall that reconstruction continues to run inference rules until no new literals are produced. "New" is defined relative to syntactic equality. If a literal is produced that is equal to an existing literal, then we say that a new derivation was found for an old literal; a new literal was not produced. Equality of literals depends crucially upon the definition of regions. Let us define the top boundary of a region to be halfway between that region and the next region in the positive y–direction. If there is no such region, then the boundary is set at infinity, which is represented by "*." Define the bottom, left and right boundaries similarly. Thus, "+" in the expression "2 + 3" would be represented by the literal *plus ([35,\*,45,\*])* because the top and bottom boundaries are at infinity.

With this definition, the literal *sum([\*,\*,\*,\*])* represents either "2 + 3" or "2 + 3x" written alone on a page. This makes the two terms syntactically equal, which is just what we want. A goal whose argument refers to "2 + 3" will not be made obsolete by stage change. Both before and after the state change, the goal's argument will be *sum ([\*,\*,\*,\*])*.

Let us see how the TMS handles the state change from "2 + 3" to "2 + 3x." The parse tree for "2 + 3" consists of the following literals:

    1.  *sum ([\*,\*,\*,\*])*
    2.    *term ([\*,\*,35,\*])*
    3.      *two ([\*,\*,35,\*])*
    4.  *plus ([35,\*,45,\*])*
    5.    *term ([45,\*,\*,\*])*
    6.      *three ([45,\*,\*,\*])*

When the writing operator puts an "x" in region [55,\*,\*,\*], it must retract primitive literals whose regions have been overlaid and assert new literals with smaller regions. In this case, the literal on line 6 above must be retracted and a new literal *three ([45,\*,55,\*])* is asserted. Retracting the literal on line 6 causes the TMS to retract the literals on lines 5 and 1, since their derivation depends on the literal of line 6. However, the addition of the new literals for "x" and "3" causes reconstruction, which leads ultimately to a new parse tree, which is:

    1.  *sum ([\*,\*,\*,\*])*
    2.    *term ([\*,\*,35,\*])*
    3.      *two ([\*,\*,35,\*])*
    4.  *plus ([35,\*,45,\*])*
    5.    *term ([45,\*,\*,\*])*

7.    *term ([45,\*,55,\*])*
8.    *three ([45,\*,55,\*])*
9.    *term ([55,\*,\*,\*])*
10.    *x([55,\*,\*,\*])*

The literal on line 5 has been reconstructed. Although it has a different derivation now, it occupies the same region as before, so it is equal to the old version. The un-outing mechanism of the TMS will detect this and cause the literal on line 1 to be reinstated.[8]

It appears that the updating problem has at least been solved. By using a TMS–based method, only parse nodes that are truly different are changed. This means that only goals whose arguments have really changed must be reconstructed.

Moreover, by using the TMS-based method of updating, we obtain the same seamless blend of recall and reconstruction that characterizes human recall behavior. If parts of the parse tree are forgotten, then the TMS-based updating method will simply reconstruct them without even "noticing" that they were forgotten.

## Summary: When Is Reasoning Really Perceptual?

In this section, we have descended into the ugly details of mathematical notation in order to find out what would happen if the problem space approximation was dispensed with and something more like real perception was modeled. It turned out to be much more difficult than it first appeared. There were two interacting sources of difficulty. The first was the fact that mathematical notation cannot be defined locally, but only by finding the most globally coherent parse of the visual plane.

The second difficulty occurs when updating the state after an operation is executed. This problem, which includes the frame problem of AI, can be solved in the problem space framework using Strips operators and a TMS. However, it is more difficult when perception is modeled. The global coherence of a perceptual parse means that the individual parts of the parse depend on each other in subtle ways. A change to one small piece of the visual plane can ripple through the parse and change large amounts of it. After a noble but ill-fated attempt at ducking the problem (the annotated grammars approach), a method was found for representing mathematical notation so that the propagation of changes died

---

[8]The old parse tree, which treats "2 + 3" as a sum, is still available, but now it has *sum([\*,\*,55])* as its root instead of *sum([\*,\*,\*,\*])*. This literal does not participate in a parse that covers all the symbols. In order to avoid generating it, the inference mechanism should only produce literals that participate in the derivation of a literal whose argument is [\*,\*,\*,\*]. This restriction would be simple to implement in a backwards chaining control structure; a forwards chainer would require a filter.

out quickly. This allowed perceptual parsing to be updated by roughly the same TMS-based method that successfully updates state changes when problem spaces are used.

Stepping back still further, one sees that the two computations, one supposedly procedural and the other supposedly perceptual, are nearly identical. The perceptual calculation updates a "state," which is a set of existing objects and their relationships to each others. The procedural calculation updates a "goal structure," which is a set of desired things and their relationships to each other. In order to obtain a reasonable solution to the frame problem, the same TMS-based method is used to update both the state and the goal structure. This method also yields robustness to forgetting, even the kind of massive forgetting caused by answering long telephone calls.

From a computational point of view, nearly the only way to tell that one calculation is perceptual and the other is procedural is to read the English names of the predicates, which is something that only a human observer can do. The situated action theorist would probably call the whole calculation perceptual. Traditional problem-solving theorists would call the whole calculation problem solving. Planning theorists would call it planning or perhaps reactive planning. As far as we can see, what you call it does not change what it is and does. As with many of the great binary distinctions in AI (e.g., procedural vs. declarative, logic vs. knowledge engineering), the distinction between situated action and planned action may turn out to be too ill-defined to be useful.

## DISCUSSION: MULTIPLE LEVELS
## AND EXTRA CAPABILITIES

Two claims are made in this chapter. One claim is that goal reconstruction solves at least three problems: allowing intelligent problem solving within a limited capacity store for goals, providing non-LIFO access to goals, and creating a seamless blend of situated and planned action. The other claim is that most current problem-solving architectures already have the capability to do simple goal reconstruction or could easily add that capability with a few changes. These are primarily computational claims, although we have indicated at several points the similarities of goal reconstruction and human cognition, and particularly the way a TMS–based goal maintenance system mimics the way human memory blends recall and reconstruction. Most of this section discusses the psychological status of goal reconstruction, but first we present one further claim.

Goal reconstruction is useful in building AI systems. This claim is based on our experience with our newest problem-solving architecture, Cascade. Cascade is a simplified version of Teton. The major simplification is that it can only represent monotonic state changes (i.e., all the operators have empty del-lists). While constructing an expert system in Cascade for solving physics problems, we discovered that goal reconstruction was quite useful during debugging. The usual cycle during debugging is to try a computation, detect a mistake, find the buggy piece of knowledge, correct it, and redo the computation. Goal reconstruction makes redoing the computation much faster because the problem solver can begin more–or–less from where it left off. We are currently adding a learning engine to Cascade that will act roughly like a programmer would in debugging the knowledge base. We suspect that goal reconstruction will aid the learning engine just as it aided the programmer. If our experience generalizes, then there are some unexpected practical benefits to adding the little bit of extra code to problem-solving architecture that allows it to reconstruct goals.

It is time to address the psychological status of goal reconstruction. Is it a part of the real human cognitive architecture? Newell (1990) and Pylyshyn (1984) define the cognitive architecture to be those parts of cognition that are innate, subject-universal (i.e., common to all subjects) and cognitively impenetrable. We think that goal reconstruction is subject-universal, but neither innate nor cognitively impenetrable. For instance, instructions to the subject can probably cause them to modify the way they do goal reconstruction, which would imply that goal reconstruction is cognitively penetrable and hence not a feature of the true cognitive architecture, according to Pylyshyn (1984). Thus, computational architectures such as Teton that have goal reconstruction built into them are not good models of the cognitive architecture. A better computational model would represent goal reconstruction as knowledge—a program in the model's library.

However, there are problems with modeling goal reconstruction as a cognitive procedure that has the same form as a procedure for arithmetic or physics. A procedure for goal reconstruction would have to take two inputs, the perceptual situation and the task's procedure (e.g., multiplication), and produce a goal structure as output. This procedure would not only have to be a meta-level procedure, because it reads other procedures and produces goal structures, but it would have to duplicate most of the functionality of the architecture's interpreter. The goal reconstruction procedure would essentially be a copy of the interpreter with a few extra lines of code added. This position is not only unparsimonious, but nearly self-contradictory. How could a person learn a procedure that is a copy of their architecture when the architecture is not open to introspection? In short, there are grave technological and developmental problems with the position that goal reconstruction should be modeled as a cognitive procedure rather than a feature of the architecture.

The fact is that cognitive modelers are not free to set the architecture/program boundary anywhere they want. Even the Soar group, with its emphasis on aligning Soar's architecture with the human cognitive architecture, finds it convenient to provide a selection problem space as part of the bare, "innate" Soar. In its format, the selection problem space is identical to problem spaces for acquired capabilities, such as a solution procedure for a puzzle, but the selection problem space is considered to be a model of a capability that is innate, subject–universal and cognitively impenetrable.

Rather than label Soar, Teton and other architectures as failures, let us reconsider the research object proposed by Newell and Pylyshyn, which is to develop an computational architecture that models all and only the human capabilities that are innate, subject universal and cognitively impenetrable.

First, not everyone cares about innateness, universality and penetrability. More typically, learning theorists begin by defining a set of tasks that they intend to explain. For instance, Anderson (1983) chose memory tasks (mostly), Berwick (1985) chose English syntactic analysis tasks and we chose problem solving tasks. In order to explain the observed learning behaviors, the theories assume specific *prior* cognitive capabilities. These are processes and structures that are assumed to exist at the time the tasks' acquisition begins. For instance, one of Anderson's theory's prior capabilities is a semantic network with specific functions for spreading activation and strengthening connections. Berwick's theory assumes a fixed parser as one of its prior capabilities. We assume that goal reconstruction is a prior capability. Although all these theorists seem to believe in the subject–universality of their prior capabilities, none have addressed cognitive penetrability and their claims about innateness are made tentatively if at all. This is quite reasonable. The objective of their investigations is an explanation of human behavior in the chosen task domains. Assuming that a prior capability is innate or impenetrable adds little to the explanatory adequacy of their theories. Logically, an explanation for some acquisitional behavior does not have to involve ascriptions of innateness and penetrability, but only assumptions about what capabilities existed prior to the observation period.

If the cognitive theorist expresses the learning theory as a computer model, it often takes the form of an architecture and some programs. Some of the theory's prior capabilities are expressed as programs and some are features of the architecture. There is no logical reasoning why the prior capabilities must be part of the architecture alone. Indeed, it is hard enough to formulate a detailed computational model without being saddled with this superfluous restriction. What matters is developing a scientifically adequate explanation of the phenomena, and that does not entail any particular alignment of prior capabilities with distinctions inherent in the modeling technology.

Cognitive modeling has produced relatively isolated computer-based models, which, as Newell (1973) points out, leaves psychology with no unified theory of cognition. It seems to us that there are three approaches to a unified theory:

1. Reduce all the models to the lowest common denominator. A model of the lowest-level cognitive processes is selected (or developed) and models of higher level processes are (re-)implemented on top of them. ACT* is an example of such a unified theory of cognition. As Anderson discovered, actually implementing a model of a higher level process on top of a model of lower-level processes is

technologically difficult, to put it mildly. Even if it could be done, the model would produce unusably complex "explanations" of high level human behavior. In order to achieve integration, this approach sacrifices the explanatory adequacy of the higher level models.

2. Develop models at different levels, and indicate explicitly how they relate to each other. This approach seems to characterize Anderson's recent computational models (Anderson, 1989). Grapes and Pups are high-level architectures that omit spreading activation and other memory mechanisms, but are intended to be homomorphic to ACT* in all other respects. Exactly how these higher level architectures map onto ACT* is not made fully explicit, although it should be if the ensemble is to quality as a unified theory of cognition.

3. Develop models at different levels, where each level is a copy of the one below it. This approach seems to characterize the Soar work (Newell, 1990). Soar has been used as a model of lower level processes, such as stimulus response compatibility and transcription typing (John, 1988; Rosenbloom & Newell, 1987), where its cycle times correspond roughly to the frequency of updates to human memory. Soar has also been used for modeling computer configuration, algorithm design and other higher level problem solving tasks (Rosenbloom, Laird, McDermott, Newell, & Orchiuch, 1985), where its cycle times correspond to seconds or minutes of real time. In principle, the primitives provided by the authors of these higher level models could be replaced by Soar programs that are similar to those used in the modeling of the lower level processes.

We think that the second approach is the best. It allows models of higher level processes to be expressed in any way that optimizes the clarity and productivity of the explanations. The third approach forces the theorist to use the same architecture for both low level and high level models, and that seems analogous to forcing the quantum physicist and the biologist to use the same mathematics for their models. In principle it could be done, but the clarity of the models would be sacrificed.

In summary, Teton and similar architectures should not be viewed as claims about innateness, universality or penetrability. They should be viewed as part of a model that explains problem solving and skill acquisition. The model contains assumptions about what capabilities are possessed by subjects prior to training. Some, but not all, of those capabilities are modeled by features of the architecture. The others are modeled by pre–existing programs. Eventually, this model should be related via explicit mappings to models of lower–level processes, notably memory, attention, perception and motor control.

The remainder of this chapter contains another explanation of the psychological status of goal reconstruction. We claim that goal reconstruction is a *prior capability* of problem solving, which means that all subjects possess this capability prior to learning the given problem solving procedure. One way to see what this means is by seeing what other prior capabilities would be needed in a model of skill acquisition. The following sections list capabilities that, in our estimation, are prior capabilities for the tasks usually studied in the problem-solving literature: physics, blocks world, Tower of Hanoi, algebra, eight puzzle, etc.

## Goal Reconstruction

The key property that makes goal reconstruction a candidate for a prior capability is that it does not have to be learned, or at least that it does not have to be learned each time a new procedure is learned. To demonstrate this, consider a gedanken experiment. Suppose we train subjects in an entirely novel procedure, being careful never to interrupt them while they are executing the procedure. When they have mastered it, we perform the telephone test: we interrupt them in the middle of solving a problem, have them engage in an interference task sufficient to wipe out goal memory, then have them resume their original task. Presumably, they would all be able to reconstruct their internal state for this procedure, even though they had never done reconstruction on this procedure before. This gedanken experiment shows that their reconstructive capability was acquired prior to the acquisition of the procedure.

As the discussion earlier in the chapter indicated, some cases of goal reconstruction seem to require task-specific knowledge. These kinds of goal reconstruction would have to be acquired along with the task's procedure. Although we claim that some goal reconstruction is a prior capability, we are not claiming that *all* goal reconstruction is due to prior capabilities. Teton's architecture embeds specific claims about what kinds of goal reconstruction are prior and what kinds would have to be learned.

## Explanation of Worked Examples

Another capability that seems to come "for free" when one learns a procedure is explanation of worked examples. A worked example is a problem that has been solved in such a way that a partial trace of the solution process is available. Math and physics textbooks have many worked examples. Usually, the textbooks print only the results of visible actions of the procedure, the actions that the students would write if they were solving the procedure. The invisible actions, such as deciding which goal or strategy to pursue, are usually left out. Often the exact nature of the visible actions is underspecified, too. For instance, the textbook might print an algebraic equation but not say what operation was used to produce it. *Explaining* a worked example entails producing all the information that is necessary for solving the problem but has been left out of the printed material.

There is ample evidence that people can explain worked examples even when the procedure they are using to explain the example is new to them (Chi, Bassok,

Lewis, Reimann, & Glaser, 1989; Pirolli & Bielaczyc, 1989). This indicates that the ability to explain a worked example is a prior capability. That is, after one has learned a procedure well enough to execute it, then one can automatically explain examples with it as well. The converse may also be true (Chi et al., 1989).

It could be objected that explaining an example is exactly the same as solving the example's problem. This is true only of simple cases. In more complicated cases, the example might not use exactly the same order of steps as the subject would use. It might produce intermediate steps that the subject would not, or use less efficient strategies than the subject would. The subjects most control their own processing so as to reproduce the same steps as the example. So example explaining really is a different process than interpreting a procedure. Thus, it should be viewed as a distinct prior capability.

## Impasse Handling

When people are executing a procedure, even a fairly well-known procedure, they sometimes get stuck. For instance, if you normally make a white sauce using butter, flour and milk, and you discover, after mixing the butter and flour together and cooking them for a while, that you are out of milk, then you are at an impasse. People seem to have a fairly standard set of capabilities for handling impasses. For instance, one standard so–called *repair strategy* is substitution (Brown & VanLehn, 1980). In the case of the white sauce procedure, the cook might substitute for the milk something that is liquid, edible, mildly flavored and otherwise quite similar to the milk. Another repair is backing up. In the case of the white sauce, one might back up to the procedure that required the sauce (e.g., your favorite moussaka recipe) and reconsider the need for the sauce.

Repair strategies seem to be somewhat independent of the impasse and the procedure that they are applied to (VanLehn, 1990). For instance, the two white sauce repair strategies, substitution and backing up, are also applied by arithmetic students to arithmetic procedures (VanLehn, 1990). This illustrates the claim that people have a stock of general purpose repair strategies that can be adapted for use with any procedure's impasses. The impasse-repair process is a prior capability because it does not have to be learned as each new procedure is learned.

## Rule Acquisition Events

It is often conjectured that human problem solvers can interrupt their procedure, reason about the procedure and its efficacy, make a modification to the procedure, and resume execution of the modified procedure. In early work, the existence of these rule acquisition events was inferred from changes in the person's problem solving behavior (e.g., Anzai & Simon, 1979; Neches, 1987). Recent fine-grained protocol analyses have shown that people tend to pause and/or make unusual verbal comments during a rule acquisition event (Siegler & Jenkins, 1989; VanLehn, 1991, 1989). For instance, in one 90-minute protocol (VanLehn, 1991) there were 11 rule acquisition events of which 10 were accompanied by either long pauses, reflective comments (e.g., "It's just like moving four, isn't it?") or negative comments (e.g., "Wrong . . . this is the problem and . . ."). These detailed analyses support the hypothesis that people can reason about and modify their procedures even in the midst of using them.

We are currently developing detailed simulations of rule acquisition events taken from protocols of students learning college physics. It is already clear that the subjects have a large variety of rule acquisition methods that they use to analyze and modify their procedures. For instance, a particularly powerful and common method is *explanation-based learning of correctness* (VanLehn, Ball & Kowalski, 1990). When subjects try to explain a worked example and their knowledge of the target procedure is incomplete, then they will sometimes be unable to complete an explanation of the example. There will be segments of the example's solution that cannot be parsed by the student's procedure. One rule acquisition method is to invent new rules that will complete the example's explanation (Ali, 1989; Danyluk, 1989; Fawcett, 1989; Pazzani, 1988; Schank & Leake, 1989; VanLehn, 1987; Wilkins, 1988). In general, there are combinatorially many ways to build a syntactically correct an explanation (Nowlan, 1987). Rather than exhaustively searching for the semantically correct completion, the physics students seem to specialize an overly general rule that they would not normally use. For instance, one student could not explain where a certain minus sign came from in a physics equation. She eventually formed an explanation after noting that the quantity bearing the minus sign came from a vector whose x–projection lay along the negative x-axis. She said, "The reason the negative is there is because the X component is in the negative direction on the X axis." Apparently this subject used the overly general rule that mathematical manipulations conserve negations. On this reasoning, the negation in her equation had to come, ultimately, from some existing negation, such as the negative part of the X–axis. This kind of explanation completion is halfway between syntactic explanation completion (e.g., VanLehn, 1987), where completions are chosen based on their size or other structural characteristics, and explanation-based learning (Mitchell, Keller, & Kedar-Cabelli, 1986), where new rules are created by specializing general rules that are used in an explanation. In explanation-based learning of correctness, the subject normally avoids certain rules because they are known to be overly general. However, such rules will be used to bridge an impasse, and if this ultimately results in a correct solution, a specialization of the overly general rule is kept as a new, hopefully correct rule.

Explanation-based learning of correctness is just one of many rule acquisition methods that seem to be used by people in order to improve their understanding of a task domain. Since they are used in the course of acquiring a procedure, they must have existed before the procedure. Thus, they are a prior capability.

## Conclusions

This list has illustrated just a few prior capabilities that a theory of skill acquisition would need to assume. Some capabilities, such as goal reconstruction and explanation of worked examples, are best modeled as features of the architecture. Other prior capabilities, such as reading and writing English, are best modeled as procedural knowledge. Still other capabilities, such as repairing impasses, are best modeled as a mixture of architectural features and procedural knowledge.

Whether a capability is modeled as procedural knowledge or a feature of the architecture is independent of whether it is a prior capability or acquired during the observation period. Indeed, we see no logical problems with hypothesizing that some features of the architecture are acquired. (Although we *do* see interesting technical challenges in developing a learning mechanism that modifies the architecture.)

Having distinguished prior capabilities from architectures, both computational and cognitive, we hope we have clarified the main psychological claim of the chapter, which is simply that goal reconstruction is a prior capability for classical problem solving and skill acquisition.

## APPENDIX: TETON

Teton is a von Neuman machine, so it has two kinds of memory. The *knowledge base* is a large, slowly changing memory that holds general knowledge, such as procedures for solving problems, inference rules and general facts. The *working memory* is a rapidly changing memory that holds information produced in the course of a computation. Like all von Neuman machines, Teton has an built-in *execution cycle* that interprets procedural knowledge stored in its knowledge base. The execution cycle consists of (a) deciding what to do, based on the current states of the working memory and the knowledge base, and (b) doing what it decided to do. The execution cycle is an algorithm that treats the information in the working memory and the knowledge base as formatted data. The format of the data is called the *representation language.*

This description of Teton has, so far, said nothing that would distinguish it from any other von Neuman machine. To define Teton per se, the following three sections will describe, respectively, its representation language, its execution cycle and its memories.

### Knowledge Representation

Teton's representation language is appropriate for procedural knowledge, but clumsy at best for representing declarative knowledge. For instance, it is simple to represent addition and subtraction algorithms, but it is difficult to represent that addition and subtraction are inverses. This is *not* intended to be a claim that the mind has only clumsy ways to represent declarative knowledge. It means only that we have not investigated tasks where declarative knowledge has a major influence, so we have not yet included a language appropriate for representing declarative knowledge.

In working memory, the main unit of information is the *goal*. A goal serves many purposes. It can represent an action that has already been completed, or an action that is planned but not yet begun, or an action that is in progress. A goal has slots for indicating a state to be achieved, an operation, the state resulting from the operation, subgoals created by the operation, the supergoal of this goal, the time that the goal was created, and so on.

In the knowledge base, there are two kinds of knowledge: *operators* and *selection rules*. Operators have the following parts:

1. A goal type, which indicates what kinds of goals this operator is appropriate for. This description usually has variables that must be instantiated before the operator can be executed.

2. A set of preconditions. If all these predicates hold of the current state of working memory, then the operator can be executed. If not, then the architecture will automatically create subgoals for each of the unsatisfied preconditions. Operators may have an empty set of preconditions.

3. A body, which describes what is to happen when the operator is executed. If the operator is a primitive, the body describes the changes that will occur to the situation and/or the rest of working memory. If the operator is non-primitive (i.e., a macro–operator), the body describes what subgoals the operator will create when it is executed.

4. A shortcut condition, which is true if the operator can be assumed to be completed.

Teton's operators allow both deliberate subgoaling and operator subgoaling. The execution of the body of an operator can create subgoals (deliberate subgoaling), and the architecture will create subgoals if an operator's preconditions are unsatisfied (operator subgoaling).

Selection rules are the other type of knowledge in Teton's knowledge base. They are used for selecting a goal to work on and for selecting an operator to use for achieving the selected goal. There are three types of selection rules. *Consideration* rules indicate that a goal or operator should be considered. These rules are consulted first. They usually produce a large set of items. *Rejection* rules are consulted next, and cause some of the item to be removed from the set of items under consideration. *Preference* rules are consulted last. They partially order the set of items under consideration. Normally, one item will be preferred over all the others. It is the one selected. Teton's selection rule mechanism is similar to the ones used by Soar (Rosenbloom et al., chap. 4, in this volume) and Prodigy (Carbonell et al., chap. 9, in this volume). All three systems use this type of mechanism because it makes it easy to implement the acquisition of strategic knowledge: just add new selection rules.[9]

## The Execution Cycle

The main loop of Teton's interpreter is shown in Table 6.2. Most of it is quite standard: Goals are selected by goal selection rules. Operators are selected by operator selection rules. Unsatisfied preconditions cause subgoaling. Execution of macro-operators causes subgoaling. Execution of primitive operators causes state changes. However, there are two facilities, impasses and shortcut conditions, that are not standard and deserved some explanation.

Whenever the architecture needs to select a goal or operation, it enumerates all possible candidates, filters this set with the rejection–type selection rules, then rank orders the set with the remaining selection rules. If one choice is better than all the others, then Teton takes it. However, if the selection rules fail to uniquely specify a choice (e.g., they reject all possibilities, or they cannot decide between two possibilities), then an *impasse* occurs. As in Soar (Rosenbloom et al., chap. 4 in this volume) and Sierra (VanLehn, 1987; VanLehn, 1990), an impasse causes the architecture to automatically create a new goal, which is to resolve the impasse. Typically, such resolve-impasse goals are tackled by task-general knowledge. For instance, one of Sierra's methods is: If the selection rules

TABLE 6.2
The Main Loop of Teton's Interpreter

1. Select a goal from working memory using the goal selection rules. If there is no unique selection exists, then create an impasse goal describing that and select it.
2. If the selected goal has an operation selected for it already, then skip the next step.
3. Select an operation (a partially instantiated operator) for the current goal using the operator selection rules. if there is no unique operation, then create an impasse goal describing that, make it a subgoal of the selected goal, select it, and repeat this step.
4. If the selected operation has unsatisfied preconditions, then create a new goal for each such precondition and link it to the selected goal as a subgoal. Leave the selected goal marked "pending," and return to step 1.
5. If the selected operation has a shortcut condition and it is true, or it has subgols and they are all completed, then mark the selected goal "completed" and return to step 1.
6. If the operation is primitive, then execute the operation, mark the selected goal "completed", and return to step 1.
7. Otherwise, the operation is non-primitive, so execute the operation and return to step 1. Execution will cause new subgoals to be created and linked to the seleted goal as subgoals.

cannot decide among several possible candidates, then choose one randomly. Another popular impasse-resolving method is: If the selection rules rejected all operations for the current goal, then mark the goal as accompanied even though it is not. This causes the architecture to "skip" planned actions that it does not know how to accomplish. Brown and VanLehn (1980) exhibited a collection of such impasse-resolving methods (called "repairs") and showed how they could explain the acquisition of many students' bugs (procedural misconceptions).

Shortcut conditions play an important role when Teton reconstructs goals that have been forgotten (i.e., deleted from working memory). In order to recover from such working memory failures, Teton has to reconstruct some of the goals it once had. It is assumed that there is some top-level goal that is not forgotten. The remaining goals are reconstructed by simply executing the procedural knowledge with the interpreter of Table 6.2. However, when the situation corresponds to a half–completed problem, some of the goals created are superfluous because they have already been achieved. In such cases, the appropriate shortcut conditions are true, and goals are marked "completed" before any attempt is made to execute them.

One mechanism that is common in other architectures is missing in Teton. Teton goals need not be selected in last-in-first-out (LIFO) order. For instance, if there are two pending goals, A and B, and A is selected and leads to a subgoal C, then a LIFO restriction would rule out selecting goal B since C is more recently created. Most architectures, including Soar and Grapes, place a LIFO restriction on goal selection, but Teton does not. In the case just mentioned, it allows either B or C to be selected.

## Memories

As mentioned earlier, Teton has two memory stores, the knowledge base and the working memory. Working memory is composed of four distinct memories:

1. The *main working memory* is the one that holds the goals and other data structures generated by the execution cycle.
2. The *situation* holds a representation of the external environment. Its contents model the subjects' interpretation of what they see, which is task-specific, like a problem space's current state. For instance, an arithmetic problem is represented as a grid of rows and columns in the situation, whereas an algebra equation is represented as a tree.
3. The *scratchpad* is just like the situation, except that the contents represent something that the subject is imagining, rather than actually seeing. For instance, some subjects imagine the result of a move during problem solving before actually making the move in the real world. In order to model such events, Teton distinguishes the situation from the imagination.

4. The *buffer* is a limited capacity store for items that have simple verbal encodings, such as numbers

The latter two memories are a novelty in computational models of the architecture, so they are worth a little explanation. They are designed as simple versions of the two slave memories described by Baddeley (1986) and called the *articulatory loop* and the *visio-spatial scratchpad*. According to Baddeley, the articulatory loop consists of a passive storage medium, called the phonological store, and a mechanism for "rehearsing" its contents (analogously to a dynamic RAM). The phonological store can hold a phonological code for about 2 or 3 seconds (Zhang & Simon, 1985). If it is not rehearsed in that time, it becomes inaccessible. The time required to rehearse a code is linearly related to the time required to read the equivalent lexical item. Thus a person can store a given list of stimulus items if the time required to rehearse them once is less than 2 or 3 seconds. This accounts for the often-cited finding that untrained subjects can store and immediately recall about 7 plus or minus 2 chunks (Miller, 1956). Because rehearsal can go on relatively independently of most cognitive tasks (Baddeley, 1986), the articulatory loop acts like a short term store with a capacity of a few phonologically encoded chunks. Teton uses this much simpler model, and allows N chunks to be stored in the articulatory loop, where N is a parameter of the architecture. Typically, the articulatory loop is used for temporary storage of numbers.

The visual–spatial scratchpad contains the same kind of items as the situation does, but it is meant to model a scene that the subject is imagining, rather than the real world. Teton's version of the scratchpad is only used for one purpose, which is looking ahead during problem solving in order to project the consequences of contemplated moves. Consequently, Teton supports only a simple model of the scratchpad. There is a switch in the architecture, which can be set by a primitive operation to either "normal" or "imaginary." When the switch is thrown from "normal" to "imaginary," the scratchpad is initialized with a copy of the items in the current situation. Thereafter, all reading and writing operations that would normally access the situation access the scratchpad instead. The volatility of the scratchpad is modeled, again quite crudely, by counting the number of operations applied to it. After a threshold is crossed (the threshold is a parameter of the model), the contents of the scratchpad become inaccessible.

This facility was used to simulate look-ahead search in the Tower of Hanoi, which plays a crucial role in Anzai and Simon's (1979) account of strategy acquisition. In the course of developing a similar account of strategy acquisition, we discovered that learning the more advanced versions of the disk subgoaling strategy would require looking ahead 12 moves in the scratchpad. Not only is this implausible, but setting the stability parameter of the scratchpad to 13 caused learning of earlier versions of the strategy to go awry. This led us to look for methods of strategy acquisition that did not use the scratchpad. We found not one but several, along with good support for them in the protocol data (VanLehn, in press, 1989).

## ACKNOWLEDGMENTS

This work was supported by the Personnel and Training Research Program, Psychological Sciences Division, Office of the Naval Research, under contract N00014-88-K-0086 and by the Information Sciences Division, Office of Naval Research, under contract N-00014-K-0678. Reproduction in whole or in part is permitted for any purpose of the United States Government. Approved for public release; distribution unlimited.

## REFERENCES

Agre, P. E., & Chapman, D. (1987). Pengi: An implementation of a theory of activity. In K. Forbus & H. Shrobe (Ed.), *Proceedings of the Sixth National Conference on Artificial Intelligence.* Los Altos, CA: Morgan Kaufman.
Ali, K. M. (1989). Augmenting domain theory for explanation-based generalisation. In A. Segre (Ed.), *Proceedings of the Sixth International Workshop on Machine Learning.* Los Altos, CA: Morgan Kaufman.
Anderson, J. R. (1983). *The architecture of cognition.* Cambridge, MA: Harvard.
Anderson, J. R. (1989). A theory of the origins of human knowledge. *Artificial Intelligence, 40,* 313–352.
Anzai, Y., & Simon, H. A. (1979). The theory of learning by doing. *Psychological Review, 86,* 124–140.
Baddeley, A. (1986). *Working memory.* Oxford, UK: Clarendon Press.
Berwick, R. (1985). *The acquisition of syntactic knowledge.* Cambridge, MA: MIT Press.
Brown, J. S., & VanLehn, K. (1980). Repair Theory: A generative theory of bugs in procedural skills. *Cognitive Science, 4,* 379–426.
Charniak, E., & McDermott, D. (1986). *Introduction to artificial intelligence.* Reading, MA: Addison-Wesley.
Chi, M. T. H., Bassok, M., Lewis, M., Reimann, P., & Glaser, R. (1989). Self explanations: How students study and use examples in learning to solve problems. *Cognitive Science, 13,* 145–182.
Danyluk, A. P. (1989). Finding new rules for incomplete theories: Explicit biases for induction with contextual information. In A. Segre (Ed.), *Proceedings of the Sixth International Workshop on Machine Learning.* Los Altos, CA: Morgan Kaufman.
de Kleer, J. (1986). An assumption-based truth maintenance system. *Artificial Intelligence, 28,* 127–162.
de Kleer, J., Doyle, J., Steele, G. L., & Sussman, G. J. (1977). Amord: Explicit control of reasoning. *Sigplan Notices, 12*(8), 116–125.
Doyle, J. (1979). A truth maintenance system. *Artificial Intelligence, 12*(3), 231–272.
Ernst, G. W., & Newell, A. (1969). *GPS: A case study in generality and problem solving.* New York: Academic Press.
Fawcett, T. E. (1989). Learning from plausible explanations. In A. Segre (Ed.), *Proceedings of the Sixth International Workshop on Machine Learning.* Los Altos, CA: Morgan Kaufman.
Fikes, R. E., Hart, P. E., & Nilsson, N. J. (1972). Learning and executing generalized robot plans. *Artificial Intelligence, 3,* 251–288.

John, B. (1988). *Contributions to engineering models of human-computer interaction*. Doctoral dissertation, Dept. of Psychology, Carnegie Mellon University.

Laird, J. E., Newell, A., & Rosenbloom, P. S. (1987). Soar: An architecture for general intelligence. *Artificial Intelligence, 33*, 1–64.

Miller, G. A. (1956). The magic number seven plus or minus two: Some limits on our capacity for processing information. *Psychological Review, 63*, 81–97.

Mitchell, T. M., Keller, R. M., & Kedar-Cabelli, S. T. (1986). Explanation-based generalization: A unifying view. *Machine Learning, 1*(1), 47–80.

Neches, R. (1987). Learning through incremental refinement of procedures. In D. Klahr, P. Langley, & R. Neches (Ed.), *Production systems models of learning and development*. Cambridge, MA: MIT Press.

Newell, A. (1973). You can't play 20 questions with nature and win. In W. G. Chase (Ed.), *Visual information processing*. New York: Academic.

Newell, A. (1990). *Universal theories of cognition*. Cambridge, MA: Harvard University Press.

Newell, A., & Simon, H. A. (1972). *Human problem solving*. Englewood Cliffs, NJ: Prentice-Hall.

Nowlan, S. (1987). *Parse completion: A study of an inductive domain* (Technical Report PCG11). Department of Psychology, Carnegie Mellon University.

Pazzani, M. (1988). Integrated learning with incorrect and incomplete theories. In J. Laird (Ed.), *Proceedings of the Fifth International Workshop on Machine Learning*. Los Altos, CA: Morgan Kaufman.

Pirolli, P., & Bielaczyc, K. (1989). Empirical analyses of self-explanation and transfer in learning to program. In G. Ohlson & E. Smith (Ed.), *Proceedings of the Eleventh Annual Conference of the Cognitive Science Society*. Hillsdale, NJ:Lawrence Erlbaum Associates.

Pylyshyn, Z. W. (1984). *Computation and cognition: Toward a foundation for cognitive science*. Cambridge, MA: MIT Press.

Rosenbloom, P. S., Laird, J. E., McDermott, J., Newell, A., & Orchiuch, E. (1985). R1-Soar: An experiment in knowledge-intensive programming in a problem solving architecture. *Pattern Analysis and Machine Intelligence, 7*, 561–567.

Rosenbloom, P., & Newell, A. (1987). Learning by chunking: A production system model of practice. In D. Klahr, P. Langley, & R. Neches (Ed.), *Production system models of learning and development*. Cambridge, MA: MIT Press.

Schank, R. C., & Leake, D. B. (1989). Creativity and learning in a case-based explainer. *Artificial Intelligence, 40*, 353–386.

Siegler, R. S., & Jenkins, E. A. (1989). *How children discover new strategies*. Hillsdale, NJ: Lawrence Erlbaum Associates.

Suchman, L. A. (1987). *Plans and situated actions: The problem of human-machine communication*. New York: Cambridge University Press.

VanLehn, K. (1983). *Felicity conditions for human skill acquisition: Validating an AI-based theory* (Tech. Report CIS-21). Xerox Palo Alto Research Center. Out of print, but available as publication number 9018167 from University Microfilms, 300 North Zeeb Road, Ann Arbor, MI 49106.

VanLehn, K. (1986). Arithmetic procedures are induced from examples. In J. Hiebert (Ed.), *Conceptual and procedural knowledge: The case of mathematics*. Hillsdale, NJ: Lawrence Erlbaum Associates.

VanLehn, K. (1987). Learning one subprocedure per lesson. *Artificial Intelligence, 31*(1), 1–40.

VanLehn, K. (1989). Learning events in the acquisition of three skills. In G. Ohlson & E. Smith (Ed.), *Proceedings of the Eleventh Annual Conference of the Cognitive Science Society*. Hillsdale, NJ: Lawrence Erlbaum Associates.

VanLehn, K. (1990). *Mind bugs: The origins of procedural misconceptions*. Cambridge, MA: MIT Press.

VanLehn, K. (1991). Rule acquisition events in the discovery of problem solving strategies. *Cognitive Science, 15*(1), 1–47.

VanLehn, K., Ball, W., & Kowalski, B. (1989). Non-LIFO execution of cognitive procedures. *Cognitive Science, 13,* 415–465.

VanLehn, K., Ball, W., & Kowalski, B. (1990). Explanation-based learning of correctness: Towards a model of the self-explanation effect. In *Proceedings of the 12th Annual Conference of the Cognitive Science Society.* Hillsdale, NJ: Lawrence Erlbaum Associates.

Vere, S. (1975). Induction of concepts in the predicate calculus. In *Proceedings of the Fourth IJCAI.* Los Altos, CA: Kaufmann.

Wilkins, D. C. (1988). Knowledge base refinement using apprenticeship learning techniques. In R. Smith & T. M. Mitchell (Ed.), *Proceedings of the Seventh National Conference on Artificial Intelligence.* Los Altos, CA: Morgan-Kaufman.

Winston, P. H. (1975). Learning structural descriptions from examples. In P. H. Winston (Ed.), *The Psychology of Computer Vision.* New York: McGraw-Hill.

Zhang, G., & Simon, H. A. (1985). STM capacity for Chinese words and idioms: Chunking and acoustical loop hypotheses. *Memory and Cognition, 13*(3), 193–201.

# 7 The Role of Cognitive Architecture in Theories of Cognition

Zenon W. Pylyshyn
*Centre for Cognitive Science, University of Western Ontario*

## INTRODUCTION

This conference is about cognitive architecture and its role in theories of intelligent processing. I follow the tradition established in the past for commentators of these conferences and take this as an opportunity to discuss the general theme of the conference, as well as to comment on some of the specific theses that have emerged in the papers that have been presented.

I begin by saying what I mean by cognitive architecture, and why I believe that paying attention to cognitive architecture is essential to the business of taking computation seriously as a way of understanding mental activity. I do this by presenting several independent ways of looking at the role of cognitive architecture in providing explanations of intelligent behavior. But before I do that I want to lay out what I take to be some ground rules or shared assumptions in this discussion; otherwise, meta–cognitive–science discussions can easily degenerate into arguments about the mind–body problem.

First, I take it for granted, as I believe most of us here do, that the goal of cognitive science is to provide explanations of certain phenomena associated with intelligent activity. Of course, not all phenomena associated with such activity will naturally fall into the category of cognitive science, and indeed one of the things we expect to discover as the science progresses is exactly which phenomena do cluster into a science, in the sense that they fall under some common principles. The set of phenomena that constitute *cognition,* in this technical sense, is a long-term empirical question: we have no right to stipulate in advance which phenomena will succumb to the set of principles and mechanisms that we develop in studying what appear pretheoretically to be clear cases of cognition. The precise cluster of phenomena that define a natural scientific domain is always discovered, not stipulated. At the outset we only assume that there does exist such a (nonempty) scientific domain and that it probably subsumes the clear "core" cognitive phenomena (though even this assumption is provisional).

Second, I take for granted that one of the defining criteria of intelligent processing (or cognition) is that it is *representational*. By this I mean that explaining the behavior of cognitive processes requires that we talk about what certain states of the cognitive system represent, what they are about, what they mean, what they refer to, and so on: In other words, *knowledge,* or more generally *semantic content,* is an indispensable notion in cognitive science. Every now and then (and almost entirely when researchers are playing at philosophy rather than doing their work) some arguments arise concerning precisely what this means, whether it is real or merely an approximate way of speaking, and so on. I will not go into such issues at this time because I consider them only marginally relevant. Notwithstanding these occasional arguments, I think it is correct to say that no serious theory of intelligent activity, at least since Turing, has failed to assume that an intelligent system functions the way it does because of what it represents and because of the way representations are materially instantiated (or physically encoded) and transformed.[1] Certainly nobody here comes to the subject with a different assumption—including the people who represent the connectionist approach to understanding cognition.

Finally, I will assume that *explaining* intelligence involves much more than just correctly predicting certain kinds of observed behavior: it also involves, among other things, giving a detailed account of "how" that behavior was caused. Here matters can get a bit more tendentious so I will pause to elaborate on this point later. One reason it may be tendentious is that there is more than one viable sense of "how" a behavior is caused. Even here, there is strong agreement among cognitive scientists that the "how" need not involve giving a detailed physical or biological description, and indeed that such a description is unlikely to touch on the question of how certain patterns of intelligent behavior come about. There are good reasons for this, which relate to the need to capture certain generalizations or systematic patterns of behavior: different generalizations require different levels of abstraction over the underlying physical mechanisms.

Again, I do not discuss these general issues here, although I do devote considerable space to them elsewhere (Pylyshyn, 1984b). To simplify this exposition I will capitalize wherever I can on some generally shared assumptions. In this case I think there is general agreement that we want to explain "how" the behavior was caused by reference to information processing mechanisms and methods,

---

[1]In saying this I am of course ignoring a 50 year behaviorist tradition in American and British psychology, but since this tradition really did not address the phenomena of intelligent behavior it is not a counterexample of my claim.

rather than by reference to physics or neuroscience. Although, as I said, I will not defend this view, I will return to certain aspects of it briefly later because the issue of the right level of abstraction for describing cognitive processes sometimes surfaces in connection with issues of cognitive architecture.

## Background: Cognitive Architecture

Most cognitive scientists understand the term *architecture* roughly in terms of the parallel with computer architecture, where it refers to the resources and organization that is made available by the machine's design. There is also a natural extension of this notion to "virtual machine" architectures, where the latter are architectures (such as LISP, PROLOG, OPS5, ACT*, SOAR, and so on) that are simulated on some conventional machine in software. However, as Al Newell never tires of pointing out, there is no principled distinction between a virtual and a real architecture: they are all equally real physical architectures. The only different between them may come down to something like the theoretically irrelevant fact that after the power has been turned off (or the system reset) some machines do revert to a different architecture, such as the one described in the computer manual—a fact that is clearly incidental for our purposes.

For any particular computational process there is only one level of the system's organization that corresponds to what we call its cognitive architecture. That is the level at which the states (datastructures) being processed receive a cognitive interpretation. To put it another way, it is the level at which the system is representational, and where the representations correspond to the objects of thought (including percepts, memories, goals, beliefs, and so on). In other words, the semantic interpretation of these states figures in the explanation of the cognitive behavior. Notice that there may be many other levels of system organization below this, but these do not constitute different *cognitive* architectures because their states do not represent cognitive contents. Rather, they correspond to various kinds of implementations, perhaps at the level of some abstract neurology, which realize (or implement) the cognitive architecture.[2] Similarly, there may be various levels of organization above this, and these may or may not be cognitive architectures. Some of this organization may represent the way that a

---

[2]Connectionists (e.g., Smolensky, 1988) sometimes talk about distributed representations as involving a level somewhere between implementation and full semantic representations—a sort of subcognitive level of representation. But this is a very misleading way of speaking. What so-called distributed representations do is encode some semantic objects in terms of sets of features (or "microfeatures", frequently statistically derived). They do this as a way of (i.e., in lieu of) representing the concepts or objects themselves. This is a feature–decomposition or a componential view of representation. However, in this case the components into which the represented objects are decomposed *are* the semantically interpreted symbols, not some special lower level of quasi-representation. In that case the theory merely claims that the symbols represent certain kinds of primitive semantic features that are finer in detail than, say, those captured by words in the (nontechnical) language.

particular cognitive process happens to be structured, say in terms of sub-routines, where the structure is not required by the architecture itself (i.e., it could have been organized differently within the same architecture). Such an organization, then, does not constitute an architectural organization. On the other hand, other large scale organizations may constitute architectural properties because they are fixed with respect to what can be done symbolically. A good candidate for large scale architectural organization is the putative "modular" nature of some cognitive processes, since the claim in that case is that the architecture itself restricts the sort of inter–modular communication that can take place. (The difference between architectural constraints and constraints that arise from habit, learning, or some other contingent character of the system's history, needs to be made with care. I give a brief sketch of a way to try to do this in terms of "cognitive penetrability" of the process).

I argue that for purposes of cognitive science, the difference between cognitive architecture and other levels of system organization is fundamental; without an independently motivated theory of the functional architecture, a computational system cannot purport to be a literal model of some cognitive process. There are three important reasons for this, which I will try to sketch:

• *Architecture–relativity of algorithms and strong equivalence.* For most cognitive scientists a computational model is intended to correspond to the cognitive process being modeled at what might roughly be characterized as the level of the *algorithm* (this view of the proper level of correspondence is what I refer to as "strong equivalence"). Yet we cannot specify an algorithm without first making assumptions about the architecture: algorithms are relativized to architectures. This means that discovering the cognitive architecture of the mind must be a central concern of cognitive science.

• *Architecture as a theory of cognitive capacity.* Another way of looking at the role of architecture is as a way of understanding the set of possible cognitive processes that are allowed by the structure of the brain. This means that to specify the cognitive architecture is to provide a theory of the *cognitive capacity* of an organism. The architecture provides the *cognitive constants* while the algorithms and representations provide the free empirical parameters set by the incoming variable information.

• *Architecture as marking the boundary of representation–governed processes.* Finally, for many of us, a fundamental working hypothesis of cognitive science is that there exists an autonomous (or at least partially autonomous) domain of phenomena that can be explained in terms of representations (goals, beliefs, knowledge, perceptions, etc) and algorithmic processes that operate over these representations. Another way to put this is to say that cognitive systems have a real level of organization at what Newell (1982) has called the "knowledge level." Reasoning and rational knowledge-dependent principles apply at this level. Because of this, any differences in behavioral regularities that can be shown to arise from such knowledge-dependent processes do not reveal properties of the architecture, which remain invariant with changes in goals and knowledge. Although this is really another way of saying the same thing as was already said above, the different emphasis leads to a novel methodological proposal; namely, that the architecture must be cognitively impenetrable.

In what follows I elaborate on these three points.

## THREE WAYS OF VIEWING COGNITIVE ARCHITECTURE

### Architectures and Algorithms

Cognitive algorithms, the central concept in computational psychology, are understood as being executed by the cognitive architecture. According to the strong realist view, a valid cognitive model must execute the *same algorithm* as that carried out by the subject being modeled. But it turns out that *which* algorithms can be carried out in a direct way depends on the architecture of the machine in question. Machines with different architectures cannot in general *directly* execute the same algorithms.[3]

This point is best illustrated by considering examples of several simple architectures. Perhaps the most primitive machine architecture is the original binary–coded Turing machine introduced by Alan Turing (Turing, 1937). Although this machine is universal, in the sense that it can be programmed to compute any computable function, anyone who has tried to write procedures for it will have noticed that most computations are extremely complex. More importantly, the complexity of the sequence of operations it must go through varies with such things as the task and the nature of the input; moreover it varies with the input in ways that are quite different from the ways it would in machines with a more conventional architecture.

To illustrate this point, notice that the number of basic steps required to look up a string of symbols in a Turing machine increases as the square of the number of strings stored. By contrast, in what is called a register architecture (an archi-

---

[3]We can take this claim as a point of definition for present purposes, although there are some technical issues here that would have to be addressed in a more detailed discussion. The criterion for being the same algorithm is closely linked to the idea of *direct* execution. For example, we can trivially change an algorithm (say by adding a fixed number of redundant operations such as "no ops" to each original operation), yet for our purposes we may not want to count this variant as a distinct algorithm—i.e. we may want to count any machine executing the variant as carrying out the same process as the original machine executing the original algorithm. To develop this idea we may need concepts such as that of a canonical description of a process (e.g. along the lines that I tried to sketch in Pylyshyn, 1984b).

tecture that has what is usually referred to as random access memory, in which retrieving a symbol by name or by "reference" is a primitive operation) the time complexity for looking up a symbol in a table can, under certain conditions, be made independent of the number of strings stored. Moreover, in a register architecture an arbitrary string of symbols can be looked up in what is called "real time" (i.e., the lookup is complete after the last symbol in the string has been read). Because of this, a register architecture can directly execute certain algorithms (e.g., hash-coding or discrimination–tree lookup algorithms) which are impossible in the Turing machine—in spite of the fact that the Turing machine is universal, and therefore can compute the *same function* as computed by these algorithms. In other words, the Turing machine can be programmed to be "weakly equivalent" to these algorithms. A Turing machine can thus compute the same lookup function as a register machine, but not with the same complexity profile, and hence not by using the same algorithm.

Now of course a Turing machine could be made to mimic the sequence of states that the register machine goes through by first arranging for it to compute the functions realized by *each individual operation* of the register machine, or in other words by simulating each individual step that the register machine takes in executing its algorithm. But in that case the Turing machine would first be *emulating* the architecture of the register machine and then executing the algorithm in the emulated architecture, a very different matter from computing it directly by the Turing machine.

The distinction between directly executing an algorithm and executing it by first emulating some other functional architecture is crucial to cognitive science. It bears on the central question of which aspects of the computation can be taken literally as part of the cognitive model and which aspects are to be considered as part of the implementation of the model (like the color and materials out of which a physical model of the double helix of DNA is built). We naturally expect that we shall have to have ways of implementing primitive cognitive operations in computers, and that the details of how this is done may have no empirical content.

## Being Explicit about the Architecture: Strong Equivalence

From the point of view of cognitive science it is important to be explicit about *why* a model works the way it does, and to independently justify the crucial assumptions about the cognitive architecture. That is, it is important for the use of computational models as part of an explanation, rather than merely in order to mimic some performance, that we not take certain architectural features for granted simply because they happen to be available in our computer language.

We must first explicitly acknowledge that we are making certain assumptions about the cognitive architecture, and then we must attempt to empirically motivate and justify such assumptions. Otherwise important features of our model may be left resting on adventitious and unmotivated assumptions.

This issue frequently arises in connection with claims that certain ways of doing intellectual tasks, for example by the use of mental imagery, bypasses the need for knowledge of certain logical or even physical properties of the represented domain, and bypasses the need for an inefficient combinatorial process like logical inference. The proposal is often stated in terms of the hypothesis that one or another mental function is carried out by an "analogue" process. From the present perspective this would be interpreted as the claim that some cognitive function was actually part of the cognitive architecture.

Consider cases such as the following. People have occasionally suggested that subjects do not need to have knowledge of relational properties such as, say, transitivity, in making certain inferences, such as in the three-term series problems ("John is taller than Mary and John is shorter than Fred. Who is tallest?"). According to this view, all subjects have to do is arrange the three items in order (either in a list or in an image) and read the answer off—they simply *notice* which objects are, say, first on the list. But of course even if a subject can solve the problem in this way, that does not mean that tacit knowledge of formal properties (e.g., transitivity) of the relation "taller than" is not needed.

There are at least two reasons why one might have to postulate knowledge of formal relations. First, the decision to represent "taller" by something like "further on the list" must have been based on the tacit recognition that the two relations were of the same formal type (a list would not, for example, have been suitable for representing the relation "is married to"). Second, while ordering three names in a list and then examining the list for the position of a particular name may seem straightforward and free from logical deduction, a little thought will show that the ability to carry out this operation mentally, as distinct from physically, presupposes a great deal about the available primitive mental operations. In particular, appealing to the existence of a "mental list" (or some such structure) involves certain assumptions about the properties that such a structure *intrinsically* possesses. For example, if the subject has a mental representation of items A, B, and C and reasons (according to the theory) by placing A and B in a certain order and then adding C next in the sequence, the model must assume that (a) placing C next to B leaves the relation between A and B unchanged, and (b) the relation of A to C (with B between them) will remain the same with respect to the relevant represented relation (i.e., tallness) as that between A and B. Assumptions such as these are justifiable only if there exists an operation in the cognitive architecture which has the same formal mathematical properties (i.e., falls under the same system of logical axioms) as the relations "taller" and "further along the ordering."

## Architecture and Cognitive Capacity

Explaining intelligence is different from predicting certain particular observed behaviors. In order to explain how something works we have to be concerned with sets of *potential* behaviors, most of which might never arise in the normal course of events. Such a potential (or counterfactual) set constitutes the organism's *cognitive capacity*. In order to make this simple point more concrete, consider the following oversimplified example from by book (Pylyshyn, 1984b).

Suppose I showed you a black box into which I had inserted an electrode (Figure 7.1). As we observe the box go about its usual function we discover that the ensuing record exhibits certain regularities. For example, we observe that either individual short pulses or pairs of such short pulses frequently occur in the record, and that when there are both pairs and single pulses (as sometimes happens) the pair appears to regularly precede the single pulse. After observing this pattern for some time we discover that there are occasional exceptions to this order—but only when the whole pattern is preceded by a pair of long and short pulse sequences. Being scientists we are interested in explaining this regularity. What kind of explanation will be most appropriate?

The answer depends upon what sort of device the black box is—and in particular on what its *capacity* is beyond the particular behavior we have just been observing. It depends not just on what it is doing, or what it typically does, but on what it *could* be doing in certain counterfactual (perhaps even quite unnatural) situations—that is, on what I have been calling its "counterfactual set." In this particular example, chosen deliberately to illustrate a point, I can tell

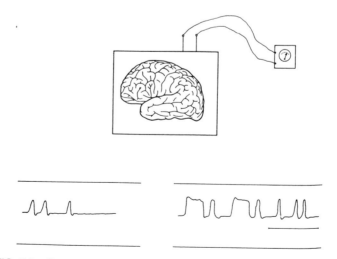

FIG. 7.1.    Systematic patterns of behavior recorded from an unknown black box. The problem is to explain the observed regularity.

you that we would not find the explanation of its behavior in its internal structure, nor in any properties intrinsic to the box or its contents.

But how can the behavior of a system not be due to its internal construction or its inherent properties? What else could possibly explain the regularities it exhibits? It is certainly true that the properties of the box determine the totality of its behavioral repertoire, or its counterfactual set; that is, its capacity. But as long as we have only sampled some limited subset of this repertoire (say, what it "typically" or "normally" does) we may not be in any position to infer what its intrinsically constrained capacity is, hence the observed regularity may tell us nothing about the internal structure or inherent properties of the device. It is easy to be misled by a sample of a system's behavior into assuming the wrong sample space or counterfactual set (a trick well known to some people who sell "expert systems" software).

Let us make this point more concrete by considering the question of why the black box in our example exhibits the particular regularity I told you about. The real reason the black box exhibits this regularity is simply that it is a box for transmitting English words encoded in International Morse Code. Thus the regularity we have discovered is attributable entirely to a spelling rule of English (viz. *i* before *e* except after *c*), together with the IMC code convention. And the reason that providing a detailed description of the component structure and the operation of the box would not explain this regularity is that the structure is capable of exhibiting a much greater range of behaviors—*the observed constraint on its behavior is not attributable to its intrinsic capacity but to what its states represent, which in turn reflect constraints in the represented domain.*

Let's now take another example, which is more directly relevant to cognitive capacity. Consider the regularities of color mixing (e.g., perceived yellow light and perceived red light mix to produce perceived orange light). What sort of account might we expect as an explanation for these regularities: One which appeals to the intrinsic *capacity* of the system, to certain internal biological mechanisms, or one which (as in the Morse Code example) appeals to properties of *what is represented* rather than of the system itself? The question is an empirical one and I wish simply to point out what is at issue and on what kinds of empirical considerations the answer depends. In this case all the evidence points to there being a biological or biochemical mechanism responsible for the regularity. One of the reasons for expecting such an account (apart from the fact that we have quite a large fragment of the account already in hand) is the fact that the regularities appear to be largely insensitive to what subjects think they are looking at, to what they believe about the actual color of these objects and the principles of color mixing, and to what they think the purpose of the experiment is.

Contrast this with the case in which a researcher studies the principles of what might be called "imaginal color mixing" (or the "internal psychophysics of color"). The experimenter might ask subjects to imagine certain colors and to superimpose them in their mental image. The instructions might be something like this: "Imagine a transparent yellow filter beside a transparent red filter. Now imagine that the two filters are slowly moved together until they overlap. What color do you see through the overlapped portion?" Suppose that the investigator discovers a set of reliable principles governing the mixing of imagined colors (in fact, experiments quite similar to this exist in the psychological literature; see the critical discussion in Pylyshyn, 1981). What sort of explanation is likely to be the correct one in this case: one which appeals to biological or biochemical principles—to the intrinsic capacity of the system—or one based on what is represented in the mind of the subject—including what the subject tacitly knows about the principles of color mixing and what the subject assumes the task to be?

Again it is an empirical question, though this time it seems much more likely that a knowledge-level ("tacit" knowledge, to be sure) explanation will be the correct one. The reason for this is that it seems likely that the way colors mix in one's image will depend on what one knows about the regularities of perceptual color mixing[4]—after all, we can make our image of a certain region be whatever color we want it to be!

A test for the validity of this explanation is to determine whether changing what the subject believes *by providing information* (possibly false information) will change the regularity in a logically explicable way. If it is, we say that the regularity is "cognitively penetrable" and conclude that no account based on appeal to intrinsic properties of a mechanism will by itself be adequate to explain the regularity or the way it can be altered. We draw this conclusion (just as we did in the Morse code example earlier), because we know that the evidence does not reveal a cognitively-fixed *capacity;* the underlying mechanism permits a wider range of behaviors than embodied in the empirically observed regularity. What the biological mechanism does provide is a way of *representing* or *encoding* the relevant knowledge, inference rules, decision procedures, and so on—not the observed regularity itself.

The view that I have been sketching (and which is worked out in much more detail in Pylyshyn, 1984b) is implicit in most of contemporary cognitive science practice, and indeed much of psychology generally. For example, while one might consider searching for a neural or biochemical explanation for certain cognitively impenetrable psychophysical capacities (e.g., the Weber function or the acoustical sensitivity curve or the Gestalt principles of perception), it is most

---

[4]Note that one needn't always use what one knows in doing some particular task. Thus, for example, if the experiment described above is carried out people frequently do such things as free associate to the color names, guess, or do just about anything depending on how the task is presented to them. Nothing much follows from this concerning the nature of their imagery mechanism. This can be easily be seen by observing that the same thing happens when the experiment involves imaging a sequence of a number, a plus sign, another number and an equal sign, and the instructions are to imagine the number that comes next. Here too subjects can easily refrain from using their knowledge of arithmetic and imagine any number. But that, of course, tells us nothing about the mechanisms of imagery either: making valid inferences is not the only thing we can do with our knowledge!

unlikely that there could be a biochemical or neurophysiological explanation of how we decide what the italicized pronoun refers to in the following sentence pairs:

1. John gave the book to Fred because *he* finished it.
2. John gave the book to Fred because *he* wanted to read it.

In this case we would expect the explanation to refer to one's knowledge of what books are for and where things end up when they are loaned. Only factors like this would explain why in particular cases the pronouns are assigned different referents in the two sentences and why the reference assignment could be easily changed in a logically coherent way by altering the belief context.[5] In other words the cognitive penetrability of the observed regularity marks it as being knowledge-dependent and as involving reasoning—even if one is not aware of such reasoning taking place. It is within the cognitive capacity of the organism to assign a different referent to the pronoun, with the new assignment being explicable in terms of the same principles that explained the original assignment, namely in terms of an inference from general background beliefs. The difference between the cases would be attributed to a difference in the state of knowledge or belief of the cognizers, and not to a difference in their capacity or cognitive architecture.

Here is another way of looking at why one needs a distinction between cognitive capacity—which remains fixed as the organism's goals and beliefs change with new information—on one hand, and the representation-governed regularities that depend crucially on these goals and beliefs, on the other.

In choosing a particular architecture one makes a commitment concerning which functions are the free parameters that can be tailored to fit specific situations, and which ones are fixed over a certain class of variation of antecedent conditions. And just as having fewer free parameters increases the explanatory power of one's theory, so the more constraining the architecture, the greater the explanatory power of resulting models. This is just the problem of reducing the degrees of freedom available for fitting a model to observations. Whenever some function can be attributed to the cognitive architecture rather than to the rationally modifiable representations, that function attains the status of a constant rather than a free empirical parameter, for purposes of formulating the cognitive model. One goal in developing explanatory cognitive models, then, would be to try to fix as many properties as possible by building them into the cognitively fixed architecture.

---

[5]For example, suppose that we knew that John was trying to encourage Fred to learn to read and had promised Fred the book as a reward if Fred finished reading all of it; or if we knew that John was blind and that Fred would often read to him. In such cases we might well assign the pronouns differently in these sentences.

Opposing this goal, however, is the need to account for the remarkable flexibility of human cognition. This plasticity leads us to attribute the behavioral regularities to the way in which the architecture is used—that is, to the programs and knowledge that allow the relatively rigid architecture to be exploited in generating behavior that is highly plastic. The stimulus-independence of cognition provides one of the strongest reasons for attributing much of its regular behavior patterns to tacit knowledge of various kinds rather than to the sorts of fixed functional properties that have frequently been proposed.

## Architecture and the Autonomy of the Cognitive Level

The need for an independently-motivated theory of the cognitive architecture can also be viewed as arising from the fundamental hypothesis that there exists a natural scientific domain of representation-governed phenomena (or an autonomous "knowledge–level"). The hypothesis that principles at this level can be expressed in terms of the nature of the representations and the structure of programs running on the cognitive architecture, entails that the cognitive architecture itself will not vary in ways that demand the same sort of *representational* or what might be called, without doing too much violence to the term, a *cognitive* explanation. In other words we assume that the architecture forms a cognitive "fixed point" so that differences in cognitive phenomena are explained by appeal to the arrangements (sequences of expressions and of basic operations) among the fixed set of operation; to the way that the resources provided by this architecture are exploited in a particular case. Though the architecture might vary as a function of physical or biochemical conditions, it should not vary directly and in logically coherent ways with changes in the content of the organism's goals and beliefs; it must be what I refer to as *cognitively impenetrable*.

This is often a straightforward criterion to apply in practice. In order to determine whether certain observed regularities favor a particular hypothesized architectural property, we carry out experiments to see whether the regularities in question can be systematically (and rationally) altered by changing subjects' goals or beliefs. If they can, then this suggests that the phenomena do not tell us about the architecture, but rather they tell us about some representation-governed process; something which, in other words, would remain true even if the architecture were different from that hypothesized.

For example, this appears to be the case with certain kinds of imagery phenomena, such as the linear relation between reaction time and the distance on a mental image that is mentally "scanned" (for more on this case, see Pylyshyn, 1981). That's because the linear increase can be made to disappear by changing the instructions; for example, by asking subjects to imagine a situation in which they do not believe there would be any increase in reaction time as a function of distance (that is, in which they believe there would be no relation between time and distance in the *real* situation which they are to imagine).

In general, if we can show that a certain regularity is cognitively penetrable we have good reason to believe that it involves reasoning. This, in turn, provides strong grounds for assuming that it is attributable, at least in part, to the nature of the representations and the cognitive processes operating over these them.[6] Thus cognitive penetrability is an important methodological tool for determining whether certain patterns reflect properties of the architecture or of the rational treatment of goals, beliefs, and knowledge—that is, of decision–theoretic considerations.

This, then, is a rough sketch of some reasons why I consider the study of cognitive architecture to be of central concern in cognitive science. Now I turn to the chapters that have been presented earlier in this volume to see how they contribute to this enterprise and how they fit in this scheme. Two of the chapters (by McClelland & Jenkins and by Oliver & Schneider) are concerned with certain problems posed by the connectionist approach to architecture. Another two (by VanLehn & Ball and by Anderson) are concerned with the possibility that some of the phenomena that have been attributed to either architectures or to representations may in fact belong to certain properties of the world outside (to the "situation" in the case of VanLehn & Ball, or to the rational demands of the task in the case of Anderson). Although there is a lot of meat in all four of these chapters I concentrate of some of the themes that they share with their intellectual neighbors in order to try to get at the more general messages that they provide.

## SOME COMMENTS ON THE CHAPTER THEMES

### Connectionist Architectures

Two of the chapters are on issues concerned with connectionist architectures. Since Jerry Fodor and I recently published a 69 page critique of this approach (Fodor & Pylyshyn, 1988), I do not attempt to give you all my views on that subject. I do, however, point to a few things that we discuss which relate directly to general remarks I made earlier concerning the nature of cognitive architecture.

### Architecture and Levels

A number of different arguments have been made in favor of connectionist networks, and against what Fodor and I call "classical architecture" (i.e., architectures which carry out computations by operating on semantically interpreted, structured symbolic expressions), some of which are repeated in this volume.

---

[6]Of course, in practice there is always the question of exactly which stage of the process is affected by the instructions or other cognitive manipulations, but this is not a problem unique to the penetrability criterion. All interpretations of observations in science involve the provisional acceptance of ancillary assumptions.

Almost none of these, however, are actually arguments about *cognitive architecture,* but are either about typical implementations of classical architectures in contemporary machines (e.g., that they are serial, sensitive to physical damage, etc.) or they are about certain characteristics of contemporary classical models—characteristics that are not constitutive of classical symbol processing systems. Thus, for example, the "hundred step constraint," or the "resistance to damage" property, which is supposed to favor a connectionist architecture both apply only to certain kinds of implementations of classical architectures, not to the architectures themselves. In fact, the discussion of these issues systematically confuses implementation and architecture. For example, even contemporary electronic computers are "massively parallel" at their implementation level (e.g., they involve simultaneous parallel electronic activity throughout the CPU and even in much of the memory during every clock cycle), and could quite easily be implemented to be resistant to physical damage (say by using holographic instead of electronic media for memory, but keeping the same register architecture). Moreover, there is nothing about symbol-processing architectures that prevents them from being stochastic, from using continuous magnitudes, or from supporting parallel execution, nor is there anything that requires them to have explicitly encoded rules (i.e., rules that are executed interpretively). These are not the issues that divide symbol–processing from connectionist proposals. The relevant level is the one at which the system transforms semantically interpreted representations. Keeping this firmly in mind would go a long way towards cleaning up much of this "levels" confusion.

## Systematicity of the *Capacity* for Representing and Inferring

If the knowledge level description of intelligent systems is correct (and, as I said, virtually everyone assumes it) then we have to explain how it is possible for a physical system, like a human being, to behave in ways that correspond to the knowledge-level principles, while at the same time being governed by physical laws. At the present time there is only one candidate explanation for how knowledge-level principles can be causally realized, and that is the proposal that builds on a set of ideas going back to the insights of Boole, Hilbert, Turing, Frege, and other logicians. It says that knowledge is *encoded* by a system of symbolic codes, which themselves are physically realized, and that it is the physical properties of the codes that cause the behaviors in question.

What Fodor and Pylyshyn (1988) have added to this general statement is an argument that the system of codes must be *structured* much like a language (as, indeed, it is in the various logical calculi that have been developed). The argument stems in part from the observation that both representational capacity and inferential capacity in intelligent systems is *systematic*. Representational or inferential capacities are not punctate—they do not occur in isolation: The capacity for representing certain things or for drawing certain inferences goes along with the capacity for representing other things and for drawing other inferences. For example, an intelligent system that is capable of representing certain situations (e.g., that John loves Mary, or that a small red ball is in a large blue box), must also be capable—whether or not this capacity is exercised—of representing other situations involving the same conceptual components (e.g., that Mary loves John or that a large blue ball is in small red box). More abstractly, an intelligent system that is capable of representing P&Q is also able to represent P alone or Q alone. Similarly, any intelligent system that can draw certain inferences (e.g., can infer that it is sunny, from knowing that it is sunny and warm and humid; i.e., infer P from P and Q and R), can also draw other related inferences (e.g., can infer that it is sunny, from knowing that it is sunny and warm; i.e., infer P from P and Q alone).

This sort of systematicity follows automatically from the use of structured symbolic expressions to represent knowledge and to serve as the basis for inference. That's because to represent P&Q is to "write down"[7] an expression that has both P and Q *as parts*. In other words systematicity of representational capacity is a side–effect of a classical architecture. In contrast it is a property that must be stipulated and enforced by the theorist (i.e., it is a free empirical parameter) in other non-symbolic architectures, such as connectionist architectures. Hence the classical architectures provide a natural explanation for a property of cognitive capacity that is left unexplained in other architectures.

## Connectionism and Learning

Connectionist models have concentrated on issues of learning, over issues of sufficiency—that is, over question of whether they have sufficient expressive and computational power. I have already comment on the latter. But how well do they fare in their analysis of learning? Let's look first at the kind of learning studied by connectionists and at the kinds of mechanisms that they have proposed for dealing with the problems of acquisition of knowledge.

The first thing to note is that connectionist learning is learning by assimilating variance among the set of stimuli (i.e., it is statistical). Internal parameters (weights) are increased or decreased to reflect certain (high order, to be sure)

---

[7]The notion of "writing" symbols is a familiar one to computer people, and it can me made mathematically quite precise. What it entails is that there exist a mapping from inscriptions to physical properties of the system which preserves the theoretically relevant properties of the expressions—for example which preserves their structure (see, for example, footnote 9 of Fodor & Pylyshyn, 1988).

statistical patterns that have occurred in the inputs.[8] What kinds of human learning experiences fit this paradigm? Well, some of them do. Perhaps some motor skill learning does. I was going to say that rote paired–associates learning and classical or operand conditioning do, but even that's not so clear. There is good reason to believe that conditioning in humans may be best explained in terms of subjects' discovery of the reward contingencies (e.g., by being told, or by seeing the apparatus being set up, or by drawing inferences from what they see and hear, together with what they know) and then simply acting in their best interests—that is, acting rationally, given their beliefs and utilities (Brewer, 1974).

Putting such cases aside for now, what about the cases more typically studied—for example, learning to read (Sejnowski & Rosenberg, 1987), learning verb morphology (McClelland & Rumelhart, 1986), or learning the operation of logical gates, as in the Oliver and Schneider studies reported at this conference? Can these be explained in terms of some sort of sophisticated statistical pattern-

---

[8]Although many connectionist networks models, such as the Boltzmann machine described by (Hinton & Sejnowski, 1986), are quite explicitly designed to reflect the statistical patterns in their inputs, the assertion that connectionist learning systems in general are "statistical pattern matchers" frequently raises strong objections. It's quite true that what connectionist networks do is different in many interesting ways from what you get from a multiple regression curve-fitting procedure. The process is non-linear, it involves higher-order statistics, it allows patterns to be inferred between inputs that have never occurred together before (although that is standard in statistical devices because of the transitivity of correlations among stochastic variables), it allows feedback to be used to bias the process in a direction dictated by the instructor (analogously to the use of "marker variables" in certain statistical procedures), and so on. Moreover, the system has some initial structure and dynamic principles which allows the statistically data to be assimilated into what amounts to a certain a priori *similarity metric* that may be quite non–obvious.

However, there are two aspects of the learning that lead me to refer to it as "statistical". One is that it is typically frequency-sensitive. Everything else being equal, more frequent events are given higher weight in the learning. The other is that although the structure of the network contributes to the learning, the inputs affect the state of the system in a way that is *interpretation independent*. Unlike the learning that a scientist engages in when observing nature, the input and the system's knowledge do not interact through a process of inference or *reasoning*. That's because the only mechanisms we know that can model general reasoning—reasoning from an open-ended database of knowledge—do it by *proof theoretic* or symbolic means. For more on the latter, see Fodor and Pylyshyn (1988).

Because of this, the equivalence classes into which inputs are assigned when the system has learned to some level of proficiency—or the similarity space to which stimuli are assigned—are the wrong ones; they are not *semantically defined* classes, such as classes that correspond to some stimuli having been interpreted the same way, say as the same distal object. Such partitions of stimuli into equivalence classes would not, for example, distinguish two views of the Necker Cube since the objective input is identical for both. Consequently the wrong generalizations are bound to occur, exactly as they do in models of perception when the products of perception are characterized extensionally in terms of the objective stimulus, without recourse to a process of inference (cf. Fodor & Pylyshyn, 1981).

matching mechanism? The answer depends on how seriously one takes intransigent counterexamples, as opposed to percent variance accounted for, as a measure of the adequacy of such theories.

The problem is this: Learning is not only varied in its types and mechanisms, but most cognitive learning is like the learning that goes on when scientist learn about the world around them. It is not learning by changing probability estimates, but learning by framing hypotheses and reasoning about the way that evidence bears on those hypotheses. It is learning that combines what one is told, what one sees, and what one already believes. Moreover, the combining is done in a rational way, not haphazardly. If I tell you that in my house the coffee is kept in the refrigerator, and you happen to be in my house wanting a cup of coffee, you will put together what I said, with your recognition (i.e., learning) that a certain piece of equipment on the kitchen shelf is a coffee maker (even if it is one you have not seen before), your general knowledge of how to make coffee, your knowledge that water comes out of taps, your expectation that the tap on the right is for cold water, and countless other items of both general and particular knowledge. You will put all these diverse things, including your desire for a cup of coffee, together in a rational manner and you will come to know how to make coffee in my house. In the course of this quite legitimate kind of learning, you will also be learning things about the locations of objects, about the operation of things, about the fact that some of your expectations will be violated, and so on. All this clearly involves reasoning. A theory of learning which does not contain a theory or reasoning is doomed to leave out almost everything interesting about (at least human) learning.

Even where the domain appears to be relatively closed, as in the case of, say, learning to read by converting strings of letters into sounds, it is easy to show that a procedure which attends only to the statistical distributions of stimuli will not learn correctly in general. An argument that Jerry Fodor is fond of citing is directed against statistics–based learning–to–read models, such as NetTalk (Sejnowski & Rosenberg, 1987). He points out that such a system could never learn certain phonological patterns of English which every native English speaker has implicitly mastered, such as the pattern that determines whether a consonant is soft or hard. The reason is that the basis for this regularity is not found in the statistics of letter-sound combinations, but involves a rule which must have access to other information. For example, the different /g/ sounds in the two words "Swingle Singers" arises because of a phonological rule that says that /g/ is hardened if it occurs in a noun derived from a verb. Moreover, this rule is productive, so that if we knew that there were workers, called "longers" who stretched things to make them long, and we came across a reference to the tallest of these workers, we would read the novel phrase "the longer longer" with the correct phonetic shape. Similarly, the stress that we place at various points in reading a sentence reflect both syntactic and semantic factors and cannot be inferred from samples of text alone.[9]

The same is true of perception more generally. The point is that what we see something *as* (what we take it to be) is context-dependent in a particular way. It depends not only on the context of the stimulus set, but also on more general knowledge, expectations, and inference. In other words, perception is knowledge-dependent and inference-dependent, and so cannot be induced from sets of visual stimuli together with their classifications. Of course, there is an earlier stage of vision (sometimes called "early vision") for which this is not true, so it is at least possible that some early vision processes could be learned this way, although the evidence in the case of mammalian vision offers little support of a perceptron-like learning mechanism at this level either.

## Some Compromise Connectionist Alternatives

There are several natural options available for anyone who wants to preserve the techniques of connectionism in the case of higher level cognition. One, which is a step towards dealing with the systematicity issue, is to design the connectionist network to implement recursive symbol structures. This appears to be the option that some people, including Touretsky (1986) or Hinton (1988), have taken. The attempt here is to develop ways for the network to implement complex symbols with a part-whole structure. Although I do not believe the particular way that Hinton (1988) has chosen to implement such hierarchies will work,[10] there is no doubt that there is *some* way to do it within a connectionist network (since one can, after all, simulate a Turing Machine tape in a network). Another closely related option, required this time to deal with the complexity-scaling problem, is one that Oliver and Schneider take: Break the phenomena onto stages and intro-

---

[9]Of course one might reply that even if the information is not present in the learning-to-read trials alone, it *is* there in the total sample of sentences that a person ever hears, because that's what allows us how we learn the grammar of a language. This, however, presumes that a connectionist network can first learn the grammar from presentations of sentences alone, and then can use the grammar to learn the right phonological rules. This is more than a little dubious, given the results of learnability theory (Osherson, Stob, & Weinstein, 1984; Wexler & Cullicover, 1980), the combinatorial nature of parsing, and the constituent-structure of sentence representations (discussed in Fodor & Pylyshyn, 1988).

[10]The reason that such a network will not work is, in part, that there is an important difference between a representation *having* a constituent structure, and merely having a way to *represent* a part–whole hierarchy. The systematicity argument sketched earlier requires that a representation of P be *part of* the representation of P&Q in order for the required representational systematicy to be exhibited. Moreover, the attempt to achieve the effect of having symbol structures (as required, for example, in order to represent sentences) without having stored symbol structures, say by encoding sets of symbol-position pairs in the network, runs into other serious problem: Again, see Fodor and Pylyshyn (1988).

duce control mechanisms, including mechanisms for focusing attention and for binding variables. This strategy appears to be on the right road to developing enough computational power to allow the resulting system to meet certain performance criteria and perhaps even to scale up reasonably.

However, one should note several things about this approach. One is that it is the beginning of a road that ends just where one would expect—with connectionist mechanisms implementing a classical symbol processing architecture. All you need to do is introduce structured expressions, break the process into many subprocesses, and introduce a control apparatus, and you will have not only a classical computer, but even a highly conventional serial architecture which separates the executive from the memory—an architecture explicitly denied by connectionist polemics (e.g., McClelland, Rumelhart, & Hinton, 1986). The second thing to note is that the critical aspects of the new design, the structured symbols in Hinton's case and the articulated subprocesses and control apparatus in Oliver and Schneider's case, are not themselves *learned*. What is learned are the contents of memory; whatever is in the pattern-based lookup table. Whether or not this is empirically sustainable I don't know, but at least the learning has been circumscribed to a plausible part of the system, the memory. The architecture of the system itself has now become a pretty conventional one. Moreover, only the way the memory is *implemented*—that is, its subcognitive (nonsemantic) workings—is connectionist. All of which is just what we should have expected.

## Some Miscellaneous Remarks on the Connectionist Chapters

Before closing this discussion of the connectionist chapters, I would like to add a remark about a claim made in the Schneider and Oliver chapter as well as to remark on one aspect of the McClelland and Jenkins chapter.

With respect to the Schneider and Oliver chapter, the claim is made that this is an example of a "hybrid" model, wherein elements of connectionist techniques are blended with some classical symbolic computing ideas. Although there is a sense in which this is true, inasmuch as their model does use some connectionist learning principles, it is also a misleading way to put it since, from the perspective of the broader argument between connectionist and classical architectures, the Schneider and Oliver model is a clear example of a classical model. The only thing that is hybrid is the level at which the model is described. Schneider and Oliver describe both the information processing carried out by the system *and* the way in which they believe some of the basic architectural facilities are implemented. I have no comments to make concerning the likelihood that these proposals are correct (except for the general remarks I have already made regarding learning), but there is nothing about their story that is at variance with standard information-processing methodology and classical architectures. It is very much the sort of story you might give if someone asked how a bubble-sort algorithm works on a VAX computer. You might give the algorithm in some canonical notation. But you might also say something about how the VAX actually carries out some of the basic instructions in this algorithm, because that might be relevant to such questions as the precision with which matches are made, or the size of arrays that can be handled without swapping, and so on. The fact that you give a hybrid story of this kind in no way implies that you are departing from a classical symbol-processing architecture. It's just that implementations do affect some aspects of observed behavior; something that should come as no surprise to either supporters or detractors of the classical position, since it is plainly true of ordinary electronic computers.

Let me try once again to make the point that Fodor and I have been trying to make for some time. There is a principled level of description that defines the cognitive architecture, and hence the distinction between symbolic processes and their implementation in some physical system. However, when you explain how a computational system works, you may wish to describe more than the functional architecture and the symbol structures it processes; you may also want to describe how the architecture is physically or biologically realized. For many purposes it may be crucial to describe such things. For example, you can't make sense of why a computer acts differently when the temperature gets too high or when it swaps to a slow disk, or why a person acts differently under the influence of alcohol or drugs unless you do give such a mixed description. Nobody knows exactly which features of behavior will require such a description; perhaps frequency-based learning is such a property. That's all perfectly reasonable and routine in both psychology and computer science and hardly to the credit of connectionist theorizing.

Schneider and Oliver also cite the complexity of cognitive processes as an argument for paying attention to implementation issues. However, I find the appeal to complexity as an argument for connectionist modeling to be more than a little beside the point. The concern for complexity is not only compatible with the classical symbol-processing approach, it has always been its bread and butter. That's precisely why the study of cognitive architecture (though not necessarily its implementation) is an important part of information processing psychology (e.g., it is the main concern of the analysis in Pylyshyn, 1984b). The reason is precisely the one given by Schneider and Oliver, namely, cognitive science is interested not only in what can be computed in principle, but also in what can be computed within realistic time and memory constraints, as well as any other constraints that we discover to be intrinsic to the human cognitive architecture. Far from being a discovery of, or an advantage of, the connectionist approach, it has been the mainstay of the classical symbolic approach and is the reason that "strong equivalence," which I spoke of earlier, is the goal of model builders working in the information processing tradition.

Let us turn now to the McClelland and Jenkins chapter. McClelland and Jenkins offer a connectionist simulation of the developmental sequence exhibited by children dealing with the balance-beam problem, a simulation which matches well the sequence described by Siegler's rules.

But it is surely not much of an accomplishment to get a connectionist network to learn to simulate the behavior of a system of rules, once you know what the rules are. There are enough degrees of freedom in these models to simulate a wide range of functions (though, in fact, we don't know *how* wide a range of functions they can learn to realize, and that too is one of their problems—but this is a topic for another occasion). A more useful approach would be to start off with a well defined and independently constrained architecture and then observe that any model built to carry out the task in this class of architecture would lead naturally to behavior which conforms to Siegler's rule system.[11] That's not what happens here and it is not what happens in the Rumelhart and McClelland (1986) model of verb morphology learning, as Lachter and Bever (1988) have documented in detail. What happens in both cases is that a lot of arbitrary decisions are made and the system is finely tuned until the desired behavior, the one correctly described by some system of rules, is exhibited. McClelland and Jenkins themselves note some of these design decisions. For example, a great deal of the credit for the order in which the model develops its skill should be ascribed to the choice of the order and frequency of presentation of the examples, rather than to the structure of the model. In the absence of independent empirical confirmation that children have more experience with weight differences than distance differences, the decision to provide more examples in which weight is varied than ones in which distance is varied is a rather transparent way of ensuring that the role of weight is learned first. Moreover, dealing with this criticism by elevating the decision to the status of an "environment assumption" does not diminish the fact that it is another free parameter that can be used to fit experimental data.

The basic problem is that the process of applying connectionist ideas to particular models is enormously underconstrained. Consequently a vast number of arbitrary decisions have to be made (which Lachter & Bever, 1988, call "TRICS," for "*T*he *R*epresentations *I*t *C*rucially *S*upposes") and it is these *arbitrary decisions,* rather than the architecture itself, that should be credited with the close match that the resulting system exhibits to the system of rules.

There are other features of the connectionist approach which point to its ultimate inadequacy for dealing with intellectual problems of the balance-beam sort. In discussing the putative advantage of this approach, McClelland and

---

[11]This, by the way, is exactly what happened in Newell's (1973a) model of rapid memory scanning experiments. By trying to build a model of memory scanning within the constraints of the production system architecture, Newell was led quite naturally to an alternative novel model that predicted the linear memory scanning results.

Jenkins emphasized that the model was able to simulate some of Siegler's results *without using or "consulting" explicit rules* of the kind that Siegler himself had formulated. Now, as Fodor and I have pointed out repeatedly, classical symbolic models do not require all rules to be executed in "interpreted" mode—i.e., they do not require that the rules be explicitly encoded and accessed in generating the behavior. Note however, that the converse is not true: connectionist architectures do not provide a way of explicitly representing rules and accessing them in generating behavior (except, of course, by first simulating a classical rule system architecture, as is done, for example, by Touretsky, 1986, 1989). Nor do they provide a way to deal with other explicit items of knowledge, such as the torque rule, which can be taught. While it might be argued that one should first model the simpler aspects of development—that the model must learn to walk before it learns to fly—the generality of this shortcoming suggests that there will be no way to scale the model up in intelligence to include anything requiring reasoning or appeal to known general principles. Even with the subjects studied by Siegler there is a suggestion (cited in the McClelland & Jenkins paper) that some subjects could verbalize something of what they were doing. In other studies it has been found that although tacit knowledge often cannot be articulated, when it can it frequently corresponds to what subjects are in fact doing. But these kinds of articulatable—and teachable—principles cannot be accommodated in a connectionist architecture, for reasons discussed at length in Fodor and Pylyshyn (1988).

Besides not being able to accommodate explicit rules and principles, connectionist models such as that of McClelland and Jenkins typically do not have a rich set of concepts to work from. While this may not be a principled limitation, as is the case with the inability to encode rules and expressions, it is nonetheless endemic to models (like McClelland & Jenkins') that attempt to learn with minimal intellectual structure. In the present case, the model has no concept of multiplication or even of magnitude. So far as it is concerned, what is learned is a pattern of distance-weight combinations. Thus in the present case it learns that the weight-distance pairs, say, 20-1, 10-2, and 5-4 balance one another. But it could equally easily learn that weight-distance combinations 10-5, 20-2, and 5-1 balance one another if those were the examples presented. That's because although we call one of the inputs distance and the other weight, they are just different elementary "units" in the model. They have no intrinsic metrical properties nor any natural arithmetical relations. Although I know of no experimental data on this question, I would be very surprised if the same were true of children learning the balance beam. In fact I would be surprised if children could learn arbitrary patterns which could not be given a simple arithmetical characterization, for example, in terms of such relations as multiplication or addition. It may even be that children approach this problem with some rough concept of torque already available to them. As I have tried to point out on many occasions, the frequency-based notion of learning that pervades connectionist models is extremely impoverished and very likely plays only a minor role in intellectual development.

Now one might reply that there is a sense in which these are unfair criticisms of an approach that is so new; one needs time to explore these ideas in a general and unbiased manner before passing judgment on their value. I agree with this position. I do believe that the connectionist architecture should be empirically explored over a range of tasks to see whether it has anything to offer certain (though clearly not all) areas of cognition. One of the discoveries one might hope to make is that certain tasks that were thought to require rules and representations can be carried out without this cognitive apparatus—that these tasks are carried out by the architecture itself. As I said earlier, precisely *which* phenomena fall under knowledge-level principles cannot be prescribed in advance, but remain to be discovered. The only thing I would add to this is that the results that have emerged to date in the exploration of the capacities of connectionist networks hardly merit the excitement that has been engendered. In fact, the results suggest that a certain degree of modesty may be appropriate when stating the claims for this architecture—a modesty that is not apparent in the introductory parts of the essays in the PDP volumes (e.g., McClelland, Rumelhart, & Hinton, 1986) or in most other connectionist manifestos.

## Some Comments About the SOAR Project

Before closing these comments about different architectural proposals, I want to add some comments on one of the most ambitious attempts to design a general architecture (in this case a "classical" one) for intelligence, the SOAR project. This project is intended, in part, to meet Newell's challenge issued at an earlier Carnegie Symposium on Cognition (Newell, 1973b): instead of addressing empirical questions one by one (in what Newell characterized as the "twenty questions" style of research), try to design a system whose goal is to (eventually) be adequate for the entire range of intellectual tasks. I have a great respect for this extremely ambitious research program (for it is a research program, rather than a model designed to fit particular experimental data). Since SOAR is one of the approaches featured at this meeting, I want to make some general remarks concerning the basic assumptions which implicitly guide the project. I want to suggest that some of them may turn out to be on the wrong track, if the recent history of other areas of cognitive science can serve as a guide (particularly visual perception and psycholinguistics). I am not claiming that SOAR is irrevocably wedded to these assumptions, but they do reflect the spirit of the project as it has proceeded so far.

The assumption I want to question concerns the uniformity of the cognitive architecture, both in its structure and in the way in which its behavior is modified, that is, the way it learns. Uniformity of the cognitive architecture and uniformity of learning principles appear to be general working assumptions. Yet neither, it seems to me, is warranted on the face of it. There are a number of areas of cognitive science that have seen some progress in recent decades and where it appears reasonably clear that cognitive processes are going on which are not of the sort that SOAR addresses—in particular, they are not processes that can reasonably be thought of as driven by a single large database, using a recognize–act cycle of rule application, and they do not appear to be processes which change by chunking rules into larger units.

In the first category I have in mind evidence of cognitive modularity. By modularity, I mean that the cognitive database appears to be systematically partitioned; there appear to be processes that are systematically prohibited *by the architecture itself* from accessing information that is *relevant* to carrying out their task efficiently. The evidence is now reasonably persuasive that in spatial vision, the perceptual system does its work without availing itself of what the rest of the cognitive system expects (or even knows with certainty) to be in the visual field. No amount of knowledge about the various visual illusions will make the illusions disappear. Moreover, it is pretty clear that certain perceptual-motor actions (such as reaching or locomotion) proceed without using relevant knowledge that the cognitive system has concerning the spatial layout of the world around it (Goodale, 1988). It is also pretty clear to those who follow the details of the experimental literature in psycholinguistics, that the human sentence parser does not avail itself of knowledge that the cognitive system has about the discourse topic while it is parsing phrases. While the data are not uncontrovercial, there is surely enough converging evidence by now that parts of the cognitive system are cognitively impenetrable, and yet are complex enough to not be single operations in the cognitive architecture. In particular, the view that has rules being matched against all of the cognitive database is surely untenable.

Of course SOAR provides a mechanism for dividing up the database. All that is required is that some subset of the productions contain a designated symbol as part of its condition. Then the productions in this subset will only be available if that particular symbol occurs in working memory. Thus one might conclude that a partitioned database is the rule, rather than the exception in SOAR. But notice that this partitioning is in terms of the content of knowledge—it's the sort of thing that the system knows or learns about; it's not a consequence of the architecture itself. In other words, it's not a consequence of the structurally fixed property of the mental mechanism that we call its architecture. SOAR also has a way of creating automatic behavior from exposure to deliberate behavior (the rule chunking mechanism)—so it has a way by which the system can arrive at insulated subsets of rules. But that too is not an insularity that is architectural—it can differ willy-nilly depending on the system's experience. The modularity claim is that the insularity, the cognitive impenetrability, is architecturally given. Although it need not be entirely innate, the claim is that it is principled and can't be changed by anything so ephemeral and individual as the experience of past problem–solving episodes.

As an architecture, SOAR may not be irrevocably committed to the single uniform database view. Yet that seems so far to be in the spirit of the enterprise.[12] Even if SOAR is viewed as the architecture of the central processor only (which is not the way it is viewed, see Laird, Rosenbloom, & Newell, 1988), it is still not clear that a uniform architecture is warranted. For example, there is reason to believe that processes such as reasoning using mental images may involve a different set of architectural mechanisms.[13] Where that spirit seems most ill advised (as, for example, in spatial vision) is where there is also the most reason to question whether the production system architecture (together with the uniform memory and single working-memory context) is the right one. In these cases, for example, some topographically-organized representation, together with a parallel constraint-satisfaction processes operating over topographically-local neighborhoods appears most natural (which, I hasten to add, does not implicate a non-symbolic connectionist architecture: constraint satisfaction by parallel label–propagation is classical symbol–processing).

Of course SOAR can be used to implement a parallel constraint-satisfaction process, inasmuch as it is a universal architecture (modulo assumptions about

---

[12]Since this was written I note that in Newell's William James Lectures (Newell, 1990) provision is made for a somewhat special medium of representation for the inputs and outputs of *Perception* and *Motor* productions in SOAR. In particular, Perception is said to put its elements into a part of working memory that is organized as topographical fields with intrinsic metrical properties, whereas the Motor productions provide inputs to *coordinative structures* built up of composed dynamic systems. Whether these sorts of deviations from uniformity represent a significant movement in a direction away from a single architecture is not clear since these are the least developed aspects of the SOAR architecture. However they are the sorts of directions in which we can expect a system to develop which is responsive to the modularity of the cognitive architecture. The communications restriction between modules (which is the hallmark of modular design) may turn out to be a consequence of the different media or the different symbolic "vocabularies" that they are perforce required to adopt.

[13]There are those, I am told, who are surprised to hear me endorse this idea, in view of the energy I have spent criticizing what is sometimes called the "imagery view". But I have always held that there is something special about reasoning with the aid of images. The problem is, nobody has been able to articulate what that special thing is. My criticisms over the years (e.g., Pylyshyn, 1973, 1981) have always been directed at particular proposals which, in my view, fell far short of providing an adequate account of what goes on when people "use" mental images. One litmus test of whether the accounts add anything new is to ask whether they explain anything that could not be explained just as naturally in terms of a single-architecture model which contained only propositional information (or, as some would put it (Paivio, 1986), a "single code" model—although that way of putting it is even more problematic since it is far from clear how we should individuate *types* of codes). The fact that the answer has invariably been "no" means that the natural null hypothesis has not been supplanted—it does not mean that the null hypothesis is correct. In fact I feel quite sure it is false, but it is the default hypothesis: One does not discard the hypothesis that all cognition arises from common architecture without both empirical evidence that such an architecture is inadequate *and* at least some sketch of one that might fare better. This we do not have for different types of reasoning, including imagistic reasoning, as of the time of this writing.

resource bottlenecks), but this runs counter to the spirit of the "blackboard" type of control structure it uses. The point of the blackboard is that every rule has an equal opportunity to examine every state of knowledge; there are no principled barriers to information flow. Yet such principled barriers appear to be exactly what is required for both parallel relaxation methods and for a modular design. The constraint satisfaction processes that appear useful in early vision lend themselves nicely to an implementation involving many processors each of which has access to very circumscribed "local" information. That, indeed, is what makes it possible to implement constraint satisfaction efficiently under certain conditions.

The second aspect of uniformity that I think is ill-advised concerns learning. The study of learning has been one of the saddest episodes in the history of psychology. The attempt, in this century, to build a science of psychology around a priori assumptions concerning the mechanisms which must be used to get into some final state of performance, has been a resounding failure. The mechanism that has been assumed (and is still assumed in connectionist theorizing) is that of association, a pairing of states derived from co-occurrences of properties or events in the environment. The SOAR system improves on this proposal by using a more structured mechanism: learning occurs when the system discovers that goals can be satisfied by taking certain short-cuts through the problem trace, thus leading to new and more aggregated rules (giving rise to chunking).

There is nothing wrong with this proposal that I can see. There have been many attempts to develop similar ideas in the past (e.g., the original "chunking" idea of Miller, the use of "well-formed subgraphs" by "chart parsers," the STRIPS MACROPS, and so on) and this one improves on these by offering an elegant way for the macro-rules to be compiled automatically through experience. Moreover, the partial nature of these learned rules results in an interesting form of generalization. The problem lies not with the details of the particular proposal, but with the implicit assumption, which it shares with all other theories of learning in psychology, that this, finally, is *the* mechanism by which organisms learn. But I see no reason to think that there is such a thing as *the learning mechanism*. Organisms alter their behavior as a result of problem-solving experience, as assumed in the SOAR model; but they also alter their behavior as a result of passive exposure, as a result of being instructed, as a result of trial and error, as a result of single exposures to the right stimulus, as a result of reasoning, as a result of perceptual reorganization (as in the case of "insight learning" such as studied by Kohler) and as a result of who knows what other kinds of processes (including, if Chomsky is right, of plugging in the right parameter values in a highly restricted innate schema). Which of these is *real learning?* The question is surely misstated: there may well be no such natural kind as "learning." There may, instead, be various ways in which organisms and environments interact to change the state of the organism.

This does not mean that the SOAR chunking mechanism does not have an important role to play. But it does mean that an architecture may have to have a lot more innate structure and many more ways, besides chunking, for changing in response to experience. Recent work in the theory of learnability (Osherson, Stob, & Weinstein, 1984; Wexler & Cullicover 1980) shows clearly that "poverty of the stimulus" considerations require that the learning system be extremely restricted in what possibilities they entertain and what they are prepared to get out of their experience. Again, the SOAR approach does not preclude any of this, but such considerations do appear to go against the spirit of the enterprise, which attempts to design a *uniform* architecture for learning, reasoning and performance. I doubt very much that such a uniform architecture is in the cards, at least not at the cognitive level. There may, of course, be a uniform structure at the cellular or biochemical level, or at some other non-cognitive biological level; indeed it's hard to see how this can fail to be the case, given that the science of biology is, by definition, concerned with discovering the principles by which all organic objects operate. Thus I do believe that there is a grain of truth in the connectionists' intuitions; many of the problems that people pretheoretically feel to be problems of cognition will turn out not to be problems that fall within that domain, that is, they may turn out not to be representation-governed symbol-processing problems. My own hunch is that a lot of what we call learning, especially concept attainment, will be in that category (see Pylyshyn, 1984a).

## Externalizing the Constraints

There is quite a long tradition in psychology that attempts to explain many of the patterns of behavior in terms of principles and constraints located outside the organism. One of the best known of these schools is J. J. Gibson's "direct realism" approach to perception, which itself derives from the ecological psychology of Egon Brunswick. This approach attempts to finesse some of the hard problems of perception by redefining both what serves as the "stimulus" and what the perceptual task is. I will not go into the reasons why this extremely ambitious and far-reaching approach is doomed to failure (see, however, Fodor & Pylyshyn, 1981). However, the idea that we should attribute many of the organism's regularities to properties of the environment is an attractive one that keeps resurfacing. In fact, the idea has an important place in the work of Newell and Simon (1972) (see, also, Simon's chapter in this volume), and is the point of Simon's famous ant-on-the-beach parable (Simon, 1969). More recently it has reappeared as a new attempt to provide a naturalized semantics, in Barwise and Perry's (1983) "situated semantics." So far the "situational" approach has not had a large impact in cognitive science, although I note that at least some the terminology has made its way into the chapter by VanLehn and Ball.

There is a lot that I agree with in both the VanLehn and Ball chapter and the Anderson chapter. It is important that we acknowledge the role of factors other than the organism's capacity in determining its performance. That, in fact, was the point of my code-box example earlier. Like Anderson, though in a very different context and to a quite different purpose, VanLehn and Ball suggest that we have overlooked the importance of the environment itself in serving both the functions of memory and retrieval cues. They show, quite convincingly, that "goal reconstruction" is an important activity in planning and is also one that can be greatly aided by "situating" the plan formation process among the objects of perception. However, in my view some writers have taken this idea too far (e.g., in Suchman's externalization of the plan, or in Rosenschein's (1985) and connectionists' eliminativist position on explicit knowledge representation).

In explaining performance in the exercise of such skills as arithmetic, there is always an empirical question of just what subjects do know and how they index this knowledge so as to bring it to bear when it is relevant. What VanLehn and Ball appear to have demonstrated, and also to have successfully modeled, is that in doing arithmetic, subjects may index their knowledge of their goals in terms of certain intermediate states of the written problem-solution trace. This enables them to retrieve the relevant knowledge by examining the partially-solved problem. This is, of course, a very useful way to index the knowledge since one can easily be distracted while working on a long multiplication problem.

All this seems quite sensible. But it does not entail that a plan is not stored in these cases. All it means is that some of the plan is in the form of implicit generative procedures that can be indexed from visual information. But it is still a stored plan: it is still a cognitive representation. In fact, it is just the sort of representation that must be involved in all generative capacities, like mathematics and language.

The finding that arithmetic knowledge may in part be stored as procedures indexed to visual cues, is a useful and interesting one, even if it does not mark a radical departure into "situated" rather than stored plans. In fact, the proposal in Teton, that subjects use locations in the visual stimulus as placeholders for parts of their plan, is very close to some ideas I have been developing recently in connection with a model of visual attention and tracking (e.g., Pylyshyn, 1989; Pylyshyn & Storm, 1988). The proposal is that the visual system provides a limited number of internal pointers (which we call FINSTs) that can keep track of simple features or feature-clusters in the visual field (even if the eyes or the features themselves move). The hypothesis is that in order to evaluate a visual predicate—like COLLINEAR(x,y,z) or INSIDE(x,y) or PARALLEL(L1,L2)— over certain visual objects, the arguments of the predicates must first be bound to these visual objects. The FINST indexes provide this binding function, and also serve to bind the visual features to parts of an evolving internal representation of the scene. Thus they act like natural language indexicals (like the English words "here" or "there"). The FINST hypothesis is an architectural proposal which happens to serve one of the functions needed by Teton, though it was designed to deal with quite different problems.

Finally, VanLehn & Ball present an argument for wanting to blur the distinction between architecture and symbolic process. They introduce an interesting notion of "prior capability". They appear to agree with my earlier statement that in order to develop an explanatory model one needs to distinguish the fixed from the variable aspects of a model, or the parameters that are in some sense fixed from the ones that function as free empirical parameters for the purpose at hand, that is, for fitting the relevant observations. The notion of prior capability is intended as way of making this distinction which is an alternative to the notion of architecture. Although VanLehn and Ball's distinction has some useful consequences, it in no way displaces the much more fundamental distinction between the architecture and the symbolic processes. I have already given some of the reasons for this earlier when I discussed the importance of studying the functional architecture, but with your indulgence I would like to briefly review one of these in the context of the VanLehn and Ball chapter.

The distinction between prior and subsequent capability is a deliberately relative one: it is a distinction between what a particular model intends to address—what phenomena it is intended to explain—and what principles, mechanisms, habits, knowledge, and so forth it presupposes already exist. Of course in practice any model will be restricted in the range of phenomena it will address, and it is clearly better to be explicit about what the model presupposes. But the important point is that whereas some demarcations of phenomena are purely a matter of convenience, others constitute an empirical hypothesis about the range of phenomena that form a natural class, a class to which a uniform theoretical vocabulary and set of principles will apply.

VanLehn and Ball's discussion confounds issues of practical convenience with issues of principle. Of course in practice we provide explanations by citing various sorts of generalizations at many levels of abstraction. And we do distinguish what we intend to cover with some particular model from what we are willing to take for granted for the time being. I am not advocating a uniform level of theoretical or observational analysis of psychological phenomena. We note and record regularities wherever we can find them. But when all is said and done we do find that there is an essential difference between phenomena that are attributed to what subjects believe and what their goals are (i.e., to their representations) and those that are attributed to how the organism is built—to the kind of machine it is, to put it bluntly. In the introduction to this chapter I tried to give some examples to illustrate this distinction. I remind you that one reason we need the distinction, and the reason that the criterion of cognitive penetrability is invoked is, roughly speaking, that we can change one type of regularity by telling subjects something or in some rational way changing their beliefs or goals, but we cannot change the other type of regularity in the same way. If computation is to be taken as a literal way of characterizing how an organism works, then we must respect and independently validate these two types of factors because they have very different effects and are organized according to very different principles.

Teton, as it turns out, is a nice example of the progressive refinement of some theoretical ideas about architecture, together with some additional ideas, whose status is perhaps less clear, about what subjects know and what things they are able to do with their knowledge—including recursively apply their (probably tacit, but certainly more general) knowledge of problem solving to search in new spaces when they fail to achieve one of their current goals. The fact that it is not always clear whether some feature of the evolving theory is part of the architecture, or part of the knowledge base, or just an old habit, need not hold up VanLehn and Ball in their investigation (and I am glad to see it has not), but it is one that will have to be faced sooner or later. A good example of the consequences of glossing over the distinction occurred in the case of a parallel puzzle concerning the explanation of certain phenomena in mental imagery, which I cited earlier. The result was that it was not clear which of two very different claims was being made. One possible claim was that humans have a certain cognitive capacity, or certain mechanisms, which they use when they reason with the aid of mental images. The other, much less interesting because it is pretty obviously true, is that people can generate certain sequences of representations in their mind (i.e., they are able to think certain sequences of thoughts), with appropriate temporal durations, when they believe that the corresponding sequence would occur in the world (say, the sequence of locations occupied by a fly moving across a map). The reason that it matters is that in the latter case the observed phenomena would be expected to be quite different if the person's beliefs or goals were to change, whereas in the former case, since the regularity arose from a property of the architecture, it could not be so rationally and coherently altered. And that is clearly a difference that needs explaining. For more discussion of this point, see Pylyshyn (1981).

## Comments on Anderson's Chapter

I agree with Anderson that human cognition is characterized by rationality. In fact, if it were not for some notion of rationality, the entire contemporary approach to cognition as a representation-governed process would fall apart. The reason we believe that cognition involves the processing of representations is that we can make sense of human cognition as a semantically interpreted sequence of states and the reason we believe that states have to semantically interpreted is because that's the only way we can capture a certain class of regularities that appear to hold of sequences of mental states; namely, these sequences generally *preserve semantic properties* such as truth, plausibility, and general semantic coherence. And the preservation of such semantic properties is the mark of rationality.

I also agree with Anderson that we need to examine task demands before plunging into a model to account for behavioral regularities. The reason, as I noted when we discussed the mental image scanning results, is that some reliable regularities in behavior tell us nothing about the intrinsic nature of the mind and of its architecture (except perhaps to confirm that it is rational and that it has certain psychophysical abilities, such as being able to generate known time intervals). Many regularities merely tell us that the organism is responding appropriately to the task requirements, as Newell and Simon (1972) have repeatedly emphasized. Anderson is certainly right that it does not hurt to be frequently reminded of this lesson inasmuch as it is often forgotten in the haste to construct models that mimic some observed behavior.

Having said that, I do want to take issue with the proposal to raise this excellent research strategy to the status of what Anderson refers to as a "principle of rationality"[14], and to view architectural issues as somehow secondary or subservient to task demands. Anderson is correct to relate this "principle" to David Marr's injunctions about how to understand cognitive processes (Marr, 1977, 1982). Marr, like Anderson, assumes that nature adopts the most efficient solution to problems, and therefore that asking what the most efficient way is to achieve a goal will lead you to the correct characterization of the function being computed. This idea is put in various different terms in Marr's writings and in Anderson's chapter. It is an appealing idea for many people who believe implicitly that the most satisfactory kind of explanation is fundamentally teleological: that if we can show that a certain hypothesized cognitive process is the most efficient or the most robust or otherwise the best possible process for accomplishing a certain goal, then we really have rooted our explanation in the most secure ground, namely evolution.

The trouble with such teleological groundings, however, is that they are notoriously quixotic. In the first place the determination of what constitutes the most efficient way of accomplishing a certain goal stands on two rather weak pillars. One pillar is determining a measure of efficiency. Measures of efficiency depend upon how one does one's cost accounting. And that, in turn, depends as much on the organism's architecture as it does on the task. The other weak pillar is the determination of the goals of the task, a step that cannot be avoided since measures of efficiency are relative to design goals. Other than the survival of the species, there are few goals that can be taken as given. In fact claims of design goals in various domains of cognition are generally no more than statements of philosophical prejudices. For example, the often heard claims that perception is

---

[14]Anderson's use of the phrase "principle of rationality" differs from the way it is used in Pylyshyn, 1984b, or in the chapter in the present volume by Rosenbloom, Laird, and Newell. In the latter uses it is the *individual* who is claimed to be rational, at least to a first approximation. However, Anderson's use goes quite a way beyond that to claim, in effect, that the organism is designed to work *optimally*. I see no reason to believe in that sense of rationality (the rationality of the design), for reasons that I give later.

designed for optimal action or that language is designed for optimal communication are far from being obvious, and indeed are quite likely false (for reasons I will not burden you with today). In any case, unless you have a strong independently motivated statement of the goals of a certain cognitive skill, any talk of efficiency (or what Anderson calls a rational analysis) is bound to be little more than a heuristic research strategy.

Even if you could give some reasonable story about what function a certain skill is intended to accomplish, linking this story to an understanding of *how* an organism carries out a process is fraught with problems. Organisms operate within the constraints imposed by their biological structure. But most of the details of the biological structure, as Gould and Lewontin (1979) have very nicely argued, can hardly be viewed as *designed for* some particular function. Much of the structure is simply a side effect of the interaction of biological or physical requirements with something else which itself may be useful for (or at least not harmful to) procreation or competition for food or escape from predators. Moreover, an infinite number of properties of an organism are the way they are for no better reason than that they had to be *some way*. Clearly the way an organism is constituted must neither violate physical/biological principles, nor place the organism at a disadvantage in the race for survival. Yet that leaves an enormous range among which no teleological story will cast any light. That's true of an indefinite number of the organism's physical properties, and it will also be true of an indefinite number of its functional properties—in particular, properties of its cognitive architecture.

When an organism sets about to solve some cognitive problem, the only thing we can be sure of is that it does so within the constraints imposed by its cognitive architecture. We cannot assume that it will do so by the most efficient means, nor can we even assume that the architecture itself is the most suitable one for the job, since it quite likely did not evolve for the task to which it is currently being applied. For example, the particular human skill at mathematics is quite likely a byproduct of brain structures that were either accidental correlates of something more basic and useful, or are parasitic on evolutionarily useful cognitive capacities. It is hard to see where mathematical ability per se (particularly the strong intuitions of number and of succession to which Intuitionistic Mathematics appeals) could have played a role in the survival of our species.

So my point, viz-a-viz John Anderson's chapter is this:   John has presented a number of examples where some behavior we thought should be accounted for by positing special features of the architecture, may in fact be better accounted for in terms of the way more general features of the architecture are used appropriately to meet the requirements of the task. On the assumption that the subject is acting rationally to achieve his or her goals, this shows that we can subsume several disparate behavioral patterns under a single more general principle (some sort of a cost-saving or utility-maximization principle). While I am skeptical about the details of some of his examples[15], the general point of the examples is, I think, correct. On the other hand, nothing follows from this concerning the cognitive architecture. As Anderson notes, the same rational adaptation to the demands of the task can be achieved within almost any architecture. From this Anderson draws the following quite unwarranted conclusion;

> Choice among architectures is then not to be determined by veracity of empirical predictions. Rather it is to be determined by how easy it is to work out the optimal behavior in the architecture. Ease of use is the classic criterion for selecting among notations. Empirical veracity is reserved for theories.

What's wrong with this conclusion is its assumption that the choice of architecture, like choice of the notation, is not an empirical matter. This position is consistent with Anderson's indeterminism thesis, which he has espoused elsewhere (Anderson, 1978), and which I have criticized at length (Pylyshyn, 1979). This position seriously misunderstands the nature of intentional or representational explanations. In fact, the choice of *both* notation and architecture are central empirical issues in cognitive science, and for reasons that go right to the heart of the computational view of mind. It's true that in the physical sciences, theoretical notation is not an empirical issue. But in cognitive science our choice of notation is critical precisely because the theories claim that representations are written in the mind in the postulated notation: that at least some knowledge is explicitly represented and encoded in the notation proposed by the theory. The architecture is likewise important because the claim is that these are literally the operations that are applied to the representations, as I argued at the beginning of this essay.

Sure, it is the theory which makes empirical claims. But in cognitive science, theories claim that the mind works the way the model does, complete with notation and architecture. What is sometimes not appreciated is that computational models are models of what literally goes on in the mind. The fact that most of the current models are doubtlessly wrong, and that it is hard to decide among them, should not blind people to the fact that they are literal empirical hypotheses, much like the physicists' hypotheses about the atomic structure of matter. And, also like the physicists' hypotheses, they are empirically determinate, at

---

[15]I don't, for instance, think that Anderson's categorization example is a good one for this purpose. I doubt very much that people develop certain natural or "basic level" categories in order to maximize predictability or discriminability, or any other *statistical* criteria. In fact there is no evidence that individuals develop such natural concepts in response to statistical properties of their experience at all (cf. Demopoulos & Marras, 1986; Fodor, 1981; Osherson, 1978). I don't even believe that a case can be made that this is how evolution did it either, although as I remarked above, it is almost impossible to speak for nature's intentions or to provide a teleological justification for particular features of the current biological makeup of the species.

least within the limits of the inductive method, yet they are very hard to test in practice. All we can conclude from that is that science is hard.

## REFERENCES

Anderson, J. R. (1978). Argument concerning representations for mental imagery. *Psychological Review, 85*, 249–277.

Barwise, J., & Perry, J. (1983). *Situations and attitudes.* Cambridge, MA: MIT Press/Bradford Books.

Brewer, W. F. (1974). There is no convincing evidence for operant or classical conditioning in adult humans. In W. B. Weiner & D. S. Palermo (Eds.), *Cognition and the symbolic processes.* Hillsdale, NJ: Lawrence Erlbaum Associates.

Demopoulos, W., & Marras, A. (1986). *Language learning and concept acquisition: Foundational issues.* Norwood, NJ: Ablex.

Fodor, J. A., & Pylyshyn, Z. (1981). How direct is visual perception? Some reflections on Gibson's 'Ecological Approach'. *Cognition, 9,* 139–196.

Fodor, J. A., & Pylyshyn, Z. (1988). Connectionism and cognitive architecture: A critical analysis. *Cognition, 28,* 3–71.

Fodor, J. A. (1981). The present status of the innateness controversy. In J. A. Fodor, *Representations: Philosophical essays on the foundations of cognitive science.* Cambridge, MA: MIT Press/Bradford Books.

Goodale, M. (1988). Modularity in visuomotor control. In Z. Pylyshyn (Ed.), *Computational processes in human vision: An interdisciplinary perspective.* Norwood, NJ: Ablex.

Gould, S. J., & Lewontin, R. (1979). The spandrels of San Marco and the Panglossian paradigm: A critique of the adaptationist programme. *Proceedings of the Royal Society (London), B205,* 581–598.

Hinton, G. E. (1988). Representing part-whole hierarchies in connectionist networks. *Proceedings of the Tenth Annual Conference of the Cognitive Science Society, Montreal, Canada.* pp 48–54. Hillsdale, NJ: Lawrence Erlbaum Associates.

Hinton, G. E., & Sejnowski, T. (1986). Learning and relearning in Botzmann machines. In D. Rumelhart, J. McClelland, & the PDP Research Group (Eds.), *Parallel distributed processing: Volume 1.* Cambridge, MIT Press/Bradford Books.

Lachter, J., & Bever, T. G. (1988). The relation between linguistic structure and associative theories of language learning: A constructive critique of some connectionist learning models. *Cognition, 28,* 195–247.

Laird, J., Rosenbloom, P., & Newell, A. (1988). *Universal Subgoaling and Chunking: The Automatic Generation and Learning of Goal Hierarchies,* Boston, MA: Kluwer Academic Publishers.

Marr, D. (1977). Artificial Intelligence—a personal view. *Artificial Intelligence, 9,* 37–48.

Marr, D. (1982). *Vision.* San Francisco: Freeman.

McClelland, J. L., Rumelhart, D. E., & Hinton, G. E. (1986). The appeal of parallel distributed processing. In D. E. Rumelhart, J. L. McClelland, & the PDP Research Group (Eds.), *Parallel Distributed Processing: Volume 1.* Cambridge, MA: MIT Press/Bradford Books.

Newell, A. (1973). Production systems: Models of control structures. In W. Chase (Ed.), *Visual information processing.* New York: Academic Press.

Newell, A. (1973). Why you can't play twenty questions with nature and win. In W. Chase (Ed.), *Visual information processing.* New York: Academic Press.

Newell, A. (1980). Physical symbol systems. *Cognitive Science, 4,* 135–183.

Newell, A. (1982). The knowledge level. *Artificial Intelligence, 18,* 87–127.

Newell, A. (1990). *Unified theories of cognition.* Cambridge, MA: Harvard University Press.

Newell, A., & Simon, H. A. (1972). *Human problem solving.* Englewood Cliffs, NJ: Prentice-Hall.

Osherson, D. (1978). Three conditions on conceptual naturalness. *Cognition, 6,* 263–289.

Paivio, A. (1986). *Mental representations: A dual coding approach.* New York: Oxford University Press.

Pylyshyn, Z. (1979). Validating computational models: A critique of Anderson's indeterminacy of representation claim. *Psychological Review, 86,* 4, 383–394.

Pylyshyn, Z. (1981). The imagery debate: Analogue media versus tacity knowledge. *Psychological Review, 88,* 16–45.

Pylyshyn, Z. (1984a). Plasticity and invariance in cognitive development. In J. Mehler & R. Fox (Eds.), *Neonate cognition: Beyond the blooming, buzzing confusion,* Hillsdale, NJ: Lawrence Erlbaum Associates.

Pylyshyn, Z. (1984b). *Computation and cognition: Toward a foundation for cognitive science.* Cambridge, MA: MIT Press.

Pylyshyn, Z., & Storm, R. (1988). Tracking multiple independent targets: evidence for a parallel tracking mechanism. *Spatial Vision, 3,* 179–197.

Pylyshyn, Z. (1989). The role of location indexes in spatial perception: A sketch of the FINST spatial-index model. *Cognition, 32,* 65–97.

Rumelhart, D. E., & McClelland, J. L. (1986). On learning the past tenses of English verbs. In J. L. McClelland & D. E. Rumelhardt (Eds.), *Parallel distributed processing, Volume II.* MA: MIT Press/Bradford Books.

Sejnowski, T. J., & Rosenberg, C. R. (1987). Parallel networks that learn to pronounce English text. *Complex Systems, 1,* 145–168.

Simon, H. A. (1969). *The sciences of the artificial.* Cambridge, MA: MIT Press.

Smolensky, P. (1988). On the proper treatment of connectionism. *Behavioral and Brain Sciences, 11,* 1–23.

Touretsky, D. S. (1986). BoltzCONS: Reconciling connectionism with the recursive nature of stacks and trees, *Proceedings of the Eighth Annual Conference of the Cognitive Science Society,* Amherst, Mass. August, 1986. Hillsdale, NJ: Lawrence Erlbaum Associates.

Touretsky, D. S. (1989). Chunking in a connectionist network. *Proceedings of the 11th annual conference of the Cognitive Science Society.* Hillsdale, NJ: Lawrence Erlbaum Associates.

Turing, A. (1937). On computable numbers with an application to the Entscheidungsproblem. *Proceedings of the London Mathematical Society, 42,* 230–265.

Wexler, K., & Cullicover, P. (1980). *Formal principles of language acquisition.* Cambridge, MA: MIT Press.

# II ARTIFICIAL INTELLIGENCE

# 8 How to Build Complete Creatures Rather than Isolated Cognitive Simulators

Rodney A. Brooks
*Massachusetts Institute of Technology,*
*Artificial Intelligence Laboratory*

## INTRODUCTION

How can we build artificial creatures which inhabit the same world as us? To me this has always been the romance of Artificial Intelligence.

Artificial Intelligence as a discipline has gotten bogged down in subproblems of intelligence. These subproblems are the result of applying reductionist methods to the goal of creating a complete artificial thinking mind. In Brooks (1987) I have argued that these methods will lead us to solving irrelevant problems; interesting as intellectual puzzles, but useless in the long run for creating an artificial being.

Thus, my goal over the last few years has been to build complete creatures that can exist in a dynamic people–populated world.

But having rejected reductionism as an approach how can this goal be achieved? We can begin by making the following observation inspired by nature.

Trying straight up for human level intelligence is obviously difficult and is not necessarily the only valid approach. Evolution, after all, built a large number of prototypes less intelligent than humans before incrementally reaching the intelligence of *homo sapiens*. In building artificial creatures we might well make progress by starting with low expectations and gradually building upon our experience. Note that we are not saying we should build creatures in simple worlds and then gradually increase the complexity of the worlds. Rather we are arguing for building simple creatures in the most complex world we can imagine and gradually increasing the complexity of the creatures.

One approach then, is to aim initially for the intelligence level of lower animals (e.g., insects) and respect the constraints that biology seems to have worked under. This approach may not produce the "optimal" intelligence in some sense, but it may have a chance where other approaches have failed.

In looking at lower animals one sees that most of their activity is concerned with rather mundane aspects of simply existing in the world (e.g., Moravec, 1984). Very little of their activity has an obvious component that would match any piece of existing work in Artificial Intelligence. To list just of few examples, it seems highly unlikely that a house fly is:

- recovering three dimensional surface descriptions of all the objects within its field of view,
- reasoning about threats from a human poised with a fly swatter, in particular about the human's goal structures, intents or beliefs,
- representing prototypes and instances of humans (or coffee pots, or windows, or napkins),
- making analogies concerning suitability for egg laying between dead pigs and other dead four legged animals, or
- constructing naive physics theories of how to land on the ceiling.

It seems much more likely that:

- there is very close connection of sensors to actuators (especially given the low speed of neural hardware and the fast reaction time of the fly)
- there are pre-wired patterns of behavior
- the fly uses simple navigation techniques
- and it is almost characterizable as a deterministic machine.

In this chapter we show how systems with such capabilities can be built from a collection of simple machines, with no shared representations, no central control, and only very low switching rates and low bandwidth communication.

Agre and Chapman (1987) have gone further and argued that much of human activity is simply a matter of following routines and that in fact very little of the traditional AI sorts of processes mentioned above go on in humans for much of their mundane day to day activity. They implement their systems in combinational circuits.

Like Minsky (1987) we believe that human level coherence during many activities may only be in the eye of the beholder; the behavior is generated by a large collection of simpler behaviors which do not have the rationality generating them that we might normally attribute to humans.

In fact, we hypothesize that all human behavior is simply the external expression of a seething mass of rather independent behaviors without any central control or representations of the world. Maybe there is only chaos from which order appears to emerge.

# THE SUBSUMPTION ARCHITECTURE

The subsumption architecture Brooks (1986) is a parallel and distributed computation formalism for connecting sensors to actuators in robots. A traditional way of describing these connections would be to say the subsumption architecture provides a way of writing intelligent control programs for mobile robots.

One writes a subsumption program by specifying layers of networks of *augmented finite state machines*. These are finite state machines augmented with timers which can be set to initiate a state change after some fixed time period has passed.

The two key aspects of the subsumption architecture are that (a) it imposes a layering methodology in building intelligent control programs, and that (b) within each network the finite state machines give the layer some structure and also provide a repository for state.

## Subsumption Details

Although there are a number of variations of the subsumption architecture in active use (see below), they all share a common base.

Each augmented finite state machine has a number of states and a set of input and output ports. Each input port has a buffer register that always contains the most recently arrived message on that port. The networks are built by wiring output ports of machines to inputs of others. Messages are sent over these wires. The messages on a given wire are all the same number of bits long (or wide).

Beside input registers a finite state machine can have additional *instance variable* registers in which extra state can be stored.

There are four types of states possible in a finite state machine:

• An *output* state outputs a message to a designated port, then switches to a specified state. The message is a *peripheral function* of input and instance variable registers. In the early versions of the subsumption architecture a peripheral function was allowed to be an arbitrary supplied piece of Lisp code.

• A *conditional-dispatch* state tests the value of a peripheral function and conditionally branches to one of two designated states.

• A *self* state computes a peripheral function of input and instance variable registers, sets an instance variable register to the new value and branches to a designated state.

• An *event-dispatch* state waits in parallel for a number of different events and when one happens branches to the designated state. Each event is a boolean combination of message arrivals on input ports and the expiration of a timer initialized when the state was first entered.

Examples of all these types of states can be seen in Figure 8.1. Additionally there

```
(defmodule avoid 1
  :inputs  (force   heading)
  :outputs  (command)
  :instance-vars  (resultforce)
  :states
    ((nil  (event-dispatch  (and  force  heading)  plan))
     (plan  (setf  resultforce  (select-direction  force  heading))
            go)
     (go  (conditional-dispatch  (significant-force-p  resultforce  1.0)
                                  start
                                  nil))
     (start  (output  command  (follow-force  resultforce))
             nil)))
```

FIG. 8.1.

is a *reset* line into each finite state machine; a message arriving on this line forces the machine into a distinguished state without resetting any of the register contents.

There are two other types of connection interaction allowed. An output port can have an *inhibiting* side tap added, where any message arriving on the side tap inhibits all output on the port from some specified time period. Any existing wire can have a *suppressing* side tap placed on it, where a message arriving on the side tap is propagated along the wire as though it had originated at the original source, and furthermore all messages from the original source, for some specified time period, are totally suppressed and discarded.

Figure 8.2 shows a schematic representation of a finite state machine with inputs, outputs and a reset, along with a suppressed input and an inhibited output.

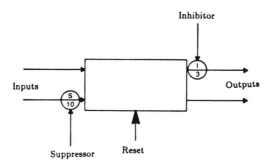

FIG. 8.2.  A module has input and output lines. Input signals can be suppressed and replaced with the suppressing signal. Output signals can be inhibited. A module can also be reset to state NIL.

## Variations on the Theme

The details of the subsumption architecture are very fluid, and indeed many people now use distinct versions, although all are strongly of the above described flavor.

Connell (1987) and Brooks (1988a) have explored the idea of simplifying all peripheral computations to the point where they are implementable in combinatorial logic or table lookup. For creatures with insect level intelligence this has not proved to be a serious constraint. It removes an ugly wart on earlier versions of the subsumption architecture by removing an escape mechanism into Turing-equivalent arbitrary computations, and hence puts a bound on the computational power necessary to implement a subsumption program.

Connell (1988a) has proposed a subsumption model where all messages have a continuous nature. When one layer wants to subsume another it must continually send messages to keep control. Messages might have the flaor of "go forward," "go forward," "go forward," etc. Once the higher layer is satisfied it stops sending this message and hence relinquishes control. This version of the subsumption architecture does not make use of inhibition or resetting and suppression nodes have no timeout period. The new version is implementable in the original version however. Viola (1988) has reimplemented a number of earlier creatures in the continuous model of the subsumption architecture. It seems to simplify the subsumption programs markedly.

Cudhea (1988) has added a layer of abstraction to the subsumption architecture which lets users define programs in terms of instantiating finite state machine schemas. This makes it easy to write subsumption programs where there are many instances of a single finite state machine.

Horswill and Brooks (1988) have augmented the underlying subsumption architecture with high bandwidth vision busses. Simple means of combination (such as MUXes and logical combination) of vision signals, along with local operators, delay elements and region to coordinate mapping functions, allow the implementation of a number of low level visual navigation techniques useful for insect level navigation. Standard subsumption architecture finite state machines monitor and switch the visual pathways, and translate the outputs into actuator commands.

## THE PHILOSOPHY AND CONSEQUENCES OF SUBSUMPTION

Given these mechanics of the subsumption architecture a wide range of programming styles are possible. However there are some underlying considerations which distinguish a "good" subsumption program from a "bad" subsumption program.

The design of the subsumption architecture has been influenced by a philosophy of no global world models and no traditional AI planning. In turn, the experiments we have done with real robots controlled by the subsumption architecture have fed back on this philosophy, refining it and our understanding of the essential aspects of the subsumption architecture.

The underlying architecture is very distributed. There is no "free" communication network or any shared memory between computational elements. Any communication path must be made quite explicit by specifying a wire. It is thus difficult to maintain a central world model. Indeed it often becomes easier to use the world as its own model, and sense the pertinent aspects of the world when it is necessary. This is a good idea as the world really is a rather good model of itself. It automatically adds robustness to the system as there is neither a tendency for the world model to be out of date, nor are large amounts of computation poured into making sure that its not. We take this idea even further and often actually use the world as the communication medium between distributed parts of the subsumption program. Thus one layer senses what really happened in the world, rather than being told what another layer expects to happen.

Given that there is no world model there is also no place for traditional AI planning which examines a world model and reasons about consequences of actions. Rather, in the subsumption architecture it is more natural to locally react to sensed aspects of the world, and let a pre-wired priority scheme resolve any conflicts generated within the distributed system. It is entirely plausible for different parts of the system to "believe" wildly inconsistent things about the world. Of course belief is all in the mind of an outside observer as there are no explicit symbolic representations of any believed facts within the subsumption architecture.

Lastly, with no central world model there is no need for sensor fusion in the usual sense of the phrase. There is no "perception" system which delivers descriptions of the world to a "central" system which controls and "actuation" system. In the subsumption architecture the fusion of data from different sensors, or even from different processing applied to the same sensor (e.g. stereo and motion algorithms applied to the same camera inputs) data, does not happen in the "perception" end at all. Individual strands of perceptual data are delivered to individual subsumption layers and then actuator commands are generated. Fusion happens in resolving conflicts between these commands.

## EXAMPLES

In this section we briefly review some successful creatures built with the subsumption architecture and highlight the ways in which they have exploited or epitomize that architecture. Finally we outline a subsumption program for a complex visually guided creature (named Seymour) that is currently under development.

## Allen

Our first robot, Allen, had sonar distance sensors and odometry onboard and used an offboard lisp machine to simulate the subsumption architecture. In Brooks (1986) we described three layers of control implemented in the subsumption architecture. The wiring diagram is shown in Figure 8.3.

The first layer let the robot avoid both static and dynamic obstacles; Allen would happily sit in the middle of a room until approached, then scurry away, avoiding collisions as it went. The internal representation used was that every sonar return represented a repulsive force with an inverse square drop off in strength. The vector sum of the repulsive forces, suitably thresholded, told the robot in which direction it should move. An additional reflex halted the robot whenever there was something right in front of the robot and it was moving forward (rather than turning in place).

The second layer made the robot randomly wander about. Every 10 seconds or so, a desire to head in a random direction would be generated. That desire was coupled with the instinct to avoid obstacles by vector addition. The summed vector suppressed the more primitive obstacle avoidance vector, but the obstacle avoidance behavior still operated, having been subsumed by the new layer, in its account of the lower level's repulsive force. Additionally the halt reflex of the lower level operated autonomously and unchanged.

The third layer made the robot look (with its sonars) for distant places and try

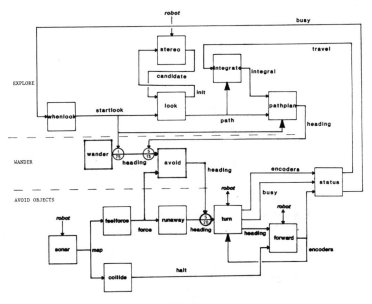

FIG. 8.3.

to head towards them. The third layer monitored progress through odometry, generating a desired heading which suppressed the direction desired by the wander layer. It was thus fed into a vector addition with the instinctive obstacle avoidance layer. The physical robot did not therefore remain true to the desires of the upper layer. The upper layer had to watch what happened in the world, through odometry, in order to understand what was really happening in the lower control layers, and send down correction signals.

In Brooks and Connell (1986) we described another set of layers for the robot Allen. See Figure 8.4 for the wiring diagram. The first was identical; avoiding obstacles both static and dynamic. The second layer implemented wall following by treating a wall to the right, say, of the robot as an attractive force slightly ahead and to the right of the robot. This attraction fought with the repulsive force of the wall, and together they formed an attractive vector which made the robot hug the wall. The wall follower breezes right past open doors. A third layer examines the sonar data looking for doorways. When it sees one it sets up a goal as in the previous set of experiments, and servoes through the doorway using odometry. Now however the repulsive forces from the lowest obstacle avoidance layer are crucial to line the robot up with the center of the doorway so that it can squeeze through. The door finder only has a very rough idea of where the door is, so the third layer only has a very crude world model. The lowest layer uses the

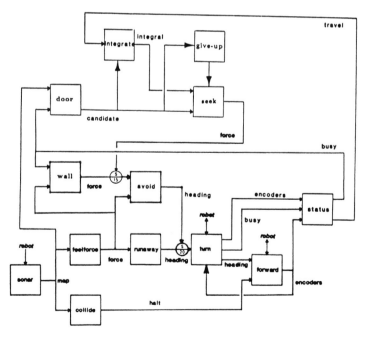

FIG. 8.4.

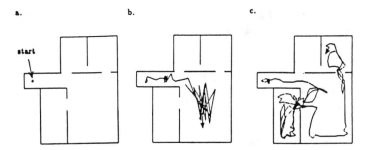

FIG. 8.5.  The path followed by the robot. a. The starting point in a suite of four rooms. b. The wandering system. c. The wall following system.

world as its own best model in order to get the robot through the door. Note that the upper layer does not involve the lower layer as a subroutine. The lower layer is just doing its job as best it understands it as it always has. Figure 8.5 shows the behavior of a simulated version of Allen with one, two, and three control layers activated.

## Tom and Jerry

Tom and Jerry (Connell, 1987) were two identical robots built to demonstrate just how little raw computation is necessary to support the subsumption architecture. A three layer subsumption program for the robots is shown in Fig. 8.6. All data paths are one bit wide, and the whole program is implemented on a single 256 gate PAL (Programmable Array of Logic). Tom and Jerry physically are toy cars with three one bit infrared proximity sensors mounted on the front of them, and one identical sensor mounted at the rear. The sensors are individually tuned to a

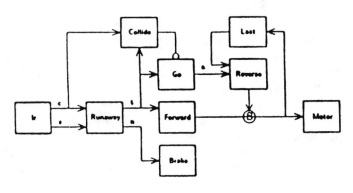

FIG. 8.6.

proximity distance at which they will fire. The central front sensor fires only on much closer objects than the two others which point slightly outwards.

The lowest layer of Tom and Jerry implements our standard pair of behaviors, using a vector sum of repulsive forces from obstacles and a halt reflex to stop when something is too close ahead, as detected by the central front looking sensor. There are extra complications in that we need to use the subsumption architecture to implement an active braking scheme because of the high speed of the robots relative to their sensor sensitivities. Tom and Jerry's second layers are much like Allen's original second layer—an urge to wander about, implemented by an attractive force which gets added to the repulsive forces from obstacles. The third layer detects relatively moving objects using the front three sensors. When something is detected it is attracted towards them. The lower level collide behavior stops the robot from actually hitting the target however. While the robot is chasing a target the wander behavior is suppressed.

We see with Tom and Jerry both the notion of independent behaviors combining without knowing about each other (chasing obstacles but staying back from them a little ways) and the idea again of using the world as its own best model. It demonstrated that the subsumption architecture could be compiled (by hand) down to the gate level, and also that it could be run at clock speeds of a few hundred Hertz. This has inspired us to automate the compilation process (Brooks, 1988b).

## Herbert

Herbert (Brooks, Connell, & Ning, 1988) is a physically much more ambitious robot which is now physically complete. It has a 24 processor distributed loosely coupled onboard computer to run the subsumption architecture. The processors are slow CMOS (low electrical power; an important consideration when carrying batteries around to power them) 8 bit microprocessors, which can communicate only by slow serial interfaces (maximum 10 packets each 24 bits wide per second). Onboard Herbert the wires in the diagrams shown in this paper for subsumption programs have physical embodiments as copper wires which provide the medium to support the serial sensing of messages.

Herbert has 30 infrared proximity sensors for local obstacle avoidance, an onboard manipulator with a number of simple sensors attached to the hand, and a laser light stripping system to collect three dimensional depth data in 60 degree wide swath in front of the robot out to a range of about 12 feet. A 256 pixel wide by 32 pixel high depth image is collected every second. Through a special purpose distributed serpentine memory, some number of the onboard 8 bit processors are able to expend about 30 instructions to each data pixel. By linking the processors in a chain we are able to implement quite good performance vision algorithms.

Connell (1988b) is programming Herbert to wander around office areas, go into peoples offices and steal empty soda cans from their desks. He has demonstrated obstacle avoidance and wall following, real-time recognition of soda can like objects and desk like objects, and a set of 15 behaviors (Connell, 1988b) which drive the arm to physically search for a soda can in front of the robot, locate it and pick it up. These fifteen behaviors are shown as fifteen separate finite state machines in Figure 8.7.

Herbert shows many instances of using the world as its own best model and as a communication medium.

The laser–based *table–like–object* finder initiates a behavior which drives the robot closer to a table. It doesn't communicate with any other subsumption layers. However when the robot is close to a table there is a better chance that the laser-based *soda-can-like-object* finder will trigger. In turn it centers the robot on the detected object, but does not communicate anything to other subsumption layers. The arm control behaviors notice that the robot is stationary, and reach out looking for a soda can. The advantage of this approach is that there is no need to set up internal expectations for what is going to happen next; this means that the control system can both (a) be naturally opportunistic if

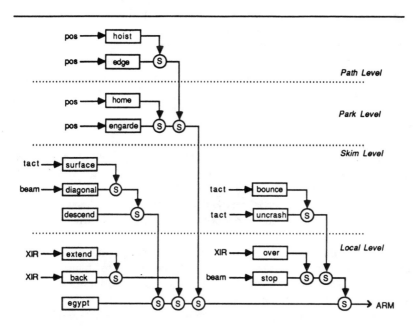

FIG. 8.7.

fortuitous circumstances present themselves, and (b) it can easily respond to changed circumstances, such as some other object approaching it on a collision course.

Likewise the arm and hand do not communicate directly. The hand has a grasp reflex that operates whenever something breaks an infrared beam between the fingers. When the arm locates a soda can with its local sensors it simply drives the hand so that the two fingers are on either side of the can. The hand then independently grasps the can. Given this arrangement it is possible for a human to hand a soda can to the robot. As soon as it is grasped the arm retracts—it doesn't matter whether it was a soda can that was intentionally grasped, or one that magically appears.

## Seymour

Seymour is a new robot we are building with all onboard processing to support vision processing of 8 to 10 low resolution cameras at approximately 10 frames per second. The cameras will feed into different subsumption layers which will act upon those aspects of the world they perceive. For instance, one layer might use a camera looking at ceiling lights to direct the robot down a corridor. Another might use motion stereo to detect obstacles in the path of the robot and force deviations from the simple corridor following path.

While the robot and its computers are under construction we have begun testing a number of low level visually guided navigation routines on Allen using an offboard Lisp machine to do the computations. We will transfer these routines to the robot when it is built.

Horswill and Brooks (1988) describe a subsumption program that controls two simple and unreliable visual processing routines to producer a reliable behavior which follows moving objects using vision. The subsumption network is shown in Figure 8.8. One vision process tracks a single moving blob. It gets bootstrapped by another process which overlays the blob image with an indication of where motion is seen. The robot then tries to servo a selected blob to stay in a fixed location in image coordinates. The blob tracker often loses the blob it is tracking. The motion finder produces a lot of noise especially when the robot is moving. But between the two of them they let the robot reliably follow a moving object (any moving object; we have seen the robot chase a pink plastic flamingo and a black trash can dragged by a string, a radio controlled toy blue car on a blue floor, a grey notebook on a grey carpeted floor, and a drinking mug moved around by hand), by switching back and forth between the visual routines as either one fails. The subsumption program nowhere has the notion of an identifiable object internally, but to an outside observer it certainly appears to follow a moving object well.

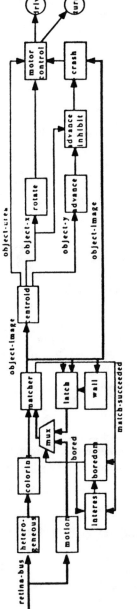

FIG. 8.8. Diagram of approach-and-follow system.

# CONCLUSION

By trying to build complete creatures we have found it useful to place a different emphasis on many aspects of intelligence than has been traditional in AI research. The key problems in building a complete creature are:

- providing fast and adequate response in a dynamic changing environment,
- providing a way to make sense of sensory data in an incompletely understood world, and
- providing a mechanism where the goals of a creature are not routinely overwhelmed in dealing with the interruptions provided by the world.

At least for simple creatures we have found little use for complete world models, planning, search, explicit knowledge representation, truth maintenance or control of reasoning.

Inspired by Minsky (1986) we hypothesize that the same will hold true as we move up the evolutionary train in the complexity of creatures we build. In our more radical moments we believe that this will hold true all the way through to human level intelligence. We are further inspired by the following observation.

Nature has shown us that intelligence is possible with very low switching speeds in the substrate used for computation. Indeed *every single example* of biological systems with any form of cognition operates on hardware that can propagate signals at no more than a kiloHertz or two. Yet all of these systems can react and operate in a fraction of a second. But they can do more than just react in those time frames. Humans, for instance, can often perceive, reason, understand and plan actions in subsecond time frames. In fact they can produce continuous streams of speech at many words per second. Thus we have an existence proof that it is possible to achieve intelligence with very shallow computational processes. Interestingly we have no existence proof that it is possible to do it any other way. The subsumption architecture similarly provides intelligence to simple creatures with hardware that need only be clocked at a few hundred Hertz (Brooks, 1988b).

# ACKNOWLEDGMENTS

This report describes research done at the Artificial Intelligence Laboratory of the Massachusetts Institute of Technology. Support for the research is provided in part by the University Research Initiative under Office of Naval Research contract N00014-86-K-0685, in part by the Advanced Research Projects Agency under Office of Naval Research contract N00014-85-K-0124.

# REFERENCES

Agre, P., & Chapman, D. (1987). Pengi: An implementation of a theory of activity. *AAAI-87*, Seattle, WA, 268–272.

Brooks, R. A. (1986). A robust layered control system for a mobile robot. *IEEE Journal of Robotics and Automation*, RA-2, April, 14–23.

Brooks, R. A. (1987). Intelligence without representation. Preprints of the *Workshop on Foundations of Intelligence*. MIT: Endicott House.

Brooks, R. A. (1988a). Simple Computations Suffice, *in preparation.*

Brooks, R. A. (1988b). A Silicon Compiler for the Subsumption Architecture, *in preparation.*

Brooks, R. A., & Connell, J. H. (1986). Asynchronous Distributed Control System for a Mobile Robot. *SPIE Vol. 727 Mobile Robots*, 77–84.

Brooks, R. A., Connell, J. H., & Ning, P. (1988). Herbert: A Second Generation Mobile Robot. Report No. MIT AIM-1016.

Connell, J. H. (1987). Creature Building with the Subsumption Architecture. *IJCAI-87*, Milan, Italy, 1124–1126.

Connell, J. H. (1988a). A Behavior-Based Arm Controller, *to appear SPIE Mobile Robot Conference*, Cambridge, MA, Nov.

Connell, J. H. (1988b). Task Oriented Spatial Representations for Distributed Systems. MIT Ph.D. thesis in preparation.

Cudhea, P. H. (1988). Describing the Control Systems of Simple Robot Creatures. MIT S.M. thesis, June.

Horswill, I. D., & Brooks, R. A. (1988). Situated Vision in a Dynamic World: Chasing Objects, *to appear AAAI-88*, St. Paul, MN.

Minsky, M. L. (1986). Society of mind. New York: Simon and Schuster.

Moravec, H. P. (1984). Locomotion, vision and intelligence. In Brady & Paul (Eds.), *Robotics Research* (pp. 215–224). Cambridge, MA: MIT Press.

Viola P. (1988). A Syntax for Mobot Description with Strong Semantics: Evolution the Easy Way. MIT S.B. thesis.

# 9 PRODIGY: An Integrated Architecture for Planning and Learning

Jaime G. Carbonell
Craig A. Knoblock
*School of Computer Science, Carnegie Mellon University*

Steven Minton
*NASA Ames Research Center, Sterling Federal Systems*

## INTRODUCTION: WHAT IS PRODIGY?

Artificial intelligence has traditionally favored a reductionistic approach, studying intelligent behavior by analyzing each component independently: Knowledge representation, search-intensive problem solving, knowledge-intensive expertise, concept acquisition from examples, performance improvement due to experience, and so forth. Such a divide-and-conquer approach has been historically quite appropriate, providing many useful results. However, artificial intelligence is evolving from an exploratory endeavor to a quantitative science, and part of the maturation process is the emergence of unifying theories and integrated computational architectures. This chapter describes one such investigation, the PRODIGY system, an integrated architecture unifying problem solving, planning and multiple learning methods. The learning methods in PRODIGY encompass learning control rules through explanation-based learning (EBL) and static search–space analysis, learning plan knowledge through analogical transfer, learning abstraction hierarchies through domain–definition analysis, and acquiring new domain knowledge through goal-oriented experimentation and dynamic interaction with a human expert.

Before endeavoring to describe PRODIGY in depth, let us situate it in the space of integrated computational architectures. There are multiple dimensions one can use to contrast and compare the architectures. We list each dimension, situating PRODIGY and contrasting it to SOAR (Laird, Newell, & Rosenbloom, 1987; Rosenbloom, Newell, & Laird, chap. 4 in this volume), THEO (Mitchell et al., chap. 12 in this volume) and occasionally ICARUS (Langley, Thompson, Iba, Gennari, & Allen, 1989). TETON (VanLehn & Ball, chap. 6 in this volume) is an architecture that is very similar to PRODIGY, although its purpose is the study of human problem solving rather than machine learning. Each dimension in the design space addresses a major component of the architecture:

• Central problem solver—Each architecture relies on problem solving. Whereas THEO has no general problem solver (it is guided by the acquisition of domain–specific methods, overriding more general ones), PRODIGY and SOAR each have an architecturally-defined general problem solver whose performance improves incrementally through the acquisition of factual and control knowledge for each domain.

• Representational transparency—All the knowledge used or acquired in any PRODIGY module is open for inspection and use by every other module, a discipline made possible by the use of a uniform logic-based representation of all control and factual knowledge. This *glass–box* philosophy contrasts sharply with SOAR's *black-box* discipline; once a SOAR chunk is formed, its contents are not open to inspection or modification, nor are the SOAR domain operators available across problem spaces.

• Deliberative vs reflexive learning—PRODIGY acquires new knowledge only when it believes that knowledge will be useful; learning is a deliberate meta-reasoning process. SOAR, on the other hand, cannot help but learn; chunking is a reflex process in the architecture. THEO's caching mechanism is closer to SOAR's chunking, but more recent developments indicate some motion towards the PRODIGY philosophy. ICARUS grows its decision trees as an incremental reflex process, much like SOAR's chunking philosophy.

• Multiple vs single learning strategies—PRODIGY employs multiple learning strategies: explanation-based learning, analogy, abstraction, experimentation, static analysis, tutoring, and so on. SOAR employs only chunking, through which it attempts to emulate some of the other learning methods. THEO takes an intermediate position with a couple of learning mechanisms: caching and explanation-based learning.

• Inductive vs analytical learning—Only ICARUS employs purely inductive learning techniques. THEO and SOAR use only deductive methods, and PRODIGY combines both, relying more heavily on the EBL–like deductive methods for acquiring control knowledge. Induction is employed only in the experimentation techniques and in extensions to purely deductive derivational analogy.

The rest of this chapter presents PRODIGY in some detail, describing the basic architecture, the central problem solver, the knowledge representation, and the learning methods. We focus primarily on PRODIGY's EBL method and on learning abstractions for efficient hierarchical planning, as these two learning components have been validated empirically over substantial populations of problems.

# THE GENERAL ARCHITECTURE

The PRODIGY architecture can be depicted graphically as a core planner/problem solver tightly integrated with a cluster of learning modules (Carbonell & Gil, 1987; Carbonell & Veloso, 1988; Knoblock, 1989a; Minton, 1988a; Minton et al., 1989). The PRODIGY system was designed both as a unified testbed for different learning methods and as a general architecture to solve interesting problems in complex task domains, such as robotic path planning, discrete machine-shop scheduling, assembly and configuration planning, logistics planning, and matrix algebra problem solving.

As illustrated in Figure 9.1, the central core of PRODIGY is a general problem solver whose behavior is determined by knowledge about the domain (objects, relations, operators and inference rules), and by control knowledge to guide search. The problem solver searches a space defined by a set of operators (i.e., rules with specified preconditions and effects). It produces a complete trace of the search, encapsulating all decisions and hypotheses made in the reasoning process—right ones and wrong ones—as well as the final solution. The information in the problem-solving trace can then be used by the learning components. Search is guided by explicit control rules (both domain-independent and domain-specific), defaulting to traditional means-ends analysis in the absence of any guiding control knowledge. All of PRODIGY's learning modules share the same

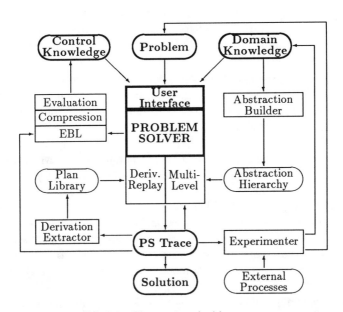

FIG. 9.1. The PRODIGY Architecture

knowledge representation and all have access to the full knowledge sources of the problem solver, including the problem solving trace. To complete the picture, we summarize each PRODIGY module:

- An explanation–based learning module acquires control rules from a problem-solving trace. Explanations are constructed from an axiomatized theory describing both the domain and the problem-solver's architecture. Then, explanations are compressed into operational control-rule form, and control rules whose utility in search reduction outweighs their application overhead costs are retained.

- An abstraction generation module creates a hierarchy of abstraction spaces based on operator interactions. The planner uses the hierarchy to build abstract solutions and then refines them into progressively more detailed solutions.

- A derivational analogy engine can solve new problems by storing and replaying entire solutions to similar past problems. The stored solutions are augmented with explicit justifications, which allow the problem solver to recreate past lines of reasoning.

- A static analysis module acquires control knowledge from the operator descriptions given to the problem solver. In contrast to explanation-based learning, static analysis does not require any example problem-solving traces in order to produce control rules.

- A learning–by–experimentation module refines domain knowledge that had been incompletely or incorrectly specified. Experimentation is triggered when the plan execution monitor detects a divergence between internal expectations and external observations. The main focus of experimentation is to refine factual domain knowledge, rather than control knowledge.

- A dynamic knowledge–acquisition user-interface participates in an apprentice-like dialogue, enabling the expert user to evaluate and guide the system's problem solving and learning.

These modules are integrated into a unified architecture in several ways: They all use a common representation based on first order logic. They all access the global knowledge sources (domain knowledge, control knowledge, problem solving trace, etc). Any learned knowledge produced by one module is directly exploitable by the general problem solver and open to examination by any other learning module. In other words, all learning modules are synergistic with the problem solver and compatible with each other. In future work, we would like direct synergism among the learning modules themselves (e.g., analogical transfer at multiple levels of abstraction).

Before presenting the problem solver and learning modules in depth, a few shared concepts need to be defined clearly:

- Operator: Operators map states into new states, corresponding to actions that affect the external world. PRODIGY operators consist of an FOL expression describing the operator's preconditions, coupled with conditional *add* and *delete* lists representing the resulting changes to the state when the operator is applied.

- Inference rule: Inference rules add information explicitly to the state that was implicitly in its deductive closure. PRODIGY represents inference rules as simplified operators, without *delete* lists, and matches them in the same manner; although their epistemological status differs.

- Control rule: Control rules map a set of candidate decisions (e.g., which legal operator to apply, or which goal to work on next) into a smaller or prioritized decision set. Control rules can access any knowledge source because they have access to the internal state of the problem solver (e.g., the pending goals, current domain description, and history of past planning actions). PRODIGY represents control rules with an FOL condition side, followed by a control action which is applied when the condition side is true. The possible control actions are described later. Control rules may be entered by hand or acquired by the learning processes.

- Control knowledge: Any kind of information that reduces search constitutes control knowledge. Control rules are the primary encoding of control knowledge in PRODIGY, but heuristic evaluation functions, abstract plans, problem-solution analogs (from the case library), and macro-operators are also forms of control knowledge.

- Solution: A sequence of instantiated operators which, if applied to the initial state, will produce a state satisfying the goal.

- Problem solving trace: The entire search tree, including failed attempts, generated in the process of discovering the final solution sequence.

## THE PROBLEM SOLVER

PRODIGY's basic reasoning engine is a general-purpose problem solver and planner that searches for sequences of operators (i.e., plans) that accomplish a set of goals from a specified initial state description. Search control in PRODIGY is governed by a set of *control rules* that apply at each decision point: selection of which node to expand, of which goal to work on, of which operator to apply, and of which objects to use. Search control rules may be general or domain specific, hand–coded or automatically acquired, and may consist of heuristic preferences or definitive selections. In the absence of any search control, PRODIGY defaults to depth–first means–ends analysis. But, with appropriate search control rules it can emulate other search disciplines, including breath-first search, best-first search, and knowledge-based plan instantiation. A new version of PRODIGY undergoing preliminary testing is capable of complete nonlinear planning (Veloso, 1989), while retaining the ability to exploit all available control knowledge and integrating with the various learning mechanisms.

PRODIGY has been applied to many different domains: Robotic path planning and assembly, the blocksworld, the STRIPS domain, an augmented version of the STRIPS domain, matrix algebra manipulation, discrete machine-shop scheduling, telescope-mirror production, distribution planning, multi-agent robotic planning, etc. In order to solve problems in a particular domain, PRODIGY must first be given a specification of that domain, consisting of a set of operators and inferences rules. To illustrate the knowledge used by the basic PRODIGY problem solver, we introduce a simple machine–shop scheduling domain. Other domains are introduced later to provide a varied set of examples.

Let us suppose that the shop contains a variety of machines, including a LATHE and a ROLLER (which are used to reshape objects), a POLISHER, and other simple machines. For simplicity, we assume that each machining operation takes one time unit. Given a set of objects to be drilled, polished, reshaped, etc., and a fixed amount of time, the task is to schedule the objects on the machines so as to meet these requirements.

Each operator has a precondition expression that must be satisfied before the operator can be applied, and an effects-list that describes how the application of the operator changes the world. Precondition expressions are well-formed formulas in PDL, a form of predicate logic encompassing negation, conjunction, disjunction, and existential quantification, as well as universal quantification over sets. (Constants are shown in upper case and variables are in italics. Quantifiers are omitted for universally quantified variables whose scope extends over the entire operator.) The effects-list indicates atomic formulas that should be added or deleted from the current state when the operator is applied, reflecting the actions of the operator in the "world."

Let us take a close look at one of the operators given in the domain specification, the operator for scheduling the LATHE:

```
(LATHE (obj time new-shape)
 (preconditions
  (and
   (IS-OBJECT obj)
   (LAST-SCHEDULED obj prev-time)
   (LATER time prev-time)
   (IDLE LATHE time)))
 (effects
   (delete (SHAPE obj old-shape))
   (delete (SURFACE-CONDITION obj old-condition))
   (delete (PAINTED obj old-paint))
   (delete (LAST-SCHEDULED obj prev-time))
```

                (add (SURFACE–CONDITION *obj* ROUGH)
                (add (SHAPE *obj* CYLINDRICAL)
                (add (LAST–SCHEDULED *obj* *time*))
                (add (SCHEDULED *obj* LATHE *time*))))

At any particular moment, the current state of the world is represented by a database containing a set of ground atomic formulas. There are two types of relations used in the system, primitive relations and defined relations. Primitive relations are directly observable or "closed-world". This means that the truth value of these relations can be immediately ascertained by a call to the state database. Primitive relations may be added to and deleted from the state database by operators. Thus, in our machine shop domain, the primitive relations include SCHEDULED and SHAPE. Primitive relations that are *static* (i.e., they cannot be changed by any operator in the domain), such as (LATER TIME–5 TIME–2), can be computed on demand.

Defined relations, such as IDLE and CLAMPABLE, are inferred on demand using inference rules. The purpose of defined relations is to represent useful abstractions in the domain, allowing operator preconditions to be expressed more concisely. Inference rules only change the system's internal knowledge state, whereas operators change *both* the external world and the system's internal state. For example, the following inference rule defines the predicate IDLE by specifying that a machine is idle during a time period if no object is scheduled for that machine during that time period.

                (IS–IDLE (*machine time*)
                 ( preconditions
                   (not (exists *obj* (SCHEDULED *obj machine time*))))
                 (effects
                   (add (IDLE *machine time*))))

Because inference rules are encoded and applied in a manner similar to operators, PRODIGY can use a homogeneous control structure, enabling the search control rules to guide the application of operators and inference rules alike.

## An Example Problem

Once the domain has been specified, problems are presented to the problem solver by describing an initial state and a goal expression to be satisfied. The goal expression for our example problem is:

(and (SHAPE OBJECT–A CYLINDRICAL)
     (SURFACE–CONDITION OBJECT–A POLISHED))

This expression is satisfied if the object named OBJECT–A is polished and has a cylindrical shape.

| | TIME-1 | TIME-2 | TIME-3 | TIME-4.... | | | | TIME-20 |
|---|---|---|---|---|---|---|---|---|
| LATHE | OBJECT-B | | | | | | | |
| ROLLER | OBJECT-C | | | | | | | |
| POLISHER | | OBJECT-B | | | | | | |

FIG. 9.2.  Initial State

The initial state for the example, illustrated in Figure 9.2, contains OBJECT-B and OBJECT-C already scheduled, and OBJECT-A which has yet to be scheduled. Let us suppose that the schedule consists of 20 time-slots, and that OBJECT-A is initially unpolished, oblong-shaped, and is cool. The problem solver searches for a sequence of operators that transforms the initial state into a state where the goal is achieved, producing the search tree in Figure 9.3.

The left side of each node shows the goal stack and the pending operators at that point. The right side shows a subset of the state that is relevant to our discussion. For example, at Node 3, the current goal is to clamp the object. This is a precondition of the POLISH operator, which is being considered to achieve the higher goal of being polished. The predicates like CYLINDRICAL and HOT in the figure are shorthand for the actual formulas, such as (SHAPE OBJECT-A CYLIN-DRICAL) and (TEMPERATURE OBJECT-A HOT).

If an expression does not match in the current state, the unmatched conditions become subgoals. The system selects a subgoal to work on first, then selects a relevant operator (or inference rule), matches the preconditions against the database, and subgoals further if the match does not succeed. Any of these choices can be mediated by control rules, as described later.

In our example, the first top-level goal (SHAPE OBJECT-A CYLINDRICAL) is not satisfied in the initial state. To achieve this goal PRODIGY considers the operators LATHE and ROLL, since these operators add effects which unify with this goal. At this point PRODIGY arbitrarily decides to try ROLL first; there are no control rules which indicate otherwise. In order to satisfy the preconditions of ROLL, PRODIGY must infer that OBJECT-A is available and the machine is idle at the desired time. Assume that previously acquired control knowledge indicates a preference for the earliest possible time slot, TIME-2. After rolling the object at TIME-2, PRODI-GY attempts to polish the object, but the preconditions of POLISH specify that the object must either be rectangular, or clamped to the polisher. Unfortunately, clamping fails, because rolling the object has raised its temperature so that it is too hot to clamp without deforming the object or clamp. Since there is no way to make the object rectangular, the attempt to apply POLISH fails.

Backtracking, PRODIGY then tries rolling the object at TIME-3, and then TIME-4, and so on, until the end of the schedule is reached at TIME-20. Each of these attempts fails to produce a solution, because the object remains HOT (or cools down insufficiently, if the domain specification was a bit more realistic). As we will see, when learning is interleaved with problem solving, PRODIGY can reason

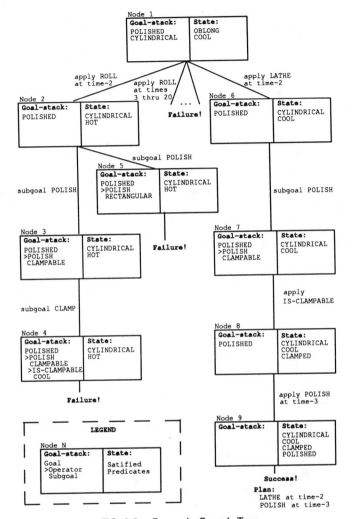

FIG. 9.3. Example Search Tree

about the failures and therefore backtrack more intelligently. In any event, the problem–solver finally succeeds when it eventually backs up and tries LATHING rather than ROLLING.

## Control Structure

Here, we describe the control structure of the PRODIGY problem solver. A problem consists of an initial state and a goal expression. To solve a problem, PRODIGY must find a sequence of operators that produces a state satisfying the goal expression. The search tree initially starts out as a single node representing the initial state and the initial set of goals that need to be achieved to satisfy the goal expression. The tree is expanded by repeating the following two steps:

1. Decision phase: There are four types of decisions that PRODIGY makes during problem solving. First, it must decide what node in the search tree to expand next, defaulting to a depth-first expansion. Each node consists of a set of goals and a state describing the world. After a node has been selected, one of the node's goals must be selected, and then an operator relevant to this goal must be chosen. Finally, a set of bindings for the parameters of that operator must be decided upon.

2. Expansion phase: If the instantiated operator's preconditions are satisfied, the operator is applied. Otherwise, PRODIGY subgoals on the unmatched preconditions. In either case, a new node is created.

The search terminates after creating a node whose state satisfies the top-level goal expression.

## Control Rules

As PRODIGY attempts to solve a problem, it must make decisions about which operator to use and which subgoal to pursue. These decisions can be influenced by control rules for the following purposes:

1. To increase the efficiency of the problem solver's search. Control rules guide the problem solver down the correct path so that solutions are found faster.

2. To improve the quality of the solutions that are found. There is usually more than one solution to a problem, but only the first one that is found will be returned. By directing the problems solver's attention along a particular path, control rules can express preferences for solutions that are qualitatively better (e.g., more reliable, less costly to execute, etc.).

3. To direct the problem solver along paths that it would not explore otherwise. As with most planners, for efficiency PRODIGY normally explores only a portion of the complete search space. This is accomplished through the use of default control rules. For example, PRODIGY will not normally explore all permutations of conjunctive sets of subgoals. However, when these default heuristics prove too restrictive, they can be selectively overridden by additional rules.

PRODIGY's reliance on explicit control rules, which can be learned for specific domains, distinguishes it from most domain independent problem solvers. Instead of using a least–commitment search strategy, for example, PRODIGY expects that any important decisions will be guided by the presence of appropriate control knowledge. If no control rules are relevant to a decision, then PRODIGY

**IF**: (and (CURRENT-NODE *node*)
   (CURRENT-GOAL *node* (SHAPE *obj shape*))
   (CANDIDATE-OPERATOR *node* ROLL)
   (CANDIDATE-OPERATOR *node* LATHE))
**THEN**: (prefer operator ROLL to LATHE)

FIG. 9.4.   An Operator Preference Rule

makes a quick, arbitrary choice. If in fact the wrong choice was made, and costly backtracking proved necessary, an attempt will be made to learn the control knowledge that must be missing. The rationale for PRODIGY's *casual commitment* strategy is that for any decision with significant ramifications, control rules should be present; if they are not, the problem solver should not attempt to be clever without knowledge, rather, the cleverness should come about as a result of learning. Thus, our emphasis is on an elegant and simple problem solving architecture which can produce sophisticated behavior when given the appropriate, domain-specific control knowledge, coupled with the automated acquisition of that knowledge through experience.

Control rules can be employed to guide the four decisions described in the previous section "Control Structure." Each control rule has a left-hand side condition testing applicability and a right-hand side indicating whether to SE-LECT, REJECT or PREFER a particular candidate. For example, the control rule depicted in Figure 9.4 is a preference rule used in deciding which of the candidate operators at a node to attempt first. In this case the rules state that if ROLL and LATHE are candidate operators at the current node, ROLL should be preferred over LATHE.

To make a control decision, given a default set of candidates (nodes, goals, operators, or bindings, depending on the decision), PRODIGY first applies the applicable selection rules to select a subset of the candidates. (If no selection rules are applicable, all the candidates are included.) Next rejection rules further filter this set by explicit elimination of particular remaining candidates, and finally preference rules are used to order the remaining alternatives. The preferences among the remaining alternatives can be viewed as a directed graph.[1] Cycles in the preference graph are ignored. (That is, if A is preferred over B, and B is preferred over A, then PRODIGY actually considers neither to be preferred over the other.) The most preferred candidate is one over which no other candidate is preferred, after taking into account the rule for cycles. If backtracking is necessary, the next most preferred candidate is attempted, and so on, until all selected and non-rejected candidates are exhausted, or a global solution is found.

Notice that the left-hand-side of the control rule is written in PDL, the same language as the preconditions for operators and inference rules, though different

---

[1]PRODIGY also allows preferences to be prioritized, but this capability is not used by the EBL system.

predicates are used. Meta-level predicates such as CURRENT–NODE and CANDI-DATE–NODE are used in control-rules, whereas the predicates used in operators and inference rules are domain-level predicates, such as SHAPE and IDLE. A stock set of meta-level predicates is provided with PRODIGY.

Another example control rule is shown in Figure 9.5. This operator rejection rule states that if the current goal at a node is to reshape an object and the object must subsequently be polished, then we should reject the ROLL operator. Notice the use of the meta-level predicate ADJUNCT–GOAL; if a goal is an ADJUNCT-GOAL at a node, then it will be achieved after the current goal. (The adjunct goals at a node are the goals that have not been selected as the current goal.)

The example problem from the previous section illustrates why this rule is appropriate: polishing OBJECT–A after rolling it turned out to be impossible. Had the system previously learned this rule, the problem would have been solved directly, without the costly backtracking at Node 1.

## EXPLANATION-BASED LEARNING IN PRODIGY

The capability to learn and exploit search control knowledge is critically important for domain-independent problem solvers. Without control knowledge such systems are grossly inefficient and impractical for all but the simplest problems. Their poor performance is due to the exponential nature of the search spaces they typically confront, and consequently even highly parallel hardware cannot make up for a lack of control knowledge. In practice, a problem-solving system must be given enough information about the problem and how to solve it so that its search is restricted to a tractable space.

Unfortunately, human experts find it difficult and time consuming to provide appropriate control information, and consequently domain–independent problem solvers are rarely used. In the ideal world, a problem solver would take a description of the actions possible in the world, and learn methods for effectively solving problems based on its own experience, much as a human would. Recent progress on a knowledge-intensive learning approach, explanation-based learning (EBL), appears to bring us closer to this possibility. By analyzing problem-solving traces, EBL programs have learned macro-operators (Fikes, Hart, & Nilsson,1972), chunks (Rosenbloom & Laird, 1986), heuristics (Mitchell, Utgoff, & Banerji, 1983) as well as other knowledge structures (DeJong & Mooney,

IF: (and (CURRENT-NODE *node*)
    (CURRENT-GOAL *node* (SHAPE *obj shape*))
    (CANDIDATE-OPERATOR *node* ROLL)
    (ADJUNCT-GOAL *node* (POLISHED *obj*))))
THEN: (reject operator ROLL)

FIG. 9.5. An Operator Rejection Rule

1986; Silver, 1986) that can be used to control a problem solver. However, EBL is not *guaranteed* to improve problem solving. Indeed, in many cases performance may even degrade. The problem is that control knowledge has a hidden cost that can often defeat its purpose—the cost of testing whether the knowledge is applicable as the search is carried out. To produce real efficiency improvement, an EBL program must generate control knowledge that is *effective*—its benefits must outweigh its costs. Recent experience with systems such as MORRIS (Minton, 1985), SOAR (Tambe & Newell, 1988), and PROLEARN (Prieditis & Mostow, 1987) have indicated that EBL can actually degrade performance if the costs and benefits of learned knowledge are ignored. Previous research in EBL has largely ignored this issue, which we refer to as the *utility* issue. PRODIGY's EBL component was designed specifically to produce control knowledge that is effective. The system considers what type of concepts are worth learning from a problem-solving trace, how to best represent the learned knowledge, and how useful the learned knowledge is with respect to the set of training problems. In this sense PRODIGY is a *deliberative* rather than a *reflexive* learner such as SOAR.

## EBL and the Utility Problem

Figure 9.6 shows a high-level specification of the input and output of the EBL process as described in (Mitchell, Keller, & Kedar-Cabelli, 1986). As indicated by the figure, EBL begins with a high-level *target concept* and a *training example* for that concept. Using the *domain theory,* a set of axioms describing the domain, one can explain why the training example is an instance of the target concept. The explanation is essentially a proof that the training example satisfies the target concept. By finding the weakest conditions under which the explanation holds, EBL will produce a *learned description* that is both a generalization of the training example, and a specialization of the target concept. The learned description must satisfy the *operationality criterion,* a test which insures that the description will serve as an efficient recognizer for the target concept.

As an example (adapted from Mitchell et al., 1986) consider the target concept (SAFE-TO-STACK $x$ $y$), that is, object $x$ can be safely placed on object $y$ without object $y$ collapsing. Let us suppose our training example is a demonstration that a particular book, "Principles of AI", can be safely placed upon a particular table, Coffee-Table-1. If our domain theory contains assertions such as those shown below, we can construct a proof that "Principles of AI" is safe to stack on Coffee-Table-1, because all books are lighter than tables. The resulting learned description would therefore be (AND (IS-BOOK $x$) (IS-TABLE $y$).

### DOMAIN THEORY:

(IS-BOOK PRINCIPLES-OF-AI)
(SAFE-TO-STACK $x$ $y$) if (OR (LIGHTER $x$ $y$) (NOT-FRAGILE $y$))
(LESS-THAN $w$ 5-LBS) if (AND (IS-BOOK $x$) (WEIGHT $x$ $w$))

. . . . .

Given:

- Target Concept: A concept to be learned.

- Training Example: An example of the target concept.

- Domain Theory: A set of rules and facts to be used in explaining how the training example is an example of the target concept.

- Operationality Criterion: A predicate over descriptions, specifying the form in which the learned description must be expressed.

Determine:

- A description that is both a generalization of the training example and a specialization of the target concept, which satisfies the operationality criterion.

FIG. 9.6.    Specification of EBL (from Mitchell et al., 1986)

As our example illustrates, the actual purpose of EBL is not to learn more about the target concept, but to re-express the target concept in a more "operational" manner. While the exact definition of operationality may vary depending on the learning system, efficiency for recognition is normally the implicit basis for any operationality criterion. (Otherwise, if efficiency is of no concern, the target concept could be used as is, since it is exactly defined by the domain theory.)

One can visualize a standard EBL program operating as follows. After being given a training example, EBL produces a learned description which is a generalization of the example. If the next training example is not covered by this description, another learned description is produced. If the third example is not covered by either of the two previous examples, another learned description is produced, and so on. Thus, the program incrementally re-expresses the target concept disjunctively, where each disjunct is one of the descriptions learned from an individual trial.

Supposedly, the operationality criterion insures that the learned disjuncts can be efficiently employed by the problem solver. However, in practice the operationality criteria used in EBL systems to date have been trivial and unrealistic, or even nonexistent. Thus, if we consider EBL systems that learn control knowledge (and almost all implemented EBL systems fall into this category), it is possible that learning may actually slow down the system. The following factors can contribute to performance degradation:

- Low Application Frequency: A learned description may be useful when applied, but rarely applicable (i.e., overly specific). Thus the accumulated cost of repeatedly testing whether the description is applicable in the current state may outweigh the amortized benefit, even if the average cost of the test is low.

- High Match Cost: A learned description may be useful when applied, and may indeed be applied frequently, but the average cost of determining whether it is applicable may overwhelm any potential benefits. For example, the cost of matching the preconditions of a STRIPS-style macro-operator (Fikes et al., 1972; Minton, 1985) can be prohibitively expensive when the macro-opertor represents a long chain of operators. If each individual operator in the system has approximately ten preconditions then an operator chain of length ten may have up to one hundred preconditions. This can cause serious difficulties, since the matching problem for precondition lists is NP–complete (Minton, 1988a).

- Low Benefit: The learned description may be of such marginal utility so as not to be worth the application overhead. For instance, consider a control rule in a robot navigation domain that selects amongst all possible paths to find one that has the fewest obstacles. This rule may not provide appreciable benefit if the robot can easily push obstacles out of the way.

## Addressing the Utility Problem

PRODIGY addresses the utility problem by searching for highly useful explanations that are inexpensive to match. After each problem-solving episode, explanations are generated in a three stage process. First, the system considers what to learn from a problem-solving trace, then it considers how to best represent the learned information, and finally it empirically tests the utility of the resulting control rules to insure that they are indeed useful.

- Selecting a Target Concept: Unlike earlier EBL problem-solving systems, PRODIGY can not only explain why a path succeeded, but can also choose to describe why a path failed, or why other significant properties hold, such as one solution path being shorter than another. The set of target concepts, as well as the theory used to construct explanations, is declaratively specified and extensible. Thus, control rules can be learned that capture a specific reason for making a control decision. Equally important, the right-hand sides of the control rules in PRODIGY are very expressive, enabling greater control than is possible with mechanisms such as macro-operators. (For example, preference and rejection rules are difficult to encode as macro-operators.) Therefore the capability to specify multiple target concepts is not wasted on an inflexible control structure.

- Compression: Representing an Explanation. In PRODIGY, we recognize that there can be multiple ways to express an explanation. The control rules resulting from some expressions of an explanation will have lower match costs than others. Consequently, after constructing an initial explanation, PRODIGY attempts to improve it using a simplifier. The simplification process can be regarded as a search through a space of alternative formulations of an explanation in order to find a formulation with a low match cost.

- Evaluating the Utility of an Explanation. PRODIGY has an explicit utility metric for evaluating control rules, enabling the system to measure the tradeoff between search and knowledge. The utility of a rule is determined by the cumulative time cost of matching the rule, versus the cumulative savings in search time it produces. When a rule is learned from an example, the costs and benefits for that rule can be estimated from the example and validated during subsequent problem solving. Only learned rules that have high utility are kept.

Large-scale experiments with PRODIGY's EBL module (Minton, 1988a, 1988b) have shown that all three of these features are necessary in order for PRODIGY to produce effective control knowledge. The following sections describe the EBL module in more detail.

## Selecting a Target Concept and Generating An Initial Explanation

In PRODIGY, explanation-based learning can either be interleaved with problem solving, or postponed until after the current problem has been solved. In either case, PRODIGY's explanation-based learning process begins by examining the problem-solving trace in order to pick out examples of PRODIGY's target concepts. Below we list the four types of target concepts currently implemented in PRODIGY. (Each type of target concept has a variation for nodes, goals, operators and bindings.)

1. SUCCEEDS: A control choice (of a node, goal, operator or bindings) succeeds if it leads to a solution. Learning about successes results in preference rules.
2. FAILS: A choice fails if there is no solution consistent with that choice. Learning about failures results in rejection rules.
3. SOLE-ALTERNATIVE: A choice is a sole alternative if all other candidates fail. Learning about sole alternatives results in selection rules.
4. GOAL-INTERFERENCE: A choice results in goal interference if all solutions consistent with that choice delete a condition that must subsequently be reachieved. Learning about such goal interactions results in preference rules.

The set of target concepts is specified declaratively to the system. Each target concept is represented by a predicate, and each is accompanied by a template for building a search control rule. Because there can be many training examples for the various target concepts in a single trace, target concepts are associated with *training example selection heuristics* that are used to pick out examples that appear to offer the most promise of producing useful control rules. For example, the success of an operator is deemed to be interesting only if other operators failed.

After an example of a target concept is selected, PRODIGY constructs an explanation. To do so, it is necessary to have a theory that describes the problem-solver, as well as a theory that describes the task domain. Therefore PRODIGY contains a set of *architecture–level* axioms that serve as its theory of the problem solver, and a set of *domain–level* axioms that are automatically derived from the domain operators.

PRODIGY constructs an explanation by specializing the target concept in accordance with the example using a method called *explanation-based specialization* (EBS) (Minton, 1988a; Minton et al., 1989). To specialize a target concept, EBS retrieves an axiom that implies the concept (all axioms are implications) and recursively specializes all its nonprimitive subconcepts. The algorithm operates in a manner that is similar to a top-down parser. In order to choose which axiom is appropriate when more than one is available, PRODIGY allows explicit *discriminator functions* to be associated with the theory. These functions aid the explanation construction process by examining the search tree and selecting the axioms that correspond to the example. The explanation process is therefore controlled by the discriminator functions, in that they provide a mapping from the example to the explanation.

## Discussion

A significant difference between PRODIGY and most other EBL problem-solving systems lies in the range of target concepts that are employed. PRODIGY's target concepts are meta-level concepts, such as SUCCEEDS, FAILS, and GOAL–INTER-FERENCE, that describe arbitrary problem-solving phenomenon. Earlier EBL problem-solving systems, such as STRIPS (Fikes et al., 1972) and LEX2 (Mitchell et al., 1983) focused on learning from solution sequences, and it is only recently that EBL has been used to learn from failure (Hammond, 1986b; Mostow & Bhatnagar, 1987). PRODIGY provides a uniform, extensible framework for producing explanations about any phenomenon encountered in a problem-solving trace. Each target concept corresponds to a separate strategy for optimizing problem-solving performance based on the observed phenomenon.

## Compression: Improving An Explanation

The purpose of EBL in PRODIGY is to produce a form of the target concept that is operational (i.e., one that can be evaluated efficiently). Simplification and other representational transformations play an important role in this process; one cannot simply specialize a target concept without worrying about how the result is expressed. We call these processes *compression*.

The purpose of compression is to reduce the match cost of the learned description (and thereby increase the utility of the resulting search control rule). After the initial phase of the EBL process creates the initial learned description, it is processed by PRODIGY's compression module which first employs partial evaluation and simple logical transformations, and then calls a theorem prover which can take advantage of domain-specific simplification axioms.

For example, suppose PRODIGY generates the description shown below. The description (taken literally) states that PRODIGY will fail at a node if the goal at that node is to achieve the condition (TEMPERATURE *obj y*) where *y* equals COLD, and for every current temperature of the object, that temperature is not equal to COLD. In fact, the compressor can simplify the description into the equivalent description (also shown) stating that PRODIGY will fail at a node if the goal is to change an object's temperature to COLD. (In other words, the goal (TEMPERATURE *obj* COLD) is unachievable.) To do so the compressor employs a domain specific simplification axiom stating that every object has a unique temperature, as well as a domain independent axiom indicating that if a condition is a goal then that condition is not KNOWN (i.e., true) at the current node.

(FAILS *node*)
      IF (AND (CURRENT-GOAL *node goal*)
           (MATCHES *goal* (TEMPERATURE *obj y*))
           (EQUAL *y* COLD)
           (KNOWN *node* (FORALL (*x*) SUCH-THAT (TEMPERATURE *obj x*)
                        (NOT (EQUAL *x* COLD)))))))

reduces to:

      (FAILS *goal node*)
        if (CURRENT-GOAL *node* (TEMPERATURE *obj* COLD))

In addition to simplifying individual descriptions, the compressor can also combine multiple descriptions in order to reduce total match cost. In general, this process tends to be successful only when the descriptions share common terms; simply joining two descriptions with an "OR" does not reduce match cost. If combining descriptions does not reduce match cost appreciably, then PRODIGY will stay with the original individual descriptions. (The individual descriptions are typically easier for the user to understand.)

## *Discussion*

The compression process, which rewrites a description to reduce its match cost, can be viewed as a search process to find the most useful form in which to express the description. In practice, we have found that compression is crucial for making EBL work in PRODIGY. The majority of the simplifications involve very simple reductions and reorderings, however, without these operations, the learned control rules would have hundreds, if not thousands of terms. For example, the architecture–level axioms used to explain failures take up several pages of fairy dense logical notation. Without compression, the descriptions learned by analyzing failures tend to be several pages long.

## Evaluating the Utility of an Explanation

The utility of a control rule learned by PRODIGY's EBS process can be measured in terms of the speed up resulting from using the rule. Specifically, utility is given by the ideal cost/benefit formula:

Utility = (AvrSavings × ApplicFreq) − AvrMatchCost

where AvrMatchCost = the average cost of matching the rule,
AvrSavings = the average savings when the rule is applicable,
Applicfreq = the fraction of times that the rule is applicable when it is tested.

After learning a control rule, the system produces an initial estimate of the rule's utility based on the training example that produced the rule. PRODIGY compares the cost of matching the rule with the cost of exploring the portion of the search tree that need not be considered due to the new control rule. If the new rule appears useful, it is included in the active set of control rules. During subsequent problem solving, the utility estimate is empirically validated by maintaining statistics on the use of the rule. If the system eventually determines that the rule's utility is negative, the rule is deactivated. (In the current version of sc prodigy deactivated rules are "forgotten." A more sophisticated system might reactivate rules for specific contexts.)

## *Discussion*

Traditionally, EBL systems have not attempted to evaluate the effect of the learning process. PRODIGY's utility evaluation enables it to prevent ineffective rules from impairing the performance of the system. As shown by experiments with the MORRIS system (Minton, 1985), the capability to be selective about what is learned can provide significant advantages to a learning system.[2] Despite the fact that PRODIGY deliberately attempts to find the best explanations it can in the first two stages of the learning process, it is still the case that most of the explanations that are produced are ineffective (Minton, 1988b) and must be eliminated by utility evaluation.

---

[2]In addition to PRODIGY's utility evaluation, selectivity is also exhibited by PRODIGY's training example *selection heuristics* that pick out promising examples of target concepts from the problem-solving trace, as mentioned previously.

## An Example: Learning from Failure

As previously indicated, PRODIGY's EBL method can either be interleaved with problem solving, or it may be used after the problem solver has finished. For purposes of discussion, we will assume that the learning is invoked post-hoc, although it makes little difference to the nature of the method.

Our example is taken from the scheduling episode described previously, where the problem solver constructed a plan to lathe and polish an object in order to make it cylindrical and polished. The reader will recall that the problem solver did not immediately find this solution, but first explored the possibility of rolling the object and then polishing it. This possibility failed because the object could not be clamped to the polisher once it had been rolled due to its high temperature. From this experience PRODIGY will learn a control rule that enables it to avoid repeating the mistake in the future.

Figure 9.7 illustrates the portion of the search tree analyzed by PRODIGY as it explains the failure of ROLL. PRODIGY begins the learning process by starting at the bottom left-most portion of the search tree and working upwards. The final result of the analysis, describing why ROLL failed, is shown alongside Node 1. In addition the figure shows the intermediate results describing why each of the lower-level nodes failed. The intermediate results serve as lemmas in explaining the higher level failures.

Let us walk through the learning process. As shown in Figure 9.7, PRODIGY attributes the failure at Node 4 to the fact that there is no way to achieve a goal that requires cooling an object. (Objects can only be heated.) This failure is propagated up the tree to Node 3, at which point PRODIGY can state that CLAMP-ING an object will fail if the object is not cool. Continuing the postorder traversal of the failed subtree, PRODIGY concludes that the failure of Node 3 is due to the fact that it is impossible to make an object rectangular. Thus Node 2's failure is attributed to the fact that polishing an object is impossible if the object is not rectangular and not cool. (Under these conditions, the precondition stating that either the object must be RECTANGULAR or it must be CLAMPED to the polisher is unachievable.) This also immediately explains why the other attempts to apply POLISH at later time periods also failed. Finally, the top-level failure of ROLL is attributed to the fact that object had to be subsequently polished; as evidenced by the example, polishing is impossible after applying ROLL.

The top–level result, which describes why applying ROLL at Node 1 failed, can be converted directly into an operator rejection rule. The resulting control rule is the same one shown in Figure 9.5. (In fact, all of the node failure descriptions in Figure 9.7 can be converted into node rejection control rules, although this top–level result is by far the most useful.)

The learned rule is highly effective because its match cost is low and there is a large payoff when the rule is applicable. Consider, for example, similar problems that involve reshaping and polishing an object. By eliminating the need to con-

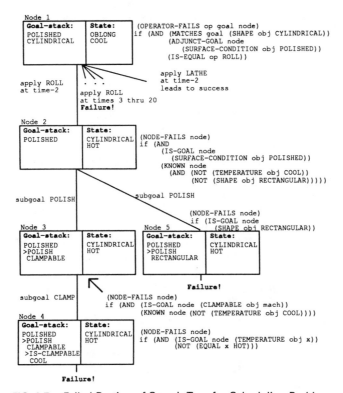

FIG. 9.7.    Failed Portion of Search Tree for Scheduling Problem

sider the ROLL operator, the rule produces a savings on the order of $n \times t$, where $n$ is the size of the schedule, and $t$ is the cost of considering ROLL for a particular time-period (e.g., the cost of searching nodes 2 through 5 in Figure 9.7). For problems where there are intervening goals that are achieved after rolling the object, but before attempting to polish it, the benefit can be as high as $O(n^k)$ where $k$ is the number of intervening top-level goals. Empirically speaking, this rule has been observed to increase the performance of the system by over an order of magnitude on certain problems. As illustrated by this example, failure-driven learning is most beneficial when the reason(s) for the failure can be expressed by a concise, easily evaluated description.

Our example also demonstrates that it is not always necessary to analyze the entire search tree in order to learn from failure. To learn why applying ROLL at Node 1 fails, it was only necessary to analyze the subtree rooted at Node 2. Once the reason for the failure was discovered, it immediately followed that the other applications of ROLL (at TIME−2 through TIME−20) fail for the same reason. In fact, had learning been interleaved with problem solving, PRODIGY could have avoided these subsequent attempts to apply ROLL. In effect, when learning and problem solving are interleaved, PRODIGY carries out a very general form of dependency–directed backtracking.

## Results

Figure 9.8 summarizes the system's performance on one hundred randomly generated problems from the machine–shop domain. Three conditions are shown: the problem solver running without any control rules, the problem solver running with learned control rules, and the problem solver running with hand-coded control rules. The learned control rules were acquired during a separate training phase consisting of approximately one hundred problems. The hand–coded control rules were written by the authors. (They took about eight hours to code.) The graph shows how the cumulative problem-solving time grows as the number of problems solved increases. The cumulative time is the total problem-solving time (*over all problems*) up to that point. Thus, the slopes of the curves are positive because the y–axis represents cumulative time. Because the problems were ordered according to size (i.e., number of objects to be scheduled, etc.), and therefore are progressively more difficult, the second derivatives of the curves are also positive.

As the graph shows, PRODIGY performed approximately fifty percent worse with the learned rules than with the hand–coded rules, but much better than without control rules. Similar results were obtained in other domains as well. A detailed discussion of these experimental results can be found in (Minton, 1988a).

## ABSTRACTION IN PRODIGY

PRODIGY is capable of planning at different levels of abstraction; that is, ignoring certain details to get an overall plan structure and progressively refining the plan into a fully operational one. Abstraction planning often improves the performance of the problem solver by reducing search; it makes no sense to commit to details in a plan that will later be scrapped as unsound for global reasons. Moreover, the top–down abstraction planning approach can produce more elegant and concise plans than an opportunistic bottom-up approach.

There are two main issues in using abstraction in a planning system: first, how the planner uses abstractions to control search, and second, how the abstractions can be produced automatically from the domain definition.

The basic approach in using abstraction hierarchies to control search is to plan in an abstract space then refine the abstract plans into more detailed plans. Many existing hierarchical problem solving systems exploit this basic technique, but vary how the abstraction spaces are defined. The various methods for defining an abstraction space include specifying a new set of abstract operators (Newell &

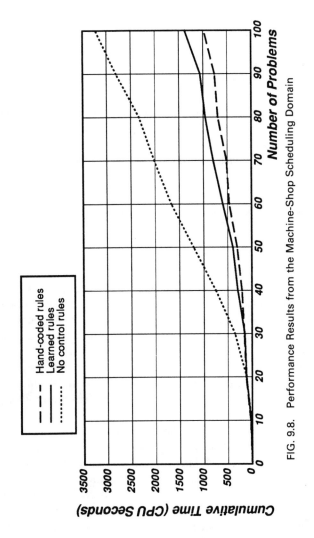

FIG. 9.8. Performance Results from the Machine-Shop Scheduling Domain

263

Simon, 1972), dropping some of the preconditions of the existing operators (Sacerdoti, 1974, 1977), using constraints (Stefik, 1981; Wilkins, 1984), forming macro operators (Korf, 1985, 1987), creating aggregate objects (Campbell, 1988; Flann, 1989), and dynamically abstracting goals (Unruh, 1988; Unruh & Rosenbloom, 1989).

The issue of automatically generating abstractions for hierarchical planning has been ignored until recently; most of the earlier systems that used abstractions were simply provided with the appropriate abstractions. The more recent work on this topic includes creating abstractions spaces by forming macro operators (Korf, 1985) and learning abstractions through experimentation in SOAR (Unruh, 1988; Unruh & Rosenbloom, 1989).

In this section, we first describe how abstractions are used for planning in PRODIGY, then we describe how abstractions are automatically generated for PRODIGY by a system called ALPINE (Knoblock, 1989a, 1989b), and finally we present some results demonstrating the effectiveness of this approach.

### Hierarchical Planning in PRODIGY

Before problem solving begins, PRODIGY selects an abstraction hierarchy that is appropriate for solving the given problem. The abstraction spaces are formed by selectively ignoring certain properties in the original problem space. Thus an abstract space does not involve simply dropping preconditions or goals; instead an abstract space is an abstract model (or reduced model (Tenenberg, 1988)) of the original problem space, where both the operators and states are simplified. The next section describes in more detail how the abstraction spaces are formed and selected. The remainder of this section describes how PRODIGY uses abstractions for planning.

To plan hierarchically, PRODIGY first maps the problem into the highest level of the abstraction hierarchy by removing details from the initial and goal states to form legal states in the abstract space. Next the system produces a plan that solves the given problem using the operators in this abstract space. This produces an abstract plan that correctly solves the problem for the most important conditions. The abstract plan is then mapped into successively more detailed levels by forming subproblems where each intermediate state in an abstract plan forms an intermediate goal at the next level of detail. Planning at successive levels of abstraction is always guided by the master plan passed from above. When the problem has been refined into the base space (the original problem space), the problem is solved. If an abstract plan cannot be refined (e.g., new conditions introduced at the current level of abstraction cannot be satisfied), PRODIGY backtracks to reformulate the plan at a higher level of abstraction.

Consider the high-level robot-planning domain described in ABSTRIPS (Sacerdoti, 1974) and shown in Figure 9.9. In this domain there are a number of rooms, a robot, a small set of blocks, and doors between connecting rooms which can be

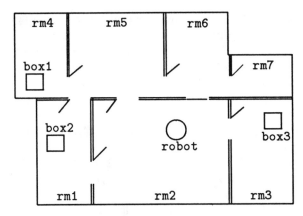

FIG. 9.9.   Robot-Planning Domain

open or closed. The domain contains operators for moving the robot, pushing boxes, and opening and closing doors. A problem in this domain might be to place several blocks next to each other in a particular room. A useful abstract plan to solve this problem might only consider moving blocks among rooms, ignoring the placement within each room, the location of the robot, or whether the doors are open or closed. The abstract plan could then be expanded to include moving the robot successively to each room that contains a box to be moved. Eventually, the plan would be refined down to the base space and all of the details would be considered. The abstraction enables the planner to focus on the difficult parts of the problem first, and then work on successively easier details.

## Automatically Generating Abstractions

To be useful, an abstraction must distinguish the important aspects of a domain from the details. A desirable feature of an abstraction is that in the process of refining the abstract plan into a plan that includes the detailed paths, the abstract plan is not altered (i.e., refining the abstract plan should not involve altering the path through the rooms). For example, in the path planning domain described in the previous section, after planning a path at the abstract level of rooms, one can plan the detailed paths within the rooms without altering the abstract plan. The invariance of the abstract solution is important because the abstract solution is used as a template for a solution at the next level of detail.

We define a refinement of an abstraction plan to be *monotonic* if the refinement does not alter the abstract plan, but only inserts additional details into the plan without undoing those conditions that have already been achieved. We define an abstraction space to be monotonic if for every solvable problem the abstraction space contains a solution that can be monotonically refined. Thus, if a solution exists it will be found by searching through the set of abstract plans and their corresponding refinements. Knoblock (1989b) provides a formal definition of the monotonicity property.

The abstraction spaces of the example described in the previous section are monotonic. At an abstract level, a plan is produced which only specifies which rooms the blocks are to be pushed through. This abstraction space is monotonic since once the plan for moving between rooms has been produced, the plan can be refined to deal with the details (i.e., path of the robot, placement of the blocks within a room, etc.) without altering the abstract plan. Once the paths for the blocks have been determined, that part of the plan is considered fixed and is then used to expand the rest of the details. If an abstraction space did not have the monotonicity property, an abstract plan could be produced only to become invalid in the process of refining the plan. The planner would then be forced to repair the old plan or backtrack across abstraction levels and find a new abstract plan. Although it may prove useful to allow altering abstract plans in certain limited situations, in general, alterations can be costly, possibly requiring more work than simply solving the problem without using abstraction. Thus, we focus on finding monotonic abstraction spaces.

Table 9.1 presents a simplified algorithm for producing monotonic abstraction spaces. This algorithm forms the basis of the more complex algorithm that ALPINE uses for generating abstractions. The algorithm is given the operators of a domain and it produces a hierarchy of monotonic abstraction spaces represented as a directed graph. Abstraction spaces are formed by removing literals from the domain. The resulting abstraction spaces can be viewed as abstract models, in which both the operators and states are simplified. The algorithm makes use of the fact that many domains have an implicit structure where the literals in a domain will only interact with some of the other literals. Thus, the algorithm partitions the literals into classes and orders the classes to exploit this structure. The ordered classes are used to form a hierarchy of abstraction spaces by remov-

TABLE 9.1
Algorithm for Producing Monotonic Abstraction Spaces

---

Input:    The set of operators for a domain.
Output:   A hierarchy of monotonic abstraction spaces.

Create_Abstraction_Hierarchy(OPERATORS)
1. ForEach OP in OPERATORS
       ForEach LIT1 in Effects(OP)
           i. ForEach LIT2 in Effects (OP)
                  Add_Directed_Edge(LIT1,LIT2,GRAPH)
          ii. ForEach LIT2 in Preconditions(OP)
                  Add_Directed_Edge(LIT1,LIT2,GRAPH)
2. Combine_Strongly_Connected_Components(GRAPH)
3. Topological_Sort(GRAPH)

---

ing successive classes of literals from a domain. The literals removed at each level only interact with other literals that are in the same class or those already removed from the domain. The final hierarchy consists of an ordered set of abstraction spaces, where the highest level is the most abstract and the lowest level is the most detailed.

The algorithm is given as input the operators of a domain, which are specified in terms of their preconditions and effects. In this simplified version of the algorithm, the preconditions and effects are restricted to conjunctions of ground literals.[3] The algorithm forms a directed graph, where the vertices of the graph are the literals and the edges are constraints between literals. A directed edge from one literal to another indicates that the first literal must be higher than or at the same level in the abstraction hierarchy as the second literal. The steps of the algorithm are as follows:

• Step 1 creates the directed graph from the operators. This step adds constraints that guarantee the achievement of a particular literal could never require adding or deleting a literal higher in the abstraction hierarchy. The constraints force all the effects of an operator into the same abstraction level and force the preconditions of an operator into the same or lower level as the effects.

• Step 2 combines the strongly connected components of the graph using a depth-first search algorithm described in (Aho, Hopcroft, & Ullman, 1974). This step eliminates cycles in the graph by partitioning the literals into classes. The remaining constraints between classes specify the order in which the literal classes can be removed from the domain to form abstraction spaces. Thus, the partially-ordered literal classes represent a partial order of abstraction spaces.

• Step 3 transforms the partial order into a total order using a topological sort. The total order represents an abstraction hierarchy by defining the order in which the literal classes are included in successive refinements of an abstract plan.

The complexity of this algorithm is quadratic in the number of literals in the domain (the proof is given in Knoblock, 1989b).

The ALPINE system uses an extended version of this algorithm (Knoblock, 1989a). This extended algorithm handles a more sophisticated language and uses additional knowledge of the domain. ALPINE deals with the full PRODIGY description language (PDL), which includes variables, disjunction, quantification, and conditional effects. In addition, ALPINE exploits additional domain knowledge to increase the likelihood of finding fine–grained abstractions. This additional knowledge includes specifying the primary effects of operators to avoid adding unnecessary constraints, typing of the arguments to increase the granularity of

---

[3]A ground literal is a possibly negated atomic formula that is fully instantiated.

the literals, and providing domain axioms to allow more sophisticated reasoning about possible interactions in a domain.

Not all of the constraints generated by the algorithm above are necessary to guarantee monotonicity. ALPINE exploits this fact by relaxing unnecessary constraints to produce additional abstraction levels. Consider a simple example. The operator for moving the robot from one room to another requires that the robot is in the first room, next to the door, and the door between the rooms is open. Similarly the operator for opening the door requires that the robot is in the room standing next to the door. If the open door operator is only used to achieve a precondition for moving between rooms, we can guarantee that the robot will already be in the room standing next to the door. Therefore, the abstraction space formed by dropping the literals involving the door status will be monotonic. ALPINE avoids adding unnecessary constraints of this type by considering the contexts in which an operator will generate particular subgoals. If an operator will not generate a subgoal, then the corresponding constraint becomes unnecessary in that context.

Figure 9.10 shows the constraints produced by ALPINE for the example domain. The boxes placed around one or more literals indicate which literals are placed in the same class based on the strongly connected components. The literal classes are ordered such that those classes at the top of the figure must be placed

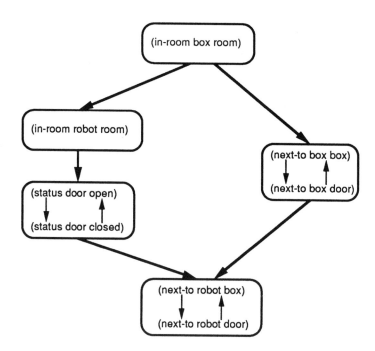

FIG. 9.10.   Partial Ordering of Literals Produced by ALPINE

higher in the abstraction hierarchy. The result is a partial order of literal classes that represents a number of possible abstraction spaces.

In addition to using context information to create the partial order, ALPINE further refines the possible abstraction hierarchies based on each goal to be solved. The system first does a one-time analysis to determine the possible abstraction spaces, represented by the partial order of literal classes. Then it transforms the partial order into an abstraction hierarchy for solving a particular problem, by adding additional constraints based on the problem, and then performing the topological sort to produce the hierarchy. The first three levels of an example abstraction hierarchy are shown in Figure 9.11.

## Results

ALPINE has been implemented and successfully run on a number of domains, including the robot-planning domain described in this section of the paper. On this domain, ALPINE produces a finer grain abstraction hierarchy than the one provided manually to and then refined by ABSTRIPS. The system generates the partial order of abstraction spaces for this domain in 3.8 seconds of CPU time on a 3 MIPS workstation.

The abstraction spaces that ALPINE produces are used in the hierarchical version of the PRODIGY system. Figure 9.12 shows the performance of PRODIGY without using abstraction, using the abstractions produced by ABSTRIPS, and using the abstractions produced by ALPINE on two hundred randomly generated problems in the robot-planning domain. The problems were ordered by increasing size and ranged from problems with goals that contained between two and nine conjuncts. PRODIGY was run in each configuration and given six minutes of CPU time to solve each of the problems. The graph shows the cumulative time spent over all the problems up to the given problem number for each of the three configurations.

As the graph shows, the ALPINE configuration performed better than both the

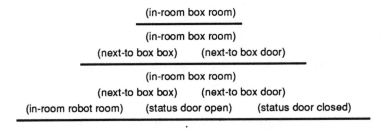

FIG. 9.11. One Possible Abstraction Hierarchy Produced from the Partial Order

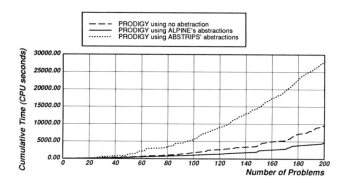

FIG. 9.12.   Performance Results from the Robot-Planning Domain

nonhierarchical configuration and the ABSTRIPS configuration in terms of CPU time. The graph does not reflect the fact that the ALPINE configuration produced shorter solutions and solved more of the problems than the other two configurations. Out of the 200 random problems, 197 of the problems were solvable. The ALPINE configuration was able to solve all of the solvable problems within the time limit, while PRODIGY without using abstraction was unable to solve 20 of the problems and the ABSTRIPS configuration was unable to solve 70 of them. The success of ALPINE in these experiments can be attributed to the fact that the abstraction spaces that ALPINE generates are monotonic. This allowed the ALPINE configuration to ignore details and focus on the more difficult parts of the problem first. In contrast, the ABSTRIPS configuration performed poorly in these experiments because only some of the abstraction spaces were monotonic. Thus, in many of the harder problems, the ABSTRIPS configuration produced plans that violated the monotonicity property and resulted in costly backtracking across abstraction levels. (We note that the abstraction spaces produced by ABSTRIPS were originally intended to be used by the STRIPS planner, not the PRODIGY planner. Because PRODIGY employs a depth-first search the ABSTRIPS configuration performed worse than it would have with STRIPS.)

Future work on abstraction in PRODIGY will focus on extending the techniques for producing abstractions, using knowledge of the population of problems encountered in a domain to bias the selection of the abstraction spaces, extending the techniques for exploiting the abstraction spaces during hierarchical planning, and combining abstraction with explanation-based learning and derivational analogy.

## ADDITIONAL LEARNING METHODS IN PRODIGY

In addition to acquiring effective control rules through explanation-based learning and automated formation of abstraction levels for efficient hierarchical planning, PRODIGY employs several other machine learning methods. In fact, a central motivation for developing the PRODIGY architecture is precisely the open–

ended opportunities for developing, testing, measuring, and contrasting multiple machine learning methods on a common knowledge representation language, a general problem solver, and a shared suite of test-bed domains. This section briefly describes the other learning components, which are under various stages of development.

## Derivational Analogy and Case–Based Learning

In contrast with explanation-based learning, which strives to acquire maximally general control rules, case–based learning stores a library of past problem-solving experience for later reuse. In essence, the case-based approach favors the storage and indexing of vast amounts of specific experiences that are retrieved, modified and extended each time new problems of a similar nature arise (Carbonell, 1983; Hammond, 1986a; Kolodner, 1980). In PRODIGY we are implementing a flexible means of recycling past cases called *derivational analogy* (Carbonell, 1986; Carbonell & Veloso, 1988). This mechanism requires that the problem solver be able to introspect into its internal decision cycle, recording the justifications for each decision taken while searching for a solution to the problem. These justifications augment the solution trace and are used both for indexing and to guide the reconstruction of the solution for subsequent problem solving situations where equivalent justifications hold true (Carbonell & Veloso, 1988).

The derivational analogy engine is able to replay entire solutions to similar past problems, calling the problem solver recursively to reduce any new subgoals brought about by known differences between the old and new problems. Alternatively, the problem solver can call the derivational analogy module to address any familiar subproblems encountered in the process of solving a new problem in an otherwise unfamiliar situation. Thus derivational analogy and operator–based problem solving are mutually recursive, exploiting analogy when possible and relying on the general problem-solving safety net when no previous cases come to mind.

Learning in the context of derivational analogy consists of adding cases to the episodic library and refining the similarity metric (in the memory organization and retrieval) as PRODIGY incrementally determines which are the contextually relevant features for reducing goals in each domain. Generalization methods group together collections of cases that share analogous features with respect to specific goals. Commonly recurring problems produce generalized plans, whereas those problems with few, if any, analogs continue to retain their full derivational traces as ground-instance cases (Veloso & Carbonell, 1989).

## Control Rules from Static Analysis

As an alternative to EBL, which acquires control rules dynamically from problem-solving traces, we are investigating when control rules can be learned statically by analyzing PRODIGY's domain descriptions. The program STATIC represents an attempt to study when examples are required and when they are superfluous in the acquisition of control knowledge. Since static analysis can be performed a priori, it may be preferable to EBL, although there are domains in which useful control rules can only be acquired dynamically.

To understand how STATIC works it is useful to think of PRODIGY's domain as a fully expanded AND/OR graph. The nodes of the graph are literals and the edges are uninstantiated operators. STATIC searches the graph for failures and pairwise goal interactions, and forms control rules that enable PRODIGY to avoid these when problem solving. STATIC considers each literal separately, and backchains on the operators that unify with the literal until it encounters failure, goal interaction, or recursion. Since recursion is detected, STATIC's search is guaranteed to terminate. The search corresponds to learning with the FAILS and GOAL–INTER-FERENCE target concepts in the explanation-based learning module. In essence, STATIC is a partial evaluator of PRODIGY's domain descriptions.

The structure of the AND/OR graph for a domain largely determines the extent to which effective control rules can be acquired (Etzioni, 1990). When this graph can be searched effectively, examples prove unimportant in learning control knowledge. Since STATIC does not utilize examples, running it in a given domain and comparing its control knowledge to that acquired by EBL amounts to an empirical test of the suitability of the domain to static learning. The control rules produced by STATIC in PRODIGY's Blocksworld compare favorably with the explanation–based rules, lending credence to the utility of static analysis. Additional experiments are underway in other domains.

## Acquiring Domain Knowledge by Experimentation

Whereas explanation-based learning, derivational analogy, formulation of abstraction hierarchies, and static control-rule acquisition all strive to improve system performance given a fixed domain knowledge base, experimentation addresses the issue of growing and refining domain knowledge through interaction with the external world (Rajamoney, 1986; Shen, 1989). There are four basic phases to experimentation:

1. Triggering–PRODIGY must determine *when* it is lacking some domain knowledge crucial to completion of its current task. Thus far experimentation is triggered when the plan execution monitor detects a divergence between internal expectations and external observations (caused by unknown side-effects of previous actions, for instance). Other triggering mechanisms include the need to learn properties of unknown objects (which may be blocking the robot's path, for instance) or establishing numerical thresholds (just how strong must the plank be to hold the robot's weight, for instance).

2. Design–PRODIGY must plan a sequence of actions that will perturb the environment minimally and yet produce the desired observations (for instance,

applying the new actions to objects not required in the plan in order to observe their side effects without interfering with the continued plan execution). This is perhaps the most difficult aspect of experimentation, and one being addressed centrally.

3. Observation–PRODIGY must instrument the experimentation process in order to observe all the important effects (a chemical reaction inside an opaque container will not inform the experimenter of a color change or a precipitated solid, for instance).

4. Assimilation–PRODIGY must change its domain knowledge to capture the new information (add new postconditions to the new operator that predict the previously unforeseen side effects, for instance).

In a test domain for planning the construction of reflector-telescope mirrors, we developed the *operator refinement method* (Carbonell & Gil, 1987, 1990) that fleshes out an incomplete domain theory through experimentation (i.e., learns new pre and post conditions of incompletely specified operators). In a second domain, we integrated PRODIGY with a 3D Newtonian robotic simulator (Carbonell & Hood, 1986) to acquire new operators through direct experimentation with the simulator.

## Semi-Automated Knowledge Acquisition

The transparent and uniform knowledge representation in PRODIGY facilitates the development of semi–automated knowledge acquisition techniques that minimize the need for intermediary knowledge engineers. In particular, we are developing the APPRENTICE system (Joseph, 1989), a visually-oriented interface to acquire knowledge of new domains, and to extend and refine knowledge of existing domains. The APPRENTICE system is intended to aid experts in acquiring both factual and control knowledge, statically and dynamically.

The static part of APPRENTICE permits graphically-oriented definition and editing of domain objects, relations and operators—the latter may be defined pictorially by *before* and *after* world states and further refined through a structure editor. In this fashion, we facilitate the initial acquisition of domain knowledge. However, much of the development time for complex knowledge–based systems (planners, expert systems, etc.) is of a more dynamic nature: knowledge–base refinement and extension, acquisition of control knowledge for more efficient problem solving, debugging both factual and control knowledge, and other aspects of general lifecycle maintenance. The initial static domain definition, important as it may be to launch the project, plays a central role only in the early phases of a software engineering effort (van de Brug, Bachant, & McDermott, 1986).

To address the extension and debugging issues, we are currently extending APPRENTICE to accept advice during problem solving. This is a process directly analogous to one–on–one coaching (or tutoring), where PRODIGY is the student and the expert user is the teacher. This work is based upon the earlier PRODIGY knowledge-refinement interface (Kuokka et al., 1987). APPRENTICE is designed to replay and analyze earlier solution attempts, all-the-while aiding in the refinement of factual or control knowledge. This interface differs from existing knowledge acquisition work in its dynamic nature: new domain or control knowledge is acquired when needed, as a problem solution unfolds, and later tested with historical replay on PRODIGY's problem library. Dynamic knowledge acquisition provides similar benefits over standard static KA to those that interactive languages and environments provide over batch-oriented edit/compile/execute systems in classical software development.

## CONCLUDING REMARKS

This paper described the PRODIGY architecture, including the uniform representation language (PDL), the general problem solver, and the various learning modules. These modules are integrated at the *representational level* in that they all employ the PDL language and the general matcher for PDL expressions, and have common data structures for states, goals, operators, inference rules and control rules. Moreover, the modules are integrated at the *reasoning level* in that all share data and interleave control with the problem solver. But, the integration does not extend to the *learning level*. Each module manifests its own deliberative learning process, unlike SOAR's pervasive and architecturally–reflexive chunking mechanism.

Underlying the design of PRODIGY are several implicit hypotheses, which we now attempt to make explicit:

• *Unified architecture hypothesis*—True intelligent behavior arises out of a unified reasoning system, rather from a collection of independent stimulus–response elements as proposed by Brooks (Brooks, 1986). This hypothesis is widely accepted in the artificial intelligence community.

• *Maximum rationality hypothesis*—Intelligent agents will behave so as to maximize the likelihood of achieving their goals. In other words, all decisions are made so as to favor the most progress towards one or more goals (whether it be the immediate task at hand, gathering information for future situations, or planning for multiple goals simultaneously). Newell stipulated this principle in (Newell, 1982), and most AI reasoning systems are designed so as to adhere implicitly to the maximal rationality hypothesis.

• *Deliberative reasoning hypothesis*—Unlike most other research projects on integrated architecture where learning is an uncontrollable reflex action of the architecture (e.g., SOAR's chunking (Laird, Rosenbloom, & Newell, 1986),

THEO's caching (Mitchell et al., chap. 12 in this volume), and ICARUS' classification-tree expansion (Langley et al., 1989)), PRODIGY decides *what* to learn about, *when* to learn it, and PRODIGY knows *why* it learned it. Thus PRODIGY can direct its learning to maximize utility, and can perform selective forgetting (e.g., if the reasons underlying a learned concept are later proven invalid, or if a new control rule is subsequently demonstrated to exhibit low utility in spite of earlier estimates to the contrary). In other words, PRODIGY elevates the maximal rationality hypothesis to the learning level, as well as applying it at the reasoning level.

• *Glass box hypothesis*—Each PRODIGY module is visible to the other modules and shares data with them: the learned control rules, the problem-solving traces, etc. All of PRODIGY's domain knowledge (and self knowledge via the architectural axioms in EBL) is available to any reasoning process, unlike SOAR's black-box philosophy where the internal structure of chunks is not open to inspection or modification.

• *Multiple learning methods hypothesis*—Factual and control knowledge can be acquired through many different mechanisms. There is no *universal learning method,* as hypothesized in SOAR's chunking mechanism, but rather a variety of methods that coexist and apply depending on the source and type of knowledge.

• *Environmental consistency hypothesis*—The external environment, the goals that arise, and the states of the world in which the system finds itself behave such that information gathered in the past is indicative of things to come in the future. Although in principle PRODIGY can track a changing environment (different problem populations, for instance), the change should be slow with respect to the time required by the learning process for adaptation. Virtually every other learning system also makes this assumption, especially inductive systems, requiring many examples to learn new concepts.

As should be evident from the list of hypotheses incorporated in the design and philosophy of PRODIGY, it is meant as a model of an idealized rational intelligence much more than a cognitively-plausible architecture emulating human reasoning. Other architectures such as SOAR differ in their design hypotheses as they strive for a closer match to human cognition.

## ACKNOWLEDGMENTS

This research was sponsored in part by the Defense Advanced Research Projects Agency (DOD), ARPA Order No. 4976, Amendment 20, under contract number F33615-87-C-1499, monitored by the Air Force Avionics Laboratory, in part by the Office of Naval Research under contracts N00014-84-K-0345 (N91) and N00014-86-K-0678-N123, in part by NASA under contract NCC 2-463, in part by the Army Research Institute under contract MDA903-85-C-0324, under subcontract 487650-25537 through the University of California, Irvine, and in part by small contributions from private institutions. The views and conclusions contained in this document are those of the authors and should not be interpreted as representing the official policies, either expressed or implied, of DARPA, ONR, NASA, ARI, or the US Government. The second author was supported by an Air Force Laboratory Graduate Fellowship through the Human Resources Laboratory at Brooks Air Force Base, and the third author was supported by an AT&T Bell Labs Ph.D. Scholarship.

The authors gratefully acknowledge the contributions of the other members of the project, past and present: Daniel Borrajo, Oren Etzioni, Yolanda Gil, Robert Joseph, Dan Kuokka, Henrik Nordin, Alicia Perez, Santiago Rememteria, Hiroshi Tsuji, and Manuela Veloso, and the help of Dan Kahn, Michael Miller, and Ellen Riloff in implementing the PRODIGY system.

## REFERENCES

Aho, A. V., Hopcroft, J. E., & Ullman, J. D. (1974). *The design and analysis of computer algorithms.* Reading, MA: Addison-Wesley.

Brooks, R. (1986). A robust layered control system for a mobile robot. *IEEE Journal of Robotics and Automation, 2(1),,* 14–23.

Campbell, M. S. (1988). *Chunking as an abstraction mechanism.* Ph.D. thesis, Computer Science Department, Carnegie Mellon University, Pittsburgh, PA.

Carbonell, J. G. (1983). Learning by analogy: Formulating and generalizing plans from past experience. In R. S. Michalski, J. G. Carbonell, & T. M. Mitchell (Eds.), *Machine learning: An artificial intelligence approach* (pp. 137–162). San Mateo, CA: Morgan Kaufmann.

Carbonell, J. G. (1986). Derivational analogy: A theory of reconstructive problem solving and expertise acquisition. In R. S. Michalski, J. G. Carbonell, & T. M. Mitchell (Eds.), *Machine learning: An artificial intelligence approach, Volume II* (pp. 371–392). San Mateo, CA: Morgan Kaufmann.

Carbonell, J. G., & Gil, Y. (1987). Learning by experimentation. In P. Langley (Ed.), *Proceedings of the Fourth International Workshop on Machine Learning* (pp. 256–266). San Mateo, CA: Morgan Kaufmann.

Carbonell, J. G., & Gil, Y. (1990). Learning by experimentation: The operator refinement method. In *Machine learning: An artificial intelligence approach, Volume III* (pp. 191–213). San Mateo, CA: Morgan Kaufmann.

Carbonell, J. G., & Hood, G. (1986). The World Modelers project: Learning in a reactive environment. In T. M. Mitchell, J. G. Carbonell, & R. S. Michalski (Eds.), *Machine learning: A guide to current research* (pp. 29–34). Boston, MA: Kluwer.

Carbonell, J. G., & Veloso, M. M. (1988). Integrating derivational analogy into a general problem solving architecture. In J. Kolodner (Ed.), *Proceedings of the First Workshop on Case-Based Reasoning* (pp. 104–124). San Mateo, CA: Morgan Kaufmann.

DeJong, G. F., & Mooney, R. (1986). Explanation-based learning: An alternative view. *Machine Learning, 1(2),* 145–176.

Etzioni, O. (1990). *A structural theory of explanation-based learning.* Ph.D. thesis, School of Computer Science, Carnegie Mellon University, Pittsburgh, PA.

Fikes, R. E., Hart, P. E., & Nilsson, N. J. (1972). Learning and executing generalized robot plans. *Artificial Intelligence, 3(4)*, 251–288.

Flann, N. S. (1989). Learning appropriate abstractions for planning in formation problems. In A. M. Segre (Ed.), *Proceedings of the Sixth International Workshop on Machine Learning* (pp. 235–239). San Mateo, CA: Morgan Kaufmann.

Hammond, K. J. (1986a). *Case-based planning: An integrated theory of planning, learning and memory*. Ph.D. thesis, Computer Science Department, Yale University, New Haven, CT.

Hammond, K. J. (1986b). Learning to anticipate and avoid planning problems through the explanation of failures. In *Proceedings of the Fifth National Conference on Artificial Intelligence* (pp. 556–560). San Mateo, CA: Morgan Kaufmann.

Joseph, R. L. (1989). Graphical knowledge acquisition. In *Proceedings of the Fourth Knowledge Acquisition For Knowledge-Based Systems Workshop*, Department of Computer Science, University of Calgary, Calgary, Alberta, Canada.

Knoblock, C. A. (1989a). Learning hierarchies of abstraction spaces. In A. M. Segre (Ed.), *Proceedings of the Sixth International Workshop on Machine Learning* (pp. 241–245). San Mateo, CA: Morgan Kaufmann.

Knoblock, C. A. (1989b). A theory of abstraction for hierarchical planning. In P. Benjamin (Ed.), *Proceedings of the Workshop on Change of Representation and Inductive Bias* (pp. 81–104). Boston, MA: Kluwer.

Kolodner, J. L. (1980). *Retrieval and organizational strategies in conceptual memory: A computer model*. Ph.D. thesis, Computer Science Department, Yale University, New Haven, CT.

Korf, R. E. (1985). Macro-operators: A weak method for learning. *Artificial Intelligence, 26(1)*, 35–77.

Korf, R. E. (1987). Planning as search: A quantitative approach. *Artificial Intelligence, 33(1)*, 65–88.

Kuokka, D. R., Etzioni, O., Carbonell, J. G., Gil, Y., Knoblock, C. A., & Minton, S. (1987). *Interactive knowledge refinement*. Working Paper. Carnegie Mellon University, Department of Computer Science, Pittsburgh, PA.

Laird, J. E., Rosenbloom, P. S., & Newell, A. (1986). Chunking in soar: The anatomy of a general learning mechanism. *Machine Learning, 1(1)*, 11–46.

Laird, J. E., Newell, A., & Rosenbloom, P. S. (1987). soar: An architecture for general intelligence. *Artificial Intelligence, 33(1)*, 1–64.

Langley, P., Thompson, K., Iba, W., Gennari, J. H., & Allen, J. A. (1989). *An integrated cognitive architecture for autonomous agents*. Technical Report 89-28, Department of Information and Computer Science, University of California, Irvine, CA.

Minton, S. (1985). Selectively generalizing plans for problem solving. In *Proceedings of the Ninth International Joint Conference on Artificial Intelligence* (pp. 596–599). San Mateo, CA: Morgan Kaufmann.

Minton, S. (1988a). *Learning effective search control knowledge: An explanation-based approach*. Boston, MA: Kluwer.

Minton, S. (1988b). Quantitative results concerning the utility of explanation-based learning. In *Proceedings of the Seventh National Conference on Artificial Intelligence* (pp. 564–569). San Mateo, CA: Morgan Kaufmann.

Minton, S., Carbonell, J. G., Knoblock, C. A., Kuokka, D. R., Etzoini, O., & Gil, Y. (1989). Explanation-based learning: A problem solving perspective. *Artificial Intelligence, 40(1–3)*, 63–118.

Mitchell, T. M., Keller, R., & Kedar-Cabelli, S. (1986). Explanation-based generalization: A unifying view. *Machine Learning, 1(1)*, 47–80.

Mitchell, T. M., Utgoff, P., & Banerji, R. (1983). Learning by experimentation: Acquiring and refining problem-solving heuristics. In R. S. Michalski, J. G. Carbonell, & T. M. Mitchell (Eds.), *Machine learning: An artificial intelligence approach* (pp. 163–190). San Mateo, CA: Morgan Kaufmann.

Mostow, J., & Bhatnagar, N. (1987). Failsafe—a floor planner that uses EBG to learn from its failures. In *Proceedings of the Tenth International Joint Conference on Artificial Intelligence* (pp. 249–255). San Mateo, CA: Morgan Kaufmann.

Newell, A. (1982). The knowledge level. *Artificial Intelligence, 18(1)*, 87–127.

Newell, A., & Simon, H. A. (1972). *Human problem solving*. Englewood Cliffs, NJ: Prentice-Hall.

Prieditis, A., & Mostow, J. (1987). PROLEARN: Toward a Prolog interpreter that learns. In *Proceedings of the Sixth National Conference on Artificial Intelligence* (pp. 494–498). San Mateo, CA: Morgan Kaufmann.

Rajamoney, S. A. (1986). *Automated design of experiments for refining theories*. M.S. thesis, Department of Computer Science, University of Illinois, Urbana, IL.

Rosenbloom, P. S., & Laird, J. E. (1986). Mapping explanation-based generalization onto SOAR. In *Proceedings of the Fifth National Conference on Artificial Intelligence* (pp. 561–567). San Mateo, CA: Morgan Kaufmann.

Sacerdoti, E. D. (1974). Planning in a hierarchy of abstraction spaces. *Artificial Intelligence, 5(2)*, 115–135.

Sacerdoti, E. D. (1977). *A structure for plans and behavior*. New York: American Elsevier.

Shen, W. (1989). *Learning from the environment based on percepts and actions*. Ph.D. thesis, School of Computer Science, Carnegie Mellon University, Pittsburgh, PA.

Silver, B. (1986). Precondition analysis. In R. S. Michalski, J. G. Carbonell, & T. M. Mitchell (Eds.), *Machine learning: An artificial intelligence approach, Volume II* (pp. 247–270). San Mateo, CA: Morgan Kaufmann.

Stefik, M. (1981). Planning with constraints (MOLGEN: Part 1). *Artificial Intelligence, 16(2)*, 111–140.

Tambe, M., & Newell, A. (1988). *Why some chunks are expensive*. Technical Report CMU-CS-88-103, Computer Science Department, Carnegie Mellon University, Pittsburgh, PA.

Tenenberg, J. D. (1988). *Abstraction in planning*. Ph.D. thesis, Computer Science Department, University of Rochester, Rochester, NY.

Unruh, A. (1988). Thesis proposal: Abstraction in SOAR. Computer Science Department, Stanford University, Stanford, CA.

Unruh, A., & Rosenbloom, P. S. (1989). Abstraction in problem solving and learning. In *Proceedings of the Eleventh International Joint Conference on Artificial Intelligence* (pp. 681–687). San Mateo, CA: Morgan Kaufmann.

van de Brug, A., Bachant, J., & McDermott, J. (1986). The taming of R1, *IEEE Expert, 1(3)*, 33–39.

Veloso, M. M. (1989). *Nonlinear problem solving using intelligent casual-commitment*. Technical Report CMU-CS-89-210, School of Computer Science, Carnegie Mellon University, Pittsburgh, PA.

Veloso, M. M., & Carbonell, J. G. (1989). Learning analogies by analogy—the closed loop of memory organization and problem solving. In *Proceedings of the Second Workshop on Case-Based Reasoning* (pp. 153–159). San Mateo, CA: Morgan Kaufmann.

Wilkins, D. E. (1984). Domain-independent planning: Representation and plan generation. *Artificial Intelligence, 22(3)*, 269–301.

# 10 A Comparative Analysis of Some Simple Architectures for Autonomous Agents

Michael R. Genesereth
*Computer Science Department, Stanford University*

## INTRODUCTION

Ever since the early years of Artificial Intelligence, there has been argument about the advantages and disadvantages of building agents that use declarative knowledge at runtime (e.g., in analyzing sensory data and planning actions). Proponents claim that this approach provides great flexibility. Critics complain about the computational cost.

In this chapter we undertake a comparative analysis of several simple architectures, some of which use declarative knowledge and some of which do not. We show that there is indeed no advantage to declarative knowledge at runtime if we have unlimited space and ignore the costs of agent design. However, we also show that, in the face of space limitations or considering design costs, the runtime use of declarative knowledge is sometimes superior to preprogramming.

In order to focus our analysis, we look at a particular class of problems, viz. those in which a designer wishes to construct an agent to achieve one of a set of desirable goal states. We assume that the designer starts with complete knowledge of the goal and the agent's perceptual and effectory capabilities, but he has only partial information about the state of the agent's initial environment. We also assume that there are no bounds on the time the agent can spend in deciding to act.

Much of the argument about declarative knowledge has centered on one particular representation for declarative knowledge, namely first–order predicate calculus. However, our question about the utility of declarative knowledge is a broad one and can equally well be asked of any declarative representation. In this chapter we concentrate on a direct representation in which (a) there is a symbol for every state of the agent's environment, every percept, and every action and (b) there is a tabular encoding of information about the agent's environment and goal—one table that encodes the effects of every action in every state, one table that gives the percept corresponding to each state, a list of possible beginning states, and a list of satisfactory goal states. Obviously, we can use first order predicate calculus to represent this information, in some cases enlarging both space and processing time, in other cases saving both space and processing time. However, the analysis with our direct representation (and, therefore, the corresponding subset of predicate calculus) is easier than the analysis with arbitrary predicate calculus databases.

To illustrate our analysis, we use an application area known as the *Square World*. The geography of this world consists of a set of four cells laid out on a 2-by-2 square. There is a robot in one of the cells and some gold in another. One state of the Square World is shown in Fig. 10.1. The robot is in the first cell in the first row, and the gold is in the second cell in the second row. Figure 10.2 illustrates another state. In this case, the robot is in the second cell of the first row, and the gold is in the first cell of the second row. If we concentrate on the location of the robot and the gold only, then there are 20 possible states. The robot can be in any one of four cells, and the gold can be in any one of four cells or in the grip of the robot (five possibilities in all).

Given *our* point of view, we can distinguish every one of these states from every other state. By contrast, our robot, without this bird's eye view, can see only whether the gold is in its grasp, in the same cell, or elsewhere. This sensory limitation induces a partition of the Square World's 20 states into three subsets. The first subset consists of the four states in which the gold is held by the robot. The second subset consists of the four states in which the gold and the robot are in the same cell. The third subset consists of the 12 states in which the gold and the robot are located in different cells (three gold locations for each of the four robot locations).

The Square World has four possible actions. The agent has a single movement action *move,* which moves the robot around the square in a clockwise direction one cell at a time. In addition, the agent can grasp the gold (if the robot and gold

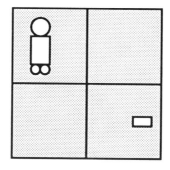

FIG. 10.1.   One state of the square world

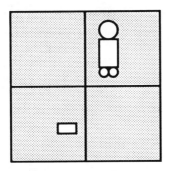

FIG. 10.2.   Another state of the square world.

are in the same cell), and it can drop the gold (if it is being held), leading to two more actions *grab* and *drop*. Finally, it can do nothing, i.e., execute the *noop* action.

Figure 10.3 presents the 20 states of the Square World. The background pattern of each state indicates its percept. White indicates that the robot and gold

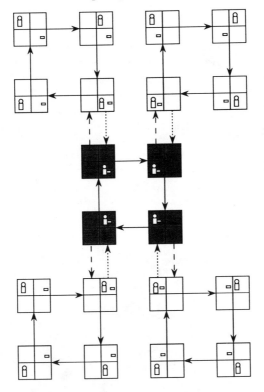

FIG. 10.3.   Percept-action state graph for the square world.

are in different cells; light grey indicates that the robot and the gold are in the same cell; and dark grey indicates that the robot is grasping the gold. The arrows in the graph indicate the effects of the world's actions. Solid arrows denote instances of the *move* action; dotted arrows represent instances of the *grab* action; and dashed arrows represent instances of the *drop* action. Actions with no effects are omitted.

In a typical Square World problem, we start out with partial knowledge about the initial state of the world. In all cases, we assume that this information is given extensionally, i.e., as a list of possible initial states. For example, if we know that the robot is in the upper left cell but we do not know the whereabouts of the gold (except that it is not in the same cell as the robot), this would be represented as a list of three states (one location for the robot and three possible locations for the gold).

A Square World goal is a set of states, any one of which is equally desirable. Again, we assume an extensional representation. The most common goal is the set containing the single state in which the robot and the gold are both located in the upper left cell of the Square.

## AGENTS

An *agent* is a tuple $\langle P,A,I,in,out \rangle$, where $P$ is a set of input objects (percepts), $A$ is a set of output objects (actions), $I$ is a set of internal states, *in* is a function from $P \times I$ into $I$ (the agent's input function), and *out* is a function from $P \times I$ into $A$ (the agent's output function). See Fig. 10.4.

We define an agent's environment to be a tuple $\langle A,P,W,see,do \rangle$, where $A$ is the set of outputs from the agent, $P$ is the set of inputs to the agent, $W$ is a set of

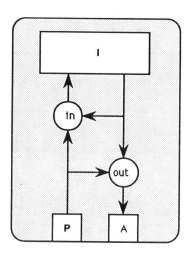

FIG. 10.4.  Agent.

states, *see* is a function from $W$ into $P$, and *do* is a function from $A \times W$ into $W$. See Fig. 10.5.

The behavior of an agent in its environment is cyclical. At the outset, the agent has a particular state $i_1$, and the environment is in a particular state $e_1$. The environment presents the agent with a percept $p_1$ (based on *see*), and the agent uses this percept and its internal state to select an action $a_1$ to perform (based on the *out* function). The agent then updates its internal state to $i_2$ (in accordance with *in*), and the environment changes to a new state $e_2$ (in accordance with *do*). The cycle then repeats.

In order to formalize this behavior, we define the following functions. The function $i_n$ maps an internal state $i$ and an external state $e$ into the internal state of the agent on cycle $n$ when started in internal state $i$ and external state $e$. The function $e_n$ maps an internal state $i$ and an external state $e$ into the external state of the agent on cycle $n$ when started in internal state $i$ and external state $e$. The function $p_n$ produces the agent's percept on the $n$-th cycle of operation. The function $a_n$ produces the action executed by the agent on cycle $n$.

The initial values for these functions follow. The internal state on the first cycle of the agent's operation is the given internal state, and the external state on the first cycle of operation is the given external state. The agent's first percept is obtained by applying the *see* function to the initial external state, and the agent's first action is obtained from this input and the initial internal state.

$$i_1(i,e) = i$$
$$e_1(i,e) = e$$
$$p_1(i,e) = see(e)$$
$$a_1(i,e) = out(see(e),i)$$

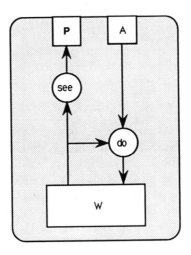

FIG. 10.5.  Environment.

The values for these functions after the first cycle are as follows. The internal state on each cycle is the result of applying the agent's state function to the preceding percept and the preceding internal state. The external state is the result of applying *do* to the action determined on the preceding cycle and the preceding external state. The agent's percept is gotten by applying *see* to the current external state. Finally, the action to be executed is obtained by applying the agent's output function to the current input and the current internal state.

$$i_n(i,e) = in(p_{n-1})(i,e), i_{n-1}(i,e))$$
$$e_n(i,e) = do(a_{n-1}(i,e), e_{n-1}(i,e))$$
$$p_n(i,e) = see(e_n(i,e))$$
$$a_n(i,e) = out(p_n(i,e), i_n(i,e))$$

Analyzing the behavior of an agent is easy if we know everything about its environment. Unfortunately, this is not always the case. Sometimes, we do not know all of the effects of an agent's actions. Sometimes, we do not know all of the characteristics of its perceptual hardware. Frequently, we do not know the exact world state in which the agent starts operation.

In this chapter we are concerned with the analysis of agents in the face of such partial knowledge. Although we could look at all of these types of uncertainty, for reasons of simplicity we concentrate on just one, namely uncertainty about the initial external state. To this end, we define a *beginning state set* to be a set of external states, any one of which may be the state in which our agent begins operation.

A *goal* is a set of environment states, all of which are equally desirable. Of course, there are other types of goals. We might, for example, have a function from initial state to sets of possible goal states; or we might have a set of acceptable sequences of states. We could have looked at any one of these cases, but for reasons of simplicity we have chosen to concentrate on simple achievement goals.

We say that an agent with initial internal state *i* *achieves* a goal *G* in an environment with a beginning state set *B* if and only if the environment, when started in any external state in *B*, eventually enters a state in *G*.

$$\forall e\ e \in B \Rightarrow \exists n\ e_n(i,e) \in G$$

In the Square World example described in the preceding section, the beginning state set contains three elements (the three states in which the robot is in the upper left cell and the gold is elsewhere), and the goal set has just one element (the single state in which the robot and the gold are both in the upper left cell). It is relatively easy to define an agent that is guaranteed to achieve this goal from this beginning state set. Consider, for example, the agent $\langle\{ig,sc,ew\}$, $\{move,grab,drop,noop\},\{1,2,3,4\},in,out\rangle$ with *in* and *out* defined as shown below. We have omitted entries for the case in which the internal state is 4 and the percept is *ew*, since that combination is impossible, given our beginning state set and the physics of the Square World.

| *in* | 1 | 2 | 3 | 4 | | *out* | 1 | 2 | 3 | 4 |
|------|---|---|---|---|---|-------|---|---|---|---|
| *sc* | 1 | 2 | 3 | 4 | | *sc* | *noop* | *grab* | *grab* | *grab* |
| *ew* | 2 | 3 | 4 | | | *ew* | *move* | *move* | *move* | |
| *ig* | 1 | 3 | 4 | 1 | | *ig* | *drop* | *move* | *move* | *move* |

To see how these definitions work, consider the execution of this agent in an initial external state in which the gold is in the lower right cell. On the first step of operation, the agent has internal state 1 and percept *ew;* and, therefore, according to the definition of *out,* its first action is *move*. The agent changes its internal state to 2, in accordance with the definition of *in;* and the external state changes to one in which the robot is in the upper right cell. The agent once again has percept *ew*, and once again its action is *move*. The internal state is updated to 3, and the external state changes to one in which the robot is in the lower right cell. After this change, the robot finds itself in the same cell as the gold, leading to percept *sc;* and, in this case, its action is *grab*. The next percept is *ig,* and so the agent decides to *move*. Afterward, its percept is *ig* once again, and so it executes the *move* action again. Finally, with percept *ig* and internal state 1, the agent knows to *drop* the gold.

## AGENT SYNTHESIS

Figure 10.6 illustrates the process of agent design. There is a client, a designer, and a piece of perceptual–effectory hardware. The designer starts out with information about the sensory and effectory capabilities of the available hardware, and the client presents the designer with a beginning state set and a goal set. The designer uses this information to invent input and output functions and an initial internal state for an agent that achieves the given goal, and he then implements the agent on the available hardware. (More precisely, the designer observes and acts upon *his* environment to bring about a state in which the desired agent exists.) Finally, the hardware is activated; and, provided that the design was correct, it achieves the client's goal.

In thinking about this scenario, it is important to note that the designer's activities are limited to the choice and implementation of the agent's input and output functions and its initial internal state. He is not permitted to modify the given perceptual or effectory hardware.

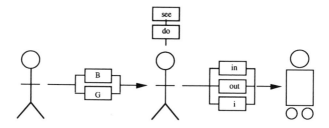

FIG. 10.6.    Synthesis scenario.

In fact, in most applications the designer is not permitted to modify any hardware at all. Rather, there is often a general purpose computer connecting the sensors and effectors, with its own input and output functions. In a case like this, the designer's sole job is to invent a program to run on this computer. So, agent design comes to be computer programming. See Fig. 10.7.

It is, of course, in theory possible to automate the process of design. We can build a machine (at least in principle) to design hardware, and we can build a machine (at least in principle) to design software. Of course, there may be no design that is guaranteed to achieve a given goal, in which case our machine may fail or, what's worse, run forever; however, we can be assured that, if a design exists, our machine will eventually find it. The possibility of automated programming leads us to consider the scenario shown in Fig. 10.8.

Since both agents in this last scenario are machines, it is tempting to consider them to be a single agent, particularly if they are implemented on the same hardware. This view is especially attractive since, in our analysis of agent architectures, we consider the costs incurred by both agents. However, for the purposes of this paper, it is more appropriate to treat the agents as distinct, and so we forego this possibility in what follows.

In the next few sections, we present a variety of different agent architectures and some techniques for automatically designing agents with those architectures. Afterward, we analyze the performance of the architectures and the corresponding design techniques.

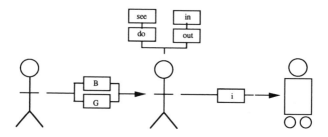

FIG. 10.7.    Programming scenario.

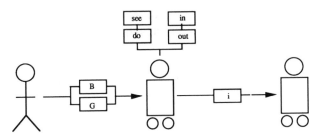

FIG. 10.8.  Automatic programming scenario.

## SEQUENTIAL ARCHITECTURE

An agent with *sequential architecture* is one in which every internal state is a data structure denoting a sequence of actions. On each cycle of its operation, the agent executes the first action in the sequence denoted by this data structure and changes the internal state to a data structure denoting the remainder of the sequence. If and when the sequence becomes empty, the agent halts operation.

As an example, consider a sequential agent for the Square World. First, we define a suitable set of data structures, hereafter called *programs*. Then, we give the semantics of these programs in the form of a mapping from our data structures into sequences of actions. Finally, we exhibit an interpreter capable of executing our programs correctly.

The basis of our language is a set of symbols for the Square World's allowable actions. For simplicity, we use the same names as in our earlier discussion, but we use a different font to emphasize that these are symbols for our actions, not the actions themselves. Since the Square World has only four actions, we need a set A of just four symbols—move, grab, drop, and noop.

Having established this basic vocabulary, we define the set $S(A)$ to be all linear labelled directed graphs in which the arc labels are symbols from A. The following graph is an example.

The meaning of each symbol in a program is given by an interpretation function $f$ that maps the symbol into an available action. We let the symbol move denote the *move* action; we let grab denote the *grab* action; we let drop denote the *drop* action; and we let noop denote *noop*.

The meaning of a sequential program is the sequence of actions denoted by the arcs in the graph. For example, under interpretation $f$ the preceding program denotes the action sequence shown below.

$$\langle move, move, grab, move, move, drop \rangle$$

If the robot starts out in the upper left cell and the gold starts out in the lower right cell, this program solves the Square World problem, as discussed in section

2. The agent first moves to the upper right cell and then to the lower right cell. It grabs the gold. It moves to the lower left cell and then to the upper left cell. It drops the gold, thereby achieving the desired state.

Given a formal definition for our agent's programs, we can design a suitable interpreter for these programs. Consider, for example, the agent $\langle\{\perp\}, A, S(A),$ $in, out\rangle$, with $in$ and $out$ defined as follows.

$$out(\perp, \bullet \overset{a}{\longrightarrow} \bullet\text{---}\cdots\text{---}\bullet) = f(a)$$
$$in(\perp, \bullet \overset{a}{\longrightarrow} \bullet\text{---}\cdots\text{---}\bullet) = \bullet\text{---}\cdots\text{---}\bullet$$

This agent is guaranteed to execute correctly any sequential program it finds in its initial internal state. Furthermore, it executes the program in unit time, that is, it executes one program action on every cycle of its operation.

Given the existence of a unit-time interpreter for sequential programs, designing a sequential agent for the Square World reduces to the problem of synthesizing a suitable sequential program. This problem has been discussed extensively in the AI literature, and numerous solution methods have been proposed. In what follows, we examine the simplest of these methods, namely state–space programming and program–space programming.

In state-space programming, we search the percept–action–state graph for a path connecting the initial state to a goal state. If such a path exists, a guaranteed program can be formed from the actions named along the path.

For example, looking at the graph in Fig. 10.3, we see that there is a path connecting the Square World state in which the robot is in the upper left cell and the gold is in the lower right cell to the state in which both are in the upper left cell. Consequently, there is a program for achieving the latter state from the former, namely, the one shown above.

Obviously, there are many ways to conduct this search—forward, backward, bidirectional, and so on. If the search is done in breadth-first fashion, the shortest path will be found first. Although none of these methods is best for all graphs, they all work.

The absence of complete information about the agent's beginning state makes it more difficult to find a plan that is guaranteed to achieve a given goal. Nevertheless, this does not mean that such plans do not exist. For example, the following Square World program achieves the goal, no matter what the beginning state.

In order to deal with partial knowledge, we can use an alternative programming procedure, called *sequential programming*. Instead of a percept–action–state graph, this approach uses a data structure called a *sequential program graph*. Each of the nodes in this graph denotes a state set, and there is an action-labelled arc from one node to another if and only if the corresponding action maps every state in the set denoted by the source of the arc to some member of the set denoted by the destination of the arc.

In sequential programming, we start with the beginning state set and build the sequential program graph in breadth–first fashion. As we add each action arc to the graph, we compute the effects of that action on the states in the source node and connect it to a node denoting the resulting states. This process continues until we reach a node denoting a set of possible states that are all in the goal set.

If there is a sequential program that solves the problem, this procedure is guaranteed to find it. If there is no guaranteed sequential program, the procedure may or may not terminate. If the set of possible states is finite, the search can be stopped after considering all programs up to length $2^n$ where $n$ is the number of states of the environment. If the set is infinite, there is no general stopping criterion.

Figure 10.9 illustrates the sequential program graph for the Square World problem introduced previously. The labels inside the nodes of the graph enumerate the states denoted by that node. The first letter of each label denotes the location of the robot. The letter a denotes the upper left cell; the letter b denotes the upper right cell; the letter c denotes the lower right cell; and the letter d denotes the lower left cell. The second letter denotes the location of the gold, using the same notation as for the robot, with addition of i indicating that the gold is in the grip of the robot. A node with an open triangle on its right hand side means that search is cut off at that node, since it is a repeat of an earlier node. A black triangle indicates a node that satisfies the goal. The heavy arrows in the figure illustrate the program mentioned earlier.

Unfortunately, sequential architecture is not perfect. Although it is sometimes possible to find guaranteed sequential programs, this is not always the case. Consider, for example, a variation of Square World in which the agent can only grab for the gold once, after which any attempt to grab will fail. For such a world, there is no sequential plan guaranteed to achieve the goal in the face of uncertainty about the initial location of the gold.

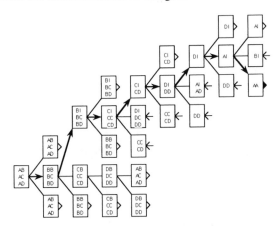

FIG. 10.9.  Sequential program graph.

Although the utility of sequential architecture is limited, it does have applications. It is ideal whenever complete information about the initial state is available, since in these cases all sensory data is redundant with what is already known. The architecture is also useful in many primitive robotic applications, where sensory data is simply not available. This idea of trying to find a sequential program to achieve a goal in the face of partial information is the subject of some interesting research by Matt Mason and Michael Erdmann in the area of motion planning for sensory–deprived robots.

## CONDITIONAL ARCHITECTURE

Conditional architecture expands the capabilities of sequential architecture by allowing an agent to use sensory information in guiding its actions. In an agent with conditional architecture, every internal state is a nested conditional program. On each cycle of operation, the agent compares its current percept to the conditions in the program, performs the associated action, and updates its internal state to be the conditional program nested at that point.

Again, to be concrete, let us define an agent for the Square World, this time one with conditional architecture. As in the last section, we first define our agent's programs, then their semantics, and, finally, a suitable interpreter.

As our basic vocabulary, we take the set $A$ of action names introduced in the last section. To these we add a set $P$ of three additional symbols—ig, sc, and ew—as names for the three Square world percepts. Using this vocabulary, we define the set $C(P,A)$ of conditional programs recursively.

1. ● is a conditional program.

2. is a conditional program, provided that (1) each $p_i$ is a member of $P$ and each $p$ in $P$ occurs at most once, (2) each $a_i$ is a member of $A$, and (3) each $c_i$ is a conditional program.

member of $P$ and each $p$ in $P$ occurs at most once, (2) each $a_i$ is a member of A, and (3) each $c_i$ is a conditional program.

Given a formal definition for our programming language, we can design an interpreter for programs in that language. Consider, for example, the agent $\langle P,A,C(P,A),in,out \rangle$, with $in$ and $out$ defined as follows.

$$out(p_i, \text{}) = f(a_i)$$

$$in(p_i, \text{}) = c_i$$

The following data structure is an example of a conditional program. If on its first cycle the robot perceives the gold in the same cell, then it need not do anything, since the goal is already satisfied. If the robot is grasping the gold, then the robot should drop it. If the gold is elsewhere, the agent should move to the next cell. And so forth.

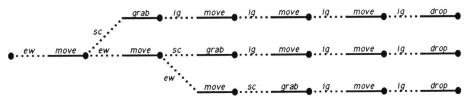

The process of synthesis for conditional programs is similar to that for sequential programs; however, instead of searching a sequential program graph, we search a conditional program graph. A conditional program graph is a labelled directed graph, in which the labels on arcs are the names of percepts and actions. There are two types of nodes and two types of arcs. Percepts arcs are labelled with percept names, and action arcs are labelled with action names. Every node is either a perceptual node or an effectory node. A perceptual node has only percept arcs emanating from it and action arcs leading to it. An effectory node has only action arcs leading from it and percept arcs leading to it. Each percept arc connects the node for a set of possible states to the node representing the subset of that set characterized by the associated percept. Each action arc connects a node for a set of possible states to a node representing the set of states resulting from the execution of the associated action in those states.

Figure 10.10 illustrates the conditional program space for the Square World problem discussed earlier. The perceptual node on the left denotes the three possible beginning states. The arcs emanating from this node denote the percepts *ig, sc,* and *ew.* Since we know, by definition of the problem, that the robot and the gold are initially in different cells, all three possible states share the same percept, and so only the *ew* successor is non–empty. The action arcs emanating from this effectory node denote the three Square World actions *grab, move,* and *drop.*

As with sequential programming, we search this space to find paths from the perceptual node representing the beginning state set to effectory nodes representing state sets entirely contained in the goal set. The difference is that we terminate the search only after we have found at least one path to the goal down every percept branch. The resulting conditional program is formed from these paths. Like our sequential programmer, this procedure is guaranteed to find a program, if there is one. Its computational properties are discussed later.

The conditional program shown above corresponds to the heavy arcs in figure conditional. Note that the program contains every percept arc whenever the successor of a node is non–empty. By contrast, there is only one action arc taken from any node in the graph.

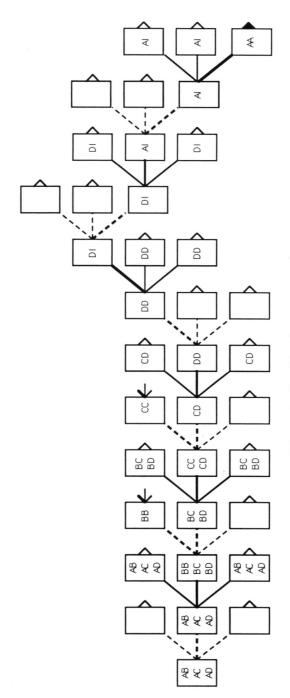

FIG. 10.10.  Conditional program graph.

292

## SEQUENTIAL PLANNING ARCHITECTURE

In each of the architectures we have seen thus far, programming precedes execution. The designer uses its declarative knowledge to create a guaranteed program and then places the program in the agent's memory. In the next two architectures, the designer places its declarative knowledge in the memory of the agent and allows the agent to select its actions for itself. In order to emphasize this difference, we use the term *planning* to refer runtime programming, and we use the term *plan* to refer to a program developed at runtime.

Of course, if upon starting operation an agent's first activity were to produce a complete plan, this would be little different from the preceding architectures (at least in the absence of time bounds). What makes planning architectures interesting is the potential for interleaved planning and execution. By beginning execution before the planning process is complete, an agent can gather additional information that, by eliminating uncertainties, can save it time in completing its plan.

One way of implementing a sequential planning agent is to install in the runtime agent an appropriate programming procedure, like the one discussed previously but with one simple change. In order to get the agent to interleave its planning and execution, it is necessary to add an additional termination condition, when the agent is "close enough" to the goal to stop planning and start executing. When the planner finds a situation in which this condition is true, it returns the plan it has pieced together up to that point terminated by a list containing a specification of the current set of states. This list can be used by the agent in restarting the planning process when it is encountered during execution of the partial plan.

The primary problem an agent faces in interleaving planning and execution is knowing when it is "close enough" to the goal to stop planning and start executing. If a plan is not yet complete, how does the agent know that there *is* any completion? Perhaps its partial plan leads to disaster, while some other partial plan works well. In some cases, this is exactly the situation, as illustrated by the horizon problem in chess. In other cases, it is possible to show there is a plan to achieve the goal without constructing a complete plan that covers all possible initial states.

There is a particularly simple stopping criterion for the Square World. As it proceeds with sequential programming, the agent simultaneously explores the *conditional* program graph, ignoring any percept arcs that lead to empty state sets and ignoring any action arcs that lead to repeated state sets. If the agent encounters a situation in which there is just one possible state set and that state set has more than one non-ignorable percept arc emanating from it, it stops planning. Since there is just one state set under consideration, it has not lost anything by stopping; and, since the branching at that point is perceptual, it can gain efficiency by waiting until the perceptual information is available and ignoring other branches.

As an example of this, consider the conditional program graph in Fig. 10.10. There are percept arcs from the initial state set to three possible successors. Two of these are empty and can be ignored. The other successor has three action arcs. Two of these lead to repeated state sets and can be ignored. The other leads to a new state set. This state set is the only one under consideration at this time, and it has two non–empty perceptual arcs emanating from it. Consequently, the agent can stop planning; it can execute the single step plan it has found thus far; and it can restart planning after it has the perceptual information to decide which branch to take. Let us say that the percept at this point is *ew*. In this case, the agent would take the middle percept arc. Once again, there are three actions branches, two of which can be ignored; then, two possible percept successors; so planning can be halted again. Once the *move* action is executed, the agent begins planning yet again, in this case completing the plan. This approach allows the agent to get to the goal in a guaranteed way, while pruning out at least two thirds of the search space.

As will be seen below, there is much computational advantage to be gained by interleaving planning and execution. Although some of this advantage is lost in determining whether it is okay to stop planning, the savings often outweigh this cost.

## CONDITIONAL PLANNING ARCHITECTURE

An agent with *conditional planning architecture* is just like one with sequential planning architecture except that the runtime planner is capable of generating conditional plans. We might use, for example, a suitably modified version of the programming procedure described previously.

Conditional planning architecture is like conditional architecture and unlike sequential planning architecture in that it is guaranteed to succeed in achieving the goal in cases where there is no sequential plan.

## TIME ANALYSIS

In comparing these different architectures, we consider not only the architectures themselves, but also their corresponding programming procedures. To emphasize this, we use the word *approach* in what follows to refer to the combination of an architecture and a programming procedure.

In our analysis of time cost, we take as our measure the sum of the time taken by the programmer to program the agent and the "nonproductive" time taken by the agent in executing the resulting program. Since the agent may be activated multiple times, the total cost is a sum over all of these activations. If we assume that each execution has the same cost (bad assumption sometimes), then we get the following expression for total time cost $t$, where $p$ is the programming time, $e$ is the execution cost, and $n$ is the number of executions.

$$t = p + n * e$$

In computing execution cost, we take as *nonproductive time* all those steps on which the agent performs no external action (other than *noop*), during which it is presumably computing which action to perform.

We begin our analysis with the sequential programmer presented previously. The procedure in this case iterates over actions, for each action calling itself recursively until it succeeds or until it exceeds a specified program length. In the worst case, this algorithm is linear in the size of the beginning state set and exponential in the number of actions. The exponent $k$ here is the length of the program.

$$p_{sa} \approx |B|*|A|^k$$

In the sequential approach, executing any program of length $k$ takes just $k$ steps, i.e., there are no nonproductive steps, and so the cost for this approach is 0.

$$e_{sa} = 0$$

Combining the costs for programming and execution using our general formula, we get the following expression for the total cost of the sequential approach.

$$t_{sa} \approx |B|*|A|^k + n * 0$$
$$\approx |B|*|A|^k$$

Analyzing our conditional programming procedure, we get the following upper bound on runtime. As before, it is exponential in the number of actions; but, since there is also a loop over percepts, it is also exponential in the number of percepts.

$$p_{ca} \approx |B|*(|P|*|A|)^k$$

However, this is an overestimate of the actual cost. The reason is that $B$ is not a constant across all recursive calls. The set shrinks on each call to reflect the extra information provided by the conditions in the evolving program. If we use the symbol $s$ to refer to the average factor by which this set shrinks on each recursion, we can rewrite our cost expression as follows.

$$p_{ca} \approx (|B|/s^k)*(|P|*|A|)^k$$
$$\approx |B|*(|P|/s)^k*|A|^k$$

The shrinkage factor $|P|/s$ cannot be less than 1 and, of course, cannot be greater than $|P|$. In the best possible situation, the shrinkage on each recursion is equal to the size of the set of inputs, we get the following expression.

$$p_{ca} \approx |B|*|A|^k$$

The significance of the is that, in the face of partial information, with this sort of shrinkage factor, conditional programming is no more expensive than the sequential programming.

An important feature of conditional architecture is that, as with sequential architecture, there is no runtime overhead, i.e., the appropriate external action is performed on every cycle.

$$e_{ca} = 0$$

Combining the costs for programming and execution, we get the following expression for the total cost of the conditional approach (assuming no perceptual shrinkage).

$$t_{ca} \approx |B| * (|P| * |A|)^k + n * 0$$
$$\approx |B| * (|P| * |A|)^k$$

The design cost in the sequential planning approach is negligible. In the worst case, it is linear in the size of the specification. If we assume that the computer used to do the "design" is identical to the computer used at runtime, then the cost is 0 (since the specification is already resident in the machine's memory).

$$p_{spa} = 0$$

The real cost of the sequential planning approach comes at runtime. Looking at our sequential planner, we see that it is almost identical to the sequential planner analyzed above. The major difference is the termination condition by which it stops planning before having produced a complete plan. Given this similarity, we can use the same cost expression, except that the exponent, instead of being the number of steps to the goal, is the number of steps $k'$ until the appropriate termination condition applies.

$$e_{spa} \approx |B| * |A|^{k'}$$

This difference is extremely important, coming as it does in the exponent of our expression. To see this, assume that the planner manages to break the original $k$ step solution into $j$ portions (so that $k' = k/j$). We then end up with the following execution cost.

$$e_{spa} \approx j * |B| * |A|^{k/j}$$

Plugging the expressions for planning cost and execution cost into our general formula, we get the following result.

$$t_{spa} \approx 0 + n * j * |B| * |A|^{k/j}$$
$$\approx n * j * |B| * |A|^{k/j}$$

If $j$ is 1, then the cost of the sequential planning approach is similar to that for sequential programming. The only difference is that the expression is multiplied by the number $n$ of executions. This means that, in the face of multiple executions, sequential planning is inferior to sequential programming.

In the limit, as $j$ goes to $k$, we see that the exponential cost of sequential planning becomes a polynomial. By exploiting perceptual information, the agent is able to ignore possibilities that the sequential programmer must consider.

We can compute the cost for the conditional planning approach in a manner similar to that for sequential planning. Assuming zero design cost and conditional planning time similar to that for conditional programming (except for the change in exponent), we get the following total cost expression.

$$t_{cpa} \approx 0 + n*j*|B|*(|P|*|A|)^{k/j}$$
$$\approx n*j*|B|*(|P|*|A|)^{k/j}$$

We can compare this approach to the conditional programming approach by looking at the ratio of their costs.

$$\frac{t_{cpa}}{t_{ca}} \approx \frac{n * j * |B| * (|P| * |A|)^{k/j}}{|B| * (|P| * |A|)^{k}}$$

Simplifying, we get the following.

$$\frac{t_{cpa}}{t_{ca}} \approx \frac{n * j}{(|P| * |A|)^{k-k/j}}$$

Note that the relative cost of the conditional planning approach decreases exponentially in the number $j$ of chunks. Its relative cost increases linearly with the number $n$ of executions; but, if the agent caches partial plans from one execution to the next, this factor can be eliminated.

In looking at this analysis, it must be remembered that in practical settings, we rarely have a choice between pure sequential programming, pure conditional programming, pure sequential planning, and pure conditional planning. Rather, we use a mix of the two. The importance of our analysis here is to suggest where the gain from preprogramming is most likely to be found and where preprogramming effort is likely to be wasted.

## SPACE

In our analysis of space cost, we take as our measure the maximum amount $s$ of space needed in the runtime agent.

Looking at the definition of our sequential interpreter, we see that the only information saved is the sequence of actions to be performed. Consequently, we get the following expression for the maximal amount $s_{sa}$ of space needed for an agent with sequential architecture.

$$s_{sa} = k*log|A|$$

As with the sequential interpreter, our conditional interpreter needs space for the program only. However, in this case the size of the program is somewhat greater.

$$s_{ca} = \frac{|P| * (|P|^k - 1)}{|P| - 1} * log|A|$$

In sequential planning architecture, we need to provide space for the specification (beginning state set, goal set, perceptual function, and effectory function) and space for partial plans (action sequences of length $k/j$).

$$s_{spa} = |B|*log|S| + |G|*log|S| + |S|*log|P| + |A|*|S|*log|S| + k/j*log|A|$$

The space needs for conditional planning architecture are the same, except that the maximum program size is much larger.

$$s_{cpa} = |B| * log|S| + |G| * log|S| + |S| * log|P| + |A| * |S| * log|S|$$
$$+ \frac{|P| * (|P|^{k/j} - 1)}{|P| - 1} * log|A|$$

If $j$ is one, conditional planning architecture is clearly clearly worse than conditional architecture. However, as $j$ approaches $k$, the amount of space needed to store the agent's plan decreases exponentially (in the limit it reduces to just $P* log|A|$), and the space needed for the specification begins to dominate the space cost. Although this residual space requirement is non–trivial, it is still much less than the amount of space needed to store an entire conditional program; and so in this case, conditional planning architecture is superior to conditional architecture.

## CONCLUSION

One of the problems with the analysis in this chapter is that it compares architectural approaches, that is, architectures and specific design techniques, and not just architectures. If we were to vary the choice of design techniques but keep the architectures fixed, the results could be different. If we could be sure that the design techniques were the best possible on the whole (so that their runtimes were minimal), then the advantages and disadvantages of the approaches could be attributed to the architectures themselves. It seems likely that the design techniques discussed here are in some sense minimal, but this has yet to be proven.

Even if we had such a proof, our analysis would be less than completely satisfying. All we have done is to show the superiority of one architecture over another under certain conditions. We have not shown that any one of these architectures is the best of the ones considered in all cases, and we certainly have not shown that any one of these architectures is the best of all architectures in even a few cases.

Another problem with the analysis is its limited applicability. For the sake of simplicity, we make some very strong assumptions. Although there are applications that satisfy these assumptions, there are many that do not.

One such assumption is the stipulation that our agents can spend an unlimited number of cycles in selecting their actions. Unfortunately, in many applications this is simply not possible. It seems clear that, in such applications, some amount of preprogramming is desirable, even if the number of "nonproductive" cycles is thereby increased. However, our analysis here does not make clear what tradeoff is appropriate for these applications.

A related problem derives from our assumption that the designer can spend an unlimited number of cycles in programming. In some applications, the amount of time available to produce the agent is sharply limited. For such applications, runtime planning of at least a limited sort may be the only possibility.

In our analysis, we concentrate on the production of agents that are guaranteed to achieve the given goals. In many cases, it may be very expensive or impossible to produce an agent that is guaranteed to achieve the given goal from every beginning state (due either to perceptual or effectory limitations of the available hardware or due to inadequate information about the beginning state set). Unfortunately, we have no universally accepted standards for such applications. Where a guarantee is impossible, we might prefer to produce an agent that achieves the goal in as many initial states as possible (the probabilistic approach). In applications where getting the guarantee is very expensive, we might prefer to trade off correctness in some cases for lower cost on the whole.

Another shortcoming of our analysis is that it covers only one representation of declarative knowledge. Much of the argument about declarative representations rages over first-order predicate calculus in particular. Computing with first-order predicate calculus has inherent disadvantages in some situations; but in other situations it can provide not only greater expressiveness but also greater efficiency, when compared with declarative representations like the one discussed here. In a way, this paper is an attempt to separate the argument about declarative representations from the argument about predicate calculus and to provide a basis for a subsequent comparison of different declarative representations.

Finally, in going through this analysis we are adopting an engineering perspective on agents. We are studying applications in which there is a given goal and the concern is to design an agent to achieve that goal with confidence and efficiency. We are not directly concerned with the analysis of human cognition or the architecture of agents that select their own goals. This is at variance with the interests of many individuals doing research on intelligent agent architecture. However, our hope is that this sort of engineering analysis may, when extended, have value on these other problems as well.

# 11

## Making Intelligent Systems Adaptive

Barbara Hayes-Roth
*Stanford University*

## INTRODUCTION

Contemporary artificial intelligence systems exhibit important aspects of intelligence. They possess knowledge and heuristic problem-solving skills. They solve problems typically requiring sophisticated human expertise and they do so in a manner that is evocative of human problem-solving behavior. On the other hand, most contemporary AI systems are static, isolated problem solvers. They accept particular classes of problems, reason about them, perhaps request additional information, and eventually produce solutions. They perform a narrow range of reasoning functions to produce stereotypic responses to a predetermined set of situations. They are oblivious to real-time constraints on the utility of their behavior.

By contrast, human beings are versatile and flexible problem solvers that continuously adapt to the demands and opportunities presented by a dynamic environment. They encounter a great variety of unanticipated situations, decide whether and how to respond to them, and opportunistically adjust their behavior as those situations evolve. They focus attention on the most critical and most urgent aspects of the current situation and synchronize their behavior with important external events. Adaptivity figures prominently in everyday human skills, such as conducting a conversation or playing a game of tennis, as well as esoteric skills, such as monitoring critically ill medical patients or controlling a manufacturing process.

Following the model set by human intelligence, we define an *adaptive intelligent system (AIS)* as: a *knowledge-based system that reasons about and interacts with other dynamic entities in real time.* The present research involves building and experimenting with adaptive intelligent systems in particular task domains. Our goal is to develop a generic AIS architecture to support adaptive intelligent systems in a variety of task domains.

## AN ILLUSTRATIVE ADAPTIVE INTELLIGENT
### SYSTEM: Guardian

To illustrate the kind of behavior a generic AIS architecture must support, let us consider the task of monitoring patients in a surgical intensive-care unit (SICU).

Surgical intensive-care patients are critically ill individuals who require life-support devices, such as respirators or dialysis machines, to perform some of their vital functions (see Figure 11.1). These devices also measure certain physiological parameters. For example, parameters measured by the respirator include the *tidal volume* of air inhaled by the patient on each breath and the *peak inspiratory pressure.*

During a patient's stay in the SICU, medical staff gradually reduce the amount of life support provided to the patient and eventually withdraw life-support devices in accordance with a therapeutic plan. Along the way, the staff closely monitor and interpret available measurements of the patient's physiological function, detect deviations from expected progress, and diagnose observed signs and symptoms. If necessary, they adjust or modify the therapeutic plan and perform other therapeutic interventions.

The SICU situation typically presents great quantities of patient data and simultaneous demands for multiple interpretation, diagnosis, prognosis, and treatment activities. Because these demands exceed human cognitive ca-

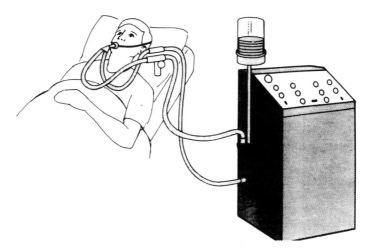

FIG. 11.1.   SICU patient with respirator-assisted breathing.

pabilities, the SICU staff must selectively attend to the most important information and perform the most urgent and important activities.

Guardian (Hayes-Roth, Washington, Hewett & Seiver, 1989) is an experimental system for SICU patient monitoring. We intend that Guardian eventually will perform all of the reasoning necessary for closed-loop control of device settings and other therapeutic interventions and exploit that reasoning in an advisory capacity. Thus, in addition to the multiple tasks performed by SICU staff, Guardian will report, summarize, and explain the SICU situation and its reasoning about that situation to physicians, nurses, and other SICU staff members.

Here is a simple scenario of the sort Guardian must handle:

1. Guardian is sensing several different respiratory parameters, including tidal volume and peak inspiratory pressure, many times per second. To insure that its interpretation keeps pace with the data, Guardian samples sensed values of each parameter once per second and bases its interpretation of the patient's condition on the sampled values.

2. Following an initial interval of normal data, Guardian detects an abnormal increase in peak inspiratory pressure and begins reasoning about probable causes. To allocate cognitive resources for this diagnosis task and avoid falling behind in its interpretation task, Guardian reduces its sampling rate to once every ten seconds for all sensed parameters except peak pressure. It maintains its once per second sampling rate for peak pressure because that is the focus of its diagnostic reasoning.

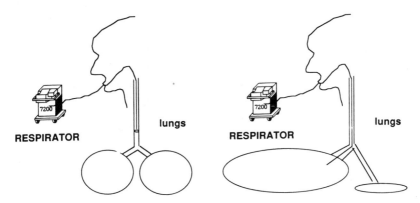

The respirator tube is positioned correctly above the bifurcation of the endotracheal tube. It delivers a constant volume of air to the two lungs on each breath.

The respirator tube has slipped into the right main stem. The respirator must apply greater pressure to deliver the same volume of air to a single lung.

FIG. 11.2.   One-sided intubation causes increased peak inspiratory pressure.

3. Guardian hypothesizes "one-sided intubation" as the most likely cause of the increase in peak inspiratory pressure. It reports this hypothesis to SICU personnel, along with a diagrammatic explanation of how one-sided intubation causes increased peak pressure (see Figure 11.2). Guardian then recommends a corrective action, "reposition the tube," and confirms the resulting resumption of normal pressure.

4. Having completed its diagnosis, explanation, recommendation, and confirmation tasks, Guardian continues to perform only its interpretation task, resuming its original once per second sampling of all respiratory parameters.

## THE CLASS OF ADAPTIVE INTELLIGENT SYSTEMS

We have studied several tasks requiring an adaptive intelligent system: intensive-care monitoring, materials processing, aircraft tactical planning and control, and tutorial instruction. Despite differences among the domains of these several tasks, they share fundamental requirements for: (a) *Perception*—interpretation of sensed data to gain knowledge of other entities; (b) *Action*—controlled actuation of effectors to influence other entities; (c) *Cognition*—symbolic reasoning to draw inferences from perceptions, solve problems, make decisions, and plan actions; and (d) *Attention*—allocation of computational resources among competing perceptions, actions, and cognitions in real time.

In the case of intensive–care monitoring, the system must continually sense and interpret important features of the patient's condition, diagnose observed signs and symptoms, predict the course of the patient's condition, plan appropriate therapies, control life–support device settings, take other therapeutic actions, and explain its reasoning to medical personnel. (We are investigating intensive–care monitoring in collaboration with Dr. A. Seiver at Stanford University).

In the case of intelligent processing of materials, the system must continually sense and interpret important material properties, diagnose exceptional properties, predict the impact of exceptional properties on the overall process outcome, revise the process plan to achieve process goals, control process environment parameter settings, and explain its reasoning and behavior to the operator (Pardee, Shaff, & Hayes-Roth, 1990). (This project is directed by Dr. W. Pardee at Rockwell International Corporation.)

In the case of aircraft tactical planning and control, the system must continually sense and interpret important environmental circumstances, diagnose exceptional events, predict the impact of events on tactical success, revise the tactical plan to achieve tactical goals, and explain its reasoning to the pilot. (This project is directed by Dr. N. S. Sridharan at FMC Corporation.)

In the case of tutorial instruction, the system must continually sense and interpret important features of the student's learning state, diagnose errors and limitations in the student's knowledge, predict the ramifications of current learning state on subsequent tutorial activities, revise the tutorial plan to achieve tutorial goals, perform tutorial actions, and explain its reasoning and behavior (Murray, 1990). (This project is directed by Dr. W. Murray at FMC Corporation.)

In each of these tasks, the AIS faces a continuing stream of demands and opportunities for potential perceptions, actions, and cognitions in real time. It generally cannot perform all potential operations in a timely fashion. Further, performing all potential operations as soon as possible is not always a system's primary objective or even a desirable one. Under certain circumstances, for example, it may be more desirable to perform only operations that meet a specified criterion or to delay performance of certain operations until specified preconditions occur. While more efficient algorithms or faster computers may enable some application systems to achieve particular real-time objectives, they will not solve the general problem of limited resources or obviate its concomitant resource-allocation requirement. For a computer of any speed, we can define tasks whose computational demands—for multiplicity of operations, computational complexity of operations, temporal responsiveness, and synchronization—exceed its computational resources. For these reasons, we view attentional power and flexibility, rather than speed *per se,* as the primary scientific challenge in developing a generic architecture for adaptive intelligent systems.

## GENERIC REQUIREMENTS FOR ADAPTIVE INTELLIGENT SYSTEMS

More specifically, adaptive intelligent systems functioning in diverse task environments share generic requirements for: cognitive versatility, interaction with a dynamic environment, management of complexity, and real-time performance. We discuss each of these different categories of requirements below, with illustrations from Guardian's patient-monitoring task.

### Cognitive Versatility

*Multi-Faceted Expertise.*   An AIS must perform multiple reasoning tasks, involving different problems, problem domains, and problem-solving methods. For example, Guardian must know how to interpret patient data, diagnose observed signs and symptoms, and plan appropriate therapeutic actions. It must know how to perform these tasks for different biological systems, such as the respiratory system and the circulatory system. It must know, for example, how to diagnose observed signs probabilitistically, using a belief network, as well as from first principles, using explicit models of system structure and function.

*Concurrent Reasoning Activities.*   An AIS must simultaneously conduct multiple reasoning activities. For example, Guardian must continue to interpret newly perceived patient parameters while diagnosing an observed sign so that it can incorporate interpretations of relevant data into its diagnostic reasoning and notice when other incidental data suggest other situations requiring its attention.

*Incremental Reasoning.*    An AIS must reason incrementally about situations observable over time. For example, in the SICU, a great variety of patient data occur asynchronously over a long period of time. Guardian must perceive and integrate relevant data, as they occur, to form a coherent, "up–to–the–minute" model of the patient's dynamic condition.

*Explanation.*    An AIS must explain its knowledge, reasoning, and behavior. To maximize the utility of its advice, Guardian must justify its recommendations to SICU staff.

## Interaction with a Dynamic Environment

*Functional Asynchrony and Parallelism.*    An AIS must perceive, reason, and act asynchronously and in parallel. For example, Guardian cannot ignore a patient, whose condition can change at any time, while interpreting previously perceived patient data. It must perceive important new patient data when they occur. Similarly, Guardian must perform planned actions at appropriate times regardless of the amount of non–relevant perception and cognition it performs during overlapping intervals.

*Continuous Operation.*    An AIS must function continuously over long time intervals. For example, a practical version of Guardian would operate continuously over periods of several weeks, accumulating patient information, building an increasingly complete and accurate patient model, and recommending therapeutic actions tailored to the patient's evolving condition.

*Functional Integration.*    An AIS must integrate perception, action, and cognition within a coherent point of view. For example, Guardian's model of a patient's condition must incorporate its perceptions of the patient's physiological parameters and its interpretation must influence its therapeutic actions. In some cases, Guardian's patient model also should influence its perceptions of particular physiological parameters. For example, since postoperative patients typically have lowered body temperatures, Guardian should adjust its perception of "normal," "high," and "low" temperatures accordingly.

## Management of Complexity

*Selective Attention.*    An AIS must differentially process sensed data in accordance with cognitive objectives and the external situation. The SICU situation presents vast quantities of data, more than a human being or Guardian could interpret in real time. It must choose among them. If, for example, Guardian perceives that the patient is suffering from hypocapnia (low $CO_2$ in the blood), it should focus on patient data relevant to its diagnosis of that problem (e.g., blood gases, temperature, respiration rate, tidal volume). It should temporarily ignore extraneous patient data whose interpretation would distract it from solving the problem at hand. At the same time, however, Guardian must remain sensitive to the possibility that extraneous data might signal a new emergency.

*Automatic Performance.*    An AIS must perform potentially complex actions without impeding ongoing perception and cognition. For example, given a decision to report recent patient data, Guardian should be able to select, format, and display those data, while continuing to perceive and interpret new patient data, diagnose new signs and symptoms, plan or replan therapeutic or other actions, and carry out unrelated actions in an appropriate and timely fashion. At the same time, it must be prepared to interrupt its reporting to perform a more important competing action, such as to alert SICU staff to a newly observed patient sign.

*Focused Reasoning.*    An AIS must dynamically control is reasoning in accordance with the current situation and its strategic objectives. The SICU presents many more "problems" than Guardian could solve in real time. It must choose among them. For example, if Guardian has decided to explore alternative diagnoses for observed hypocapnia, it should go about that task in a deliberate fashion without being distracted unnecessarily by other potential reasoning activities—e.g., reviewing the long–range therapeutic plan or preparing the day's summary report. At the same time, it must be prepared to interrupt its diagnostic reasoning to attend to a more serious emergency, should one arise.

## Real-Time Performance

*Guaranteed Inter-Operation Latencies.*    An AIS must guarantee that it will begin successive reasoning operations after a specified absolute or relative latency. Conversely, an AIS must not allocate its cognitive resources to uninterruptable processes of arbitrary durations. All real-time performance rests ultimately on an AIS's ability to redirect its cognitive resources appropriately and quickly in response to a dynamic situation. The minimum inter-operation latency required of an AIS depends upon its domain. For example, Guardian must guarantee that it will sound an alarm within a few seconds after perceiving that a patient has stopped breathing.

*Time–Stress Responsivity.*    An AIS must respond to increased time stress by reducing its response latency. For example, it Guardian is diagnosing a slight reduction in the patient's tidal volume (amount of air per breath), a few extra minutes of elapsed time will not affect the utility of its diagnosis. On the other hand, if Guardian is diagnosing a complete interruption of tidal volume (the patient is not breathing), it must complete the diagnosis, as well as recommend corrective action, within four minutes, to help save the patient's life.

*Graceful Degradation.*     An AIS must reduce response latency, in accordance with increased time stress, by gradually compromising the quality of its performance. For example, Guardian could reduce diagnosis time by exploring only the most likely possibilities and thereby reducing the certainty of its conclusions. It could further reduce diagnosis time by exploring a smaller subset of the possibilities and further reducing the certainty of its conclusions.

*Speed–Knowledge Independence.*     An AIS must produce stable response latencies despite increases in knowledge. For example, Guardian must continue to guarantee a stable diagnosis time for exploring a given subset of possibilities, even as it acquires knowledge of many other diseases. In fact, relevant new knowledge should have the potential to speed up Guardian's performance.

## A GENERIC AIS ARCHITECTURE

Figure 11.3 illustrates a generic AIS architecture that addresses the above requirements (Hayes-Roth, 1950). This section describes the elements of the AIS architecture—a *dynamic control architecture,* an *asynchronous I/O subsystem, dynamic I/O channels,* and a *satisficing reasoning cycle*—and illustrates them with examples from the Guardian system introduced earlier.

### A Dynamic Control Architecture

The rightmost section of Figure 11.3 schematizes the *dynamic control architecture* underlying the proposed AIS architecture. The architecture is implemented

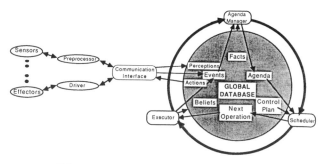

FIG. 11.3.   The generic AIS architecture.

as the BB1 system (Hayes-Roth, 1985; Hayes-Roth & Hewett, 1988) and we will use the terms "dynamic control architecture" and BB1 interchangeably. Cognitive operations take place in the context of a *global database* that contains all of the facts, beliefs, events, plans, and so forth known to the system. The architecture iterates a three–step reasoning cycle. First, the *agenda manager* produces an agenda of reasoning operations suggested by recent cognitive events. Then, the *scheduler* chooses as the next operation the one that best serves the current control plan. Finally, the *executor* executes the chosen operation, changing information in the global database and recording a corresponding cognitive event.

The BB1 knowledge base is implemented in the BB* conceptual network representation (Hayes-Roth et al., 1986). BB* provides subnetworks representing architecturally defined entities, such as actions, events, control plans, and cognitive skills. It also provides an editor for building subnetworks representing application–specific strategies, factual knowledge, and cognitive skills (discussed below). For example, Guardian's factual knowledge covers aspects of normal and abnormal anatomy and physiology, probable causes of certain signs and symptoms, and the normal and abnormal structure and function of generic flow and exchange systems. Figure 11.4 excerpts Guardian's knowledge of normal respiratory anatomy and physiology.

The dynamic control architecture provides a general-purpose reasoning environment that can support the multiple reasoning activities required of a typical

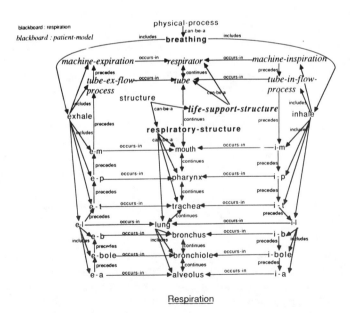

Respiration

FIG. 11.4. Excerpt of Guardian's knowledge of respiratory anatomy and physiology.

AIS. For example, BB1 has been used to build systems for design (Hayes-Roth et al., 1986; Tommelein, Johnson, Hayes-Roth & Levitt, 1987), planning (Darwiche, Levitt, & Hayes-Roth, 1989; Hayes-Roth & Hayes-Roth, 1979; Murray, 1990), signal interpretation (Brugge & Buchanan, 1987; Delaney, 1987), explanation (Schulman & Hayes-Roth, 1988), and analogical inference (Daube & Hayes-Roth, 1989). Moreover, BB1 allows an AIS to incorporate several cognitive skills. For example, Guardian currently incorporates skills for: classification of perceptual observations into temporal episodes of known semantic categories (e.g., normal, high, very high); diagnosis of observed signs based on belief networks (Ash, Vina, Seiver, & Hayes-Roth, 1990); diagnosis and explanation of observed signs based on generic system models (Hayes-Roth & Hewett, 1990). Finally, BB1 allows an AIS to perform multiple tasks concurrently by interleaving their constituent operations. For example, Guardian typically continues to classify newly sensed data while diagnosing previously observed signs. In fact, if Guardian happens to classify new data relevant to an ongoing diagnosis, it incorporates those results in its diagnostic reasoning.

The dynamic control architecture provides the strategic control required of an AIS. In general, an AIS must balance efforts to: (a) respond promptly to urgent situations; and (b) plan effective patterns of future behavior. BB1 supports this range of behavior by enabling a system to incrementally construct and modify explicit plans for its own behavior. These control plans may be short-term or long-term, abstract or specific. The system may augment or modify its plan at any time. On each cycle, the scheduler chooses an operation that best matches the current control plan. Thus, the system always behaves in accordance with plans it has previously constructed. Whenever the scheduler chooses operations that change the plan, the system's subsequent behavior changes accordingly.

For example, Figure 11.5 shows Guardian's control reasoning for the scenario described in section 2 above. The horizontal dimension in Figure 11.5 represents scenario time, partitioned into units corresponding to reasoning cycles. The top panel of the figure shows the dynamic control plan Guardian constructs during the scenario. The middle panel shows the agenda of potential operations on each cycle. The bottom panel shows the operations Guardian chooses to execute on each cycle. The actual results of Guardian's reasoning (e.g., its data classifications, diagnostic conclusions, and diagnostic explanations) appear elsewhere in the knowledge base. The episode and associated control reasoning unfold, left to right, as follows:

1. At the start of the episode, Guardian is following a long-term plan to monitor all respiratory parameters, sampling each one once per second. On subsequent cycles, it ignores potential operations of other types (symbolized as K, J, L) and executes monitoring operations (symbolized as M).

2. Upon observing an abnormal increase in peak inspiratory pressure, Guard-

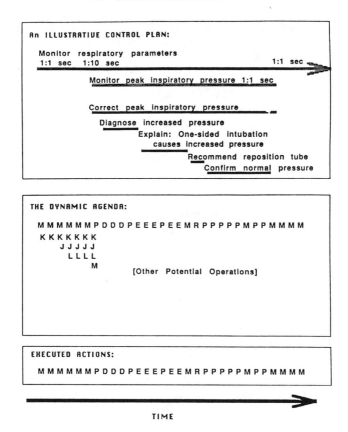

FIG. 11.5.  Excerpt from a simple control plan for Guardian.

ian decides to correct this problem. To free up computational resources for this task, it decides to reduce its sampling of all respiratory parameters to once every ten seconds, except for pressure, which it continues to sample once per second. On subsequent cycles, Guardian occasionally interleves these types of operations (symbolized as M and P, respectively) with its reasoning about the elevated peak pressure.

3.  Guardian begins its effort to correct the elevated pressure by deciding to diagnose it. On subsequent cycles, Guardian executes diagnostic operations (symbolized as D) and eventually hypothesizes that the problem is one–sided intubation.

4.  Having completed the diagnosis, Guardian decides to explain how one–sided intubation would cause elevated peak pressure. On subsequent cycles, it executes corresponding explanation operations (symbolized as E), producing the diagrammatic explanation in Figure 11.2 earlier.

5. Having completed the explanation, Guardian decides to recommend a corrective action, repositioning of the tube. On the next cycle, it makes that recommendation (symbolized as R).

6. Having made its recommendation, Guardian decides to monitor peak pressure in order to confirm that the tube has been repositioned and peak pressure has returned to normal. On subsequence cycles, it executes corresponding monitoring actions (symbolized as P).

7. Finally, having completed all tasks necessary to correct the abnormal peak pressure, Guardian continues only its monitoring activities, resuming its original once per second sampling of all respiratory parameters.

## An Asynchronous I/O Subsystem

To support an integrated approach to perception, action, and cognition the AIS architecture extends the dynamic control architecture with an *asynchronous I/O subsystem* comprising *logical I/O buffers* and a *communications interface (CI)* (Hayes-Roth & Hewett, 1989), as illustrated in Figure 11.3.

To integrate perception with cognition, the CI continuously monitors physical streams from remote sensors and records perceptual events representing sensed data in appropriate logical input buffers. In the case of Guardian, for example, the CI monitors streams from sensors attached to the respirator. The agenda–manager uses perceptual events, along with cognitive events, to update the agenda of potential reasoning operations, thereby introducing them into the reasoning process. Since input buffers are part of the global database, it is also possible for other reasoning operations to inspect them at any time. Input buffers have fixed capacities, with first–in–first–out (FIFO) overflow. Thus, if the CI relays newly sensed data faster than the reasoning system can use them, the reasoning system "forgets" old perceptions, rather than falling increasingly behind.

To integrate action with cognition, the CI continuously monitors logical output buffers for intended actions placed there by reasoning operations. The CI relays intended actions to physical streams for appropriate remote effectors. In the case of Guardian, for example, the CI monitors buffers associated with various display devices. Output buffers have fixed capacities, with FIFO overflow. Thus, in the unlikely case that the reasoning system places intended actions into the buffer faster than the CI can service them, the system "forgets" old intended actions, rather than falling increasingly behind.

The CI can run either as a background process on the host machine or on a separate machine connected to the host by Ethernet, providing concurrent and asynchronous perception, action, and cognition. The AIS architecture need not complete an entire reasoning cycle before noticing intervening perceptions or executing intended actions. It gives reasoning operations immediate access to new perceptions and it immediately executes intended actions determined by reasoning operations.

## Dynamic I/O Channels

Given real–time constraints on the utility of its behavior, an AIS must manage the computational complexity of perception and action. The environment in which an AIS operates continuously bombards its sensors with data that are more or less relevant to its current task. Interpreting these data and selecting those that are relevant or otherwise interesting is computationally intensive. Attempting to process all such data in real time could easily swamp the reasoning mechanism. Similarly, although an AIS has discretion over which actions to initiate, correctly executing actions—especially those that need to be coordinated with external events—is computationally intensive. Attempting to control the execution of several complex action programs in real time could easily swamp the reasoning mechanism. Finally, reasoning operations are, themselves, computationally intensive. Attempting to reason effectively could easily distract an AIS from perception of important events or timely performance of important actions.

To facilitate management of the computational complexity of real-time perception and action, the AIS architecture incorporates *dynamic I/O channels* (Washington & Hayes-Roth, 1989). As illustrated in Figure 11.3, each channel comprises one or more processes that mediate communications between an AIS's remote sensors and effectors and its reasoning mechanism. To provide selective attention, *preprocessors* continuously interpret and filter asynchronously arriving sensor data in accordance with their current *perceptual filters*. Preprocessors relay only task-relevant or otherwise important data to the reasoning system. To provide automatic performance, *drivers* filter and interpret asynchronously arriving actions in accordance with their current *performance filters*. They give priority to the most important and urgent actions and handle all details of action execution, including synchronization with external events. Both preprocessors and drivers apply filters determined by reasoning operations and sent to them via the communications interface.

Of course, the effectiveness of dynamic I/O channels depends on the effectiveness of the filters they apply. Our approach builds directly on the dynamic control architecture and its I/O subsystem. First, we use activity in I/O buffers as an indicator of the dynamic balance between reasoning and perception. When overflow of input buffers indicates that the system's current reasoning activities cannot keep pace with its current perceptual activities, stronger perceptual filters reduce the rate of perceptual input. When underflow of input buffers indicates that the system's current perceptual activities are underutilizing its reasoning capacity, weaker perceptual filters increase the rate of perceptual input. Guardian currently exploits this mechanism. Second, we plan to use changes in the control plan to signal changes in attentional focus and the control plan itself to characterize attentional focus. For example, having decided to monitor peak inspiratory pressure more closely than other respiratory parameters (see Figure 11.5), Guardian should send perceptual filters favoring sensor data representing that parameter over other respiratory parameters. Both of these mechanisms enable an AIS to dynamically adapt its perceptual activities to current reasoning activities in order to balance overall resource utilization.

## A Satisficing Reasoning Cycle

An AIS must satisfy real-time constraints on its performance—that is, it must perform the right operations at the right times. The AIS architecture in Figure 3 provides a good foundation for real-time performance, but it is vulnerable to open-ended computation times in each step of its reasoning cycle. In particular, the AIS architecture cannot rely upon the "best–next" version of this cycle, in which each step successively acquires control of the processor and runs to normal termination. We call this the "best–next" version because, on each cycle, it identifies, schedules, and executes the best available operation. A system that uses the best-next cycle will fail to perform important operations in a timely fashion whenever it happens to have begun execution of a time-consuming instance of one of its three steps at a critical time. Because most AI architectures use the best-next reasoning cycle, its vulnerabilities are well understood. However, efforts to address these vulnerabilities focus entirely on improving cycle *speed* through the use of efficient matching algorithms, parallelism, or compilation (Forgy, 1982; Gupta, Forgy, & Newell, 1987; Miranker, 1984; Oflazer, 1984). In aiming to place an "acceptable" upper bound on computation time for each step of the reasoning cycle, these approaches produce special-purpose solutions to limited classes of AIS applications. They will not work for systems that exceed their specifications for knowledge base size, response latency, or synchronization with external entities. Thus, they ignore the fundamental challenge of real-time computation: To guarantee a dynamically specifiable maximum latency of operations.

We are developing a *satisficing reasoning cycle* to provide the guaranteed latencies required for real-time performance (Collinot & Hayes-Roth, 1990). By "latency," we mean the elapsed time prior to beginning each successive operation. Figure 11.6 illustrates one such cycle, which differs from the traditional best-next cycle in each of its three steps. First, instead of exhaustively identifying all possible operations on each cycle, the agenda manager identifies as many operations as it can, best first, until any of its dynamic interrupt conditions occurs. Second, instead of choosing the optimal operation from a complete agenda on each cycle, the scheduler does the best it can with an incomplete agenda. Third, instead of exhaustively executing the scheduled operation on each cycle, the executor partially executes the operation until any of its dynamic

1. Update the agenda of potential operations best first until:
    (a) a criterial operation is identified; or
    (b) a criterial event occurs; or
    (c) the agenda updating deadline occurs; or
    (d) agenda updating terminates.
2. Schedule the best criterial executable operation until;
    (a) a criterial event occurs; or
    (b) scheduling terminates.
3. Execute the scheduled operation until:
    (a) a criterial event occurs; or
    (b) the interpretation deadline occurs.
    (c) execution terminates.

FIG. 11.6.  Satisficing cycle.

interrupt conditions occurs. Upon interruption, the executor saves the state of the interrupted operation in a form suitable for resumption and places a pointer to the ready-to-resume operation on the agenda. Depending upon subsequent events, the scheduler may or may not choose to resume execution of the interrupted operation on a subsequent cycle. All three steps in the satisficing cycle operate in accordance with dynamic *cycle parameters,* determined by reasoning operations.

Again, the effectiveness of the satisficing cycle depends upon the effectiveness of the cycle parameters it obeys and our approach builds directly on the dynamic control architecture and its I/O subsystem. First, as discussed above, we use activity in I/O buffers as an indicator of the dynamic balance between reasoning and perception. When overflow of input buffers indicates that reasoning activities cannot keep pace with perceptual activities, stricter cycle parameters will decrease the time spent on agenda management and select a smaller number of reasoning operations for execution. When underflow of input buffers indicates that current perceptual activities underutilize reasoning capacity, more lenient cycle parameters will increase the time spent on agenda management and select a larger number of reasoning operations for execution. Second, as discussed above, we plan to use changes in the control plan to signal changes in attentional focus and the control plan itself to characterize attentional focus. For example, having decided to diagnose an observed increase in peak inspiratory pressure (see Figure 11.5), Guardian should adopt cycle parameters favoring these kinds of operations over other kinds of operations. Both of these mechanisms enable an AIS to dynamically adapt its reasoning activities to current perceptual activities in order to balance overall resource utilization.

In contrast to best–next cycles, which invariably identify and perform the best possible operation regardless of temporal considerations, satisficing cycles enable systems to realize, combine, and alternate among different real-time reasoning policies, such as:

- Perform any operation that is "good enough" as soon as possible.
- Perform any urgent operation immediately.
- Perform the "best available" operation whenever necessary.
- Perform only operations that are "good enough."
- Perform the best possible operation regardless of the time required.

On the other hand, satisficing cycles make systems vulnerable to errors that do not occur under conventional best-next reasoning cycles. By definition, satisficing cycles allow systems to perform sub-optimal operations. In extreme cases, a system could decide prematurely to perform costly or ineffective operations or fail to notice highly desirable operations that are well within its capabilities. However, if we wish to build powerful systems that function well in dynamic environments, we must forego optimality in favor of effective management of complexity (Simon, 1969). Allowing the possibility of error is one concession we can make toward this end. Formulating execution–cycle algorithms that meet the performance requirements of adaptive intelligent systems while minimizing the impact of errors is a primary objective of our research.

## SATISFACTION OF AIS REQUIREMENTS

Table 11.1 summarizes the relationships between the generic requirements for an AIS, as described earlier, and the architectural components. Let us briefly review these relationships.

### Cognitive Versatility

*Multi-Faceted Expertise.* The dynamic control architecture provides a general reasoning framework and knowledge representation scheme. It can integrate knowledge of multiple problem classes, multiple problem-solving methods and multiple domains of factual knowledge.

*Concurrent Reasoning Activities.* The dynamic control architecture formulates reasoning as a sequence of discrete cognitive operations that incrementally generate and modify explicit solution representations. It can interleave component operations for concurrent reasoning activities.

*Incremental Reasoning.* The dynamic control architecture formulates reasoning as a sequence of discrete cognitive operations that incrementally generate and modify explicit solution representations. It can incorporate information about dynamic external situations as that information becomes available.

TABLE 11.1
Relationships between AIS Requirememts and the Proposed AIS Architecture

| | Dynamic Control Architecture | Asynchronous I/O Subsystem | Dynamic I/O Channels | Satisficing Cycle |
|---|:---:|:---:|:---:|:---:|
| **COGNITIVE VERSATILITY** | | | | |
| Multi-Faceted Expertise | X | | | |
| Concurrent Reasoning Activities | X | | | |
| Incremental Reasoning | X | | | |
| Explanation | X | | | |
| **INTERACTION WITH A DYNAMIC ENVIRONMENT** | | | | |
| Functional Asynchrony and Parallelism | X | X | X | X |
| Continuous Operation | X | X | X | X |
| Functional Integration | X | X | X | X |
| **MANAGEMENT OF COMPLEXITY** | | | | |
| Selective Attention | X | | X | |
| Automatic Performance | X | | X | |
| Focused Reasoning | X | | | X |
| **Real-Time Performance** | | | | |
| Guaranteed Inter-Operation Latencies | X | | | X |
| Time-Stress Responsivity | X | | X | X |
| Graceful Degradation | X | | X | X |
| Speed-Knowledge Independence | X | | | X |

*Explanation.*    The dynamic control architecture allows a system to generate and record explicit control plans, which it uses to determine its subsequent actions. It also can use these plans retrospectively to explain its actions and their consequences.

## Interaction with a Dynamic Environment

*Functional Asynchrony and Parallelism.*    The AIS architecture allocates independent processes for the cognitive system, the communications interface, and individual I/O channels, sensors, and effectors. It thus supports asynchronous and parallel perception, action, and cognition.

*Continuous Operation.*    The AIS architecture conceptualizes each functional component (the cognitive system, the communications interface, and individual

I/O channels, sensors, and effectors) as a cyclical, non-terminating process. This approach orients a system away from the traditional goal-directed problem solving and toward continuous operation.

*Functional Integration.*    The dynamic control architecture defines perception and action buffers as standard data structures within its global knowledge base. Its I/O subsystem automatically transfers perceptions and actions between those buffers and appropriate I/O channels. Its satisficing cycle treats perception and action events in the same fashion as internally generated cognitive events.

## Management of Complexity

*Selective Attention.*    The dynamic control architecture provides an explicit representation of a system's own control decisions and cognitive state. Dynamic I/O channels allow the system to use that knowledge to instruct perceptual preprocessors to transform and filter sensed data accordingly before relaying them to perceptual buffers in the knowledge base.

*Automatic Performance.*    The dynamic control architecture allows a system to determine intended actions at an abstract level. Dynamic I/O channels allow the system to "download" computations for controlling the execution of those actions to action drivers.

*Focused Reasoning.*    The dynamic control architecture allows a system to decide what kinds of problems it prefers to address, what kinds of reasoning operations it prefers to perform, and what kinds of knowledge it prefers to apply. The satisficing cycle uses these preferences to identify and schedule potential reasoning operations.

## Real—Time Performance

*Guaranteed Inter-Operation Latencies.*    The dynamic control architecture allows a system to decide what kinds of operations it prefers to perform and what kinds of events require immediate attention. The satisficing cycle uses these criteria to focus, limit, and interrupt processing between successive operations.

*Time—Stress Responsivity.*    The architecture allows a system to respond to time stress in several ways. First, the dynamic control architecture allows the system to modify its reasoning strategy to focus on urgent reasoning tasks and efficient reasoning methods. Second, the dynamic control architecture allows the system to modify its preferences and interrupt conditions, so that the satisficing cycle reduces the amount of processing between successive operations. Third, dynamic I/O channels allow the system to adopt stricter perceptual filters to reduce the amount of sensed data relayed to and processed by the cognitive system.

*Graceful Degradation.*    All of the above responses to time stress permit graceful degradation. First, the dynamic control architecture allows the system to postpone or discontinue individual reasoning tasks individually as required by the situation. It also permits the system to choose among alternative reasoning methods that vary in efficiency and quality of results. Second, the dynamic control architecture allows the system to modify its preferences and interrupt conditions qualitatively and quantitatively, so that the satisficing cycle can reduce interoperation processing—with associated reductions in quality of performance—by variable amounts. Third, dynamic I/O channels allow the system to vary perceptual filters qualitatively and quantitatively to reduce the relay of sensed data by variable amounts.

*Speed–Knowledge Independence.*    The dynamic control architecture allows a system to decide what kinds of operations it prefers to perform, what kinds of knowledge it prefers to apply, and what kinds of events should interrupt its search for operations and knowledge. The satisficing cycle enforces these preferences, regardless of the system's total amount of knowledge.

## ON ARCHITECTURES FOR INTELLIGENCE

In the present context, a volume on "Architectures for Intelligence," we may ask: Is the AIS architecture a theoretical contribution to our understanding of intelligence? The answer to this question depends upon what we mean by "intelligence," for example: (a) human intelligence; (b) lower forms of biological intelligence; or (c) abstract concepts of intelligence. In principle, each of these ideals can be specified further as a distinctive, although possibly overlapping, set of component functions. For example, symbolic reasoning is prominent in human intelligence, while sensory–motor adaptation is more prominent in lower forms of biological intelligence. Abstract concepts of intelligence vary widely, but a large number of them favor rational decision making. In practice, functional specifications of intelligence are, themselves, objects of research and considerable debate in fields such as psychology, biology, and decision analysis. For these reasons, to evaluate a given architecture, we must evaluate the stated functional objectives as well as the architecture's achievement of those objectives.

The AIS architecture is directed toward an evolving abstract definition of intelligence. That definition is motivated by important and challenging computational tasks and it is inspired by human intelligence as the driving metaphor. Thus, we have tried to show that our functional definition of adaptive intelligent systems is required for effective computational performance for an important class of tasks. And we would argue that our definition embodies the functionality that enables human beings to perform these tasks. Indeed, we have shown that the dynamic control architecture, which is the foundation for the AIS architecture, effectively models the details of human problem-solving protocols for an everyday planning task (Hayes-Roth & Hayes-Roth, 1979). Similarly, the architecture's use of dynamic I/O channels to achieve selective attention and automatic performance corresponds roughly to biological and information-processing models of human behavior (Broadbent, 1958; Posner, 1987; Triesman, 1969).

At the same time our definition obviously ignores many equally important elements of human intelligence, such as those related to: sensory–motor performance, a large dynamic memory, linguistic capabilities, analogue processing capabilities, and the emotional and motivational forces affecting human behavior. Moreover, given the metaphorical role of human intelligence in our research, we make no claim to model the actual psychological or biological mechanisms underlying any of the specified functionality. Nor do we claim that it is the only mechanism that can produce the specified functionality. At this stage in our research, we prefer to evaluate the AIS architecture in terms of its sufficiency to produce the specified functionality and its resulting adequacy to support a variety of adaptive intelligent systems. We reserve judgment regarding the architecture's applicability to the substantially greater scope of human intelligence.

## ACKNOWLEDGMENTS

The research reported in this paper has been supported by: DARPA Contract #N00039-83-C-0136 and gifts from Rockwell International Corporation and FMC Corporation. Thanks to Professor Edward A. Feigenbaum for sponsoring this work at the Knowledge Systems Laboratory.

Note: This chapter was written in early 1988. Since then, work on Guardian and the underlying architecture has progressed, as documented in several subsequent papers cited in this chapter.

## REFERENCES

Ash, D., Vina, A., Seivr, A., & Hayes-Roth, B. (1990). Action-oriented diagnosis under real-time constraints. *International Workshop on Principles of Diagnosis,* Palo Alto, CA.

Broadbent, D. E. (1958). *Perception and communication.* London: Pergamon.

Brugge, J., & Buchanan, B. G. (1987). *The ABC System.* (Tech. Rep.). Stanford, CA: Computer Science Department, Stanford, CA: Stanford University.

Collinot, A., & Hayes-Roth, B. (1990). Real-time control of reasoning. (Technical Report No. 90-17), Stanford University.

Darwiche, A., Levitt, R. E., & Hayes-Roth, B. (1989). OARPlan: Generating project plans in blackboard systems by reasoning about objects, actions, and resources. *Journal of Artificial Intelligence in Engineering Design, Automation, and Manufacturing.*

Daube, F., & Hayes-Roth, B. (1989). A case-based redesign system in a mechanical domain. *Proceedings of the International Joint Conference on Artificial Intelligence*, Detroit, MI.

Delaney, J. (1987). *BB1-AIRTRAC*. (Tech. Rep.). Stanford, CA: Stanford University.

Forgy, C. L. (1982). RETE: A fast algorithm for the many pattern/many object pattern matching problem. *Artificial Intelligence, 19*, 17–37.

Gupta, A., Forgy, C., & Newell, A. (1987). *High-speed implementations of rule-based systems*. (Tech. Rep.). Pittsburg, PA: Carnegie Mellon University.

Hayes-Roth, B., & Hewett, M. (1988). BB1: An implementation of the blackboard control architecture. In R. Engelmore & A. Morgan (Eds.), *Blackboard Systems*. London: Addison-Wesley.

Hayes-Roth, B., & Hayes-Roth, F. (1979). A cognitive model of planning. *Cognitive Science, 3*, 275–310.

Hayes-Roth, B., Buchanan, B. G., Lichtarge, O., Hewett, M., Altman, R., Brinkley, J., Cornelius, C., Duncan, B., & Jardetzky, O. (1986). PROTEAN: Deriving protein structure from constraints. *Proceedings of the AAAI*. Los Altos, CA: Morgan Kaufman.

Hayes-Roth, B., Johnson, M. V., Garvey, A., & Hewett, M. (1986). Applications of BB1 to arrangement-assembly tasks. *Journal of Artificial Intelligence in Engineering*.

Hayes-Roth, B., Washington, R., Hewett, R., Hewett, M., & Seiver, A. (1989). Intelligent monitoring and control. *Proceedings of the International Joint Conference on Artificial Intelligence*, Detroit, MI.

Hayes-Roth, B. (1985). A blackboard architecture for control. *Artificial Intelligence Journal, 26*, 251–321.

Hayes-Roth, B. (1990). Architectural foundations for real-time performance in intelligent agents. *Real-Time Systems: The International Journal of Time-Critical Computing Systems, 2*.

Hewett, M., and Hayes-Roth, B. (1988). Real-time I/O in knowledge-based systems. In V. Jagannathan & R. T. Dodhiawala (Eds.), *Current Trends in Blackboard Systems*. New York: Academic Press.

Hewett, R., & Hayes-Roth, B. (1990). Representing and reasoning about physical systems using generic models. In J. Sowa, S. Shapiro, & R. Brachman (Eds.), *Formal Aspect of Semantic Networks*, San Mateo, CA: Morgan Kaufmann.

Miranker, D. P. (1984). Performance estimates for the DADO machine: A comparison of treat and rete. *Proceedings of Fifth Generation Computer Systems*.

Murray, W. R. (1990). *Dynamic instructional planning*. Proceedings of the *AAAI*.

Oflazer, K. (1984). Parallel execution of production systems. *Proceedings of the IEEE International Conference on Parallel Processing*.

Pardee, W. J., Shaff, M. A., & Hayes-Roth, B. (1990). Intelligent control of complex materials processes. *Artificial Intelligence in Engineering, Design, Analysis, and Manufacturing, 4*, 55–65.

Posner, M. I. (1987). *Chronometric explorations of mind*. Hillsdale, NJ: Lawrence Erlbaum Associates.

Schulman, R., & Hayes-Roth, B. (1988). Plan-Based Construction of Strategic Explanations. In *Proceedings of the AAAI88 Workshop on Explanation*. American Association of Artificial Intelligence, Menlo Park, CA.

Simon, H. A. (1969). *The Sciences of the Artificial*. Cambridge, MA: The MIT Press.

Tommelein, I. D., Johnson, M. V., Hayes-Roth, B., & Levitt, R. E. (1987). SightPlan: A blackboard expert system for construction site layout. In J. S. Gero (Ed.), *Expert systems in computer-aided design*. North Holland.

Triesman, A. (1969). Strategies and models of selective attention. *Psychological Review, 76*, 282–299.

Washington, R., & Hayes-Roth, B. (1989). Input Data Management in Real-Time AI Systems. *Proceedings of the International Joint Conference on Artificial Intelligence*, Detroit, MI.

# 12 Theo: A Framework for Self-Improving Systems

Tom M. Mitchell, John Allen, Prasad Chalasani, John Cheng,
Oren Etzioni, Marc Ringuette, Jeffrey C. Schlimmer
*School of Computer Science, Carnegie Mellon University*

## INTRODUCTION

The research reported here seeks to develop a general framework for learning and problem solving. Over the past two decades, research on machine learning has produced a number of mechanisms that address the question of how to generalize from examples (e.g., DeJong & Mooney, 1986; Dietterich & Michalski, 1983, Mitchell, Keller, & Kedar-Cabelli, 1986). This success has lead over the past few years to a number of attempts to construct self-improving problem solvers that employ these generalization mechanisms to improve their problem solving performance at various tasks (e.g., Mitchell, 1983; Minton, Carbonell, Etzioni, Knoblock, & Kuokka, 1987; Laird, Newell, & Rosenbloom, 1987). Such attempts to construct self-improving systems raise important new research questions that go beyond the question of how to generalize from examples. A self–improving system certainly must address the issue of *how* to form general concepts from examples, but it must also address the issues of *which* concepts to learn, *when* to learn, *from what data and knowledge* to learn, *how to index* what it learns. It must be able to examine and modify most aspects of its own structure and processes in order to formulate and solve appropriate learning tasks at appropriate points in its development. In this light, the learning problem is inseparable from related issues of how the system is itself represented and what range of problem solving, reflection, indexing, and generalization mechanisms it can employ.

Theo is a framework for exploring this next level of research issues involving general problem solving, learning, and representation. As such, it draws on ideas developed in other recent research on architectures for learning and problem solving (e.g., Laird et al., 1987; Lenat, 1983; Minton et al., 1987). The design of Theo is motivated by three overlapping goals, which are only partially satisfied at present. Theo is intended as a framework to support:

- *Basic research on general problem solving, learning and knowledge representation, and especially the interactions among these three issues.* Theo is a frame–oriented architecture that supports a particular approach to knowledge representation, provides a collection of inference methods, and includes mechanisms for generalizing from examples. This initial collection of system components can be modified and augmented in order to explore more specific architectures for problem-solving, learning, and representation. For example, (Schlimmer, 1987) describes a search–oriented problem solver built on Theo.

- *Accretion of research results in a form that others may reuse and extend.* Theo is organized so that new representational features, new inference methods, and new learning mechanisms are each defined in terms of new slot definitions which can be incorporated by other users. Our hope is to move from the present era of throw-away research prototype software, to an era in which new software embodying new research results is more easily reused and research progress is more cumulative. For example, we have developed optional knowledge bases that define additional inference methods, learning mechanisms, and representation conventions.

- *An efficient framework for developing effective knowledge–based systems.* We seek to overcome one common failing of sophisticated frameworks for representation and inference: users often pay a high overhead in efficiency for a large set of system features, independent of which of these features are used in any individual program. Theo is intended to provide a range of sophistication and efficiency depending on the user's needs. For example, in defining new slots the user may specify which of Theo's inference methods should be used to infer values for instances of this slot, and whether or not Theo's learning mechanisms should be invoked for this slot. The user may also define his or her own inference procedures for inferring values of specific slots, encoding these either declaratively within the notation of Theo slot definitions (making them interpretable and modifiable by the system), or directly in Lisp code. This allows the user to choose between taking advantage of Theo's facilities for automatically refining inference methods, versus directly providing an efficient inference method encoded in Lisp.

In this chapter we focus primarily on the first of these goals, and examine Theo as an architecture for self-improving problem solvers. The next section describes Theo and its representation, inference, and generalization components. Subsequent sections describe several ongoing research experiments conducted within Theo: experiments with explanation-based learning, inductive inference of control knowledge, and use of meta–reasoning about slot properties to guide inference. We conclude with a more general discussion of the relationship of

Theo to other architectures such as Soar (Laird et al., 1987) and RLL (Greiner & Lenat, 1980).

## MOTIVATION AND OVERVIEW OF THEO

The organizing principles of an architecture may be usefully summarized at (at least!) two levels: Functional and structural. A functional characterization describes the architecture in terms of features such as the range of beliefs that it can represent, the range of problems that can be posed to it, the range of inferences that it can draw, the range of knowledge that it can learn, the portion of its initial structure that is open to learning, and the computational complexity of its memory storage and retrieval mechanisms. A structural characterization describes the particular representation conventions and data structures, as well as mechanisms for inference, learning, memory storage, and retrieval. It is the structural characteristics that determine the functional properties of the architecture, although the derivation of one from the other may be far from obvious.

### Organizing Principles

Here we summarize the structural organizing principles that underly the design of Theo. Following this, we consider the implications that these structural principles have on Theo's functional characteristics.

- Every *belief* in Theo is an assertion of the form (<entity> <slot>) = <value>, which represents the belief that some entity named <entity> stands in some relation named <slot> with another entity named <value>. For example, we might assert (fred wife) = wilma.
- Every *problem instance* in Theo is a pair of the form (<entity> <slot>), which represents the task of determining a justifiable belief of the form (<entity> <slot>) = <value>. For example, we might pose the problem "(fred wife)", whose solution is "wilma", or the problem "(current.chess.position best.next.move)". Note there is a one–to–one correspondence between beliefs and problems: each problem corresponds to a belief with a missing <value>, and each belief corresponds to the answer to some problem. Put another way, the token <slot> is the name of a relation, a belief is an instance of that relation, and a problem is a query that specifies a relation name as well as an element of its domain, and asks for the corresponding element of the relation's range.
- *Problem classes,* or sets of problem instances, are described either by a single token, <slot>, or by a pair of the form (<entity> <slot>). The form <slot> (e.g., wife) represents the class of problem instances of the form (?x <slot>) (e.g., (?x wife)), where ?x is any member of the domain of <slot> (e.g., if (wife domain) = male, then ?x may be any male). The form (<entity>

<slot>) represents the class of problem instances of the form (?e <slot>) where ?e is a member of the class represented by <entity>. For example, (stone.age.male wife) represents the class of problem instances (?m wife), where ?m is some member of the set of stone.age.males. Simply put, (<entity> <slot>) represents the subset of the <slot> relation restricted to the subdomain specified by <entity>.

• Problem instances and problem classes are themselves entities. Thus, Theo can hold beliefs about problems and pose problems regarding problems just as it can for any other entity. For example, Theo could assert its belief that the problem of determining Fred's wife is difficult by asserting ((fred wife) difficult?) = t. Here (fred wife) is the <entity>, difficult? the <slot>, and t the <value> in the belief. For convenience, we drop the nested parentheses in describing such beliefs, so that we simply write (fred wife difficult?) = t. Similarly, Theo's name for the corresponding problem of determining whether it is difficult to infer Fred's wife is (fred wife difficult?). Note we can easily state the belief that it is not difficult to determine whether it is difficult to determine Joe's wife: (fred wife difficult? difficult?) = nil.

• Theo stores all its knowledge about potential and recommended problem solving methods as beliefs about the corresponding problem class. For example, the belief (fred wife available.methods) = (inherits default.value) represents the assertion that the available methods for solving the problem (fred wife) are "inherits" and "default.value".

• Once a problem is solved, Theo may store the solution (i.e., assert the corresponding belief) in memory, indexed by the problem name. When it stores such beliefs, it also stores an *explanation* justifying the new assertion in terms of the beliefs on which it depends. Such explanations record dependencies among beliefs, so that when a belief is changed, Theo can remove dependent beliefs. This provides a simple forgetting mechanism for truth–maintenance.

• Explanations of beliefs also support a form of explanation-based learning which infers problem solving macro–methods from successfully solved problems, and stores these macro–methods as beliefs about the appropriately general problem class.

• An inductive learning method is used to acquire beliefs about the order in which available problem solving methods should be attempted for various problem classes.

The remainder of this paper explores some of the consequences of these organizing principles. In brief, the design of Theo is intended to provide three important features:

• Highly uniform representation. The one-to-one correspondence between beliefs and problems, and the fact that *every* problem is also an entity about which beliefs can be held, provide an architecture in which the same inference, learning, and forgetting methods that apply to problem solving in the task domain can also be applied to reasoning about Theo's problems, methods, capabilities, and explanations.

• Broadly applicable learning mechanisms. Theo currently has three learning mechanisms: caching of inferred beliefs, learning from explanations associated with successfully solved problems, and inductive inference for ordering problem solving methods. These mechanisms are intended to be applicable to all beliefs/problems describable by the system, so that in principle all parts of the system's knowledge and problem solving methods are open to learning.

• Effective indexing of acquired knowledge. Learning architectures must face the issue of effective indexing, or they face the problem that the more they learn the slower they become (Minton, 1988). In Theo, problem names serve as indices to the problem definition, its solution, available problem solving methods, control information, explanations, and other properties of the problem. While we do not completely understand the implications of Theo's indexing mechanisms, it is clear that once the relevant information has been learned and cached for some problem, the time to retrieve this information is only weakly influenced by the number of irrelevant facts that are subsequently acquired about other problems.

## An Introductory Example

This subsection presents a simple example of a typical Theo knowledge base, and illustrates Theo's inference and learning processes.

### Representation

As previously described, beliefs in Theo correspond to assertions of the form (<entity> <slot>) = <value>. Beliefs in Theo are stored in a frame-based representation, in which both frames and their slots correspond to entities.

Eleven simple Theo frames are depicted in Table 12.1. Each frame contains a list of slots and their values. Each sublist in the description of a frame is a slot whose value immediately follows the slot name, and whose subslots are listed after the value. Each frame and each of its slots is a Theo entity, and each entity's (sub)slots store Theo's currently explicit beliefs about that entity.

For example, the frame CUBE contains a slot called SPECIALIZATIONS, whose value is the list (CUBE1 CUBE2) (line 9). This illustrates how Theo stores the belief (CUBE SPECIALIZATIONS) = (CUBE1 CUBE2). Similarly, the frame CUBE contains a slot called HEIGHT whose value is presently unknown (as evidenced by the token "*NOVALUE*").

In general, we define an entity's *address* in the following fashion: If the entity is a top-level frame, its address is the name of the frame (e.g., CUBE). If the

## TABLE 12.1
### Fragment of a Theo Knowledge Base

```
 1 (physobj *novalue* (generalizations (frame))
 2     (specializations (box))
 3     (comment "prototypical physical object"))

 5 (box *novalue* (generalizations (physobj))
 6     (specializations (cube)))

 8 (cube *novalue* (generalizations (box))
 9     (specializations (cube1 cube2))
10     (height *novalue*
11        (definitions ((th size *de*))))
12     (length *novalue*
13        (definitions ((th size *de*))))
14     (width *novalue*
15        (definitions ((th size *de*)))))

17 (cube1 *novalue* (generalizations (cube))
18     (density 5)
19     (size 10))

21 (cube2 *novalue* (generalizations (cube))
22     (below cube1))

24 (physobj.slot *novalue* (generalizations (slot))
25     (specializations (density size height length width volume weight
26                       above below))
27     (domain physobj)
28     (available.methods (inherits defines drop.context use.inverse
29                        default value)))

31 (volume *novalue* (generalizations (physobj.slot))
32     (domain box)
33     (range reals)
34     (definitions ((* (th height *de*) (th length *de*) (th width *de*)))))

36 (weight *novalue* (generalizations (physobj.slot))
37     (range reals)
38     (definitions ((* (th density *de*) (th volume *de*)))))

40 (height *novalue* (generalizations (physobj.slot))
41     (range reals))

43 (above *novalue* (generalizations (physobj.slot))
44     (inverse below))

46 (below *novalue* (generalizations (physobj.slot))
47     (inverse above))
```

entity is a slot, its address is the sequence of slot names traversed to reach the slot from its top-level frame. For example, in Table 12.1, we say that the address of the HEIGHT slot of CUBE is (CUBE HEIGHT), and the address of the DEFINI-TIONS slot of the HEIGHT slot of CUBE is (CUBE HEIGHT DEFINITIONS). *The address of a slot is identical to the name of the Theo entity represented by that slot.* For example, (CUBE HEIGHT) is the slot address of the Theo entity named (CUBE HEIGHT) which represents the class of problems of determining the heights of cubes. The (sub)slots of (CUBE HEIGHT) represent Theo's beliefs about this problem class. In this case, the only explicitly held belief about this problem class is that (CUBE HEIGHT DEFINITIONS) = ((TH SIZE *DE*)).

Note that names of slots can also be names of top–level frames. For example, the top–level frame HEIGHT (lines 40–41) represents the class of problems of finding the height of any physical object. Theo may therefore infer beliefs about the problem class (CUBE HEIGHT) from its beliefs about the more general problem class HEIGHT. Furthermore, note that the frames VOLUME and WEIGHT also contain information defining additional slots (lines 31–38). Theo may use its beliefs about these two problem classes to infer beliefs about problem classes such as (CUBE WEIGHT) and (CUBE VOLUME), regardless of the fact that neither (CUBE WEIGHT) nor (CUBE VOLUME) is an explicitly repre-sented slot in the entity CUBE.

### Inference

The basic function of Theo is to access slot values (i.e., solve problems). If we query Theo regarding the value of (VOLUME GENERALIZATIONS) in the present example, it will return the stored value (PHYSOBJ.SLOT) (line 31). If we ask for the value of a slot which has no explicitly stored value, such as (CUBE1 WEIGHT), then Theo will attempt to infer a value based on its knowl-edge of the problem class (CUBE1 WEIGHT). All problem solving in Theo corresponds to inferring needed slot values.

A query for the value of (CUBE1 WEIGHT) leads to the sequence of subque-ries shown in Table 12.2.[1] Lines in Table 12.2 such as line 3,

>5 tget (box weight)

indicate that as a subgoal of 4 other higher level slot accesses, Theo is attempting to *get* the value of the slot (BOX WEIGHT). Similarly, lines such as line 19,

<3 tget (5 (((cube1 density))))

indicate that Theo is returning from a level 3 *get* with a value of 5 for the slot

---

[1]In fact, this is a highly selective trace showing only the slot accesses for the frames in Table 12.1. Many additional system-level slots are also accessed but are not shown in this introductory example.

(CUBE1 DENSITY). While the method for inferring slot values will be described in greater detail later, at this point it is sufficient to note that in order to determine the available methods for inferring the value of (CUBE1 WEIGHT) Theo retrieves the value of the subslot (CUBE1 WEIGHT AVAIL-ABLE.METHODS). The value of this slot is itself inferred from the value of (PHYSOBJ.SLOT AVAILABLE.METHODS) (Table 12.1, lines 28–29). The retrieved list of available methods includes the items INHERITS, which suggests inheriting a value from a generalization of CUBE1, and DEFINES, which suggests applying a definition (such as the one in (WEIGHT DEFINITIONS) listed on line 38 of Table 12.1).

As shown in Table 12.2, Theo attempts to infer the value of (CUBE1 WEIGHT) by first trying to inherit a value from (CUBE WEIGHT) (line 2), but this ultimately proves unfruitful.[2] Eventually (by line 18), Theo tries applying the DEFINES method, and this is ultimately successful.

The DEFINES method retrieves the value of (CUBE1 WEIGHT DEFINI-TIONS) and applies the definition in order to infer a value for (CUBE1 WEIGHT). Note that (CUBE1 WEIGHT DEFINITIONS) must itself be inferred, and it is obtained from (WEIGHT DEFINITIONS) in a series of slot accesses that are not included in the trace of Table 12.2. Later we discuss methods by which Theo can currently infer the value of slot DEFINITIONS on demand.

The retrieved value of (WEIGHT DEFINITIONS) indicates that the WEIGHT of some object, *DE*, can be inferred by multiplying the DENSITY of *DE* by the VOLUME of *DE*.[3] This leads Theo to attempt to retrieve the value of (CUBE1 DENSITY), as shown in Table 12.2 (line 18), and the value of (CUBE1 VOLUME) (line 20). Since this latter slot's value is not explicitly available. Theo backchains in an attempt to infer its value, and so forth. Table 12.2 summarizes the sequence of slot accesses performed to infer first (CUBE1 DENSITY) (lines 18–19), then (CUBE1 VOLUME) (lines 20–69), and finally (CUBE1 WEIGHT) (lines 1–70). Inference in Theo is typically of this fashion: methods are tried until one succeeds.

### Caching and Explanations

Once a slot's value is inferred, the value may be cached (i.e., stored) in the slot, along with an explanation of how the value was inferred. More precisely, whenever Theo successfully infers a value for some slot, S, it examines the

---

[2]Search up the inheritance hierarchy terminates at PHYSOBJ (line 4) because the domain of the WEIGHT slot is PHYSOBJ (inherited from the domain of PHYSOBJ.SLOT, Table 12.1, line 27), and thus WEIGHT is not defined for more general objects.

[3]The identifier *DE* refers to the entity whose slot value is to be computed. Slots can be viewed as relations defined over a particular domain and range, and *DE* refers to the domain element of the slot instance whose value is being inferred. Similarly, the identifier *RE* stands for the range element of the slot instance.

TABLE 12.2
Trace of Slot Accesses to Infer (CUBE1 WEIGHT)

```
 1 >1 tget (cube1 weight)
 2    >3 tget (cube weight)
 3      >5 tget (box weight)
 4        >7 tget (physobj weight)
 5          >9 tget (physobj density)
 6          <9 tget (*inferred.novalue* (((physobj density))))
 7        <7 tget (*inferred.novalue* (((physobj weight))))
 8        >7 tget (box density)
 9          >9 tget (physobj density)
10          <9 tget (*inferred.novalue* (((physobj density))))
11        <7 tget (*inferred.novalue* (((box density))))
12      <5 tget (*inferred.novalue* (((box weight))))
13      >5 tget (cube density)
14        >7 tget (box density)
15        <7 tget (*inferred.novalue* (((box density))))
16      <5 tget (*inferred.novalue* (((cube density))))
17    <3 tget (*inferred.novalue* (((cube weight))))
18    >3 tget (cube1 density)
19    <3 tget (5 (((cube1 density))))
20    >3 tget (cube1 volume)
21      >5 tget (cube volume)
22        >7 tget (box volume)
23          >9 tget (box height)
24            >11 tget (physobj height)
25            <11 tget (*inferred.novalue* (((physobj height))))
26          <9 tget (*inferred.novalue* (((box height))))
27        <7 tget (*inferred.novalue* (((box volume))))
28        >7 tget (cube height)
29          >9 tget (box height)
30          <9 tget (*inferred.novalue* (((box height))))
31          >9 tget (cube size)
               . . .
36          <9 tget (*inferred.novalue* (((cube size))))
37        <7 tget (*inferred.novalue* (((cube height))))
38      <5 tget (*inferred.novalue* (((cube volume))))
39      >5 tget (cube1 height)
           . . .
42        >7 tget (cube1 size)
43        <7 tget (10 (((cube1 size))))
44      <5 tget (10 (((cube1 height))))
45      >5 tget (cube1 length)
           . . .
54        >7 tget (cube1 size)
55        <7 tget (10 (((cube1 size))))
56      <5 tget (10 (((cube1 length))))
57      >5 tget (cube1 width)
           . . .
66        >7 tget (cube1 size)
67        <7 tget (10 (((cube1 size))))
68      <5 tget (10 (((cube1 width))))
69    <3 tget (1000 (((cube1 volume))))
70 <1 tget (5000 (((cube1 weight))))
```

TABLE 12.3
Explanation of Inferred Value for (CUBE1 WEIGHT)

---

(cube1 weight) = 5000
  ←|weight.definitions.1|—
  (cube1 volume) = 1000
    ←|volume.definitions.1|—
    (cube1 height) = 10
      ←|cube.height.deinitions.1|—
    (cube1 size) = 10
    (cube1 length) = 10
      ←|cube.length.definitions.1|—
    (cube1 size) = 10
    (cube1 width) = 10
      ←|cube.width.definitions.1|—
    (cube1 size) = 10
  (cube1 density) = 5

---

WHENTOCACHE slot of S to determine whether the value of S is to be cached. The default value for WHENTOCACHE (stored in the slot (WHENTOCACHE DEFAULT.VALUE)) is presently defined so that by default all slot values are cached.[4]

When a slot's value is cached, the slot addresses that were used to infer this slot's value are recorded in its EXPLANATION subslot. Theo's explanation for the inferred value of (CUBE1 WEIGHT) is shown in Table 12.3. This explanation indicates that the value of (CUBE1 WEIGHT) is derivable from the definition of weight and the values of (CUBE1 VOLUME) and (CUBE1 DENSITY), that the value of (CUBE1 VOLUME) is derivable from the definition of volume and the values of (CUBE1 HEIGHT), (CUBE1 LENGTH), (CUBE1 WIDTH), and so on. In this case, all slot values were inferred via definitions using the DEFINES method. For example, "←|weight.definitions.1|—" denotes the application of the first definition in (WEIGHT DEFINITIONS) (cf. Table 12.1, line 38). More generally, explanations can mention any of Theo's inference methods (e.g., INHERIT, DEFAULT.VALUE) in addition to slot definitions.

Saved explanations play two central roles in Theo. First, explanations are used for a simple form of truth maintenance. If any slot value in the system is changed, then the values of all dependent slots are uncached.[5] For example, if one changes the value of (CUBE1 DENSITY), then Theo will replace the value

---

[4]We have not yet experimented in detail with policies for when to cache slot values. Our default policy of caching all slot values tends to consume many megabytes of memory, and we expect to eventually examine this issue in greater detail.

[5]In practice, the EXPLANATION slot is accompanied by its inverse, the DEPENDENTS slot. The latter contains a list of all slots whose values depend on this slot. When any slot's value changes, Theo uncaches that slot's DEPENDENTS.

of (CUBE1 WEIGHT) with *NOVALUE*. If (CUBE1 WEIGHT) is subsequently queried, its value will be recomputed based on then current knowledge.

### Learning

The second use of the EXPLANATION slot in Theo is to support a form of explanation-based learning. In particular, Theo composes the successful inference steps mentioned in the explanation, in order to form a special-purpose macro-method for subsequent use. Table 12.4 shows the specialized macro definition for WEIGHT which Theo derives from the explanation in Table 12.3. Note that the value of (CUBE1 WEIGHT EXPLANATION) provides both the information needed to construct the macro and to compute the macro's domain of applicability. By inferring the latter, Theo determines how far up the generalization/inheritance hierarchy it may store the new macro. In this case, the macro is stored in the slot (CUBE WEIGHT SPECIALIZED.DEFINITIONS) (despite the fact that the training example was related to the more specific CUBE1). This new SPECIALIZED.DEFINITIONS will be inherited when Theo attempts to compute the WEIGHT of other SPECIALIZATIONS of CUBE. Of course, the usual downside risks of forming macro-operators (Minton, 1988) apply here, since it may turn out that the macro-operator costs more time on the average than it saves. The impact of Theo's generalized macro learning is described and evaluated in greater detail later in this chapter.

In addition to restructuring definitions in the knowledge base, Theo also improves its performance by modifying the *order* in which slot inference methods are attempted. By default, Theo attempts methods in the order in which they are listed in the AVAILABLE.METHODS slot. Of course this default ordering may not be optimal for all slot inferences, as is the case in the example of Table 12.2 where Theo attempts the unsuccessful INHERITS method before the DEFINES method (lines 2–17) and does more work than necessary to infer the value of (CUBE1 WEIGHT). In order to learn a better ordering for methods, Theo keeps a set of simple statistics on the cost and likelihood of success for each slot inference method. Table 12.5 lists the data Theo retains after inferring the value of (CUBE1 WEIGHT).

TABLE 12.4
Specialized Definition of WEIGHT Inferred
from (CUBE1 WEIGHT EXPLANATION) and
Stored in (CUBE WEIGHT
SPECIALIZED.DEFINITIONS)

```
(* (th density *de*)
   (* (th size *de*)
      (th size *de*)
      (th size *de*)))
```

TABLE 12.5
Data Collected while Inferring (CUBE1 WEIGHT)

| Computations | Odds of Success | Cost of Success | Cost of Failure |
|---|---|---|---|
| (WEIGHT INHERITS) | 0/3 | ? | 459K[6] |
| (WEIGHT |WEIGHT.DEFINITIONS.1|) | 1/3 | 883K | 113K |
| (WEIGHT DROP.CONTEXT) | 0/3 | ? | 0 |
| (WEIGHT USE.INVERSE) | 0/3 | ? | 23K |
| (WEIGHT DEFAULT.VALUE) | 0/4 | ? | 39K |

Theo utilizes the data from Table 12.5 to reorder the methods for WEIGHT, by moving DEFINES to the front of the list. If this advice could have been followed beforehand, the number of slot accesses shown in Table 12.2 to infer (CUBE1 WEIGHT) would have been reduced from 70 to 20.[7] This learning method will be described and evaluated in further detail.

The previous example is intended to illustrate the style of knowledge representation, inference, and learning in Theo. Each of these topics is discussed in greater detail in subsequent sections. The primary points illustrated by the above example are:

- All explicitly held beliefs in Theo are stored as values of slots of entities.

- All problems in Theo are queries for the value of some slot of some entity.

- Slots of entities are themselves entities which represent the problem of inferring the value of that slot. As entities, these slots have subslots (e.g., AVAILABLE.METHODS, DOMAIN, DEFINITIONS) which store beliefs about how to infer a value for the given slot. If these subslots themselves have no value, they may themselves be inferred on demand as for any other slot.

- It is useful to view Theo as an infinitely large *virtual* datastructure which is incrementally made explicit on demand. This virtual datastructure delimits the set of all beliefs which Theo can in principle represent, and therefore hold. It also delimits the set of problems which may be posed to Theo.

- When Theo is successful in inferring the value of some slot, it may cache the inferred slot value along with an explanation that justifies the value.

- Explanations of slot values are used to provide a straightforward form of truth maintenance, and to guide a form of explanation-based generalization.

- Theo currently employs three types of learning mechanisms: caching of slot

---

[6]Cost(Succeed) and Cost(Fail) are measured in terms of CPU time.

[7]In fact, reordering of methods can occur either in *guaranteed* mode, in which Theo does not reorder any methods until a statistically significant amount of evidence has been collected; or in *heuristic* mode, in which Theo reorders the methods without guarantees of statistical significance.

values, inferring macro–methods from the explanations of inferred slot values, and inductively inferring the order in which slot inference methods should be attempted.

The following sections describe Theo's inference, representation, and learning mechanisms in greater detail. Later, we consider the relation between Theo and two earlier systems: Soar and RLL.

## INFERENCE

As illustrated by Table 12.6, Theo infers the value of a given slot S based on beliefs stored in the subslots of S. This subsection describes in greater detail Theo's mechanisms for inferring slot values.

There are three layers of discipline at which the user can specify the inference method for a particular problem class (e.g., slot). At the most basic layer, each slot (i.e., problem class) has a subslot named TOGET, whose value is a Lisp function. This function takes as an argument the address of the slot whose value is to be determined, and returns that slot's value along with an explanation. The basic inference function in Theo, called TGET, simply applies this function to the address of the slot in question. Thus, the user can specify an arbitrary Lisp function to infer the value of slot S simply by storing the name of the Lisp function in the slot (S TOGET).

If the user defines some new slot, S, and does not specify a value for (S TOGET), a value will be inferred for (S TOGET) from the system-provided value of (TOGET DEFAULT.VALUE). This default value of TOGET establishes

TABLE 12.6
Summary of Theo's Layered Inference Mechanism

---

To infer (CUBE1 WEIGHT):
- Layer 1: Apply Lisp function in slot (CUBE1 WEIGHT TOGET) to the address (CUBE1 WEIGHT)
  - If unspecified, the default value of TOGET implements layer 2.
- Layer 2: Apply list of methods in (CUBE1 WEIGHT AVAILABLE.METHODS) to the address (CUBE1 WEIGHT) until a value is obtained.
  - If unspecified, the default value of available methods is: (DEFINES INHERITS DROP.CONTEXT DEFAULT.VALUE).
  - The DEFINES method implements layer 3.
- Layer 3: Interpret definitions found in (CUBE1 WEIGHT DEFINITIONS) and in (CUBE1 WEIGHT SPECIALIZED.DEFINITIONS).
  - Value of DEFINITIONS subslot may itself be inferred from knowledge of slot's INVERSE, PLURAL, SINGULAR, etc.
  - Value of SPECIALIZED.DEFINITIONS may be inferred via explanation-based learning.

---

the next higher layer of discipline for specifying inference methods. At this layer, inference methods are specified by the AVAILABLE.METHODS slot of S.[8] See, for example, the slot (PHYSOBJ.SLOT AVAILABLE.METHODS) from Table 12.1. Theo infers the value of S by sequentially attempting the methods specified in (S AVAILABLE.METHODS) until one succeeds in returning a value.[9] In fact, each method corresponds to the name of a (possibly virtual) subslot whose value is the result of applying that method to the current problem. Thus, in inferring the value for a slot such as (BOX1 WEIGHT), Theo may cache explicit values for various subslots such as (BOX1 WEIGHT DROP.CONTEXT), (BOX1 WEIGHT DEFAULT.VALUE), etc. Appendix I summarizes the legal entries in the list AVAILABLE.METHODS, as well as the definitions of the corresponding inference methods.

If the AVAILABLE.METHODS of the slot includes the token DEFINES, then Theo will attempt to utilize the DEFINITIONS and SPECIAL-IZED.DEFINITIONS[10] subslots to infer a value. DEFINITIONS provide the third, and highest level of discipline for specifying slot inference methods. The value of the DEFINITIONS slot is a list of expressions which are evaluated in sequence in an attempt to infer a value for the slot. For example, the slots (WEIGHT DEFINITIONS) and (VOLUME DEFINITIONS) in Table 12.1 illustrate the use of the DEFINITIONS slot.

For convenience in writing slot definitions, the variables *DE*, *RE*, and *ME* designate predefined slot addresses. *ME* designates the address of the slot being defined, *DE* designates the address of the domain element of this slot, and *RE* designates the address of the range element of this slot. For instance, if the value of the slot (CUBE1 VOLUME) refers to these variables, then *ME* will evaluate to the address (CUBE1 VOLUME), *DE* will evaluate to the address CUBE1, *RE* will evaluate to the address 1000,[11] (i.e., the range element, or value, associated with this slot (cf. Table 12.2, line 69)). These variables, together with the function TH,[12] provide a convenient means of specifying entity addresses relative to the address of the slot whose

---

[8]To be more accurate, layer 2 inference methods are in fact specified by a slot named METHODS, whose value is inferred from the value of the AVAILABLE.METHODS slot. However, it is easiest to think of METHODS as an implementation detail, and to think of layer 2 as logically defined by AVAILABLE.METHODS.

[9]By default, Theo attempts each method in sequence until a successful method is found. Alternatively, Theo can be directed to attempt all the specified methods for slot S and to collect the union of their values, by asserting (S TOGET) = TOGET.SET.

[10]Recall that the SPECIALIZED.DEFINITIONS subslot is inferred via explanation-based learning.

[11]Note here that we view any slot value as an entity address (even numbers), regardless of whether that entity is presently represented by an explicit datastructure with explicit slots.

[12]The function TH is described in detail in Appendix II.

value is being inferred. See, for example, the definitions illustrated in Table 12.1.

The layered inference mechanism in Theo allows the user to associate efficient Lisp procedures with selected slots (by asserting a value for the TOGET slot of that slot), to utilize a list of system standard inference methods such as INHERITS and DEFAULT.VALUE for other slots, and to utilize definitions (which may themselves be inferred by Theo) for other slots. Higher level specifications are typically more open to examination by the system. For instance, Theo is able to apply its explanation-based learning mechanism only to slots which use the default value for TOGET (i.e., slots whose inference methods are specified at levels 2 or 3).

## REPRESENTATION

This section describes in greater detail the representation conventions of Theo alluded to earlier.

*Predefined slots of slots.*    A number of slots for describing slots are defined in the initial Theo knowledge base. These slot slots describe various slot properties such as DEFINITIONS, DOMAIN, RANGE, INVERSE, PLURAL, TRANSITIVE?, and MULTIVALUED?. Other slot slots describe how to infer values of instances of the slot, such as TOGET, METHODS, and AVAILABLE. METHODS, as well as other control information such as WHENTOCACHE, WHENTOEBG. In addition, the slot slots EXPLANATION, DEPENDENTS, EXPLANATION-METHOD, and EXPLANATION-DATA describe information about the interdependencies among slot values. Table 12.7 illustrates some of the system–defined slot slots, in the context of describing the HUSBAND slot. When defining a new slot the user may omit assertions about the values of any or all of these subslots. Theo can operate successfully in the absence of any of this information, since it will infer default values for subslots that are not explicitly given in the knowledge base. For example, if the user asserts (DENSITY DOMAIN)=PHYSOBJ, then Theo will use this information to constrain its method for inheriting values of instances of the DENSITY slot, so that it searches only among specializations of PHYSOBJ. On the other hand, if the user fails to assert an explicit value for (DENSITY DOMAIN), Theo will infer its value based on the (DOMAIN DEFAULT.VALUE)=ROOT, and will therefore search more widely when attempting to inherit a value for (CUBE1 DENSITY).

*Virtual and explicit entities, slots and values.*    As described above, expressions in Theo can refer to slot values that are not explicitly described by the current datastructures in memory, but which must be inferred on demand. The same is true of entities and slots, so that if Theo is asked to infer the value of some new slot of some new entity, it will construct the entity and the slot, then

TABLE 12.7
Beliefs about the Husband Entity

---

```
(husband *novalue*
        (generalizations (spouse))
        (domain female)
        (range male)
        (definitions
                ((onewhich male
                                (equal (th wife *re*) *de*))))
        (specialized.definitions
                ((onewhich male
                                (equal *re* (th father value child *de*))))
        (default.value nil)
        (plural husbands)
        (singular nil)
        (multivalued? nil)
        (transitive? nil)
        (reflexive? nil)
        (inverse wife)
        (toget toget.first)
        (available.methods (inherits drop.context defines
                                use.inverse default.value))
        (ordered.methods (defines use.inverse inherit
                                drop.context default.value))
        (whentocache always)
        (whentogeneralize always)
        (explanation *novalue*)
        (explanation-data *novalue*)
        (explanation-method *novalue*)
        (dependents *novalue*))
```

---

infer and cache appropriate default methods for inferring the slot value. Note this relieves the user of responsibility for creating entities that define slots about which he has nothing unusual to assert. It also implies that Theo has default methods capable of inferring all essential slot values in the system.

*Slots with no value.*   Even slots that are explicitly described may have no known value. We distinguish between two situations in which no explicit slot value is recorded. If the value is not known and Theo has not yet attempted to infer a value, then the token *NOVALUE* is stored in the value field of the slot. If Theo attempts and fails to infer a slot value, then it stores the token *IN-FERRED.NOVALUE*, along with an explanation of the methods and slots which justify the absence of a value. By storing *INFERRED.NOVALUE*, Theo avoids subsequent futile searches for values of slots which it cannot infer. Because Theo records an EXPLANATION for each *INFERRED.NOVALUE*, its dependency maintenance mechanism automatically replaces an *IN-FERRED.NOVALUE* by *NOVALUE* if any change is made which could influence its ability to derive a value for the slot. In practice, we find that a great deal of wasted search effort is eliminated by this scheme of caching *IN-FERRED.NOVALUE*.

*Absolute and relative entity addresses.*    As noted earlier, the address of a slot entity is the list of entity names traversed in reaching the slot entity from the top level entity in which it appears (e.g., (CUBE1 WEIGHT DEFINITIONS) is the address of the DEFINITIONS slot of the WEIGHT slot of CUBE1). In addition to such entity addresses (which we will sometimes call *absolute addresses*), Theo also supports *relative addresses*. A relative address is a pair formed by an absolute address and a path specifying how to reach a second entity from the entity addressed by the absolute address. Such relative addresses are convenient when specifying slot DEFINITIONS which refer to addresses of other slots relative to the slot whose value is to be inferred. Appendix II describes Theo's relative address mechanism in some detail.

## LEARNING

Three learning mechanisms are presently available in Theo:

- Caching inferred slot values.
- Formulating macro-methods for inferring slot values, based on examining explanations of successful inferences.
- Ordering the methods for inferring slot values, based on inductive inference from statistics of past applications.

Here, we summarize each of these mechanisms and present experimental data illustrating their individual and combined impact on Theo's performance.

## Caching

Caching is the simplest form of learning, in which inferred slot values are stored so that they can be quickly retrieved on subsequent demand. Thus, caching provides a kind of rote learning, in which data is stored without any attempt to generalize it.

Figure 12.1 illustrates the impact of caching in Theo. Note the decreasing cost of a typical slot access in a simple knowledge base, as a result of caching, with Theo's other learning mechanisms disabled. The particular knowledge base defines a set of 12 people (e.g., MEGHAN, SHANNON), a set of 25 slots corresponding to family relations (e.g., SISTERS, UNCLES, DAUGHTERS) and an initial set of beliefs (e.g., (MEGHAN SISTERS)=(SHANNON). Initially, only 17 of the 300 describable beliefs were explicitly given. In this experiment, each

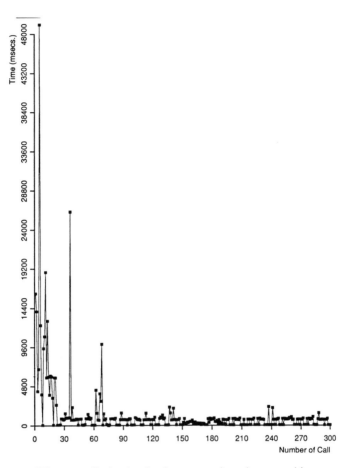

FIG. 12.1.    Reduction in slot access time due to caching.

of the 300 possible slots were queried, and the cost in seconds of obtaining an answer was measured. Figure 12.1 presents the cpu time cost of each of these 300 slot accesses, with the first slot access at the leftmost point and subsequent slot accesses progressively to the right.

Notice that the cost of the first few dozen slot accesses is quite high, with the cost of subsequent slot accesses dropping dramatically and quickly reaching a plateau. This is largely due to the high initial cost of inferring meta-level beliefs such as (MEGHAN SISTERS AVAILABLE.METHODS), (SISTERS AVAIL-ABLE.METHODS), and (SISTERS DOMAIN). It is also partly due to the need to infer additional ground level beliefs (e.g., SISTERS is defined in terms of PARENTS). Once such information has been inferred and cached during the first few dozen slot accesses, it is directly available when needed to support subsequent slot queries. Thus the high cost of relying on explicit meta–knowledge (e.g., about (SISTERS DOMAIN) is quickly reduced by caching since most instances of a slot (e.g., instances of the SISTERS slot) make use of precisely the same meta–information.

## Explanation-Based Learning of Macro-Methods

As discussed, Theo forms macro-methods by examining explanations of previously successful slot inferences. The program which achieves this within Theo is called TMAC. In particular, after Theo infers the value of some slot, S, TMAC can form a macro–method by composing the successful inference steps, computing the generalization, S', of S to which this macro–method can legally be applied, and then storing this macro–method in the SPECIALIZED. DEFINITIONS subslot of S'. Theo will then be able to inherit this macro–method when attempting to infer values for other slots that are specializations of S'.

In general, several possible generalizations may be formed from the explanation associated with a slot value. Consider, for example, the explanation of Table 12.3 for the belief (CUBE1 WEIGHT)=5000. From this example, one might apply explanation based learning (DeJong & Mooney, 1986; Mitchell et al., 1986) to infer sufficient conditions for any of the following target concepts:

- {?e | (?e WEIGHT)=5000}. By determining the general set of entities for which the explanation carries through, it would be possible to determine whether the inferred value for (CUBE1 WEIGHT) can be stored in some more general location in the inheritance hierarchy.

- {?v | (BOX1 WEIGHT)=?v}. One might alternatively generalize by determining the class of values for which the explanation still applies to the slot instance. In fact, this makes little sense for single–valued slots such as WEIGHT. However, for multi-valued slots such as HEAVIER.OBJECTS, such a generalization could result in generalizing from one legitimate slot value to a set of legal slot values.

- {<?e ?v> | (?e WEIGHT)=?v}. Alternatively, one might attempt to generalize both the entity and the value of the belief, to find a general relation between the two. This is, in fact, what TMAC computes. Its macro-methods define a relation between some generalization of CUBE1 and some generalization of 5000. This relation is defined in terms of a macro-method which allows determining the value ?v from a given entity ?e. Table 12.4 shows the macro–method for this example.

Thus, TMAC accomplishes one type of explanation-based learning, and represents an initial attempt to integrate explanation-based–learning with Theo's representation, inference, and indexing mechanisms, as well as its other learning mechanisms. At present, TMAC is applicable only to slots whose inference methods are specified in terms of layers 2 and 3 (Cf. Table 12.6).

Table 12.8 presents the results of applying TMAC. The data presented here is derived from a knowledge base defining a number of physical objects and their properties (slots) such as WEIGHT, VOLUME, HEAVIER.OBJECTS, and SAFE.TO.STACK.ON. These slots are a superset of those given in Table 12.1, and their definitions form a domain theory similar to that given in (Mitchell et al., 1986) for characterizing when it is safe to stack one physical object on another. The SAFE.TO.STACK.ON slot, for instance, is a slot whose value is a list of physical objects on which the domain element can be safely stacked.

Line 1 of Table 12.8 shows the time in seconds to infer the value of the slot (BOX1 SAFE.TO.STACK.ON), with and without invoking TMAC, but allowing caching of slot values in both cases. Note that even though TMAC carries a certain overhead cost, Theo is able to infer the slot value more quickly when TMAC is included. This is because the inference of (BOX1 SAFE.TO. STACK.ON) leads to accessing a number of additional slots (such as the WEIGHTs of other known physical objects). TMAC is able to infer macro–methods for these other slots, and Theo uses these macro–methods to complete the computation of (BOX1 SAFE.TO.STACK.ON) more efficiently. Thus, line 1 illustrates the type of within-trial learning that TMAC can produce.

Line 2 shows the results of a second, subsequent query to infer a value for (BOX2 SAFE.TO.STACK.ON). As the table shows, the cost for inferring this slot value is much less than for the first slot query. This is largely due to the effects of caching, since the WEIGHT and other features of various physical objects were cached as a result of the first slot query. In addition, TMAC reduces the cost by a factor of two over the reduction due to caching alone.

While the results in Table 12.8 are typical of those obtained for caching and TMAC, the results depend, of course, on the details of the structure of the knowledge base, the patterns of slot queries, and the frequency with which old slot values are replaced by new values. For example, we find the importance of TMAC relative to caching is minimized when the knowledge base is static (i.e., no old slot values are changed) as in the current example, and maximized when slot values are frequently updated (since this causes dependent values to be

TABLE 12.8
Impact of Forming Macro-Methods in Theo

| | Slot Query | Time in Seconds | |
| --- | --- | --- | --- |
| | | TMAC plus Caching | Caching Only |
| 1. | (box1 safe.to.stack.on) | 92 | 118 |
| 2. | (box2 safe.to.stack.on) | 1.5 | 3.1 |

removed and macro–methods are very effective for recomputing the new slot values).

## Learning to Order Methods

Since Theo usually has several methods available for inferring the value of any given slot, it is useful for Theo to attempt these methods in some appropriate order. SE is an inductive learning system which can order the AVAIL-ABLE.METHODS for any slot in Theo.[13] SE accepts as input a slot address and the corresponding list of AVAILABLE.METHODS, and produces as output a list of methods ordered in the sequence in which they should be attempted. SE may also be viewed as learning an evaluation function from statistical sampling. As such, it is closely related to the ideas developed independently by Abramson & Korf (1987).

To produce such method orderings, SE utilizes a random sample of executed Theo computations, as well as a predicate language for defining clusters of these example computations. Currently, SE clusters computations by the problem class to which they belong and the method that was used to solve the problem. Each <problem class, method> pair corresponds to a predicate in the predicate language. For example, (WEIGHT INHERIT) corresponds to the predicate satisfied by all executed instances of (WEIGHT INHERIT) such as (BOX1 WEIGHT INHERIT) and so on.

By a Theo computation we mean the application of a method (e.g., INHER-IT) to infer the value of a specific slot. For each such computation SE considers the time it required and whether it succeeded or failed. Based on this input, SE produces predictions of the probability of success and expected cost for subsequent Theo computations, then uses these predictions to order the AVAIL-ABLE.METHODS of slots. More precisely, given a query from Theo consisting of a slot address and its associated list of AVAILABLE.METHODS, SE sorts the given methods based on a simple function of their probabilities of success and failure, and their expected costs.

The function used by SE to sort the available methods is:   Cost of success + (probability of failure/probability of success)* cost of failure. Etzioni (1988) presents a general statistical model which has been used in Etzioni (1987) to analyze SE and to prove that SE's method orderings minimize the expected inference cost for Theo, if its cost data is correct. Etzioni (1987) proves that if the estimates used are good, then the ordering will be close to optimal. However, the model used for these proofs makes several assumptions that may not be realistic for Theo. In particular, the model assumes a fixed or slowly changing distribu-

---

[13]We can only give a brief high level sketch of SE in this context. See [Etzioni 87] and [Etzioni 88] for a complete description.

tion of computation costs with does not accurately model Theo when caching of slot values is active. Nevertheless, our empirical investigations of SE (see following) indicate that SE is able to significantly improve Theo's computational efficiency.

The crux of SE's problem is generating accurate predictions for the probability of success and cost of each method. To generate its predictions SE groups the sample computations into clusters. A predicate is associated with each cluster, and a computation belongs to the cluster if and only if it matches the predicate. The mean cost of sample computations in the cluster is used as the cost prediction for new computations which fall in the cluster, and the proportion of successful sample computations in the cluster is used as the probability of success prediction for new computations which belong to the cluster. Thus, the cluster's predicate implicitly defines a population of computations. A sample from the population is used to form predictions about the population.

SE attempts to find clusters which are homogeneous with respect to computational cost. That is, the cost of computations in the cluster is more or less the same. For such a cluster, the sample mean is likely to be a good prediction of the cost of new computations which match the cluster's predicate. The quality of SE's predictions depends on its ability to find homogeneous clusters, because the mean is a bad predictor for a nonhomogeneous population.

To summarize, SE is called with a slot address (e.g., (CUBE1 WEIGHT)) and an unordered list of possible methods (e.g., (INHERITS DROP.CONTEXT |WEIGHT.DEFINITIONS.1| USE.INVERSE, DEFAULT.VALUE)). It finds a predicate to match each incipient computation (<method slot> pair). The mean costs, success rate, and failure rate of the sample that matches this predicate are used to obtain predictions for the new computation. Once all such predictions have been made, the method list is sorted and returned to Theo.

Experimental results showing the impact of SE's learning are presented in the following section. Our preliminary experiments indicate that SE is able to significantly speed up Theo computations. However, SE's performance deteriorates when Theo is caching, since SE's data on expected costs becomes outdated over time. We are considering updating schemes for SE's estimates which weight recent data more heavily than older data in order to ameliorate this problem.

Table 12.9 summarizes the results of various combinations of Theo's three learning mechanisms, for the task of computing a set of slot inferences involving WIDTH, AREA, and LENGTH of various objects. Note that the longest time is required when no learning is enabled, and that any one of the learning mechanisms produces a noticeable improvement. Furthermore, combinations of the learning mechanisms produce stronger performance than individual mechanisms, and the strongest improvement is obtained when all three learning mechanisms are enabled.

Although these results are typical of Theo's behavior, the exact payoff of each learning mechanism depends in general on features such as the particular patterns

TABLE 12.9
Combinations of Learning Mechanisms
in Theo

Times in Seconds to Complete a Set of Slot
Accesses

| TMAC off | | |
|---|---|---|
| | SE off | SE on |
| Caching off | 1132 | 641 |
| Caching on | 781 | 526 |
| | | |
| TMAC on | | |
| | SE off | SE on |
| Caching off | 933 | 425 |
| Caching on | 702 | 389 |

of slot queries and updates, which slots possess inferable values, and the level of independence among slot values. In fact, it is possible to construct worst–case situations in which TMAC and SE lead to deteriorated rather than improved performance in the presence of caching. As a simple example, if one were to repeatedly query a single slot, then caching would provide the optimal learning mechanism and the overhead cost of TMAC and SE would have no offsetting benefits.

We have just begun to explore learning in Theo. Some of the observations and issues that we have identified for further exploration include:

- Each learning mechanism changes the computational environment in a way that impacts the others. The most important example of this involves the impact of caching on SE. Caching slot values changes various computational costs so that SE's estimates of costs for applying various methods can become out of date, and, thus, so can its learned method orderings. One way to deal with this issue of environmental drift might be to weight most heavily the most recent of SE's training data.

- Macro–methods can cause Theo an unnecessary amount of work by causing it to overlook available slot values. For example, when Theo forms a macro–method for HEAVIER.OBJECTS that is based on accessing values of VOLUME and DENSITY of other objects, this macro-method will fail to take advantage of subsequent situations in which Theo holds explicit beliefs about the WEIGHT of various objects.

- Theo should learn about the relative *reliabilities* of its methods. While SE learns to predict the expected costs and probabilities of success of Theo's methods, it should also learn about the reliabilities of these methods. The Default. Value method, for instance, may be highly likely to succeed when invoked, though the value it returns may be less reliable than that obtained via some other method. The control knowledge acquired by SE should take this factor into account. In general, we believe that intelligent systems cannot be constructed solely from infallible inference methods. Taking reliability into account in control knowledge, and recovering from unreliable inferences are high–priority issues on our research agenda.

- Theo should be able to use explanation-based learning as well as SE's inductive mechanisms to order available methods. Theo does not presently utilize explanation-based learning to order its slot methods (it is used only to produce macromethods). In order to achieve this, it may be useful to devise a representation of control knowledge different from the simple ordered list of methods produced by SE. This issue is discussed further in the context of comparing Theo with the Soar architecture.

- It is generally unclear which of the many possible generalizations that may be derived from a given explanation should be. In deriving a generalization from an explanation, TMAC makes a number of implicit choices that impact the generality/operationality tradeoff of the resulting learned macro–method. Consider, for example, the situation in which the original explanation refers to the default value of a particular slot (e.g., to (WEIGHT DEFAULT.VALUE)=5). When TMAC produces the resulting macro-method, should this method refer explicitly to this slot address, or simply replace the reference by the slot's value? The former leads to a more general, though slightly less operational macro-method (since it requires accessing the slot value at evaluation time). This issue is one of how thoroughly to partially evaluate (Kahn, 1984) the most general warranted macro–method in order to make it sufficiently operational.

- Theo should be able to decide when it is worth deliberating and when it is worth learning. In general, in acquiring control knowledge, how much deliberation by Theo is warranted in making control decisions? Is it best to make inexpensive unreliable guesses or expensive reliable ones? We suspect that there is no universal answer to this question, that the answer depends on the specific context, and that Theo should be made to reflect on this problem and learn slot-specific answers to the question of how thoroughly to deliberate and learn.


## PERSPECTIVE

From one perspective, Theo is a system for storing, inferring, maintaining, and retrieving beliefs, each of the form (<entity> <slot>)=<value>. Some beliefs are about entities from a particular domain (e.g., (CUBE1 WEIGHT)=5000). For each such belief, Theo may hold many more meta-beliefs about the belief itself, and about the problem of inferring the belief (e.g., (CUBE1 WEIGHT AVAILABLE.METHODS), (CUBE1 WEIGHT DEFAULT.VALUE), (CUBE1

WEIGHT EXPLANATION)). Similarly, it can hold meta-beliefs about *these* beliefs and problems as well (e.g., (CUBE1 WEIGHT AVAILABLE. METHODS DEFAULT.VALUE), (CUBE1 WEIGHT AVAILABLE.METHODS DEFAULT.VALUE EXPLANATION)). Note that even though Theo's potential beliefs cover an indefinite number of meta-levels with an increasing number of potential beliefs at each level, there is no necessary difficulty with infinite regress or with interminable meta-level reasoning. Theo need not necessarily consider the infinite number of meta-level problems which it can in principle pose, or the infinite number of meta–level beliefs which it can in principle hold.

Under this view, problem solving is the process of inferring the <value> field of a belief, given its <entity> and <slot>. Theo solves such problems by applying methods it believes to be appropriate to that problem, and by controlling the problem solving search based on yet other beliefs about the problem. Because Theo's ground and meta beliefs are described in a single notation, it can apply the same inference methods to both. This perspective raises questions about the distinction between learning and problem solving. Both are simply means for producing new beliefs about some entity.

A related perspective on Theo is that it is an infinitely large virtual datastructure which is incrementally made explicit on demand. This virtual datastructure corresponds to the set of all beliefs which Theo can in principle hold, and all problems which Theo could ever in principle pose. Furthermore, each such belief and problem has a name (i.e., its slot address) which provides an efficient means for indexing and retrieving the belief or problem in this datastructure. If this (infinite) virtual datastructure could be made completely explicit, then Theo could solve all subsequent problems it encountered by simply looking up their solutions. Of course this is not possible, but it does provide a useful perspective for understanding the significance of simple caching of inferred beliefs in a uniform representation with an efficient associated indexing mechanism. In fact, Theo can never make this datastructure completely explicit, and it simply makes those parts explicit that correspond to problems it encounters. Furthermore, its learning mechanisms seek to generalize its experience so that information is stored with problem classes rather than with the individual problem instances that constitute its experience.

This perspective raises questions about properties of this virtual datastructure as it becomes increasingly explicit. Is it possible to characterize Theo's level of competence at solving some class of problems as this datastructure becomes increasingly explicit? Can one show that Theo's indexing scheme based on absolute and relative slot addresses allows an indefinite increase in explicitness of this datastructure with a bounded increase in the cost of accessing knowledge needed to solve new problem instances? Does Theo's virtual datastructure include the deductive closure of its explicit beliefs? We are currently considering such questions about Theo's representation, inference, and indexing mechanisms.

## Comparison with Soar and RLL

The design of Theo has been influenced by several earlier efforts to develop uniform architectures for self-improving systems, especially by Soar (Laird et al., 1987) and RLL (Greiner & Lenat, 1980). Here we consider the relationship between Theo and these two systems.

Soar (Laird et al., 1987) is an architecture intended as a model for human cognition, and is organized around the notion of problem spaces. Problem solving corresponds to search in some problem space, and the decisions which must be made to guide this search (e.g., What are the legal moves? Which of these should be preferred as the next search step?) are made by applying a set of production rules to infer the information directly. When productions are not available to make such decisions, Soar recovers from this impasse by formulating the decision as a problem to be solved by search through some other problem space. Once this decision problem is solved, Soar compiles, or "chunks" the answer into a production rule which can provide the answer directly for similar subsequent problems. Thus, chunking provides the mechanism in Soar for incrementally compiling information which is in the inferential closure of Soar's knowledge, but which is not initially explicit in its productions. Soar has a *complete* set of impasses, in the sense that *every* decision involved in conducting search in a problem space can be formulated as a problem to be solved in another problem space, and Soar possesses weak methods to solve all such problems.

RLL (Greiner & Lenat, 1980) is a frame-based architecture which has been used as the basis for implementing the Eurisko program (Lenat, 1983). Eurisko extends the initial set of frames and slots that describe some domain (e.g., mathematics, VLSI structures) in order to explore the space of possibly useful new concepts in that domain. The important points here are RLL's ability to explicitly describe its own structure and its ability to support automatic generation of new frames and slots which constitute the vocabulary of its domain–specific representations.

Theo represents an attempt to incorporate impasse–driven computation similar to that found in Soar, with a self-describing frame-based representation similar to that found in RLL, along with explicit representation of explanations for beliefs, the ability to describe and index beliefs about *every* problem and belief, and a variety of inference and learning mechanisms.

Consider the correspondence between Soar and Theo:

- *Uniform problem representation.* Both Soar and Theo are organized around a uniform representation of all problems. Soar is organized around problem spaces, and Theo around problems described by pairs of the form (<entity> <slot>).
- *Problem solving knowledge indexed to problem description.* Both systems index problem solving knowledge based on the problem description. In

Soar, problem solving knowledge is stored in productions whose conditions test the problem space description. In Theo, problem solving knowledge resides in the subslots of the (<entity> <slot>). Note that in Theo, no condition matching is needed to index cached problem solving knowledge.

• *Use of impasse-driven computation.* Both Soar and Theo use impasse-driven computation to infer necessary problem solving knowledge when this knowledge is not directly retrievable. In Soar such impasses lead to solving problems in another problem space. In Theo, impasses correspond to queries of slots whose values are unknown, and result in the subtask of inferring the corresponding slot value. In both cases, an impasse in solving one problem results in formulating and solving a second problem described in the same representation.

• *Caching results of impasses.* Both systems cache the problem solutions resulting from such impasses. In Soar, solutions to impasses are stored in productions whose condition elements mention only those features of the problem which were used to resolve the impasse. In Theo, solutions to impasses are simply the inferred slot values, and are stored directly in the subslots of the problem instance. Note that chunking in Soar indexes the result of the impasse in a way that allows it to be retrieved more generally. Caching in Theo does not do this, although Theo's explanation–based learning component (i.e., TMAC) does. Thus, explanation-based learning in Theo plays a role similar to that played by the generalization step in chunking in Soar. See Rosenbloom & Laird (1986) for a discussion of the relationship between chunking in Soar and explanation-based learning.

The previous list makes clear several major similarities between Theo and Soar, and the correspondence between problems as (<entity> <slot>) pairs in Theo and problem spaces in Soar. There are also significant differences:

• *Different representations for control knowledge.* In Soar, knowledge to control search is expressed by explicitly asserted preferences (e.g., operator1 is preferred to operator2). In Theo, control knowledge is currently described by a sorted list of methods, but there are no explicitly asserted preferences between individual methods in this list. Thus, Soar's representation of control knowledge is finer grained: its individual preferences allow describing a partial rather than total ordering on the methods, and this partial ordering is often all that need be inferred in order to proceed with selecting a method. It may be advantageous to elaborate the representation of preferences among methods in Theo in a similar fashion.

• *Difference in uniformity of representation.* Theo's slots avoid the distinction made in Soar between problem spaces and attributes used in data representations (e.g., attributes used to describe problem states). This additional uniformity in Theo's representation allows it to apply the same inference mechanisms to resolving impasses that it applies to inferring the value of some attribute of the problem state. In fact, there is no fixed set of impasses in Theo, since *any* slot whose value is needed but not available can lead to attacking a new subproblem.

• *Different commitments to permanence and explicitness of explanations.* Theo records permanent explicit explanations for its beliefs, and these can be examined by the system. They are also used by Theo to maintain dependencies and to remove beliefs whose explanations cease to hold. Soar uses similar dependencies when constructing its "chunks", but it neither records these dependencies permanently, nor makes them available to the non-architecture portion of the system. Soar thus seems to have no corresponding notion of belief maintenance, and it is unclear how Soar deals with situations in which one of its productions becomes outdated because of changed beliefs that have been compiled into it.

• *Different memory indexing schemes.* Soar's long term memory consists solely of productions, while Theo's consists solely of entities and beliefs about them. These two memory organizations are similar in some sense, since one can typically translate an If-Then production into a belief about some appropriate class of entities. The differences in storage costs and retrieval speeds between these two schemes are poorly understood, however, and these issues are critical ones as we scale to larger knowledge bases.

• *Difference in use of explicit beliefs about problem classes.* Theo explicitly represents beliefs about problem classes, such as beliefs about their domain, range, inverse, generalizations, and specializations. It uses this information to infer solutions to the problems (e.g., Inheritance uses the slot's DOMAIN, Use.Inverse uses the slot's INVERSE, and Slotspecs uses a slot's SPECIALIZATIONS). This focus on problem classes as objects for reasoning is quite different from that in Soar. In Theo, approximately 80 slots, or problem classes, are predefined when the system is loaded, and Theo commonly caches new beliefs about the DOMAIN, AVAILABLE.METHODS, etc. of its taxonomy of problem classes.

• *Different learning mechanisms.* Soar presently has only one learning mechanism, and Theo three. As noted above, chunking in Soar is used to cover the same kinds of learning tasks that caching and explanation-based learning cover in Theo. Theo's third learning mechanism, the inductive inference method for inferring method orderings, has no inductive counterpart in Soar (whose control information is inferred by chunking). In some sense, Soar is more successful in integrating a single learning mechanism into the architecture (perhaps due to its representation of control information in terms of explicit preferences). However, it is not clear how Soar would accomplish the kind of statistical inference performed by SE.

This comparison between Soar and Theo is based on viewing both as instances of impasse-based architectures which incrementally make explicit information from their inferential closure. In contrast, the following comparison between RLL and Theo is based on viewing both as self-descriptive, frame-based representation systems.

As noted, RLL (Greiner & Lenat, 1980) is a modifiable and highly self-descriptive representation system which has served as the basis for implementing the Eurisko program (Lenat, 1983). RLL achieves its functionality by utilizing a highly uniform representation of frames and slots, and by possessing declarative descriptions of parts of itself. It allows describing each slot (e.g., VOLUME) by a frame whose slots describe beliefs about the slot (e.g., (VOLUME DO-MAIN)=PHYSICAL.OBJECTS), including information about how to infer values of the slot. It allows organizing such slot–defining frames into taxonomies so that their properties can be inherited, and allows defining new slots (e.g., FATHER) in terms of existing slots (e.g., SPOUSE, MOTHER). In addition, RLL attempts to provide declarative representations of methods with the goal of making it easy to create new methods by copying and editing the definitions of existing related methods.

Theo builds on many of the ideas in RLL, including the central ideas of explicit entities to describe each item in the system, and slots that specify beliefs about other slots, including information about how to infer their values. As in RLL, each slot in Theo has a corresponding top–level entity (e.g., VOLUME) whose slots define its properties in general. However, Theo also has entities corresponding to *each use of each slot*. This extension results in the important property that Theo can pose problems and hold beliefs about *every specialization and instance* of the VOLUME relation in the system. Furthermore, it can hold beliefs about these beliefs, and so on. Consider, for example, the definitions for various specializations of VOLUME:

- (VOLUME DEFINITIONS)=Integral over the surface of dx dy dz
- (PARALLELPIPED VOLUME DEFINITIONS)=Length × Width × Height
- (CUBE VOLUME DEFINITIONS)=Length × Length × Length

Without the ability to refer to the (CUBE VOLUME) specialization of the VOLUME relation, Theo would not be able to assert its specialized definition. In fact, one could create a new slot name, CUBE-VOLUME, assert that this is a specialization of the slot VOLUME, and store the specialized definition there. However, one quickly encounters an explosion of atomic slot names if this practice is followed for every specialization and instance of each slot. Consider, for example, the explosion resulting from constructing special–case names for each instance of the EXPLANATION slot (e.g., (CUBE1 VOLUME DEFINI-TIONS EXPLANATION), (CUBE2 VOLUME DEFINITIONS EXPLANA-

TION), ...). This ability to specify beliefs about beliefs and about problem classes is especially important in representing specialized problem solving knowledge about subclasses of problems.

## Conclusion

Theo is still evolving as an architecture. It constitutes the focus of our current efforts to understand the variety of representation, inference, self-reflection, learning, and memory indexing issues that arise in constructing general intelligent agents, and especially the interaction among these issues. For years, the file of Artificial Intelligence has taken a reductionist approach to addressing these issues, studying them separately with the belief that the eventual solutions could be combined later. Our working assumption is that this reductionist research strategy has reached the point of diminishing returns. Our hope is that by constructing unified architectures such as Theo, we will be able to more effectively study these issues in their full context. For example, many instances of problem solving and learning tasks occur within Theo, and for each it is possible to understand the full context in which it occurs, the full set of knowledge and data available to the system in addressing the task, and the costs and benefits of succeeding or failing at the task. Our goal is to use Theo to develop a better understanding of these individual issues in their full context, as well as the interactions among them.

## APPENDIX I

Table 1 lists the inference methods presently defined in Theo.

TABLE 1
Inference Methods that Can be Specified in AVAILABLE.METHODS

| Method | Method Definition |
|---|---|
| DEFAULT.VALUE | Retrieve a value from the DEFAULT.VALUE subslot of the given slot.<br>Example: (BOX VOLUME) ← (BOX VOLUME DEFAULT.VALUE) |
| INHERITS | Inherit values from GENERALIZATIONS of the domain element of the slot.<br>Example: (CUBE 1 VOLUME AVAILABLE.METHODS) ← (CUBE VOLUME AVAILABLE.METHODS)<br>Example: (WEIGHT DOMAIN) ← (PHYSOBJ.SLOT DOMAIN) |

| INHERITS.FROM.CONTEXT | Inherit values from a more general context, but *not* from GENERALIZATIONS of the immediate slot name.<br>Example: (BOX VOLUME DEFINITIONS) ← (PHYSOBJ VOLUME DEFINITIONS)<br>*Non*-example: (VOLUME DEFINITIONS) ← (PHYSOBJ.SLOT DEFINITIONS) |
|---|---|
| DROP.CONTEXT | Retrive a value from the slot given by the tail of the address.<br>Example: (BOX VOLUME DEFINITIONS) ← (VOLUME DEFINITIONS) |
| DEFINES | Infer a value from each of the expressions in the DEFINITIONS or SPECIALIZED.DEFINITIONS subslot.*<br>Example: (CUBE1 WEIGHT) ← (*(CUBE1 VOLUME) (CUBE1 DENSITY)) where (CUBE1 DEFINITIONS) includes (* (TH DENSITY *DE*)<br>    (TH VOLUME *DE*)) |
| SLOTSPECS | Retrieve a value from some specialization of the slot.<br>Example: (FRANK CHILDREN) ← (FRANK DAUGHTERS) where value of (CHILDREN SPECIALIZATIONS) includes DAUGHTERS |
| USE.INVERSE | Infer a value based on the value of the inverse of this slot.<br>Example: (FRED WIFE) ← WILMA where (WILMA HUSBAND)=FRED and (WIFE INVERSE)=HUSBAND |

*In fact, the procedure for DEFINES is somewhat less direct than described here. Theo uses the values of the DEFINITIONS and SPECIALIZED.DEFINITIONS subslots to construct Lisp functions which it then applies to the address of the domain element.

## APPENDIX II

Relative addresses in Theo provide a convenient means of addressing one entity relative to another. This addressing method is useful in describing general slot definitions which index other slots relative to the slot whose value is to be inferred.

A relative address is a pair formed by an absolute address and a path specifying how to reach a second entity from the entity addressed by the absolute address. The path is a list of slot names and the token "VALUE," which specifies a path of subslots or slot values. The slot names in the path specify subslots of the starting entity which are to be traversed to reach a subentity, and the token "VALUE" refers to the entity named in the value field of the current slot entity. The syntax of absolute and relative addresses may be summarized as follows (where the symbol <×>+ stands for one or more instances of <×>):

<absolute-addr> := <entity-name> | (<entity-name>+)

<relative-addr> := (<absolute-addr> <path>)

<path> :=(<path-token>+)

<path-token> :=<entity-name> | VALUE

Table 2 illustrates the use of relative slot addresses In example 2A, for instance, the relative address consists of the absolute address MARY, plus the path (MOTHER ENTITY.AUTHOR), and thus refers to the entity whose absolute address is (MARY MOTHER ENTITY.AUTHOR). In example 3A the token "VALUE" appears in the path. Thus, the relative address in this case refers to the ENTITY.AUTHOR subslot of the VALUE of the ENTITY.AUTHOR subslot of MARY. This is the entity whose absolute address is (SUE ENTITY.AUTHOR).

One useful function in Theo is the function TH, which accesses slot values via relative addresses. TH takes the relative address of a slot (in a modified syntax) and returns the value of that slot. Examples 1B through 4B in Table 2 show the use of TH for the same relative addresses as examples 1A through 4A. The arguments to TH are the <path-tokens> of the relative address given in reverse order, followed by an expression which must evaluate to the <absolute-address>. TH is especially useful in describing values of slot DEFINITIONS, since it provides a mechanism for indexing beliefs relative to the slot whose value is to be inferred.

TABLE 2
Relative Addressing

```
(mary *novalue*
  (mother sue
    (entity.author john)))

(sue *novalue*
  (entity.author frank)
  (mother ann
    (entity.author harry)))

Examples of relative addressing:
  1A. Relative address: (mary (mother))
      Equivalent absolute address: (mary mother)
  2A. Relative address: (mary (mother entity.author))
      Equivalent absolute address: (mary mother entity.author)
  3A. Relative address: (mary (mother value entity.author))
      Equivalent absolute address: (sue entity.author)
  4A. Relative address: (mary (mother value mother entity.author))
      Equivalent absolute address: (sue mother entity.author)

Examples of using TH to refer to slot values based on relative
  addressing:
  1B. (th mother 'mary) = sue
  2B. (th entity.author mother 'mary) = john
  3B. (th entity.author value mother 'mary) = frank
  4B. (th entity.author mother value mother 'mary) = harry
```

## ACKNOWLEDGMENTS

Many people have contributed ideas over a long period of time in discussions regarding the design of Theo. We thank John Laird, Allen Newell, and Ron van Kampen for useful comments on an earlier draft of this paper. This work has been supported by the National Science Foundation under grant IRI-8740522, and in part by a grant from Digital Equipment Corporation.

## REFERENCES

Abramson, B., & Korf, R. E. (1987). A model of two-player evaluation functions. In *Proceedings of the 1987 National Conference on Artificial Intelligence,* AAAI (pp. 90–94). San Mateo, CA: Morgan-Kaufmann.

DeJong, G., & Mooney, R. (1986). Explanation-based learning: An alternative view. *Machine Learning, 1*,(2), 145–176.

Dietterich, T. G., & Michalski, R. S. (1983). A comparative review of selected methods for learning from examples. In R. Michalski, J. Carbonell, & T. Mitchell (Eds.), *Machine Learning: An Artificial Intelligence Approach* (pp. 41–82). Palo Alto, CA: Tioga Press.

Etzioni, O. (1987). *A statistical approach to learning control knowledge.* Internal Theo Project Working Paper. School of Computer Science, Carnegie Mellon University.

Etzioni, O. (1988). Hypothesis filtering: A practical approach to reliable learning. In *Proceedings of the Fifth International Conference on Machine Learning* (pp. 416–429). San Mateo, CA: Morgan-Kaufmann.

Greiner, R., & Lenat, D. B. (1980). A representation language language. In *Proceedings of the First National Conference on Artificial Intelligence,* AAAI (pp. 165–169). San Mateo, CA: Morgan-Kaufmann.

Kahn, K. M. (1984, Spring). Partial evaluation, programming methodology, and artificial intelligence. *The AI Magazine 5*(1), 53–57.

Laird, J., Newell, A., & Rosenbloom, P. S. (1987, September). SOAR: An Architecture for General Intelligence. *Artificial Intelligence 33*(1), 1–64.

Lenat, D. B. (1983, March). Eurisko: A program that learns new heuristics and domain concepts. *Artificial Intelligence 21*(1), 61–98.

Minton, S. (1988). Quantitative results concerning the utility of explanation-based learning. In *Proceedings of the 1988 National Conference on Artificial Intelligence.* AAAI, Morgan-Kaufmann.

Minton, S., Carbonell, J. G., Etzioni, O., Knoblock, C. A., & Kuokka, D. R. (1987). Acquiring effective search control rules: Explanation-based learning in the PRODIGY system. In P. Langley (Ed.), *Proceedings of the Fourth International Workshop on Machine Learning* (pp. 122–133). Irvine, CA: Morgan-Kaufmann.

Mitchell, T. M. (1983). Learning and problem solving. In *Proceedings of the Fifth International Joint Conference on Artificial Intelligence.* IJCAI (pp. 1139–1151). San Mateo, CA: Morgan-Kaufmann.

Mitchell, T. M., Keller, R. K., & Kedar-Cabelli, S. (1986). Explanation-based generalization: A unifying view. *Machine Learning, 1*(1).

Rosenbloom, P. S., & Laird, J. E. (1986). Mapping explanation-based generalization onto soar. In *Proceedings of the 1986 National Conference on Artificial Intelligence,* AAAI (pp. 561–567). San Mateo, CA: Morgan-Kaufmann.

Schlimmer, J. (1987, November). *General search in Theo.* Internal Theo Project Working Paper. School of Computer Science, Carnegie Mellon University.

# 13

## The Frame of Reference Problem in the Design of Intelligent Machines

William J. Clancey
*Senior Research Scientist,*
*Institute for Research on Learning, Palo Alto, California*

### CHANGE AND CONFLUENCE IN COGNITIVE SCIENCE

What accounts for the regularities we observe in intelligent behavior? Many cognitive scientists would respond, "Mental structures which are representations, symbols of things in the world." Since at least the mid–70s there has been widespread agreement among cognitive scientists that models of a problem-solving agent should incorporate knowledge about the world and some sort of inference procedure for interpreting this knowledge to construct plans and take actions. Research questions have focused on how knowledge is represented in computer programs and how such cognitive models can be verified in psychological experiments.

But we are now experiencing increasing confusion and misunderstanding as different critiques are leveled against this methodology and new jargon is introduced (e.g., "not rules," "ready-to-hand," "background," "situated," "subsymbolic"). New robotic research is founded on the idea that knowledge does not consist of objective representations (maps) of the world; conversely, other researchers define rational behavior in terms of an observer's supposedly objective descriptions of a task environment. This diversity of approaches takes us back to fundamental issues about the nature of perception, theories, and system dynamics.

There have been many philosophical arguments posed against cognitive science and AI research over the years; what reason is there to suppose that we are making progress now on these complex issues? Most striking is the convergence of ideas and new approaches over the past five years:

- The long-standing criticism by Dreyfus (1972), for example, has been joined by insiders (Clancey, 1987a; Winograd & Flores, 1986), and is reflected in sharply divergent, new approaches by previously staid proponents of AI (Anderson, chap. 1 in this volume; Brooks, chap. 8 in this volume; Cohen, 1989; Rosenschein, 1985);

• Neural net research has reminded us of the extent of the gap between neurobiology and cognitive science models, while new hardware and programming techniques have enabled a resurgence of network modeling (Edelman, 1987; Rumelhart et al., 1986);

• Cognitive science itself has flourished and succeeded in including social scientists within the community, and their methods and analyses often starkly contrast with the AI view of human knowledge and reasoning (Lave, 1988; Suchman, 1987). They place increasing emphasis on representation construction as an activity within perceptual space, organized by social interaction (e.g., Allen, 1988), not something in memory that precedes speaking, drawing, or action in general.

Criticisms of cognitive science and AI may often fail to be effective because they aren't sufficiently grounded in computational modeling terminology and may even appear to be compatible with existing programs. For example, the current buzzword "situated" might just mean "conditional on the input data of particular situations"; hence all programs are situated. Moreover, the discourse of other intellectual traditions may appear incoherent to cognitive scientists; consider for example the claim that "representation must be based on interactive differentiation and implicit definition" (Bickhard & Richie, 1983). Experienced AI researchers believe that an engineering approach is essential for making progress on these issues. Perhaps the most important reason for recent progress and optimism about the future is the construction of alternative cognitive models as computer programs, the field's agreed basis for expressing theories:

• The AI-learning community is focusing on how a given ontology of internal structures—the designer's prior commitment to the objects, events, and processes in the world—enables or limits a given space of behavior (e.g., the knowledge-level analyses of Dietterich, 1986; Alexander et al., 1986);

• New robots ("situated automata") demonstrate that interpreting a map of the world isn't required for complex navigation; instead, maintaining a relation between an agent's internal state and new sensations enables simple mechanisms to bring about what observers would call search, tracking, avoidance, etc. (Agre, 1988; Braitenberg, 1984; Brooks, chap. 8 in this volume; Rosenschein, 1985; Steels, 1989);

• Neural networks, incorporating "hidden layers" and using back-propagation learning, provide a new means of encoding input/output training relationships, and are suggestive (to some researchers at least) of how sensory and motor learning may occur in the brain (Rumelhart, McClelland & the PDP Research Group, 1986).

In essence, this new research lead us to reconsider how the internal states in an agent derive from the *dynamics of a physical situation,* relegating an observer's later descriptions of the patterns in the agent's behavior (what has been called "the agent's knowledge" or a "knowledge-level description") to a different level of analysis. That is to say, this new research suggests that we reclassify many existing cognitive models as being *descriptive and relative to an observer's frame of reference,* and not isomorphic or literally identical to physical mechanisms internal to the agent that cause the observed behavior.

By systematically analyzing these alternative architectures, placing them in ordered relation to each other, we should be able to articulate distinctions that the researchers couldn't accomplish alone. The result will be a better understanding of the diverse approaches to "situated cognition" and "neural networks" research, contrasted against conventional AI architecture research. Thus, understanding a new approach and reconceptualizing the claims behind a traditional approach will arise together.

## SCOPE AND OUTLINE OF THIS CHAPTER

When I began gathering notes for this chapter and preparing my symposium presentation a year ago, I had a good notion of how to describe the traditional approach. I believed and still do that knowledge engineering can be fruitfully characterized as a methodology for modeling processes qualitatively, and that this is in fact the main technique and lasting contribution of AI programming, regardless of what we later discover about how the human mind works or how to build intelligent machines. I am particularly concerned that we not lose sight of this modeling methodology as a legitimate, separate discipline, and to this end have recounted the main ideas in a series of papers (Clancey, 1983a, 1985, 1987a, 1989).

It should therefore be clear that the purpose of this chapter is not to undermine or dismiss knowledge engineering, that is, the idea of representing knowledge in computer programs in order to construct useful computer tools. Rather, my analysis aims to improve our understanding of how expert systems relate to human knowledge, so qualitative modeling methods can be more systematically applied, improved, and used appropriately. However, the view that knowledge engineering is fundamentally the development and application of a modeling methodology implies that AI researchers must clearly identify whether their architecture is intended to be a contribution to knowledge engineering, or is to be taken as a general model of an intelligent agent's functional architecture (to use Pylyshyn's terminology [Pylyshyn, 1984]). That is, I draw a distinction between knowledge engineering and the study of intelligence and believe that evaluation of research, and hence progress, hinges on clearly committing to one or the other. It is fine to aim for both, but the respective contributions must be separated out.

One reason for bringing up the knowledge engineering vs. study of intelligence distinction here is to make explicit the knowledge-engineering contributions of GUARDIAN, specifically the ACCORD framework for representing knowledge and control useful for configuration tasks (Hayes-Roth, Hewett, Vaughn, Johnson, & Garvey, 1988), which has no apparent counterpart in PRODIGY, SOAR, or THEO. This curiosity might be stated as the question, What is Hayes-Roth doing? Two other challenges are posed by the papers: To resolve formalization phobia (what is Genesereth doing?) and to integrate the situated automata work with the rest of the field (what is Brooks doing?). Somewhat surprisingly, these are related: We will find that understanding Brooks' insight requires a significant reinterpretation of the observer-relativity of knowledge-level (KL) descriptions, and this in turn places a new primacy on methods of formalization. In brief, we will conclude that KL representations are a theoretician's formalizations and should therefore be stated in a proper mathematical notation; they are not to be automatically identified with physical structures possessed by the agent being studied or designed. Of course, the beauty of our investigative dilemma is that the theoretician is an agent himself, and these representations reflect his or her beliefs. In this recursion we will reconsider the fundamental nature of the understanding process and how it relates to perception, memory, and representation.

This commentary can therefore be viewed from three perspectives:

1. an attempt to integrate the symposium papers;
2. in the style of Pylyshyn, an attempt to lay bare assumptions, take a stand on foundational issues, relate current work to classical philosophical issues, and draw out the implications for the study of intelligence;
3. a relativistic reinterpretation of KL analysis, which synthesizes analyses by Newell, Pylyshyn, and Dennett.

The chapter is organized as follows:

1. I start with a simple overview of superficial distinctions in the papers, emphasizing how the word "architecture" is interpreted: what is viewed as constraining an architecture, and what an architecture is expected to support.
2. I next focus on the work of Brooks and Anderson, which is problematic from the conventional AI paradigm, and present a framework for interpreting their points of view. Related work by Agre, Rosenschein, and Harold Cohen is discussed, focusing on the relation of design specifications to observed, emergent behavior.
3. I then discuss the relation of a KL description to a functional architecture description: What system is the KL about? What is the relation of the

observer-theoretician to this system? How are perception and representation related?

With respect to these questions, I will argue the following about KL descriptions:

- A KL description is about a situated system, not an agent in isolation. That is, the systems level being described is above that of individual agents. Therefore, a knowledge-level description cannot be identified with (isomorphically mapped to) something pre-existing inside an individual head, but rather concerns *patterns that emerge in interactions the agent has in some (social) world.*

- A KL description is always ascribed by some observer, and so is relative to the observer's frame of reference and is inherently subjective. Therefore, a KL description *is only created when an act of perception has occurred* (otherwise there is no observation).

- A KL description must be expressed in some perceivable medium. Knowledge representations are always and only expressed as perceivable statements and drawings, including silent speech and imagined visualizations (mental imagery). Therefore, a theoretician's KL description cannot be identified with (isomorphically mapped to) something pre-existing inside the observer's head, it *physically exists only in the observer's statements, drawings, computer programs, or modeling medium in general.*

Further claims can be made about how KL descriptions affect later behavior. In general, statements about the world constitute an observer-agent's way of adding information about the current situation. This process is *reflective*—objectifying by commenting on ongoing activities—and it is *perceptual* in the way it leads the agent to organize the world in a new way (manifested in a new way of talking about the world). Thus, I follow cognitive science in emphasizing the generation and use of representations, but view them as something that goes on in "perceptual space," not as subconscious manipulations of grammars or other interpreted descriptions, and emphatically not via storage and indexing of preconceptions ("knowledge"). This idea stems from Bartlett's analysis of memory; its detail and nontraditional view takes us too far afield for full treatment in this paper. The idea is briefly introduced and elaborated in a separate monograph.

In summary, a year of considering the symposium papers, supported by extensive reading in fields outside AI, leads me to conclude that it is now possible to integrate views that heretofore were viewed as discrepant or even incoherent. The writers that have influenced me the most (roughly in order of consideration) are Tyler (1978), Newell (1982), Winograd (1986), Bartlett (1977), Bateson (1988), Gregory (1988), Pylyshyn (1984), and Dennett (1988). The fundamental problem I face is that I believe I have a coherent way of reformulating what we are doing, but it is so dramatically different from conventional approaches and so intermingled with many difficult problems, it is impossible to communicate convincingly without stating precisely how it influences the design of computer programs. This chapter is a contribution to the theory that bridges between how my colleagues and I have talked about AI architectures and a future, different way of designing intelligent machines.

The arguments here suggest that we need to dramatically reformulate how we talk about memory, perception, and representation. Current work on situated automata and analyses in other fields suggests that we focus on how simple mechanisms in interaction with a complex environment produce behaviors that are perceived by observers as recurrent patterns. In effect, researchers are re-discovering the heuristic value of Simon's "ant on the beach" metaphor (Simon, 1969), which in its current interpretation suggests the following changes in perspective:

- a better appreciation of the nature and capabilities of AI's qualitative model-ing methodology, relative to cybernetics and new statistical approaches,
- viewing computation in terms of self-organizing processes,
- viewing information as perceptual as opposed to objectively defined,
- viewing interaction as dialectic as opposed to linearly causal or objectively characterizable from any one frame of reference,
- viewing science as subjective and socially organized, and hence
- a different view of the observer-theoretician's relation to a machine's design and behavior.

Obviously, this cannot be fully communicated or worked out in one paper. However, as a beginning, I believe that the "design stance" (Dennett, 1988)—specifically, analyzing the design of robots from the frames of reference of designer, machine, environment, and observer—is the approach that will pro-vide the bridge between our current programs and the ideas of the writers I have cited above.

## ARCHITECTURAL VIEWS OF COGNITION

. . . [We] need to expose what by now have become some stable intuitions which cognitive science researchers share and which to a great extent guide their work, but which have been articulated only in the most fragmentary ways. (Pylyshyn, 1984, p. xix)

It is useful to begin with a simple overview of superficial distinctions in AI architecture research, emphasizing how the word "architecture" is interpreted;

what is viewed as constraining an architecture and what it is expected to be able to support. In this way, we can get started on Pylyshyn's central challenge to acknowledge our philosophical commitments. Here I focus on the architectural implications of building knowledge into a program, as emphasized in knowledge engineering, versus the evident emphasis in the symposium papers on generating knowledge (SOAR), expressing it in more primitive forms (THEO), or perhaps avoiding it entirely (Anderson, Brooks). This serves as an introduction to more basic questions about the nature of memory and information.

## Architectural Levels

Figure 13.1 organizes the AI architectures described at the symposium, according to the operations that individual researchers assume are "hardwired" or directly supported by the architecture.[1] The nesting of the three levels corresponds to a composition of functions, such that inner functions are invoked to carry out tasks required by the higher levels. GUARDIAN and INSECTS emphasize reasoning functions corresponding to the interaction of the agent with the world. The operations of their architectures are designed to support the program's role in its environment (e.g., monitoring a large amount of changing data or following a wall in a room). The internal operations of the architecture are stated in terms of this interaction between the agent and the world (e.g., the need to monitor a great deal of data simultaneously, the need to maintain a constant reading on a sensor).

More specific capabilities, which we view as lying wholly inside the agent, construct a model of the world in order to take action. It is this level—the process of forming and testing descriptions of processes occurring in the world—that I have sought to make explicit in HERACLES (Clancey, 1987a). These functions correspond to what we commonly call "model building" or "understanding." This basic pattern of inference capabilities is revealed when we abstract domain-specific inference rules and state the control knowledge separately in terms of operators for constructing a situation-specific model of the domain system being reasoned about (Clancey, 1989), such as in HERACLES (diagnostic operators) and ACCORD (configuration operators). Knowledge engineers emphasize this system-modeling level when relating tools, tasks (e.g., diagnosis and configuration), and representations (e.g., classification or causal networks).

Finally, most of the architecture descriptions at this symposium focus on the innermost functional layer, the representation, inference, and control constructs

---

[1]Interpretation of abbreviations: SOAR (Rosenbloom et al., chap. 4 in this volume), THEO (Mitchell et al., chap. 12 in this volume), PRODIGY (Minton et al., chap. 9 in this volume), BB1 (Hayes-Roth et al., 1985), HERACLES (Clancey, 1987a), ACCORD (Hayes-Roth et al., 1988), GUARDIAN (Hayes-Roth, chap. 11 in this volume), INSECTS (Brooks, chap. 8 in this volume). Author names refer to papers from this symposium: (Genesereth, chap. 10 in this volume) and (Anderson, chap. 1 in this volume). RIC is an abbreviation for representation, inference, and control.

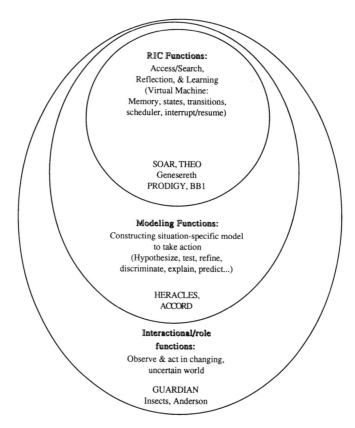

FIG. 13.1. Functional capabilities emphasized by different research-ers, shown integrated as layers in a single machine.

that enable access and search of knowledge representations, including reflection and learning. In many respects, the functional requirements of the outermost layers propagate down to these more basic functions, constituting a machine specification in terms of memory, processing states, transitions between states, scheduling, and interrupt/resume capabilities. Here AI architecture research clearly departs from the concerns of routine knowledge engineering. Researchers are wrestling with foundational issues: What sort of machine could automatically generate the modeling and interactional functions that are constructed by ad hoc means in expert systems? What are the basic memory, reflection, and learning requirements of an architecture that supports intelligent behavior?

The distinction between knowledge engineering and the study of intelligence becomes increasingly important in theories of learning, where we move from *building in* knowledge as structures (the approach of engineering efforts, such as GUARDIAN and HERCULES) to *generating or inferring* knowledge from problem-solving experience (SOAR, THEO, PRODIGY). It is just this tension—wanting to generate rather than build in—that motivates Brooks' design of INSECTS (abandoning the idea of stored knowledge structures entirely) and design trade-offs considered by Anderson and Genesereth (attempting to formally derive how an agent's behavior is constrained by the nature of the environment and task). Similarly, this tension between building in and generating motivates how the search process in SOAR is formalized (indirectly generated by a cycle of operator/operand hypothesizing and testing, rather than a directly-programmed search of static structures in memory). Here also we have competing views of the innermost level of mechanism: In contrast with SOAR's flat production rule memory, Mitchell hypothesizes that hierarchical structures are directly supported by "schema" primitives for storing knowledge. This distinction between the structure of memory and the representations manipulated during problem solving in fact becomes our central concern when we attempt to relate the knowledge-level descriptions to the functional architecture.

## "Generic Systems" Versus Functional Architecture

Pylyshyn provides a simple, useful definition for talking about architectural levels that isn't commonly used by AI architecture designers. By definition, the functional architecture concerns a level of mechanism that is *cognitively impenetrable* (Pylyshyn, 1984). Like the relation between VLSI circuits and computer programs, this level of mechanism is independent of the machine's outward behavior. Programs do not inspect or deliberately change structures at this level, nor is the program's operation dependent on how operations are implemented at this level. To turn it around, an agent's knowledge is assumed to be cognitively penetrable because by definition an agent's beliefs and goals have a direct effect on behavior. The distinction is useful here, because it suggests that operators like "test a hypothesis," which are articulated by an agent—and hence are cognitively penetrable—are not part of the functional architecture, but constitute material ("knowledge") that is represented (learned) and manipulated by the functional architecture. A functional architecture specification must be general, independent of any particular content (Pylyshyn, 1984, p. 36); its purpose is to support a variety of content and behavior, not to implement it directly in hardwired form.

This definition of functional architecture helps explain why the symposium papers don't describe their programs in terms of the task-specific operators that are emphasized in knowledge engineering. Specifically, this would explain why Hayes-Roth didn't mention the ACCORD framework that is built on top of BB1 and included in GUARDIAN, used to represent the specific knowledge and control structures required by the intensive-care unit problem. Instead, Hayes-Roth tells us about the input-output transducers and reflective monitoring cycle that constitute the most general, knowledge-independent components of her program, that is, the functional architecture.

But to turn this around, we have seen repeatedly in "generic expert system tools" like HERACLES and ACCORD, control structures that construct models of specific physical systems in the world, for diagnosis and for configuration respectively. Viewed a step back, these programs model a general understanding process, strongly guided by beliefs and goals, but described at a domain-general level. For example, the operations of "yoking," "refining," "confirming," suggest that the functional architecture should provide some direct support for achieving coherence, directly driving the problem-solving process. Describing problem solving in terms of impasses and operators may be too low-level. Might the functional architecture directly support what we commonly call "story understanding"? It is noteworthy that the view that representations are not stored but generated (or reinterpreted) freshly for every new problem would put primacy on such a capability for achieving coherence by an automatic process below the knowledge level. The idea that knowledge representations are stored and problem solving involves combining and matching primitive elements may have led researchers to inadvertently minimize this problem.[2]

To summarize, most researchers apparently take the symposium title, "Architectures for Intelligence," to be a charge to describe what Pylyshyn calls the functional architecture. This emphasis on functional architecture follows naturally from the value and priority AI researchers place on structures and processes that are generative. While we all tend to agree that successful problem solving depends on having a lot of knowledge, intelligence per se is to be characterized in terms of the memory, sensory, and learning capabilities that allow this knowledge to be acquired, stored, and accessed effectively. As Pylyshyn puts it, we don't want to find ourselves "mimicking the most frequent behavior rather than inferring the underlying mechanisms" (1984, p. 85). Nevertheless, there is some question about how directly the "explanation" or "modeling" operators in generic systems like HERACLES and ACCORD are to be supported by the functional architecture. Chandrasekaran's group has recently undertaken to redescribe MDX in these terms (Johnson et al., 1989); in general the question is not raised by the symposium papers. As a stable, widely-referenced theoretical level that appears to be between knowledge-level descriptions and theories of memory and learning, this "comprehension process" may be an important clue of how current architectures need to be improved.

## Maps and Learning

Given that knowledge is about the world, one way of characterizing the representations used by a program is the extent to which it uses map-like representations of the world, and secondarily whether these are these stored or generated. This is illustrated in a simple way by the following spectrum:

---

[2]Newell discusses comprehension operators in SOAR/UTC (Newell, 1990). My interest here is not to argue the details of the case, but just to raise the issue and how it relates to foundational concerns about memory.

maps   —(more learning required) →   no maps

"Maps" here refers to the idea of building into the program descriptions of the world. As the program reasons or manipulates objects in the world, it is constantly comparing a situation-specific description to an idealized, map-like description of how the world is supposed to appear or operate. The architectures of both PRODIGY and GUARDIAN assume that a great deal of such knowledge is provided by a person who constructs the program. As stated before, routine knowledge engineering is distinguished from the study of intelligence by not requiring commitments in this respect: Building in maps is just fine, the problem is to do it efficiently.

Aiming for machines with generative intelligence capability and not just built-in knowledge, Brooks (and his colleagues in arms, Rosenschein and Agre) reject this idea; their models disavow or minimize the agent's use of map-like descriptions of the world. Interestingly, the "no maps" approach has been advocated by people following bottom-up construction strategy like Brooks, as well as by people working top-down from studies of social organizations (Lave, 1988; Suchman, 1987). Thus, in some sense, the emphasis on maps in traditional AI is being squeezed by both the biological and social bands, as Newell labels these perspectives (Newell, 1990).

Most researchers strive for a happy medium, assuming that the problem solver needs maps, but they must be learned. In this respect, we can distinguish between researchers who rely strongly on psychological data (as in SOAR) and those who collect and study knowledge abstractions and later formulate the underlying processes of memory and learning that form such abstractions, exemplified by the generic system approach.

## FRAMES OF REFERENCE FOR DESIGNING INTELLIGENT MACHINES

When we analyze a mechanism, we tend to overestimate its complexity. In this uphill process of analysis, a given degree of complexity offers more resistance to the workings of our mind than it would if we encountered it downhill, in the process of invention. . . . The patterns of behavior described in vehicles (just illustrated) . . . undoubtedly suggest much more complicated machinery than that which was actually used in designing them. (Braitenberg, *Vehicles*, 1984, p. 21)

The work of Brooks and Anderson poses a dilemma for someone trying to understand the current state of AI architecture research. In this section, I provide a framework for interpreting their points of view, but I do this by presenting related work that was not represented at the symposium—research by Rosenschein, Agre, and Cohen. This framework (and the associated Fig. 13.2) will provide the backbone for the discussion in the rest of the paper. The central thesis is that we need a better way of talking about the design of machines. We must make explicit the different roles, point of view, and causal properties of: the designer, the specification of how the machine is to work, processes in the operational environment, and the observer who later describes and theorizes about the machine's behavior. In this respect, it is useful to talk about robots as designed artifacts, not just "intelligent agents," making the frames of reference of the designer, environment, and observer an integral part of our theory. In particular, I believe that this perspective will enable us to restate the rhetoric of "situated cognition" in terms of its implications for AI architectures. We will then be in a position to reconsider how human memory, perception, and learning are different from present-day machines.

My approach here is to characterize the ontological commitments of alternative architectures: What facts about the world are built into each program? Two useful, related questions are: *Who owns the representations* (robot, designer, or observer)? *Where's the knowledge* (in robotic memory, in a designer's specification, or in our statements as observers)? Throughout, I will use the term "robot" to emphasize that we are dealing with designed artifacts intended to be agents in some physical environment. I believe we need to distance ourselves from our programs, so we can better understand our relation to them. Our orientation here is not of philosophical discourse in the abstract, but rather an attempt to find an appropriate language to describe existing robots and the process by which they are designed, so the engineering methods for building them are clear enough to allow us to order, compare, and improve them.

## The Problem: The Ontological Commitments of Plans

When we examine the situated automata research of Brooks, Rosenschein, and Agre, we find a striking emphasis on the *nature of planning,* focusing on the precommitments made by the designer of the computer program. These commitments are characterized as *ontological,* that is, they concern the designer's view of the kinds of objects and events and their properties that can occur in the robot's world. The researchers arrive at this focus from distinctly different considerations and objectives. Agre (1988) and Kaelbling (1988) emphasize the resource and information limitations of real-time behavior—deliberation between alternatives must be extremely limited and many details about the world (e.g., will the next closed door I approach open from the left or the right?) can't be anticipated by the designer or by the robot. Rosenschein (1985) found that formal analyses of knowledge bases are problematic—how can knowledge structures in a computer program be related in a principled way to the world, when their meaning depends on the designer's changing interpretations of what the representations mean? Cohen (1988) was wedged in a designer's conundrum: Since AARON is supposed to be producing new drawings of people standing in a garden, how could he build in a representation of these drawings before they are made? Cohen was face to face with the ultimate ontological limit of traditional cognitive models: Any description of the world that he builds in as a designer will fix the space of AARON's drawings. How then can a robot be designed so it isn't limited by its designer's preconception of the world? If such limitations are inevitable for designed artifacts, how can the specification process be accomplished in a principled way? Abstracting the work of Rosenschein, Brooks, Agre, and Cohen, here are four perspectives on these questions.

## Classical Planning—Knowledge is in the Robot's Memory

In most AI/cognitive science research to date, the descriptions of regularities in the world and regularities in the robot's behavior are called "knowledge" and located in the robot's memory. A robot preferably uses a declarative map of the world, planning constraints, metaplanning strategies, etc. This view is illustrated especially well by natural language programs, which incorporate in memory a model of the domain of discourse, script descriptions of activities, grammars, prose configuration plans, conversational patterns, etc. Aiming to cope with the computational limits of combinatoric and real-time constraints, some researchers are reengineering their programs to use parallel processing, partial compilation, failure and alternative route anticipation, etc. These approaches might incorporate further ontological distinctions (e.g., preconceptions of what can go wrong), but adhere to the classical view of planning.

## Knowledge is in the Designer's Specification

Rosenschein (1985) introduces an interesting twist. Besides using efficient engineering (compiling programs into digital circuits), his methodology explicitly views the robot as a designed artifact. He formally specifies robotic behavior in terms of I/O and internal state changes, gaining the advantages of internal consistency and explicitly-articulated task assumptions. The problem of building a robot is viewed as an engineering problem, nicely delineating the designer's relation to the robot and the designed behavior.

Knowledge is not incorporated as data structure encodings; it is replaced by a design description that specifies how the state of the machine and the state of the environment should relate. Thus, knowledge is not something placed in the robot, but a theoretical construct used by the designer for deriving a circuit whose interactive coupling with its environment has certain desirable properties. These "background constraints . . . comprise a permanent description of how the automaton is coupled to its environment and are themselves invariant under all state changes" (Rosenschein, 1985, p. 12). Regardless of how program structures are compiled or transformed by learning, the program embodies the designer's ontology. Rosenschein's formal analysis can be contrasted with Brooks' analogous, but ad-hoc constructive approach (functionally–layered, finite–state automata) (Brooks, see chap. 8 in this volume); Brooks assembles circuits without spelling out his ontological commitments to world objects, machine states, and relations among them.

## Knowledge is the Capacity to Maintain Dynamic Relationships

Agre (1988) views the ontological descriptions built into his robot as *indexical* and *functional*. That is, descriptions of entities, representations of the world, are inherently a combination of the robot's viewpoint (what it is doing now) and the role of environmental entities in the robot's activity. For example, the term *the-ice–cube–that–the–ice–cube–I–just–kicked–will–collide–with* combines the indexical perspective of the robot's ongoing activity ("the ice cube I just kicked") with a functionally-directed visualization (one role of ice cubes is for destroying bees).

Agre demonstrates that an internal representation of the world needn't be global and objective, in the form of a map, but—for controlling robotic movements at least—can be restricted to ontological primitives that relate the robot's perceptions to its activities. There are two more general claims here: (a) that representations are *inherently* indexical and functional (that is, a rejection of the correspondence theory of truth, which holds that representations are objectively about the world) and (b) that the robot can get by with mostly local information about the activity around it. Agre is showing us a new way of talking about knowledge base representations, and demonstrating that a different perspective, that of "dynamics" as opposed to "objective description," can be used for constructing an ontology. It is arguable that Agre's programs aren't fundamentally different from conventional AI architectures; the use of hyphenation just makes explicit that internal names and variables are always interpreted from the frame of reference of the agent, relative to its activities. The important claim is metatheoretical: All representations are indexical, functional, and consequently subjective.

## Knowledge is Attributed by the Observer

Cohen's work nicely articulates the distinction between designer, robot, behavioral dynamics, and observer's perception that Rosenschein, Agre, and Brooks are all wrestling with.

> AARON draws, as the human artist does, in feedback mode. No line is ever fully planned in advanced: it is generated through the process of matching its current state to a desired end state. . . . All high-level decisions are made in terms of the state of the drawing, so that the use and availability of space in particular are highly sensitive to the history of the program's decisions. (Cohen, 1988)

Notably, AARON's internal, general representation of objects is sparse; it doesn't plan the details of its drawings; and it maintains no "mental photograph" of the drawing it is producing. There is no grammar of aesthetics; rather 3-d properties, *as attributed by an observer,* emerge from following simple 2-d constraints like "find enough space." The point is made by Agre, in saying that the purpose of the robot's internal representation is "not to express states of affairs, but to maintain causal relationships to them" (1988, p. 190). The internal representations are not in terms of the "state of affairs" perceived by an observer, but the immediate, "ready-at-hand" dynamics of the drawing process (again, the terms are indexical/functional, e.g., "the stick figure I am placing in the garden now is occluded by the object to its left"). The robot's knowledge is not in terms of an objective description of properties of the resultant drawing, rather the ontology supplied by Cohen characterizes the relation between states of the robot (what it is doing now) and how it perceives the environment (the drawing it is making).

## Who Owns the Knowledge?

The above analyses demonstrate the usefulness of viewing intelligent machine construction (and cognitive modeling in general) as a *design problem.* That is to say, we don't simply ask "What knowledge structures should be placed in the head of the robot?" but rather, "What sensory-state coupling is desired and what machine specification brings this about?" Figure 13.2 summarized the elements of this perspective.

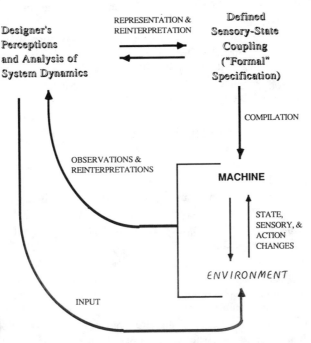

FIG. 13.2. Relation of designer's theory to machine and coupling.

Briefly, the figure illustrates that a machine specification is a representation that derives from the designer's interpretation of the machine's interaction with its environment. No "objective" descriptions are imputed—how the machine's behavior is described is a matter of selective perception, biased by expectations and purposes. The recurrent behavior attributed to the machine by the observer/ designer is a matter of how people talk about and make sense of the world. Furthermore, the specification—usually an external representation in the form of equations and networks—is itself prone to reinterpretation: What the specification means (its semantics) cannot be described once and for all. The validity of the specification lies in the over-all coherence of the designer's goals, the machine's behavior, and what the designer observes.

Cognitive science research has to date not been driven by such metatheoretical analyses. Most researchers have simply assumed that the world can be exhaustively and uniquely described as theories, and that learning itself involves manipulating theories—a correspondence view of reality. But a radically different point of view has played a central role in methodological analyses in fields as diverse as anthropology and physics. For example, one interpretation of Heisenberg's Uncertainty Principle is that theories are true only with respect to a frame of reference. AI and cognitive science research has been based on the contrary point of view that theories (representations and language) correspond to a reality *that can be objectively known* and knowledge consists of theories; consequently, alternative design methodologies have rarely entered the discussion (this is discussed further later on).

To recapitulate the emerging alternative approaches to cognitive modeling: In classical planning, epitomized by present-day expert systems, descriptions of regularities an observer will perceive in the robot's interaction with the world are stored in the robot's memory and interpreted as instructions for directing the robot's behavior. Rosenschein breaks with this idea, instead compiling a state-transition machine from a designer's specification of the desired coupling between machine and environment. Agre's work reminds us that regardless of what compilation process is used, a program still embodies a designer's ontological commitments, and these are fruitfully viewed as indexical and functional with respect to the robot's activity. As an artist, reflecting on the robot's behavior, Cohen reminds us that this indexical, functional theory is to be contrasted with an observer's statements about the robot's behavior. The essential claim is that representations in computer programs are not objective—true because they correspond to the world—but inherently indexical, functional, relationships between the agent and the world that a designer specifies should be maintained. Moving from engineering "knowledge structures" in an agent to designing on the basis of state-sensory coupling constraints is a significant theoretical advance.

However, situated automata research doesn't get to the heart of the matter: Each program still embodies the designer's ontology, which is neither fixed nor objective. Rosenschein, in particular, continues to speak of an objective physical reality, implying that perception is just a matter of processing data on fixed sensors in an axiomatic way (cf. Neisser, 1976). He fails to acknowledge that his coupling specification and background constraints are linguistic entities prone to change under his own interpretation, no less than knowledge structures built into a classical planning system. Formality is not gained by behavioral specification, because these specifications still embody the designer's perceptions of the robot's behavior and theory of the dynamics of the robot's interactions. Compilation into circuits only changes computational efficiency; the resultant physical structures formally correspond to the designer's original formal notations of "world conditions" and "behavioral correlations." And what these notations mean cannot be objectively specified.

Furthermore, while the robot's structural form is fixed after the design process, the coupling can be modified by human intervention. When a person interprets internal structures during the operation of the program (e.g., providing input by responding to the robot's queries), the coupling between robot sensation and action is changed. This interpretation is again an inherently subjective, perceptual process.

Viewing knowledge as relative to an observer/designer's perceptions of dynamic indexical-functional relations between an agent and its environment is indeed a major theoretical reconceptualization of the process of constructing intelligent agents. However, is a more radical stance possible? Further analysis might focus on the nature of the primitive ontology, specifically to restrict it to sensations inherent in the agent's peripheral sensors (if any) or to primitive perceptual structures that arise in the early developmental interactions of the agent and its environment.

From a strict sense, we could claim that the robots described above react to sensors, but never perceive, because they never form new ontologies, new ways of seeing the world. Driving this analysis would be the radical hypothesis that all perceiving is a form of learning and it is dialectically coupled to development of new physical routines. In this respect, it is highly significant that none of the above programs have any learning capability. We must explain how a string like "potentially-attacking-bee" could be created as a new way of seeing the world by the robot itself, rather than being a designed structure that determines its behavior in a fixed, programmatic way. How do we break away from modeling learning by grammatical reshuffling of grammars? In short, situated automata research has laid down the gauntlet: How far can we go in removing the observer–designer's commitments from structures built into the machine?

## Implications for the Study of Intelligence

The above discussion is only an introduction to complicated issues that require considerable elaboration. My initial objective is simply to provide a way of organizing this diverse work so we can begin to see a larger picture. In essence we need a much better articulated theoretical framework for talking about computer programs and machine behavior, emphasizing interactional dynamics and the role of human perception and representational acts. Rather than dealing directly with topics like system dynamics and emergence, I will continue my approach of grounding the discussion in the symposium papers and associated computer programs.[3] Three central issues are introduced here, then elaborated in later sections of the paper: the importance of including a formal description of the environment in a KL-theory, the impossibility of exhaustively representing what a symbolic structure means, and the inherent subjectivity of information.

## Making the Environment Explicit

First, I claim that Anderson, Rosenschein, Brooks, and Genesereth are converging on "understanding the nature of the problem being solved" by an agent (Anderson, chap. 2 in this volume), "framing" the information processing problem in a way that makes explicit the environment. We can view this work as a reaction against the complexity of AI architectures and an attempt to reground the study of intelligence in the behaviors we are seeking to explain. These researchers are looking more closely and asking, "What is the robot accomplishing from its point of view?" This question serves to refocus the description of behavior on more local, moment-by-moment interactions between the agent and the environment, as opposed to the much more varied and complex patterns of behavior an observer will see over time. The researchers of course have wildly different approaches for developing a new methodology: Anderson throws out any discussion of functional architecture; Brooks throws out discussion of representations(!); Rosenschein goes to the extreme of compiling his specification into an electronic network (as if to disavow any connection to the machine that results from his analysis); and Genesereth just forges ahead with a mathematical analysis of an assumed-objective world.

## Symbolic Interpretation as Perceivable Commentary

Second, I will give an example from MYCIN that illustrates the problem Rosenschein is struggling with and serves as an introduction to a more protracted discussion of KL descriptions. In the epistemological study of MYCIN (Clancey, 1983b), I describe a problem called *concept broadening,* in which MYCIN concepts were reinterpreted as new rules were added to the system. Rather than introducing new (intermediate) concepts, knowledge engineers wrote new rules that used existing concepts in a more general way, broadening their meaning. For

---

[3]For an elegant reformulation and extension of Brooks' work, which models cooperating agents in terms of self-organization and dissipative structures using quantitative optimality criteria, see Steels (1989).

example, several rules were of the form, "If X then the organism is significant." These rules originally used information about cultures; for example, a positive culture from a normally sterile body site is significant. However, rules added later were based on other patient findings, for example, "If the patient has a high fever, then the organism is significant." After several rules were added, it became clear that there were two categories of evidence that made an organism significant, "evidence for infection" and "evidence of non-contaminated cultures." Thus we reinterpreted what "significant" meant in the *original* rules—what MYCIN knew changed because how we talked about the rules changed. This was Rosenschein's dilemma: How can we say that the program's knowledge causes its behavior to be intelligent when the knowledge changes under our interpretation as designers?

Computer representations are human utterances; they are interpreted with respect to a background, so our interpretation of what they mean is prone to change. In this respect, they are no different than what we say or write anywhere else. From our perspective as designers, representations don't have a fixed, noncontextual, meaning-separated nature. With every use and by every observer they are under interpretation (cf. Agre, 1988). However, the program itself is constrained to manipulating these same expressions formally (literally by their form, syntactically), not their semantic interpretation. So we can say what the term "significant" means, but MYCIN cannot. Even if MYCIN had a well-structured definition of the term, it wouldn't be able to define its primitive elements. And although the designers of MYCIN could define the term, the meaning was never fixed.

This discussion quickly takes us far afield, but I want to introduce the issue early on. The essential claim is that as we speak and interpret representations we are capable of doing something that today's computer programs cannot do. This is because of the nature of human memory, learning, and perception. Put somewhat coarsely, in people these capacities are combined in such a way that, for humans, to speak is to conceive something new each time. Furthermore, the interpretative action is going on in the outward sequence of our behavior: Meaning is never defined or preconceived and then translated into an "output statement"; meaning attribution occurs only in the ongoing commentary of one behavior referring to a earlier one. Indeed, it is our talking about another utterance that makes it a representation, specifically, by providing a context (what we say the representation is about). Crucially, each statement or phrase is generated by direct recombination of processes that generated past behaviors, not from representations that describe or label these processes. Obviously, the ongoing oral and written commentary reorients behavior, but these representations must all be perceived in order to exist and have any effect (silent speech and visual imagination included). I briefly expand on this theory later. My point here is to make clear that I have a definite synthesis I am working towards, for which the present exposition provides one path of support.

I want to underscore that the essential questions facing the study of intelligence today concern the nature of representations. We have not precisely enough described how the representations of designers and observers relate to the representations used by the machine, and indeed today's machines do not create or use representations in the way people do. The key points of my argument are:

- Representations are inherently generated and used in *sequences of behaviors,* as commentary on each other. We may point to a particular drawing for example and say it represents a geometry problem, but the representation is as much in our comment as in the original drawing.

- All semantic interpretation lies outside AI computer programs, just as it lies outside any written text, diagram, or code. We cannot build in a semantic map that definitely relates notations to the world. This is because the world is not an objectively fixed thing and because our experience from which our interpretations are drawn is always changing: There is no final statement, no definitive representation, that could be built into the program and that would say, "This is everything that this program means."[4]

Putting this together, it is apparent that our use of the term *representation* in referring to something in a program has been far too loose. The symbols in programs are representations in the sense that they are statements a person has made about something else seen, heard, etc. But to the program itself, these same statements are nothing more than tokens, forms or marks that are themselves about nothing and only manipulable by their shapes. To the AI computer program, every problem is like assembling a puzzle with the picture-side facing down. In short, my solution to the "semantic interpretation problem" (e.g., see Pylyshyn, 1984, p. 39) or "how can symbols in a computer program refer to the world" is to claim that tokens refer only by virtue of what we say about them. In some crucial sense, symbols don't refer, people do. Semantic interpretation cannot be captured by a map, rather it occurs only in ongoing outward behavior.

---

[4]Here I am to clarify Winograd and Flores's analysis. Representations (e.g., a set of terms and relations) are fixed as visual and syntactic entities within a program, but they are not fixed in their meaning to us. Thus, a fixed nature is not inherent in representations, just the notations themselves and what a given program can make of them. After reading Winograd and Flores, I wrongly thought that a representation (e.g., something I say) is a fixed, unchanging statement about the world. It has a momentary property of fixing attention within a sequence of utterances, but otherwise there is no fixed meaning attached or attachable to any human statement. The meaning is always what I say it is to me (or what you say it is) in every next interpretation. Thus, people do not have to cope with a "fixed, meaning-separated" aspect of representations; that's the problem that computer programs have. Nevertheless, notations are fixed forms in themselves, and this unchanging nature may invite rote interpretations. Tyler reminds us how representations separate us from experience: "Speaking is the alienation of thought from action, writing is the alienation of language from speech, and linguistics is the alienation of language from self" (Tyler, 1978, p. 17).

It is neither objective nor ever definitive. It is always relative to an observer and the purposes at hand.

## Information as Relative

The final issue I want to introduce here concerns the notion of information. The idea of an information-processing analysis, which Anderson wants us to rededicate ourselves to, supposes that information is like a substance that every observer would objectively describe in the same way. As Reeke and Edelman (1988) put it, the AI view is that the "organism is a receiver rather than a creator of criteria leading to information" (p. 153). In describing a functional architecture, Pylyshyn rightly realizes the fundamental problem of separating what is fixed and given by the organism's input "transducers" and what can be attributed to inference. Ultimately, the problem surfaces in explaining the nature and origin of "primitive representations stored in memory" (e.g., Rosenbloom et al., see chap. 4 in this volume): By defining perception as something distinct from cognition and prior to conceptual inference, we have possibly grossly distorted how representations are created. Reeke and Edelman continue, "To place this problem [of finding a representation] in the domain of the designer rather than the designed system is to beg the question and reduce intelligence to symbol manipulation" (p. 147).

Information is relative to a point of view. There is no such thing as "all the information" in a particular situation. Information-processing analyses are strictly observer-relative. This does not detract from their analytic value; we just must be more careful in saying things like "the nature of the problem being solved" that we realize that "the problem" is our description of the situation and the information-processing formalizations are our conceptions as observer–designers, not something that necessarily resides in the head of the subject being studied.

With this preparation, we are now ready for a more detailed reconsideration of the nature of knowledge-level descriptions.

## THE RELATIVITY OF KNOWLEDGE-LEVEL DESCRIPTIONS

If we desire to explain or understand the mental aspect of any biological event, we must take into account the system—that is, the network of closed circuits, within which the biological event is determined. But when we seek to explain the behavior of a man or any other organism, this "system" will usually not have the same limits as the "self" . . . mind is immanent in the larger system—man plus environment. (Bateson, *Steps Towards an Ecology of Mind*, 1972, p. 317)

In his response to Dennett's precis of the *Intentional Stance* (Dennett, 1988), Newell asks whether there is "something about the knowledge level that makes it more in the head of the analyst than atomic physics is in the head of the physicist?" (Newell, 1988, p. 521). Why does Dennett refer to the ascription of intentions as a stance, as if it were a maneuver by the observer-theoretician? Aren't intentions an objective property of the subject? Without getting bogged down in the subjective nature of physics (which we will briefly consider later), my objective here is to bring Newell's and Dennett's analysis together, primarily by making a strong interpretation of Newell's claims in his KL paper.

My foil in this discussion is the paper by Rosenbloom, Newell, and Laird presented at the symposium, "Towards the knowledge level in SOAR." Rosenbloom et al. begin by repeating some of the key ideas of Newell's KL paper: that the KL lies above the symbol level, that rationality is defined in terms of using knowledge to accomplish a goal, and that it is the knowledge, not the internal structures, that determine behavior. However, I claim that their ensuing discussion violates Newell's own view that a KL description is an observer's attribution. Rather, the SOAR program itself is referred to as a "knowledge-level system" (as if this where an inherent, objective property of the system in isolation) and the problem reduces to showing how SOAR's structures and mechanisms provide "direct support" for knowledge. I claim that the essential matter is not "how does the architecture support knowledge," but rather, why would we ascribe knowledge to the behavior produced by such an architecture? How does our frame of reference as observers of the SOAR system, coupled to its environment, lead us to ascribe procedural competence or say that it has episodic knowledge? What are the requirements on our observations, our perceptual processes, and the sequence of behaviors available to be observed that provide the minimum support for such ascriptions?

Thus, "supporting the KL in SOAR" is as much a matter of devising an appropriate functional architecture, as devising an appropriate set of tasks, sequence of observations, and theoretical abstractions that could support our claim that SOAR has knowledge of a certain type. Indeed, we must describe the nature and properties of the perceptual and understanding process by which the theoretician sees patterns, names them, and explains them. Regarding the special kinds of knowledge we ascribe to SOAR, the question is not how to *encode* or *store* structures (Rosenbloom et al., chap. 4 this volume) that we would interpret as procedural or episodic. The KL is not a property of the architecture per se. Support for a KL, what makes it possible, comes as much from the environment, including the people who interact with and observe the program, as from the functional architecture. Claiming that knowledge of a certain type is a possible ascription that could be made about a given architecture requires specification of the world, tasks, and observers in which the architecture is embedded.

In what follows, I will characterize knowledge as structures created dynamically in the agent's working memory (and written or aural space in the world), distinguishing this from the KL description that constitutes an observer's claims about these knowledge structures and other aspects of the agent's behavior. The very idea that SOAR has four main kinds of knowledge is a theoretician's claim, which is not to be realized in a purely programmatic way as objective structure storage and retrieval, but as attributions about sequences of agent behavior. As Rosenbloom et al. (chap. 4, this volume) acknowledge at the end of their paper, "The most important missing aspect is the relationship between SOAR's mechanisms and the principle of rationality." That is to say, the most important missing aspect in their analysis is the relationship between SOAR's mechanisms, the patterns of behavior an observer will claim SOAR manifests, and how these patterns come to be interpreted as rational by the observer. In short, they have not explained the nature of rationality, because they have not explained the observer's theory-formation process.

## Newell's Knowledge Level Reviewed

Newell defines knowledge to be "Whatever can be ascribed to an agent, such that its behavior can be computed according to the principle of rationality." The essential properties of knowledge that I wish to emphasize are as follows:

Knowledge, in the form of an observer's articulated KL description of an agent, is:

- observer-relative, not an objectively defined property or structure;
- external (perceived), not encoded or stored;
- constantly reinterpreted, not fixed or definitive;
- about a social system, not agents in isolation;
- about emergent phenomenon, not linear causal interactions.

An important corollary I will have much to say about later is that to claim another agent has knowledge is to be in a position yourself to be described as having knowledge. That is, the process of making a KL attribution can be studied as an example of how knowledge is created and used. To explain the observer's theory-formation process will be to describe a functional architecture and knowledge creation and use process that human observers and agents share.

Newell's (1982) paper, particularly Section 4.3 on knowledge, is an uncanny performance. As if sleepwalking, Newell negotiates all the difficult turns with ease, yet somehow we cannot believe he would say all of these things were he fully awake, talking directly about SOAR or other AI programs. The paper is a wonderful abstraction, reaching beyond where we are, and always trying to say what we would believe if we had all our wits about us.

Consider for example the following remarks:

- The knowledge level is not realized as a state-like physical structure, "running counter to the common feature at all levels of a passive medium." Knowledge isn't embodied in structures. (p. 105)

- "It seems preferable to avoid calling the body of knowledge a memory." (p. 101) "The total system (i.e., the dyad of the observing and the observed agents) runs without there being any physical structure that is the knowledge." (p. 107)
- "Knowledge of the world cannot be captured in a finite structure." (p. 107) "Knowledge can only be created dynamically in time." (p. 108) "Knowledge is not representable by a structure at the symbol level. It requires both structures and processes." (p. 125)
- Knowledge can only be "imagined as the result of interpretive processes operating on symbolic expressions." (p. 105)
- "Knowledge remains forever abstract and can never actually be *in hand.*" (p. 125)
- "One way of viewing the knowledge level is as the attempt to build as good a model of an agent's behavior as possible based on information external to the agent." (p. 109)

Ironically, Newell anticipates in his introduction that our reaction will be, "But that is just the way I have been thinking about knowledge all along" (p. 93). This far into the analysis, steeped in observer-agent relations and non-physical encoding, Newell concludes quite the contrary, "The definition above may seem like a reverse, even perverse way of defining knowledge" (p. 106).

Newell's crucial insight is that a KL description is an abstraction made by an observer. This attribution derives from the observer's projection of himself onto the subject; he adopts the role of the other and considers what he could find out and what he would do (p. 109). Such attribution is a possible and valid prediction because the observer has the same underlying functional architecture. When the observer ascribes correctly, "the agent behaves as if he has knowledge K and goals G" (p. 106).

Dennett uses similar language, referring to the intentional stance as "the strategy of prediction and explanation that attributes belief, desires . . . and predicts future behavior from what it would be rational for an agent to do" (Dennett, 1988, p. 495). Newell is disturbed by the suggestion that such a level of description is somehow less real or is more subjective than a description of the symbolic or neurophysiological levels.

The simplest resolution of these points of view is to make clear that a KL description is not about a particular agent in the same way that a description of his circulatory system is about him. Contrary to what Newell says, a KL description is a level higher than the physical body, it is inherently about the individual agent interacting with the world. This is evident in any remark concerning the agent's knowledge: see, believe, know, and hypothesize are always predicates about the world relative to the agent, evident in the most mundane examples, "Pat knows Mike's telephone number" (Newell, 1982, p. 118). They are statements about the situated agent, not a mechanism in isolation.

A KL description for people is a description of a social system, that is, about how people perceive each other and their common activities, which would belie Newell's claim that the KL is analogous to a "register–transfer" description, just a higher level. This would easily explain why KL abstractions have no isomorphic realization as structures in the agent. KL descriptions are about interactions the agent has with its environment. Emergent patterns can result; categories for describing what is happening will lie outside the awareness or control of individual agents. Indeed, this orientation is apparent in Newell's remarks, which incidentally are a perfect summary of Anderson's approach: "Knowledge, in the principle of rationality, is defined entirely in terms of the *environment* of the agent, for it is the environment that is the object of the agent's goals, and whose features therefore bear on the way actions can attain goals" (Newell, 1982, p. 110).

By analogy with the theory of relativity in physics, the laws of rationality will be the same in every frame of reference. That is, observers might attribute different knowledge to the same agent, but coherence relations that hold between beliefs, goals, and actions, and hence the predictive laws, will be the same. Thus, identifying a KL description with an observer-theoretician is not to adopt the folk view that "it's all relative." Instead, as for physics, psychology must drop the idea that observations are objective facts that everyone will agree upon. Rather, observations, perceived patterns, and subsequent knowledge-level descriptions are dependent on the observer's frame of reference: his beliefs, goals, and actions, and more specifically how he interacts with the agent and elicits the behavior he subsequently theorizes about. The laws of rationality are the same because we share the same functional architecture and, through a common theory-formation process, are capable of projecting different perceptions and social norms onto behaviors that would otherwise be discrepant in our culture. This does not mean that our theories will agree, but rather, that we can usually find systematic justifications for behavior that are relative to an agent's presumed beliefs, goals, and knowledge. It is this metatheoretical systematicity, which we term rationality, that is invariant.

## KL Representations

The relation between knowledge and representations is no less bewildering than the relation between knowledge and an observer. Newell's key break with the conventional AI view is to say that knowledge representations are the observer's statement of his KL theory. They *represent* the knowledge ascribed to agent, they are not to be identified with the agent's knowledge itself: The map is not the territory. Yet throughout, even if Newell is not ambiguous, his point is far from clear. Readers must pick and choose the statements that speak to their own biases.

The discussions of logic and conceptual dependency provide anchoring points. The simple claim is that "logic is just a representation of knowledge" (Newell, 1982, p. 110). Surely many researchers must be bewildered when Newell then goes on to say, "It is not the knowledge itself, but a structure at the symbol level," for it is AI gospel that knowledge is encoded in the brain as symbolic structures. The way out of this, I believe, is presented in Figure 13.3. A logic statement is an observer's KL description, in the form of symbolically interpretable expressions (e.g., knowledge representations in a computer program, such as predicate calculus statements). Such knowledge representations have the same status as any other representations, such as book chapters—they are written down by an observer and they are interpretable. Crucially, they are in "perceptual space"–they are externalized in a form that can be reflected upon (otherwise they couldn't be perceived and given a subsequent semantic interpretation). (Again, I include silent speech and mental imagery as externalized expressions.) Thus, when Newell says that a logic encoding is a symbolic structure, but not the agent's knowledge, he must mean that what is encoded are the observer's representations, symbols in the observer's perceptual field, which are to be interpreted as being *about* the agent's knowledge. A knowledge representation is not the agent's knowledge, and it's not the observer's knowledge either: It is a representation of the observer's knowledge of the agent's knowledge.

Newell claims that conceptual dependency is a contribution to the KL because it expands our repertoire as theoreticians, it gives us another formalism for expressing KL theories. Similarly, calculus was a contribution to physics because

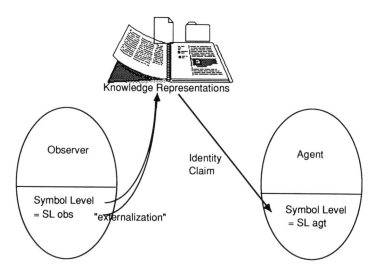

FIG. 13.3.   Relation of knowledge representations to observer and agent; adapted from Newell (1982, FIG. 4). This paper criticizes the identity claim.

it provided another means of "encoding knowledge of the world in a representation." Thus, conceptual dependency, like logic, is a theoretician's tool. It is how cognitive scientists (and robot designers) might specify an agent-environmental system in a way that allows predicting the agent's behavior (or specifying what behavior is desired in the designed machine).

Newell's analysis enables him to pinpoint the essential dilemma confusing our enterprise: What is the relation of the observer's knowledge representations to the symbol level of the agent? Some logicists (exemplified by McCarthy and Nilsson) simply assume that "the role of logic . . . (is) for reasoning by intelligent agents," rather than being "a tool for the analysis of knowledge" (Newell, 1982, p. 118). That is, these researchers identify the theoretician's expressions with physical structures that pre-existed in the body of the agent and caused the observed behavior (see Figure 13.3, "Identity claim").

The identity claim encapsulates the idea of *strong equivalence* (described by Pylyshyn, chap. 7 in this volume). It claims that our models of agents are isomorphic to structures in the agent. But the frame of reference perspective suggests that this couldn't possibly be the case. A KL description isn't even about an individual, isolated agent, let alone physical processes that are unobservable.

The argument might then take another form. Perhaps these knowledge representations are to be identified with symbolic structures lying inside the *observer?* This would be a curious move to make; it would equate "pictures, physical views, remembered scenes, linguistic texts, utterances" (Newell, 1982, p. 112) with physical structures in the head of the observer. We might be confused about many things here, but we surely know better than to say a book made out of paper is *identical* to something inside the skull. Instead, we are interested in the processes by which an observer perceives these representations and "extracts knowledge from them" (Newell, 1982, p. 113). A theory that relates an observer's KL description to the observer's symbol level (and hence his behavior) must account for this extraction or interpretation process.

## KL as Reinterpretation

The issue of semantic interpretation is probably the riskiest quagmire on the terrain of the philosophy of AI. However, it is on these grounds that the whole "symbol processing" view rests, and it is here that we must follow Pylyshyn in taking a definite stand. Given what I have just said, it is worth restating my position: Semantic interpretation goes on in our "outward" behavior, in our ongoing sequence-cycle of perceiving a representation and commenting on it through another utterance, gesture, drawing, image, or notation. Thus, symbols are interpreted semantically, but not in a hidden way, not subconsciously (dreaming aside), but always in the space of our perceptual field.

In short, it is perfectly fine to describe the mind as operating upon symbols that are interpreted semantically. However, these symbols must be perceived in order to be interpreted. Or to put it a better way: It is the perceptual process and our subsequent activity that gives a token symbolic status. Since this is something the person is very well aware of, we prefer to say that "*the person* has symbols, rules, and representations," just like we would say "the person has a book," and would feel very strange to say "the mind has a book." Representations are not stored in memory, rather they are constantly created and interpreted by the person. It is the process of perception and conceptualization that we must explain.

Pylyshyn realizes very well the dilemma of semantic interpretation. The internal symbolic codes[5] "must carry all the relevant aspects of the interpretation as part of their intrinsic and functional form" (p. 66). The symbol system does not have access to the interpretations; "only the theory provides that." We must therefore distinguish between two types of interpretation:

1. A program syntactically interprets a representation by relating its formal properties to rewrite rules for creating/modifying structures.
2. A human observer semantically interprets a perceived representation by commenting on it.

The key distinction is that it is the human's comment that gives the structure representational status. Similarly, we say that the computer program "has" representations, but this is only because they are meaningful to us. Strictly speaking, MYCIN interprets our representation of "a significant organism" by relating the formal properties of the token SIGNIFICANT to rewrite rules for creating and modifying other token structures. A human semantically interprets this same representation ("(IF (SAME CNTXT SIGNIFICANT) (CONCLUDE CONTXT INFECTION TALLY 300))") by supplying a context, relating it to other concepts in which it can be viewed as an instance, a cause, etc. For example, I might say, "This is one of a dozen rules that interpret culture results as possible evidence of disease."

A key claim is that this commentary process cannot be reduced to application of syntactic interpretation rules; rather, it is inherently a conceptualization process. Each time I talk about the SIGNIFICANT rule, I am prone to discover something new about it. My representations aren't stored in memory; they are in my speaking and what I have written down. The content of my representations is in commentary about them. Representations don't have an inherent content: they

---

[5]I strongly resist calling something internal that cannot be perceived a "symbol," for these postulated tokens/forms can never be commented on and thus can never be given symbolic status by the person. Since they aren't themselves semantically interpreted, we can't call them "codes" either. "Symbolic code" is Pylyshyn's terminology.

are prone to new interpretations by every observer on every next occasion (cf. Agre). Our essential problem is to explain (a) how this conceptualization process works (in functional architecture terms); that is, what is the process by which I create representations out where I can perceive them? and (b) how does commenting on a representation organize my ongoing sequence of behaviors? Like Rosenschein, we must reject the idea that formal structures could be formally linked to their interpretations: There is no such thing as "the content" or "the meaning" of a representation.

At the very least, viewing conceptualization as a process of storing and manipulating labels on internal structures is misguided because it puts perception into the peripherals, viewing it merely as input to a conceptual processor. To understand how a different mechanism is possible, we must show how perception/commentary organizes processes directly. Our behavioral processes aren't internally tagged and matched against rules that describe how they are to be assembled. Again and again, we find that it is impossible to take a new stand on these issues without overturning the entire cart: memory, perception, meaning. Everything must go at once. Before tackling this further, I want to say more about the KL and how it is and isn't related to the functional architecture.

## KL as Descriptive Theory

It is helpful to consider again the nature of the statements we make in our computer programs. Knowledge representations are statements about regularities. They are descriptions of and relations between *patterns of behavior*. They are not necessarily descriptions of *mechanisms* that create such behaviors in people. Indeed, the possibility and usefulness of such explanatory, but non-mechanistic descriptions is one reason why we distinguish between a KL description (an observer's theory of a social, interactive system, in terms of individual beliefs, goals, and activities) and the functional architecture (a theory of physical mechanisms implemented in a neurobiological system).

A simple example is the metarule in NEOMYCIN (paraphrased), "Generalize an inquiry, rather than request the specific finding of interest." This rule is surely part of the mechanism of the program. However, its relation to people is different. It is a description of a regularity in observable human behavior. Such rules should be viewed as *grammatical* characterizations. They are perfectly fine ways of summarizing and abstracting observations made over a variety of problems, agents, and domains. Knowledge-level attributions are therefore similar to natural language grammars. They are a theoretician's way of stating regularities; they are descriptive; they are generative; they have predictive power. However, as explanations, they aren't to be taken literally as structures and processes that are encoded in the heads of the subjects we are studying. Their explanatory power isn't (necessarily) mechanistic. As Dennett says, "We should not jump to the conclusion that the internal machinery of an intentional system and the strategy that predicts its behavior *coincide. . ."* (p. 497).

Once again, we find ourselves on familiar, controversial terrain in the philosophy of AI. The surprise is that so many people have identified every explanation with mechanism, ignoring the nature of grammatical, descriptive theories that state regularities, abstracting behavior. Such descriptions can surely be related to lower level processes of memory, learning, and perception, but they cannot be reduced or replaced by better mechanistic models. Again, to quote Dennett (1988), "There are patterns of 'behavior' . . . that are describable only from the intentional stance . . . there are no 'deeper facts' to resolve the outstanding questions of belief attribution" (p. 497).

A KL description is surely a model, but it is not a model of the physical mechanism. While we surely want to know what the functional architecture is, this KL description is not to be viewed as inferior. It is a legitimate level of explanation which has no isomorphic embodiment in physical mechanisms: It summarizes patterns and states principles that arise in the agent's interaction with the world, the theoretician's interaction with the agent, and the theoretician's perceptual process, goals, and beliefs.

Thus, we have restated the situation in Figure 13.3: A KL description is like a grammar. Just as for natural language, we must decide whether these grammars are literally encoded in the head of the agent and thus were the structures that caused the agent's behavior. The identity claim is tempting because (a) such structures really are part of the causal mechanism of computer programs, and (b) we know that articulating such representations has an effect on the agent's behavior (i.e., telling me a new grammar rule can alter how I speak). I have argued that KL descriptions should not be identified with causal mechanisms in the agent because:

• they are *attributions made by an observer,* involving his own selective interactions with the agent, his own perceptions, and his point of view;

• they *abstract a sequence of behaviors,* not single, moment-by-moment responses;

• they *characterize a social system,* not processes within an individual agent;

• the interpretation of such representations, which itself is claimed to cause behavior, is constantly changing, dependent on the observer of the representation, and in any case is always made in perceptual space;

• such interpretations patently occur only through outward behavior, and there is no evidence that the agent, despite being a theoretician of his own behavior, has any such notations (e.g., see (Stucky, 1987) for a related analysis from a linguist).

Indeed, it now seems perverse to think that a theoretician's KL descriptions (what I say about an agent after watching over time) could have caused the agent's behavior. To say that an agent follows a pattern is not to say that the pattern is necessarily a thing inside the agent.[6]

From the perspective of explanatory theory, the KL can be viewed as necessary because we need to express generalities that cannot be reduced to mechanisms at a lower level (Pylyshyn, 1984, p. 35). Pylyshyn relates this approach to the idea that there can be constraints on behavior that are above the level of "actual performance." This is consistent with my claim that the KL describes the interaction of individuals within the social environment. It follows also from the introduction of an observer's point of view and the desire to describe behavior temporally, in terms of sequences of behavior. Thus, environment, observation, and time supply the context for KL descriptions. The direct ramification for the design of intelligent machines is that the KL level is for specification of a design; it will use representations that don't causally enter into the machine's behavior, rather *they will describe what the behavior will look like* (e.g., "rational," like someone imagining a 3-D world, like someone avoiding obstacles, like someone trying to be efficient).

Furthermore, just as the existence of a KL is brought into being by our theoretician-designer's perspective, so is the very idea of regularities in the agent's behavior. When we talk about "regularities that need explaining" (Stefik, 1989, p. 242), we must keep in mind that regularities aren't substances and patently aren't objective. They are an observer's statements with respect to some behaviors perceived in some frame of reference. A regularity is not a property of an agent so much as a perception that arises in the interaction of the observer, agent, and environment.

Understanding the nature of KL descriptions therefore requires considering the nature of perception.

## KL as Perceptual, Emergent, Interactive

Imagine placing a cafeteria chair near Brooks' robot—what will happen? Suppose it jams under a rung. We must ask Brooks whether this is what he intended. Suppose the robot starts wheeling around the fat leg of a chair; Brooks says, "Ha, it thinks the leg is a wall!" There is no end to the games we can play with

---

[6]This became clear during the development of NEOMYCIN. We abstracted metarules such as "when testing a hypothesis, first seek evidence of enabling conditions" from a physician's initial questions when confirming disease hypotheses. For viral meningitis, he asked if a flu was going around; for fungal meningitis, he asked where the patient had traveled recently; for neisseria-meningitis, he asked if the patient had been living in a crowded environment (Clancey, 1988). If probed, a physician might formulate the rule that one should first seek evidence of exposure to infectious diseases, but the abstraction to causal enabling conditions is a knowledge-engineer's theoretical statement. It is intriguing to consider how such routines might evolve by mimicry of other physicians and attempts to be more efficient when interviewing a patient, without conscious formulation of a generalized rule.

the robot, introducing new elements to its environment and watching what happens. In the end, how we characterize the robot's beliefs, goals, and knowledge will depend on what obstacles are placed in its path and even whether we were watching when something occurs. After awhile, we might feel confident that we fully understand the robot's capacities and foibles. But this is just part of the stable order of our own purposes and social organizations. Someone might coat the floor with jello next week to see what happens.

A number of related issues surface here, some of which we have considered previously:

- There is no such think as "all the data" or "all the information" in a situation—this is an observer-theoretician's analysis, dependent on the measuring devices (consider for example how viewing a video in fast-forward can reveal new patterns[7]);
- Perceptual interactions among people are dialectic—such that my interpretation of your response to what I did biases my interpretation of my original intentions; thus, we define the present by interactively constructing the past (indeed, articulating intentions after the fact places the agent in the role of KL-theoretician);
- Teams of people are not merely "cooperating agents," not merely "distributed"—activities are not transmitted or conceived or planned completely (i.e., fully anticipated in all its particulars) by any individual, but arise through mutually constrained perception.

These are the kind of claims you will find in the work of Agre, Lave, and Suchman.

The bottom line (again) is that the functional architecture mechanisms supporting what we call human memory, learning, and perception are different in kind from our KL theories.[8] Furthermore, a better model of the functional archi-

---

[7]"Not many people appreciated the importance of the videocassette recorder . . . . by using fast forward and fast reverse, the radar data could be used to show not only things were going, but also where they had come *from*. Computer support made the task easier by eliminating items that moved no more than once every two hours—thus erasing the Russian radar lures—and there it was, a brand-new intelligence tool" (Clancy, *Red Storm Rising,* 1986, p. 392).

[8]Indeed, it was on a related point that Ryle introduced the idea of a *category mistake:* The total interactive system (in Ryle's example, the mind as university) is not to be found on the lower level of agent behavior and internal mechanisms: "But where is the University? I have seen where the members of colleges live, where the Registrar works, where the scientists experiment and the rest.'. . . The University is just the way in which all that he has already seen is organized" (Ryle, *The Concept of Mind,* 1949, p. 16). It is no coincidence that Ryle's examples (a University, division, team-spirit) are all descriptions of emergent social phenomena, a level above individual agents, as perceived by an observer. It is not just a matter of using words incorrectly, as Ryle was want to emphasize, but of not understanding the nature of situated systems, emergent effects, and frames of reference.

tecture (or simply not equating a KL description with a FA) will explain the plasticity of human behavior. By not building in grammatical descriptions of how people can behave, we discover a mechanism (remember AARON and PENGI) that has the potential to generate a wider range of behaviors and is more robust (capable of responding without having predefined situation types) than any KL description.

Redefining the idea of "information" will turn out to be pivotal, because it so strongly affects our ideas of perception, memory, and learning in turn. The strong claim is that information is dialectically defined by the interaction of processes in the agent and processes going on in the environment. "Dialectic" here is to be contrasted with the idea of "conditioned" or "dependent on the data," in which "data" is something objective and given (like tokens put in the slot of the machine) and conditionality is reflected by conversion of the data to internal codes that serve as labels or tags, which are stored in memory and referenced by rules. Thus, identifying information with data is the same as claiming that "situations" are enumerable (in terms of constellations of input, precisely the formal analysis Genesereth strives for).

My claim is that we will be able to relate the analyses of Agre, Lave, Suchman, et al., to SOAR by translating their discussion of "social situation" and "dialectics" into a different view of information, and hence perception. Furthermore, we should look for examples in which the social band is not a phenomenon manifested only in changes of behavior over days, as characterized by Newell (1990, p. 338), but is manifested, for example, in conversational interactions, mutually constrained over seconds (a good example to start might be patient–psychiatrist dialogues involving the transference effect). Again, this social orientation is not just a claim that our goals, beliefs, and desires are pervaded by the social organization (and hence KL descriptions are *about* a social system). Rather, the more important implication for us will be the changes it requires in how we view the functional architecture, by realizing that the KL is a description of interactive, dialectic phenomena—a description of *the result* of processes interacting within and outside individual agents.

Finally, we should relate this orientation to my earlier emphasis that representations are in the perceived environment. The cycle by which information is perceived involves a sequence of creation and interpretation of representations that are in the environment (plus imagination). Therefore symbol manipulation[9] is inherently a coupled phenomenon of the agent to its environment. Symbolic reasoning is not merely conditional on the current situation (i.e., influenced by supplied "data"), and it is not an invisible, cognitively impenetrable process.

---

[9]Here a symbol is something that is semantically interpreted not just a tokin. I make this distinction here because I want to preserve the cognitive science insight that reasoning can be characterized in terms of symbol manipulation, while arguing that it happens in a cyclical process of perception and re-representation commentary.

Rather, symbol manipulation—a KL characterization—is a characterization of the result of how the agent interacts with its environment. To say it more directly: Symbol manipulation is what agents do in their outward activities, not something happening to physical structures inside the mind (silent speech and visualization aside). People manipulate symbols. This is why social theorists place so much emphasis on the actual materials surrounding agents and how they are moved around, pointed to, and modified (e.g., see Allen, 1988; Suchman, 1987).

## KL as Sense Making

One of the most valuable twists in our analysis is to view the observer-theoretician as an agent and characterize his behavior as indicative of what agents do: Agents make observations, they articulate theories (representations), they generally attempt to understand the world in which they live. To properly characterize and improve KL descriptions, we need, as Dennett puts it, to explain the power of folk psychology.

The fact that we ascribe knowledge to agents, as well as the kinds of theories that are satisfying to us, reveals as much about the nature of our understanding processes as about the agent or system being studied. In fact the entire cognitive science enterprise reflects what agents do. We are agents after all.

Hence our use, as theoreticians, of the KL reflects back the very property we wish to study–the nature and origin of beliefs and their influence on behavior. Examining our own activity, we discover that:

• Beliefs are expressed as representations in perceivable, shared media (most notably speech and writing). Representation construction involves changes to the environment, which is then interpreted and modified by other agents.

• Theoreticians, as humans, need to view their beliefs and goals as coherent. Hence, KL descriptions reflect humans in their ordinary process of making sense: the world is described in terms of law-like statements. The complexity of many specific observations is abstracted, categorized, and parsed by grammar-like theories.

In short, KL descriptions exist because we, as agents, need to construct a coherent story about why agents interact the way they do. Put another way, a semantic level exists in our theories of intelligence because we need to explain why this system of interacting agents is meaningful. The concepts of a KL description are our categories. They need be articulated only in our theory, they exist apart from the neurobiological processes going on internally in individual agents. Of course, individual human theorizing about social behavior has profound effect on how members of the community act (i.e., intention and social theory is cognitively penetrable). This itself makes the point: The intentions ascribed are relative to each agent's point of view and there are multiple explanations, depending on where you stand, what you saw, and what you are trying to do.

As an aside, we now see how ironic it is to say that logic "is therefore a candidate . . . for the representation to be used by an intelligent agent" (Newell, 1982, p. 121). The fact is that McCarthy, et al. are intelligent agents and they indeed use logic as a representation! As I have said, their symbol manipulation is going on out where we can see it; there is no doubt that they use logic representations. This itself tells us very little about their functional architecture, except maybe we will want to account for this emphasis on tidiness and elegance in terms of how the processes inside are organized.

Similarly, it is ironic to say that conceptual dependency "made relatively little contribution to the symbol level" (Newell, 1982, p. 120), given that it provided a convenient symbolic language for expressing theories. Here again, the "symbol level" as we know it is what's going on in our perceptual space. As agents, this is how we state what we believe; conceptual dependency, like the predicate calculus, provides a more disciplined means of articulating and sharing theories.

The primary difference between a KL description and any other theoretical statement is that it is an explanation of agent behavior vs. inanimate phenomenon such as meteorology. As an aside, it is interesting to consider the attributes that human behavior and the weather share:

• Both meteorological and social systems can be described in terms of loosely coupled, interacting processes;

• Local interactions over short periods of time can be described and predicted fairly well, but emergent macro effects, while statistically correlated, are difficult to predict;

• The laws and principles describing behavior (e.g., rationality in people) describe the results of dynamic interactions, not mechanisms that are internal to the components. (For some reason, this is more obvious in physics, where we wouldn't say Newton's laws are "known" by the planets, who then changed their minds when Einstein came around.)

In general, a KL description, just like any other theoretical statement,

• arises in making sense (thus, it exemplifies the centrality of human story-telling and comprehension);
• is based on observations from a frame of reference (i.e., it is highly dependent on the measuring devices and sampling period);
• is attributed to the system being observed (i.e., it is viewed as a property that belongs to the system, not the observer);
• is realized in some perceivable form (a representation).

Putting this together, stating a KL description is creating information. A KL description, like any representation, is not translated from a prior internal representation. Thus, when we speak we are not translating from a description of what we are going to say. By this view, speaking itself is a conceptual process that is only realized in the actual physical activity of uttering a phrase. The oddity of such a strong claim is that it makes perception and activity one process. What is perceived–conceived–stated can then be perceived and commented on.

It is in this respect that semantic interpretation is going on in our outward behavior; the semantic relation is embodied in the reference one external representation makes to another. That is, semantic relations are realized in our ongoing behavior, not encoded or predescribed in some internal form. This is also why semantic relations cannot be reduced to laws or representations: Semantic relations are inherently processes realized in our interaction with the environment. As such, an observer can comment on them, but they cannot be reduced to single point-of-view, objective descriptions.

Of considerable interest is how such commentary orients and controls subsequent behavior, so the whole ongoing sequence of sense making is providing an accumulating orientation, which is composing new sequences of behavior. These ideas are again too non–traditional to be fully elaborated and digested here; I later attempt a simple presentation; a more complete story is told in Clancey (in preparation).

To summarize, KL descriptions are crucial for the sense making of any agent and appropriate for designers of intelligent machines. But they are inherently subjective and realized only in an observer's representations. We have been very confused about this because as AI researchers we have adopted mentalist arguments, specifically that representations of the world and descriptions of our own behaviors are stored in memory, indexed, and manipulated as data structures. Any description is relative to a frame of reference, so what is inside cannot be the descriptions made by the theoretician. Any descriptions (knowledge, representations, theories) are articulated with respect to and about an interactional, observational space; they presuppose a frame of reference, are perceptual in character, and inherently subjective. KL descriptions are about agents, but they belong to the theoretician. They constitute his knowledge, his beliefs.

Adding to our analytic difficulty is our observation that agents being studied do make statements about what they know, and such statements have an effect on subsequent behavior. This has led theoreticians to assume that their own attributions of beliefs and desires, which explain behavior, must be actual statements encoded in the agent, which are causing the behavior. However, beliefs and desires are expressions that only an observer can make. A theoretician–observer could attribute beliefs and desires to us, but they aren't in this sense our beliefs or desires.

Following Bartlett, expressions of beliefs and desires are reflective constructions that for the agent serve to resolve an impasse in behavior by providing a new orientation (Bartlett, 1977). Thus beliefs and desires must be stated to have effect; their causality is towards the future, not as a mechanistic account of what has already occurred. Thus, we must distinguish between:

1. an agent's expression of his own beliefs and desires (where these come from);
2. an observer's grammatical attribution of beliefs/desires to others;
3. the effect reflecting on #1 has on the agent's subsequent behavior.

Items 1 and 2 arise by the same "understanding process," the production of a KL description. Hence, for the agent as observer, we have the interesting process by which a KL account of what happened in the past has implications at the level of the functional architecture in changing future behavior. As in the conventional AI picture, a representation is causing behavior. The interesting twist is that the representation is constructed in order to create new information ("a way of turning round on its own 'schemata' " (Bartlett, 1977, p. 202)), as a reflection on past behavior, serving as an orientation (way of perceiving) that allows a present impasse to be resolved (and behavior to proceed again automatically, without reflective construction of representations).

To bring a few points together in a different way, consider that I might attribute beliefs and desires to a cat chasing a bird: "The cat believes the bird can't hear her." This takes us up short because we have never heard a cat state any beliefs and desires, yet we recognize it as a valid KL explanation of what the cat is doing. It reminds us that such attributions are the observer's statements and representations and not of the agent being studied. This case is clearer because of point #3 above, namely a cat's behavior, as far as we know, is not affected by KL descriptions.

Hence, we're studying at least two phenomenon:

1. The nature of the KL as a social system-level description, necessary to predict and explain interactional behavior. (Or, in its degenerate form, the case of a robot in isolation, this reduces to just a physical system constituting the robot and its physical environment.)

2. The effects such articulations by agents themselves have on their future behavior, what forms such explanations take, and why they seek such understanding (specifically, its origins in both the interactional environment and in the neural processes constituting the functional architecture that maintain formal relational consistency in perceptions and behaviors).

## KL as Physical Theory

To carry the analysis of the relativity of the KL a step further, it is worth making explicit connections to the philosophy of physics. The interpretation of the Uncertainty Principle has caused much debate, not surprisingly since it involves many of the same issues and complications AI is struggling with. Maybe most surprising is that Bohr and Heisenberg themselves wrote about the relativity of knowledge and the origin of theories. For example, Heisenberg said, "What we observe is not nature itself, but nature exposed to our method of questioning." Bohr wrote, "It is wrong to think that the task of physics is to find out how nature is. Physics concerns only what we can *say* about nature" (both quoted in (Gregory, 1988)). Heisenberg and Bohr saw that the metaphysical implications of quantum theory involved viewing theories as relative to a frame of reference, whose appropriateness depended on the measuring devices and purposes of the experimenter. Gregory summarizes this well: "We interact with the world and create interpretations of what this interaction means" (Gregory, 1988).

Figure 13.4 provides a summary of the interactional and perceptual aspects of theory formation, characterizing the process by which representations develop. The world ("reality") is viewed here as an undifferentiated, continuous field. Organized subsystems interact and interfere with one another. The dynamics of

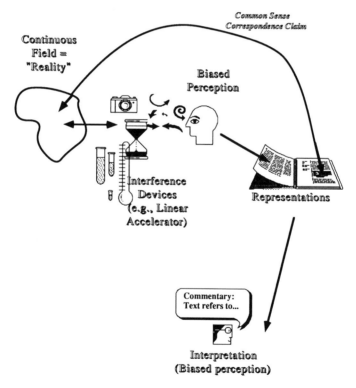

FIG. 13.4   How representations correspond to reality, illustrating first order relativity of representation construction and second order relativity of representation interpretation.

interactions result in locally–stable configurations, due partly to exchange of energy (equilibrium) and partly to the conserving effects of memory (e.g., in genes and neurons). The measurement devices we use (including our visual system) constitute another situated subsystem, which both enable observations by their interactions with the containing environment and distort these observations through their own character. Thus, human perception is biased by both the external interactive process (e.g. our use of a camera with certain recording properties) and our orientation as we interpret and make sense of stimuli.

Our representations (e.g., our written theoretical statements in some notation) are part of the dynamics of our own interaction with the environment we are studying. One way of saying this is that representations emerge as perceptions, whose construction accomplishes and maintains coherence (in the mapping between perception and action) against the dynamic interaction with the environment. Furthermore, as I have emphasized throughout this paper, these representations are subsequently interpreted by another perceptual process (e.g., performed by the reader of the scientific text), in a process of commentary which creates a secondary conceptualization.

The upper arrow in the figure illustrates the common sense view that a scientist's statements are objective descriptions of reality. The *correspondence theory of reality* holds that what we know and say is about the world (reality) and is only more or less accurate. This is the commonsense view that scientific models are only approximations of reality. This is also the commonsense view that words refer to things and events "out there." The correspondence theory underlies most theories of truth and has been the subject of volumes of philosophical debate (most notably in AI, the work of Brian Smith (1987)). In contrast, the strong claim (supported by Bohr and Heisenberg) is that there are no objects and events to be described independent of the interference effect of making an observation (which is why whether the electron is a wave or a particle depends on the experimental process that interferes with it). Indeed, the very notion of objects, categories, and time arises in our perception and language (Gregory, 1988; Tyler, 1978). The most immediate implication for AI research is that we must abandon the search for some kind of "formal semantics" that could be used to formalize the correspondence between programs (*qua* representations) and "the world." There is no independently knowable, objective world that our representations can be mapped to. This is another way of saying that the meaning of a representation depends on the frame of reference of the observer.

In short, understanding the nature of KL theories is tantamount to understanding how any theory corresponds to the phenomenon it is about. There are two forms of relativity: First-order perceptual relativity (a KL theory is no more objective than a physics theory), and second-order representational relativity (KL descriptions are always open to interpretation). To relate this to AI architectures, a knowledge base represents theories about the world. Every knowledge base contains models of one or more systems in the world (e.g., a model of an electronic circuit, a model of the physiological processes in the human body). This model constitutes the beliefs of an agent about the system in the world. As described above, these beliefs are inherently a product of how the agent has interacted with the world and the purposes at hand (how the model will be used). We say that this model constitutes the agent's knowledge.[10]

Figure 13.5 summarizes how a KL description of agent behavior can be viewed as a causal theory.

The left side of Figure 13.5 shows how I have characterized KL theories. A KL theory is something that an observer knows about an agent, who in turn has knowledge of some system in the world. The system in the world that the KL theory is about is the system containing the agent, with which it interacts, not the agent itself, in isolation. Thus, the properties of subjectivity and relativity that hold for physics (left inner box, "agent knows domain causal theory") hold as well for the observer's KL description of the agent (right box, "observer knows KL-causal theory"). This is not surprising or especially profound, but it does point out that to take a stand on the nature of the KL is to take a stand on the issues raised by Bohr and Heisenberg.[11]

It is not surprising that the same confusion about system levels has cropped up in expert systems research. Many people believe that all qualitative models can be reduced to function-structure blueprints. According to this view, the only reason physicians deal with disease taxonomies is because they don't understand how diseases are caused. After medical science improves, we would be able to describe every disease exclusively in terms of abnormal states and processes within the body. Classification models are inherently inferior, these researchers suppose; real scientists work with hardware diagrams.

However, this interpretation is false, for the same reason that the KL cannot be identified with processes within an individual person. In fact, diseases are descriptions of the result of a pattern of interaction between an individual person

---

[10]Here it should be apparent why I have emphasized that we need to view AI programming as a modeling methodology. We need to realize that every knowledge base contains models, specifically that classifications are models. Thus, the term "qualitative reasoning" covers what all AI programs do; for all contain qualitative models (primarily non-numeric relational networks representing causal, temporal, and spatial characteristics of processes in the world). The term "qualitative simulation" is to be contrasted with the kind of classification model in MYCIN. The most prevalent form of qualitative simulation is a behavioral description of internal states and processes, commonly called a "causal-associational network." See Clancey (1989) for elaboration.

[11]It is tempting to get caught in a conundrum: If "everything is relative" then this description itself can't be an objective, absolute description of the nature of reality. If the theory is right, then it must be wrong. Because it is relative to our purposes, not everyone will agree. But then, conversely, the theory must be right, for our explanation of its failure restates the theory itself (that what you perceive depends on your point of view). Trying to work your way out of this is tantamount to wanting a representation that has a defined meaning, that wears its interpretation on its sleeve. The theory says that it is open to interpretation; if that sounds like a fixed, objective statement, it is just because of the illusion that for the moment you think you know what "open" and "interpretation" mean.

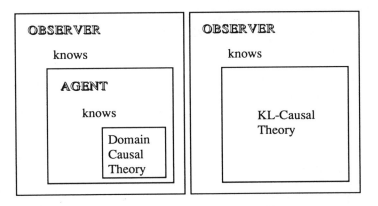

FIG. 13.5.   KL descriptions viewed as causal theories.

and his environment. Consider for example tennis elbow. This syndrome cannot be causally explained in terms of processes lying exclusively within the person or within the environment. Rather it is a result of a pattern of interaction over time. As for any emergent effect, it can't be predicted, explained, or controlled by treating the person in isolation, or even by studying the person-environment system over short periods. It is a developmental effect, an adaptation in the person that reflects the history of his or her behavior. The same claim can be made about the entire taxonomy of medical diseases—trauma, toxicity, infection, neoplasms, and congenital disorders—they are all descriptions of the agent after a history of recurrent interactions. Similar examples can be drawn from computer system failures; faults cannot reduced to changes in a blueprint, but in fact the space of possible etiologies is constantly changing with the dynamics of interaction with an open environment. For example, a favorite story at SUMEX-AIM at Stanford is how system crashes were caused every fall when the first October rains wet the phone lines going to Santa Cruz, swamping the computer with spurious control–C input attempting to get its attention.[12] Such problems aren't fixed by swapping boards.

---

[12]The same analysis applies to the controversy in student modeling research between misconception models or "bug libraries" and the assumed superior form of simulation or generative error models (by which errors are produced from a grammar during the course of problem solving, rather than being pre-enumerated) (VanLehn, 1988). Although a generative model is advantageous because it is more general and supplies an explanation of the cause of misconceptions, in fact bug libraries, like disease hierarchies, cannot be avoided. Misconceptions are KL descriptions that reflect developmental interactions in the student's and observer's experience; they cannot be replaced by more objective descriptions of the student or the environment viewed in isolation to each other. However, viewed as a mechanism in the brain, generative models point in the right direction because they don't treat knowledge as something that is stored, but as inherently manifested in problem-solving interaction. As always, treating knowledge, misconception or not, as a *thing* is where the problem begins.

It is worth restating how the KL is like any other causal theory. First, it is relative to an observer's frame of reference; it has space-time characteristics. As previously stated observers might attribute different knowledge to the same agent, but from their point of view the coherence relations (why agent behaviors appear meaningful) will be based on the same principles (concerning how the agent's goals and beliefs account for his behavior). The law of rationality holds because human observers more or less share a functional architecture that produces a sense-making process with similar characteristics:

- representation use and generation, by commentary about perceived structures;
- a process of combining past behaviors in way that maintains and achieves coherence in every action;
- plasticity, adaptability, learning rates, perceptual capability that leads to a more or less common capacity to generate new information and develop a shared domain of discourse in collaborative work.

Finally, it is intriguing to reach for an analogy with the General Theory of Relativity. In particular, an observer can't tell whether an agent's behavior is generated by a perception (influence) we cannot see (and might be just an imagined state of affairs) or an ongoing change in the environment (i.e., to maintain equilibrium, the agent's behavior is evolving with the changing dynamics of the interaction with the environment). As for inertial frames of reference, the organism responds to perceived *changes* in the environment (i.e., acceleration). Constant movement in the environment is adapted to by constant behaviors.[13] Attempts to apply dynamic systems theory to the study of intelligence must be framed in terms of development with respect to the history of environmental interactions, as opposed to local responses. Put another way, memory crucially changes the study of dynamic systems, just as onto- and philogenetics separates biology from physics.

McCarthy has said that AI research needs a few Einsteins. Applying Einstein's (and Bohr-Heisenberg's) ideas about relativity and the nature of scientific theories to the study of cognition might be a good start.

---

[13]This is analogous to the discovery that data storage requirements are substantially reduced for video images if one stores changes between sequential images, rather than full pictures. By analogy, for repeating routines the brain may only need to have the capability to recognize and generate changes, not descriptions of moment-by-moment appearances. Such embedded (relative to the particulars of the current context, but not declaratively describing them), process-oriented computation could obviate the need for maps and plans, as Brooks' INSECTS suggest.

## Summary: Relation of KL-description to Functional Architecture

I have argued that a KL description is necessary and useful, but it is not to be identified with the physical processes that cause behavior. Knowledge is an observer's characterization, not something that the agent owns. In cognitive science and AI, we have heretofore taken our *selective* (based on limited interaction with the system being studied/modeled) *perceptions* (necessarily abstractions, generalizations) and placed these *grammar-like descriptions* (formal, expressed as rewrite rules) in the heads of our subjects, claiming not only that they aren't ours, but as representations they existed before we created them, and they even existed as descriptions of what the agent was going to do, inside working memory, before he or she behaved. The strong claim is that representations do indeed play a crucial role in human behavior, but they are created fresh, out where they can be perceived; they are not manipulated, indexed, and stored by hidden, inaccessible processes.

Table 13.1 contrasts the mentalist, cognitive science or AI architecture claim against the contrary point of view that I have synthesized from a variety of fields. A KL description is about a situated, social system, the result of interacting internal and external processes, and is an interpretation by an observer; it is neither objective nor a property of individual agents.

As Newell says, the KL is a real level of description, as much as any description is real. It is a system-level description, but attributable to social systems, not individual agents. We need such a level because the behaviors we observe are emergent in interactions, and as such they could not be preconceived or pre-

TABLE 13.1
Opposing View of the Nature of the Knowledge Level Descriptions.

| Cognitive Science | Anthropology, Philosophy, Linguistics, Sociology, Physics |
|---|---|
| subject's knowledge | observer's theory |
| stored in memory | expressed, stated, written on paper |
| pre-existing plan, determining behavior | product of selective interaction and perception |
| objective, corresponding to reality | subjective, relative to a frame of reference |
| fixed, causally determining behavior | continuously interpretable (a representation, not the mechanism itself) |
| reflection = examining internal data structures | reflection = objectifying own activity, perceiving and commenting about a sequence of behavior |

described in the individual agents. Of course, agents themselves can predict what will happen and this can enter into their deliberate planning about what to do. The fact that agents have their own KL descriptions of themselves and this does affect their behavior greatly complicates our analysis. We can't tease this apart without resolving longstanding issues in psychiatry, and we should recognize that's the domain we're dealing with.

The most critical distinction between my analysis and Newell–Pylyshyn's is that I claim the three levels are not views of the same system, the individual agent, "bearing an implementation relationship" (Newell, 1982). The KL can't be reduced to (implemented as) structures in an individual. Furthermore, I claim that this is the essential insight that distinguishes traditional AI from the evolving view of situated cognition research. Figure 13.6 illustrates this difference.

This idealized diagram shows the theoretician and agent occupying one environment (or social system). For robotic design, it may be practical to view the agent as being in an idealized, closed world, and hence, not the environment of the theoretician. They share an environment at least in the sense that the theoretician has some way of observing the agent's behavior. KL descriptions are shown as being part of the environment, in a space that other agents can access. This incorrectly leaves out silent speech and mental imagery. Strictly speaking there is a private perceptual space for each agent and a shared space of sensations. As I have stressed, the whole analysis is recursive—as for any agent behavior, KL descriptions themselves are emergent, arising through the interaction of the observer–agent with his environment.

Prior to Newell's KL paper, we might have shown the mind with everything "below the line" (encoded in a program or human memory):

```
-----------------------------------------------------
Knowledge  =  symbolic  structures  in  the  program
```

Newell separated the symbol level into two parts (Newell, 1982, p. 99):

```
Knowledge  =  observer's  description
-----------------------------------------------------
      symbols  (internal  to  the  agent)
```

The effect is to redefine knowledge as an ascription made by an observer and to begin to view representations in a new way: as perceivable forms that are used by an observer to articulate his or her beliefs and theories. My move has been to claim that this is how it is for the agent as well—all symbol manipulation is

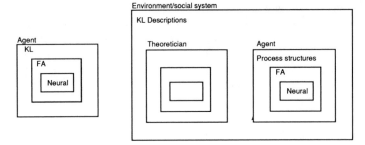

FIG. 13.6.   Newell and Pylyshyn's Knowledge-Level (left) opposed to situated, interactive, relativistic view (FA = Functional Architecture).

going on above the line, in the agent's behavior. Thus, I move the symbol level fully to the top, leaving only "syntactic" relations between neural processes inside. I claim that a KL description is just an instance of the general sense-making process by which agents produce and manipulate representations of their world and themselves:

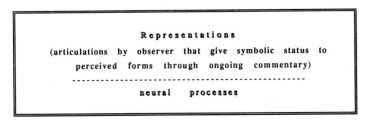

I call this the *externalization move*. In the most general sense, for example in the study of humans, the KL can't be reduced to (or restated exclusively in terms of) internal neural processes, because it's about the interactions that occur between an environment and neural processes. These interactions are manifested by agents who create and use representations. Because these representations are only interpreted within ongoing sequences of behavior and themselves emerge in an interaction between internal processes and the world, we cannot say that agent behavior is ever strictly caused by representations; rather, the sequence of behavior and changing representations are arising together, dialectically. Agent behavior is not conditional on objective characterizations of a situation, in the sense that representation creation and use could be reduced to (implemented as) rule-like mechanisms that match objectively-defined inputs.

Following Newell's lead, we have explored the hypothesis that knowledge is not stored as structures. I have brought forward arguments raised outside mainstream AI research by people in anthropology, philosophy, linguistics, and physics, specifically trying to account for the "situated" perspective. As such, this is an attempt to bridge the gap between different points of view, while remaining grounded in AI terminology as much as possible (cf. Newell, 1988, p. 521). My approach has been to retell the situated story from the perspective of designing a robot that interacts with its environment, in which the design and the observer's attributions are found to be on different levels: one a physical mechanism (the machine's design in terms of physically interacting parts), the other a description that names and accounts for patterns in how the robot and environment interact (the KL description).

The next step is to propose and implement a different kind of functional architecture, or better, show how SOAR should be modified. The trick is that we must change our understanding of three pivotal concepts: the nature of representations (what gives something symbolic status), memory (what is retained from previous activity), and perception (how input from fixed transducers is organized to constitute a new conception). The key move we must accomplish is to integrate perception into the reflective, conceptual process, rather than making it a peripheral process. I have argued that this requires a subjective notion of information, in fact, viewing information as the product created by the agent, externalized as representations, as opposed to something objective and supplied.

One approach is to now investigate the relations in a sequence of changes to representations, for example, the study of situated design (Allen, 1988). Another approach is to return to the functional architecture and ask what neural processes would support the production of (what appear to the observer as) recurrent, coherent phrases of behavior. Could we account for the practice effect and sensemaking in a way that is consistent with the strong claims that place representations only in perceptual space? This is the research program I claim we are now faced with. I sketch out one possible approach in the following section.

## A FUNCTIONAL ARCHITECTURE THAT MANIPULATES PROCESSES

All the psychological schools and trends overlook the cardinal point that every thought is a generalization; they all study word and meaning without any reference to development. (Vygotsky, *Thought and Language,* 1934)

As Pylyshyn points out, heretofore there has been "only one nonquestion-begging answer" to the dilemma of how the semantics of representations could cause behavior, given that "only the material form of the representation could be causally efficacious," namely that "the brain is doing exactly what computers do when they compute numeric functions. . ." (Pylyshyn, 1984, p. 39). I have argued that semantic attributions occur only in an ongoing sequence of behavior, in the form of commentary one representation (articulation) makes on another. That is, semantic attribution is an observer's statement about how one behavior relates to another. My objective in this section is to point the way to a new conception of the functional architecture that could in particular account for *how such representations in a sequence (the evolving commentary) are related to one another*. Specifically, I want to describe a functional architecture that could account for how phrases of behaviors are constructed, retained, and recombined (remaining fully aware that what constitutes a phrase is relative to an observer's frame of reference).

Having ruled out a functional architecture that manipulates descriptions of processes, we are left with the possibility of a mechanism that manipulates processes directly. That is to say, memory is the capacity to reenact a phrase of behavior and perception/learning, the process by which phrases are composed in an apparently hierarchical manner. Obviously, you won't find a program listing at the end of this paper that does this. Our field is at the intermediate stage of theorizing about what could be possible, using KL descriptions of the behavior the functional architecture must support. For this new beginning, special emphasis should be placed on highly-interactive behaviors like jazz improvisation, drawing, speaking, and ensemble performances of all kinds. These all place a premium on a cycle of movement, perception/reflection, and incremental modification that comments on what has come before, composing a coherent new form. Following Agre and Chapman's analysis, research should shift from geometry and algebra problem solving to examples of developing and never fully-definable routines, dialectically coupled to the agent's changing perceptions of its own interactions with the environment (recall AARON). By this, cognitive science would move from building in ontologies (however hyphenated or compiled) to finding ways that a process-oriented memory would embody and create (rather than describe) recurrent interactions the agent has with its world.

What follows is obviously speculative, but it makes the point that there is another way of talking about symbols, memory, and conceptualization, that gives perception a central place and avoids the semantic-attribution problem (how internal, unperceived representations could relate to what they are about). I start by discussing a simple example, elaborate upon Vygotsky's idea that speaking is conceptualizing, and finally attempt to pin down how phrases of behavior could be related to the neural processes that create them.

## Tokens, Symbols, and Reference

Perlis states an essential question for AI research: "If a system employs symbols, in what sense are they symbolic, of what are they symbolic, and in what sense is it the system that makes them symbolic?" (Perlis, 1987). Many discussions of symbols, meaning, and reference in computer programs are based on a misconception about the nature of symbolizing and representing in human reasoning. A token (mark, sound, or anything perceived) becomes a symbol by virtue of comments people make about it, rather than being a property inherent in the identified thing itself. Today's computer programs combine tokens according to an observer's grammar-like descriptions of how the resultant behavior will appear from outside, while human behavior proceeds at some level directly from the remembered history of the processes that directly generate physical movements.

The key changes in perspective called for here are:

- Human memory is not a store for things, but rather the functional capacity for creating and recombining phrases of activity.
- Representing, such as speaking, is a mode of perception, of claiming a new distinction, adding information that achieves coherence in the memory of processes.

My running example is how people talk about the Sydney Opera House:

The New South Whale, they called it, the Operasaurus, a pack of French nuns playing football, an opera house with eight sheets to the wind. Then it was finished. The London *Times* said it was "the building of the century," and the Aussies shut up, looked again, and saw a pearl–pale sculpture glowing suspiciously like a national symbol on their waterfront. (Godwin, 1988, p. 75).

Consider the Sydney Opera House as an example of a token (albeit larger than most). The commentary about it as it was built is precisely how any observed object or event becomes a representation. Each comment (e.g., "a pack of French nuns playing football") provides a context for interpreting the structure, for viewing it in a new way. Most strikingly, notice what happened after the Opera House was finished—it glowed "suspiciously like national symbol." That something is declared a symbol *after its creation as a thing* contradicts the typical stance of AI research. In fact, this is how it always is. Something becomes symbolic by virtue of what people say about it, not for something inherent in the thing itself. This supplied context, coming after the occurrence and observation of the token itself, is what gives it meaning (Langer, 1958). I call this the *commentary model of cognition.*

The common sense point of view is that language refers to reality (Berger & Luckmann, 1967). For example, we say that a drawing or picture refers to something other than itself and this is what makes it a representation. However, this is backwards. Meaning or reference is not in the token or in my head prior to my speaking. In speaking, I am perceiving the token in a new way, providing a context with respect to which it can be interpreted as being meaningful. Viewing the Opera House as a ship, I might say it resembles eight sails. But that's just one of many interpretations. It isn't inherently a representation of any one thing, just what someone says. Certainly, we care a great deal about the designer's interpretation, but nevertheless, even the designer's statements are apart from the structure itself and prone to change.

Two aspects of reference need to be distinguished here. Suppose I observe the

Opera House (the token, OH) then make a statement *about it,* calling it the New South Whale (the context, NSW, a pun about Sydney's location in New South Wales). The *formal* aspect of reference is the pact of mentioning or pointing to OH as a thing-in-itself when saying NSW. The *symbolic* aspect of reference is the act of saying what OH is about, what it refers to, by my comment NSW. Thus, we have a reciprocal action (Figure 13.7).

```
                    mentions/points   to
    token (OH)         <--------        comment   (NSW)

                       -------->
              acquires  meaning  in  the  context  of


             =  is  viewed  as  symbolic  within  the  context  of
             =  is  viewed  as  referring  in  the  larger  context  of
```

FIG. 13.7.   Relation of token to a comment that gives it symbolic status.

*Representing* (claiming that something symbolizes something for me) is what I do when I comment on (symbolic aspect) what has gone before (formal aspect). Our computer programs are of course full of symbols, because and only because of how we talk about them.

The phrase "attaching meaning to symbols" (Sloman, 1985) is incoherent— something becomes a symbol by virtue of our "attaching a meaning" to it. There isn't first a symbol, then the meaning. There is first something I refer to formally, as a token, in a remark, which supplies a context indicating what it is about, thus endowing it with symbolic status. We routinely say things like "the sentence implies a great deal," but such a way of talking disguises where meaning comes from, suggesting that it resides in the sentence itself.

Perhaps the most difficult "hidden matter" (Bateson, 1988) confusing our analysis is the idea that words refer to the world, that there is such a thing as objective knowledge (Tyler, 1978). This is an integral component of everyday understanding: There is something external to speakers that their meaning is about; language is not tautological; people are always trying to work through and define the contexts that shape them and that they must work within. But this orientation of common sense and science alike is not a good description of the activity of speaking itself and what people are doing when they use words. In a related analysis Perlis says, "There is a *presumption of an external object of thought,* something we take as real. Expressions or other internal forms (even images) do all the work, but at least one is momentarily taken as the thing-in-itself. We have no other way to refer, no casting our mind forward to external things" (Perlis, 1987).

By this definition, today's computer programs do not engage in symbolic reasoning or use or create representations—for any internal "interpretation" of their tokens is always grammatical and thus bounded by the axioms of combination. People speak and draw from the unformalized processes of their memory. Thus, to answer Sloman, who has struggled over these same issues, there is "a real distinction between understanding and mere manipulation." A quotation system, according to Perlis, allows a system to use "symbols" to refer: "the system itself has both symbol and symboled at hand." However, this is purely formal, grammatically defined reference. The program has no way to jump out (cf. Winograd & Flores, 1986). Human reference doesn't proceed from axioms of what kind of references are possible, that is formally, from a preclassification of behavior, but by directly recombining (the processes that generated) past sequences of behavior.[14]

The fact that we can relate to one of today's program as if it understands demonstrates our capacity to ascribe meaning, not something inherent in the program itself. Token-producing acts by a machine, just like your speaking to me or drawing a picture, or writing a note, are open to interpretation, a matter of what an observer says about them (Agre, 1988). A robot appears to obey commands, answer questions, and teach (cf. Sloman, 1985) because the observer says so. In this respect, a human user's responses to computer inquiries, for example during a consultation, creates *a combined system that is doing symbolic reasoning,* with the computer program playing a role no different from a numeric calculator as a manipulator of notations.

How then do representing actions follow from our experience, what do they do for us, how are they organized by the representations themselves?

## Speaking as Conceptualizing/Perceiving

The quote by Vygotsky which opens this section, that all speaking is generalizing, contains a crucial insight. Speaking is not an act of translating a concept but of creating one. Speaking is an act of grasping, encompassing, taking in, contextualizing. It does so by pointing or mentioning. To mention is to include, to create a composed form. This is representing: creating a new order, perceiving a higher level of organization (Bateson, 1988).

Through the act of commentary, a token is seen in a new way. It acquires a larger meaning, which is to say that it is seen no longer as just a thing-in-itself

---

[14]An obvious connection can be made to Searle's Chinese Room (Searle, 1984). The entire question about whether rule-like manipulation of symbols inside the room constitutes intelligent behavior or not is misguided. There are no symbols being manipulated by hidden processes inside the brain, rule-like or not.

(the form of the Opera House) but as part of a larger context (notion, idea, concept). This is what it is for something to have *meaning* or to be a *symbol*.

Of course, it's not "having a meaning" in the sense of a static property of a thing, but a matter of how it is perceived, by virtue of the context supplied, the comment. This context can't be defined, or rather isn't supplied as a definition. It is known tacitly, and is changed as much by the act of pointing at the token as the token is seen in a new light by the context (the idea of Australia is changed by including the Opera House). Thus, the token under interpretation becomes an "instance" of the context, a manifestation of it, tacitly changing the meaning of the context itself. This view is critically at odds with the AI view of representation and reasoning, in which the Opera House would be subsumed under an existing category as an example or instance. The commentary model holds that the act of subsumption is not a matter of matching a subsuming category, but of changing the category so that it includes the example, while changing the example so that it is included by the category.

Asking, "What is the meaning of the comment? To what does it refer?" is incoherent unless you didn't understand the comment itself. For example, it is only meaningful to ask, "What is the meaning of the statement that the Opera House is the New South Whale?" when you don't understand the connection. For you, I didn't succeed at supplying a context that gives the token meaning. Too often we assume in constructing formal knowledge representations that every question about meaning is meaningful, just because it is suggested by a formal calculus. Philosophers and linguists have argued that many questions about reference and meaning have been derived from formal analyses such as diagrams with links between words, spawning fruitless, impossible searches for a semantic calculus (rules that could generate the space of meaningful statements [Tyler, 1978; Wittgenstein, 1958]). But, to tie this to the larger themes of this paper, reference and meaning are incoherent without a notion of time and a selective, calibrating agent who perceives by naming. Time and agent constitute a frame of reference for the laws of rationality. Thus, the study of semantics is the study of the KL, of sense-making, of the conditions for generating and using representations.

If necessary, a context-supplying statement can be pinned down further by another comment, until finally the listeners (including the speaker, who is also hearing these ideas for the first time) are in a state of feeling that nothing further needs to be said, or more specifically, nothing more remains to be *done*. According to Bateson, this state is tauto-ecological—an interaction of relational consistency to what has been experienced before (the tautological processes of the brain) and the demands of the ongoing activity in which the comments are made, tacitly supplying meaning to them (the ecological processes of interaction with an environment).

The logic of an utterance is relative to how the words have been used before, the phrases they have been part of, the relations they have borne to other phrases.

These are past processes of mentioning and referring, and having been generated by the combination of them, the current utterance bears an analogical relation to them. Schemas (recurrent phrases of behavior) emerge by the coherent recombination of past speaking processes, themselves composed of other processes. In this respect, every act of speaking is an act of conceptualization, of stepping towards an understanding, of composing a story, of being coherent.

Each act of speaking is a complete act of perceiving in itself. No further act of representation is needed. However, because each act of perceiving adds new information, something more might need to be said to re-establish the tautology of our understanding, to complete the story.[15] The distinction between recognition and generation is that one perceives meaning in a given thing and the other creates the thing (such as a program, drawing, or paragraph) iteratively, reflecting and commenting on each statement and the evolving whole.

In commenting on a sequence of behavior, we unify it, making it an item. We view it as a whole, perceiving one form. *The essence of representation is converting process*—both our memory of past activities and the ongoing activity we are engaged in—*into pattern* (Bateson, 1988). Speaking is a mode of perceiving (drawing distinctions, seeing forms). Converting process into pattern involves sampling, counting, defining bounds, claiming discontinuities in an inherently continuous world.

Bateson draws on cybernetics and genetics to help us understand what happens when a digitally randomized stochastic process (e.g., a genetic process) develops by interacting with a continuously randomized stochastic process (the environment). Regularities can be perceived in the structures that result, which biologists call the phenotype of the organism. Similarly, if we take the neural processes of memory as a conserving mechanism, similar to the effect of the genes, we can understand the regularities psychologists perceive in behavior as the product of development resulting from the interaction of two stochastic processes. We call these regularities *homologies* (Bateson, 1988); they constitute our law-like statements of how people behave, our KL descriptions.

From the perspective of the agent, the tautological recombination of past processes of memory, in a developmental process of interacting with an environment, is manifested in the grammatical appearance of everything people do, in the conceptual forms of speaking as well as the routines of skilled behavior. Every statement and action is a claim that the world is regular, a new generalization, and hence should be viewed as an ongoing attempt to reduce reflectively-constructed behaviors to routines. The space of resultant behaviors can be characterized in terms of analogies, of schemas, which are neither discrete nor continuous, neither fully coherent and definable nor arbitrary, but *constantly adapted* to the history of what we have done before and the ongoing demands of

---

[15]Regarding the tautology-preserving mechanism inherent in realizing that something needs to be said, see Winograd and Flores on "breakdown" and Bartlett on impasses/reflection.

our interactions with the world around us. Bateson has characterized this as our satisficing nature. In a perverse, ever-changing world, in which no routine will work, it is experienced as the double bind of schizophrenia.

## The Neural Processes of the Functional Architecture

Here I sketch some specifications deriving from the above discussion and contrast these with Pylyshyn's and Dennett's analyses.

Pylyshyn says that to implement the cognitive science approach, we will need "a system of transformations that preserve the semantic interpretations of the codes" (Pylyshyn, 1989). This is true. However, it is not required by the commentary model because interpretation occurs only by a sequence of perception and expressed commentary. The semantic relation is always an observer's post-hoc comment about such a sequence, and there are no internal codes that *describe* either the relation or process by which this meaning is created.

The question remains, what are the internal transformations that accomplish this creation of new conceptions and account for our reaching a state of satisfaction that we understand something? More mechanistically speaking, how is a phrase of behavior constructed from previous phrases? How is a new sequence "chunked" into a remembered phrase? What accounts for the compositional character by which impasses are resolved by perceiving higher orders of organization (Bartlett, 1977; Bateson, 1972)?

The functional architecture appears to have the following mechanisms for manipulating neural processes:

- direct "playing" of a previously enacted sequence,
- subsumption of phrases in hierarchies of substitutable actions,
- continuous substitution and recombination by integrating substitutions from multiple perspectives (corresponding to multiple parents in orthogonal hierarchies),
- interruption when recombination cannot proceed automatically,
- a reflective process by which a detail (usually an image) becomes the starting point for a new perception that constitutes a new, compositional organization (Bartlett, 1977),
- a memory for sequences created in this way (by interruption and attentive reflection) so a new phrase is created from the constructed sequence.

The key idea of impasse and rationalization based on a perceived detail comes from Bartlett. He also believes that emotional experiences during an impasse, or more generally an individual's "attitude" towards his current state, is a manifestation of the capability to come to terms with himself in a global way, an aspect of how the functional architecture can get things moving again by creating a new organization of processes. Another important idea is "feed forward" (emphasized by Pribram (1971) and Minsky (1985)), by which a process once begun is enhanced by propagation above to subsuming processes, which then enhance the activation of the included process. Combining these ideas, it is significant that an emotional attitude moves forward in memory of sequences (that is, it is remembered earlier when the sequence recurs), capturing the way in which an attitude serves to orient behavior. Further theorization might focus on the discrete nature of these processes, particularly how processes are manipulated at the level corresponding to phrases of behavior (where the temporal extent of a phrase is bounded practically only by the demands of the changing environment—a symphony is a phrase to the conductor, another phrase may be how you live a typical day).

The relations among processes reflect semantically acceptable sequences of commentary (from some observer's perspective). Figure 13.8 shows a sequence of actions (e.g., statements) A and A', generated by physical processes P and P'.

The functional architecture must account for the production of process P after P'. The commentary model suggests that the primary relation is that of composition, so P' subsumes P when A' is a comment on A. The functional architecture is the underlying process that maintains coherence in the organization of neural processes (what Bateson called the "tautological relations" (Bateson, 1988)). Note again that process P doesn't represent action A—it generates it. Nor does process P manipulate any codes that describe A, just as you won't find a gene that describes a part of the body or a physiological process. The semantic relation an observer claims holds between A and A' is not pre-encoded, but rather reflects the logic of the construction of process P' from P, achieved by the functional architecture's maintaining coherence with respect to previously constructed processes. The functional architecture's transformations do not so much "preserve semantic coherence" (Pylyshyn, 1984, p. 249), in the sense of adhering to rule-like descriptions of what is possible, as create/achieve/accomplish coherence in ongoing construction of processes that maintain a subsumption relationship through (or during) their production of sequential actions.

Perception plays a key role here. The commentary model suggests that mov-

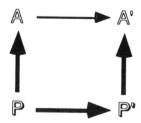

FIG. 13.8.   Two physical actions (A and A') generated by neural processes.

ing from A to A' involves constructing a process such that the perception that leads to statement A' subsumes the perception that led to statement A. For example, when someone first constructed the pun that the OH was NSW (A), a subsequent explanation that the OH was in New South Wales (A') provides a way of seeing the first action, so that A' comments on A, giving it meaning. Notice that these "semantic relations" are clearly not static relations among these words, but rather are more properly characterized as an agent's sequence of perceptions. While it might appear that the explanation A' is what generated the pun A, it is just an observer's restatement of the speaker's perception when saying A.

Another example may be helpful. Consider what happened when a colleague came up to me after a talk and said that I should reverse the order in which I presented my slides. This forced an impasse; now I couldn't see my talk as being coherent. What could be wrong? Proceeding from the idea of ordering, I viewed what as I had done and posed it as the question, "Why did I do X (show theory) before Y (examples)?" I then formulated a rule: "I usually present material in the order I conceive it." From this, I reabstracted X and Y so a new generalization would subsume what I had done in the past that worked: "Show concrete before theory." I then realized that usually I develop a theoretical description after writing programs; this was a different experience, the theory came first. That is, I went back to explain why the new rule would work in the present case—what's odd about this case?

Notice how this is related to explanation-based learning (EBL), but distinctly different. Like EBL, the orientation is entirely procedural, tracking back through a particular example to explain why a different behavior wasn't produced. However, the rule, "present material in the order conceived" was not required to generate past behaviors, it was generated after the fact, as a rationalization that describes what I do. Broadly speaking, it was a reflection over a range of individual behaviors, abstracting them in order to answer the question, "What do I generally do?" Applied to the current context, the rule fails to produce the desired behavior, so the entire sequence must be reabstracted, in a way that would produce a different behavior in the current case.

Thus, the abstraction, "Show concrete before theory" is a new way of talking about the past, subsuming those activities *as if it generated them.* It provides a useful new way of seeing the overall activity of talk preparation; that is, it provides a way of organizing the activity. In this respect, the new perception "Show concrete before theory" is about the past activities; it sees them in a new way, commenting on them, composing/grouping them in a new way, representing them. In this respect, a way of seeing or talking about behavior creates a new order, subsuming old behaviors and providing a means for organizing subsequent ones. We say, "Perception subsumes action." Ways of seeing/talking orient the particulars of what we do by directly enabling them as processes.

In the future, this new rule is likely to be remembered when making slides because a new routine has not developed yet and the process of making slides is now subsumed by this commentary. The new perception will "move forward" (it originally came after the process of making slides and giving talks) because it is about the process of making slides. That is, it will be activated by upwards propagation when the lower-level activity is engaged in (by subsumption of processes).[16] Summarizing the relation to EBL, we find that the ideas of impasse, reminding, and reasoning about cases are central, but there are no internal representations of behaviors, just the processes themselves, which are activated and recreated, and their actual or imagined results commented upon. This comment is not saved as a rule that generates behavior directly. Rather, the comment has the immediate effect of reorganizing processes it is about and its articulation in the future will provide a representation for more deliberately stepping through these processes.

A few related observations: When we as observers say that A' bears an analogic relationship to A, we must recreate for ourselves the perceptions and hence the underlying organization of processes such that P' subsumes P for us. This provocatively suggests that the functional architecture provides us with the capability to start up multiple processes and hold them active as we attempt a new organization that could subsume them. This is in essence the capability we require to deal with impasses, and as Bartlett suggests, is why consciousness is useful. Furthermore, the creation of underlying coherence involves a cycle of perception (reflection on what has been said or done before) and a new physical behavior. The only way of moving forward is incrementally, by doing something, and commenting on that. Reflection is inherently a process of actual behaving, not hidden cogitating (though you needn't talk out loud). There appears to be a connection between deliberate reflection (e.g., creating the sequence of A followed by A') and the creation of A–A' as a new phrase of behavior. We should remember that such learned "chunks" are not substances, but processes, implemented as strengthened connections between the neurons (Edelman, 1987).

All of this maintains the traditional view that symbols are semantically interpreted structures. However, by the externalization move—moving semantic relations out into the perceptual space of an observer—we can talk more coherently about relation of neural processes that produce behaviors and the relation of perception to repetition and creation of new processes. That is, there is

---

[16]An interesting question is whether the perception should be viewed as a "node"—a separate process that subsumes actions—or whether perception is the process by which an organization of actions is recreated. Under this latter interpretation, the perception is itself the organization of the neural processes. Perhaps experiencing an organizing perception, for example, articulating a rule of behavior, is what enables the organization. Or perhaps an articulation process (saying this rule) subsumes the new organization (way of seeing talks) and is simply activated (at a later time, as a "reminding") by upwards propagation prior to the application of the subsumed actions it is about.

reason to believe that cognitive science and AI research has identified enough KL phenomena so we can reasonably look to the neural process level for functional architecture mechanisms that could support the conceptualization, learning, reminding we have described at the KL.

Table 13.2 summarizes the tri-level view according to Pylyshyn-Newell, Dennett, and the descriptions given here. To bring together a few key ideas:

- The relation of the levels is not "implementational"; however, in our explanatory account it is generative; it enables predictions to be made.
- The claim that there is a semantic relation between A and A' is a KL description and is always made by an observer, relative to his or her frame of reference. Such statements (for example, that "A → A' is a rule") are representations made by an observer and are not structures that physically cause the agent's behavior (rather, that is what happens when moving from P to P').
- The semantic level concerns the result of interactions that occur as the functional architecture maintains internal coherence relative to its activities in the world; that is, the agent's resultant behavior is situated.
- Semantic or KL descriptions are expressed as categories and laws of behavior, thus they express the interaction between beliefs, goals, and activities as abstractions and rewrite rules. That is, a KL theory is analogous to a natural language grammar; more specifically, a natural language grammar is one aspect of a complete KL theory.
- We need the semantic level in order to give principled explanations of why, of all possibilities that the functional architecture allows, certain behaviors are

TABLE 13.2
The Tri-Level Architectue (Knowledge, Symbolic, and Physical Levels)
from Different Perspectives.

| Newell-Pylyshyn | Dennett | Clancey |
|---|---|---|
| representational "semantic" (Knowledge Level) | Intentional | observer's description and interpretation of perceived regularities in behavior of an agent-world system |
| symbols & symbol-manipulation rules (Symbol Level) | Subpersonal | self-organizing neural processes (subsumption & sequence relations between past processes) |
| physical, neural transducer processes (Physical Level) | | processes that create macro neural processes (feed forward & upward activation; composition & sequence creation) |

favored. These constraints, which lie outside the machine's functional architecture, are the result of emergent effects from its developmental interaction with the environment. Most notably, psychiatry often requires consideration of the agent's social organization in order to explain behavioral impasses. Thus, the principles that "prevent semantically deviant states from occurring" (Pylyshyn, 1984, p. 37) lie in the combined system, not within the individual agent.

• A KL description is an example of the perception of information, of conception in general. "Information content" is thus relative to an observer. Specifically, "input information" is not objective, but relative to the agent's perception. Without a perceptual process to create information, there is only data processing. In conclusion, placing perception prior to manipulation of representations has the process inside-out: perception creates representations.

The mistake of cognitive science has been to place observer-relative and environment-relative regularities in the machine, as pre-existing descriptive structures. I have described here how a different view of representation, memory, perception, and even language itself suggests a simpler functional architecture, with far more flexible capabilities for symbolic reasoning.

## SYMPOSIUM PAPERS RECONSIDERED

The symposium papers make a clear attempt to establish a foundation from which intelligent behavior can be characterized and generated. The authors suggest that we should:

1. Situate the program in the world; view interactive and real-time processing as the primary constraint (e.g., GUARDIAN, INSECTS).

2. Develop a formal framework of representational primitives for grounding learning or rationality; attempt to relate uniformity, expressiveness, reflection, flexibility, learning, efficiency, responsiveness, etc. (e.g., PRODIGY, THEO, SOAR, Genesereth).

My critique of this work is that it fails to address directly the frame of reference issues in the modeling of dynamic systems. Following from my proposal that a new kind of mechanism should be sought, the question naturally arises, how could we tell that an agent has a functional architecture that directly manipulates processes, versus one of today's AI programs, in which processes are labeled, stored, and grammatically recombined? This is a tricky question, for it presupposes that we could use grammatical methods to construct a program that would be so good as to resemble human capability and fool us. Of course, nothing today comes close. A better form of the original question is to ask, what precisely are the capabilities that today's programs lack?

In what follows, I characterize the contributions of the various projects, focusing on how the theoretical framework could be improved and thereby improve the capabilities of the programs.

## Mixed Architectures

As claimed in the introduction, this research falls into two categories, knowledge engineering and the study of intelligence. The knowledge engineering contributions, exemplified by PRODIGY and GUARDIAN illustrate how a KL formalization of reasoning and learning can be used to produce a useful program. Both systems make a contribution to KL theories, but they exemplify especially well how these theories can be integrated into a complex system that can control complex mechanisms in real-time (e.g., the satisficing cycle of GUARDIAN), as well as assist theorists in improving the KL descriptions (e.g., the EBL process in PRODIGY). Both systems are *mixed architectures* (Newell, 1982); the researchers make little distinction between the functional architecture and the knowledge level. For example, Hayes-Roth (this volume, chap. 11) describes "backlog monitors" and "new–focus monitors," without making clear whether these are KL descriptions or to be viewed as distinct physical mechanisms. Similarly, in PRODIGY there are both search control rules and domain-schema rules; it is not clear how these KL descriptions map onto mechanisms in the functional architecture (e.g., are there two separate memories?).

## Formal "Objective" Analysis

In the formal frameworks presented by Anderson and Genesereth, we find no mention of the observer-relativity of KL descriptions. Genesereth says, "There is a symbol for every state of the agent's environment, every percept, and every action," suggesting that an environment can be described objectively or that the agent's perceptions can be exhaustively predefined in terms of primitive symbols. (Of course, these are tokens, not symbolically interpreted representations.) In essence, Genesereth starts with the idea of a machine as a calculator operating on non-numeric tokens (a grammar calculator) and provides a formal analysis of tradeoffs in compilation (which gives speed) versus runtime processing (which gives flexibility). This is a contribution to computer science and could justify design decisions in an architecture like GUARDIAN's. The analytic techniques being developed here might later prove useful for describing a mechanism with self-organizing processes.

Anderson's paper can be viewed as a reaction against the complexity of AI architectures. He attempts to reground the study of intelligence in a study of the "information processing requirements" posed by the task and environment. The idea of incorporating a formal description of the environment is completely consistent with the view of the KL I have provided. However, Anderson is wrong to suggest that this formalization is objective, that the world somehow is given to us in predefined categories that we only have to discover and name. Information is not objectively-supplied data; Anderson is confusing the theoretician's observations with the subject's constructive acts of perception and representation (as Simon says, "It is the organism that constructs a problem space and strategy to deal with the task environment" (Simon, 1988)[17]).

However, I believe that Anderson has several valid points that Simon skips over. First, when Anderson contrasts the description of a behavioral function to mechanism, he means physical mechanism, the functional architecture. Thus his paper can be viewed as calling us to separate our theorist's perspective ("focusing on the information processing problem") from what is going on in the agent ("the information processing mechanism").

Second, Anderson strives for a more general theory, above the level of specific KL attributions, to characterize task demands in a way that could *frame* the information processing problem. However, following my analysis, we would want to focus not on an objectively-defined environment, but on *interactional* aspects of behavior. That is, following Agre, we would describe task demands in terms of how dynamic aspects of the environment constrain the use of representations and provide opportunities and resources for, or work against, the evolution of routines.

Putting this together, to frame the information-processing problem we need to consider the interaction of the observer-theorist, the functional architecture, and the environment.

## Memory

Memory is a clearly a central issue in AI architecture research. Three of the papers in particular can be viewed as attempts to take a strong stand on what memory is. Brooks rejects the idea of maps of the world, that is, static data structures that describe things in the world and are apart from the processing mechanism.[18] Rosenbloom et al. have steadily moved towards the idea that

---

[17]Reeke and Edelman put this well, "[T]he start of the chain of deductions . . . which for AI justify the notion of the brain as a computer, is the assumption that information exists in the world— that is just there to be manipulated. There is also the idea that the organism is the receiver rather than a creator of criteria leading to information. Once the prior existence of such external information is conceded, it is entirely natural to proceed without further ado to the business of programming the rules to deal with it" (Reeke & Edelman, 1988, p. 153).

[18]This provides an intriguing resolution of the "frame problem," the problem of how changes in the environment are to be noticed and stored without a time-consuming and useless combinatorial explosion of inferences. The frame problem is an artifact of viewing perception as input to cognition, suggesting that input is predigested and exists apart from the process of behaving, and that memory is a special storage for descriptions of the world which are matched against rules that describe behaviors. The frame problem is an artifact of the idea that there must be internal, unexpressed representations (maps) of the world that the organism must keep up-to-date. Indeed, the frame problem is one reason for arguing that the representational view of memory is hopelessly wrong.

representations are generated in a perceived space ("working memory"), but they retain the idea that memory consists of retrievable descriptive structures and that "knowledge is stored." Mitchell, apparently in response to a perceived weakness in SOAR, provides direct support for hierarchical organization of concepts; thus, THEO's memory is a representation of a classification of concepts. In short, Brooks sweeps a theorist's KL descriptions out the door, placing them outside the functional architecture, while Rosenbloom et al. and Mitchell still try to find clever ways of encoding an observer's descriptions inside the machine. Brooks attempts to build a robot, while the others continue to tell us how such a machine might appear.

To combine these ideas, we might follow Brooks by doing away with the idea of a separate memory store. To account for conceptualization and learning, we could find some way to dynamically reconfigure a subsumption architecture, such that prior configurations are marked in some way and more prone to reconstruction. Furthermore, higher processes would not only control how the lower processes occur, they would control the network configuration process itself. Thus subsumption of processes would support hierarchical conceptualization, memory, and learning directly.

The one weakness that is most glaring in these programs is that they never conceive of anything. The world is precarved by the designer and these elements are grammatically recombined (recall the metaphor of the inverted picture puzzle). Chunking apparently models an important aspect of how new processes are created and reenacted in human memory, however it doesn't account for the compositional aspect of process creation and control (which THEO models in KL terms). This compositional process I have claimed is at the heart of symbolic interpretation, of making sense, of conceptualization. In essence, we must return to basic issues in natural language comprehension. Recharacterizing "reminding" in terms of Bartlett's impasse-rationalization model would be a good start.[19]

## CONCLUSIONS: A SCIENCE IN TRANSITION

In this chapter I have sharply called into question our analytic techniques for specifying architectural requirements for the design of an intelligent machine. We have ignored emergent interactional effects and the observer status of our theories. The knowledge-level patterns and processes we describe are partly an artifact of our own sense-making (any theory must state regularities; it's a property of language) and partly a result of routines that have evolved in the agent's interactions with its environment. We have ignored the dynamic and selective

---

[19]Contra Schank, Bartlett argued that a "reminding" occurs when a failure-impasse occurs, in the form of a conceptualization of the past, not a literal retrieval of what happened; the later memory of this failure is secondary. A failure needn't be an emotionally dramatic quandry, but perhaps just a momentary pause in the otherwise automatic flow of activity.

aspects of perception. My claim is that the foundation of AI research is faulty. Our ideas of memory, perception, and learning have been distorted because we have viewed knowledge as objective substance, as structures that can somehow statically capture meaning and store it. In contrast, I have argued that semantic interpretation exists only as ongoing commentary, through a process of creating representations in our speaking, gestures, and notations.

The arguments given here strongly build on and emphasize the idea of intelligent behavior as symbol manipulation, however these symbols are moved outside to where they can be perceived, in what I call the externalization move. Memory is not a storage for symbols, or any kind of *place* at all, rather it is a capacity to recreate and recombine processes that have previously related perceptions to actions. By the composition of these processes, perceptions organize behaviors, and hence ways of speaking (concepts) can be *about* what we do. Through primitive capabilities to compose hierarchically and sequentially, the functional architecture creates new routines so that behavior can proceed automatically, without conscious reflection and conceptualization that must occur when impasses arise.

The arguments given here retain the materialist view that intelligent machines can be built. However, my strong claim is that we have an inadequate understanding of the phenomenon to be replicated and (very likely) an inadequate theoretical understanding of the mechanisms that would provide engineering tools for building such machines. We should take a lesson from lasers, holography, VLSI, molecular genetics, etc. that striking advances in the design of machines are built upon fundamental discoveries about microlevel processes; some crucial properties of neural-level processes may remain to be found. The entire notion of computation must be broadened beyond the idea of a stored program operating on data structures.

The guts of our robots are too rigid because we have supposed that the mechanism must operate on descriptions of how the behavior should *appear*, rather than focusing on simpler mechanisms that would directly respond to and organize stimuli in an immediate way, without intervening descriptions of what is about to occur.

The main argument of this chapter is a rejection of the idea that the functional architecture should "directly support knowledge," which the paper by Rosenbloom, et al. focuses on. Rather, building from Newell's KL paper, I have shown that knowledge is not physically realized (stored) in the structures of the machine; it is "never in hand." Knowledge, in the form of representations about something, only exists in interpretive comments, in ongoing claims about the nature of the world, which themselves are only classified and interpreted as having semantic import by an observer. In this respect, gestures exemplify the nature of representational acts. Gestures are semantically interpretable, but generally exist (are produced) without being perceived this way, at least with the same level of attention and commentary we give to what a person is actually saying.[20] Everything we call a representation (a spoken phrase, a written word, a drawing, an equation, etc.) is generated with the same immediacy as a gesture (not translated from an internal description of it, but created for the first time in the movement itself). The difference is that we generally pay attention to the ongoing sequence of representations, trying to interpret, and immediately respond with another comment. (In this respect, gestures are produced like dreams–coherent, interpretable, but not observed by agents and not commented upon.)

All knowledge–level descriptions are relative to an observer's frame of reference. "Relative" means not just that "different agents know different things" or even "different agents disagree about the world." But rather KL descriptions are:

• *Relative to an observer's view* (a perceived pattern, the result of processes interacting over time) versus an individual participant's view of moment-by-moment interactions.

• *Emergent from the dynamics of interactions,* not ascribable to an individual's action or planning. It is not just that the task environment determines behavior; rather, our law-like models describe the historical, developmental product of the interaction, not mechanisms in the agent that generated his or her moment-by-moment responses. Hence, Brooks, Cohen, Agre, and Rosenschein et al. characterize the functional architecture in terms of the dynamics of movement and internal state, characterizing perception as part of ongoing activity in some changing, interactive environment. (Indeed, Edelman and others claim that without movement or change relative to a point of view there is no perception.)

• *Interpreted in "every next use"* (Agre, 1988). The meaning of a representation can't be characterized by a static structure, rather it is recomposed, reconceived, and reperceived with every new expression.

The essence of this analysis that we should view Figure 13.2 as the framework for the study of intelligence. We should continue to develop our KL theories; for example, the work in explanation-based learning should continue to provide a useful competence model that can focus the design of a functional architecture. However, more work like Brooks' INSECTS is needed, in which the agent is a robot and sensation/movements are produced without building in maps of the world or how the robot's behavior will appear. That is, more researchers should come forward with strong claims to the effect, "My machine does not work by interpreting a KL description of its behavior." In this respect, there appears to be

---

[20]To see this, watch someone's gestures and relate them to what the person is saying. Notice how often they precede the person's words. Notice how your description in terms of a visual language is radically different from the usual way in which you pay attention to gestures. Can you categorize the gesture-concepts in a given person's repertoire? Could he or she formulate these categories without looking in a mirror?

an opportunity to combine SOAR and the INSECTS work, throwing out the idea of a production rule memory.

This chapter has also briefly introduced the *commentary model of cognition*, which has the following implications for the design of a functional architecture:

• Reformulate the nature of reflection. The construction and use of representations is inherently a process of commentary and revision in the agent's behavior; it is not "inspecting" or "reading unperceivable structures."

• Reformulate chunking as a means of re-enacting any activity, clarifying how memory is nonrepresentational and all behavior, including reflection and commentary itself, becomes regularized.

• Reformulate conceptualization, exemplified by rationalization at an impasse, as a recomposition of ways of perceiving and behaving, in the form of incremental commentary, by which sequences of behavior are viewed as a unit and hence formed into a new chunk; conceptualization is not reading out, translating, or recombining preconceived descriptions in memory.

• Adopt a more comprehensive view of understanding (making sense) as a primary high-level function that is directly supported by the hardware (relates to diagnosis, dreaming, remembering, etc. as story understanding).

A great deal of reading and synthesis underlies the arguments in this paper. Making progress requires borrowing ideas from many different fields and selectively reinterpreting what people have said. The most important works, which I strongly recommend to anyone working in this area, are those by Bartlett (the nature of conceptualization and comprehension), Tyler (relation between language, thought, and formal theory), Gregory (the subjective nature of physics), Braitenberg (ways of composing simple mechanisms to get complicated, dynamic behaviors), Agre (the open nature of representations), Newell and Pylyshyn (how to talk precisely about mechanisms and architecture), Winograd and Flores (the concepts of social commitment, breakdown, and unarticulated background), Bateson (development of interacting systems), and Wittgenstein and Ryle (the original, commonsense analysis that inspired Tyler, Gregory, and Bateson).

Much of this work has been ignored (Bartlett's being the most glaring example) because it is at odds with the cognitive science view of mind. If nothing else, I hope that my discussion here has convinced the reader that there are other perspectives—other frames of reference—that can prove useful for constructing intelligent machines. Strikingly, much of this work directly relates to our interests, yet Braitenberg isn't cited by Brooks, and Bartlett's contrary results are simply ignored by everyone. Indeed, just to realize how AI is historically related to non–linear programming, cybernetics, and general systems theory would seem to be the most basic requirement for any beginning student. If my analysis is right, the study of dynamic systems pioneered by others will soon become of central concern to AI, and most of this earlier work and its current developments (e.g., Prigogine & Stengers, 1984) will be reintegrated into the field.

## ACKNOWLEDGMENTS

I am grateful for the support and encouragement of my colleagues at the Institute for Research on Learning, without which I might not have attempted to step outside prevailing views about cognition. John McDermott and Kurt VanLehn struggled through the first working draft and helped me produce something understandable to our AI colleagues. In particular, John suggested that I look more carefully at Newell's analyses. I would especially like to thank Allen and Kurt for inviting me to be a discussant at the symposium in May 1988, and hence giving me an excuse to spend a year reconsidering the foundations of AI. Many of the ideas were also developed for a keynote address presented at AI-88, Adelaide, Australia, in November, 1988. The section entitled "Frames of reference for designing intelligent machines" originally appeared as "The frame of reference problem in cognitive modeling," presented at the Cognitive Science Annual Meeting, August, 1989. The sections entitled "Tokens, symbols, and reference" and "Speaking as conceptualizing/perceiving" have been circulated as "Symbols and Computer Programs." Paul Duguid provided useful comments on this version. This research has been supported in part by ONR Contract N00014-85K-0305 and gifts from the Digital Equipment and Xerox Corporations.

## REFERENCES

Agre, P. E. (1988). *The dynamic structure of everyday life.* Unpublished doctoral dissertation, Massachusetts Institute of Technology, Cambridge, MA.

Alexander, J. H., Freiling, M. J., Shulman, S. J., Staley, J. L., Rehfuss, S., & Messick, M. (1986). Knowledge level engineering: Ontological analysis. *Proceedings of the National Conference on Artificial Intelligence,* pp. 963–968.

Allen, C. (1988). *Situated design.* Unpublished dissertation for Master of Science in Design Studies. Carnegie Mellon University, Department of Computer Science.

Bartlett, F. C. (1977). *Remembering: A study in experimental and social psychology.* Cambridge: Cambridge University Press. (Reprint of original 1932 edition.)

Bateson, G. (1972). *Steps to an ecology of mind.* New York: Ballentine Books.

Bateson, G. (1988). *Mind and nature: A necessary unity.* New York: Bantam.

Berger, P. L., & Luckmann, T. (1967). *The social construction of reality: A treatise in the sociology of knowledge.* Garden City: Anchor Books.

Braitenberg, V. (1984). *Vehicles: Experiments in synthetic psychology.* Cambridge, MA: MIT Press.

Bickhard, M. H., & Richie, D. M. (1983). *On the nature of representation: A case study of James Gibson's theory of perception.* New York: Praeger.

Chandrasekaran, B. (1986). Generic tasks in knowledge-based reasoning: High-level building blocks for expert system design. *IEEE Expert, 1,* 23–29.

Clancy, T. (1986). *Red storm rising.* New York: Berkley Books.

Clancey, W. J. (1983a.) The advantages of abstract control knowledge in expert system design. *Proceedings of the National Conference on Artificial Intelligence,* pp. 74–78.

Clancey, W. J. (1983b). The epistemology of a rule-based expert system. *Artificial Intelligence, 20*(3), 215–252.

Clancey, W. J. (1985). Heuristic classification. *Artificial Intelligence, 27,* 289–350.

Clancey, W. J. (1987a). From Guidon to Neomycin and Heracles in twenty short lessons: ONR final report, 1979–1985. In A. vanLamsweerde (Ed.), *Current issues in expert systems* (pp. 79–123). London: Academic Press. Also *The AI Magazine, 7*(3), 40–60, Conference, 1986.

Clancey, W. J. (1987b). Review of Winograd and Flores's "Understanding Computers and Cognition." *Artificial Intelligence, 31,* 232–250.

Clancey, W. J. (1988). Acquiring, representing, and evaluating a competence model of diagnosis. In M. T. H. Chi, R. Glaser, & M. J. Farr (Eds.), *The nature of expertise* (pp. 343–418). Hillsdale, NJ: Lawrence Erlbaum Associates.

Clancey, W. J. (1989). Viewing knowledge bases as qualitative models. *IEEE Expert 4,* 9–23, Summer.

Clancey, W. J. (in preparation). Interactive control structures: Evidence for a compositional neural architecture.

Cohen, H. (1988). How to draw three people in a botanical garden. *Proceedings of the Seventh National Conference on Artificial Intelligence.* Minneapolis-St. Paul, pp. 846–855.

Cohen, P. (1989). *Why knowledge systems research is in trouble, and what we can do about it.* COINS Technical Report 89–81. University of Massachusetts.

Dennett, D. C. (1988). Precis of "The Intentional Stance." *Behavioral and Brain Sciences 11,* 495–546.

Dietterich, T. G. (1986). Learning at the knowledge level. *Machine Learning, 1,* 287–316.

Dreyfus, H. L. (1972). *What computers can't do: A critique of artificial reason.* New York: Harper & Row.

Edelman, G. M. (1987). *Neural Darwinism: The theory of neuronal group selection.* New York: Basic Books.

Godwin, J. (1988). *Frommer's Australia on $30 a Day.* New York: Simon & Schuster.

Gregory, B. (1988). *Inventing reality: Physics as language.* New York: Wiley.

Hayes-Roth, B. (1985). A blackboard architecture for control. *Artificial Intelligence, 26,* 251–321.

Hayes-Roth, B., Hewitt, M., Vaughn M., Johnson, T. R. & Garvey, A. (1988). *ACCORD: A framework for a class of design tasks.* KSL Technical Report 88-19, Computer Science Department, Stanford University.

Heisenberg, W. (1962). *Physics and philosophy: The revolution in modern science.* New York: Harper & Row.

Johnson, T. R., Smith, J. W., & Chandrasekaran, B. (1989). Generic tasks and SOAR. LAIR Tech. Rep. Ohio State University.

Kaelbling, L. P. (1988). Goals as parallel program specifications. *Proceedings of the Seventh National Conference on Artificial Intelligence.* Minneapolis-St. Paul pp. 60–65.

Langer, S. (1958). *Philosophy in a new key: A study in the symbolism of reason, rite, and art.* New York: Mentor.

Lave, J. (1988). *Cognition in practice.* Cambridge: Cambridge University Press.

Minsky, M. (1985). *The society of mind.* New York: Simon and Schuster.

Neisser, U. (1976). *Cognition and reality: Principles and implications of cognitive psychology.* New York: W. H. Freeman.

Newell, A. (1982). The knowledge level. *Artificial Intelligence, 18,* 87–127.

Newell, A. (1988). The intentional stance and the knowledge level. *Behavioral and Brain Sciences, 11,* 520–522.

Newell, A. (1990). *Unified theories of cognition*. Cambridge, MA: Harvard.

Perlis, D. (1987). How can a program mean? In J. McDermott (Ed.), *Proceedings of the Tenth International Joint Conference on Artificial Intelligence*, Milan (pp. 163–166). San Mateo, CA: Morgan-Kaufmann.

Prigogine, I., & Stengers, I. (1984). *Order out of chaos*. New York: Bantam Books.

Pribram, K. H. (1971). *Languages of the brain: Experimental paradoxes and principles of neuropsychology*. Monterey: Brooks/Cole.

Pylyshyn, Z. W. (1984). *Computation and cognition: Toward a foundation for cognitive science*. Cambridge, MA: The MIT Press.

Pylyshyn, Z. W. (1989). On "Computation and Cognition: Toward a Foundation for Cognitive Science," a response to the reviews by A. K. Mackworth and M. J. Stefik. *Artificial Intelligence, 38*, 248–251.

Reeke, G. N., & Edelman, G. M. (1988). Real brains and artificial intelligence. *Daedalus, 117*, (1) Winter, "Artificial Intelligence" issue.

Rommetveit, R. (1987). Meaning, context, an control: Convergent trends and controversial issues in current social-scientific research on human cognition and communication. *Inquiry, 30*, 77–79.

Rosenfield, I. (1988). *The invention of memory: A new view of the brain*. New York: Basic Books.

Rosenschein, S. J. (1985). *Formal theories of knowledge in AI and robotics*. SRI Technical Note 362.

Rumelhart, D. E., McClelland, J. L., & the PDP Research Group. (1986). *Parallel distributed processing*. Cambridge, MA: MIT Press.

Ryle, G. (1949). *The concept of mind*. New York: Barnes & Noble.

Searle, J. R. (1984). *Minds, brains, and science*. Cambridge, MA: Harvard University Press.

Simon, H. A. (1969). *The sciences of the artificial*. Cambridge, MA: MIT Press.

Sloman, A. (1985). What enables a machine to understand? In A. Toshi (Ed.), *Proceedings of the Ninth International Joint Conference on Artificial Intelligence*, Los Angeles, (pp. 995–1001). San Mateo, CA: Morgan-Kaufmann.

Smith, B. (1987). Two lessons of logic. *Computational Intelligence, 3*, 218.

Steels, L. (1989). Cooperation through self-organisation. In Y. DeMazeau and J. P. Muller (Eds.), *Multi-agent systems*. Amsterdam: North-Holland Publishers.

Stefik, M. J. (1989). Review of "Computation and Cognition: Toward a Foundation for Cognitive Science, by Z. W. Pylyshyn." *Artificial Intelligence, 38*, 241–247.

Stucky, S. (1987). *The situated processing of situated language* (Tech. Rep. No. CSLI-87–80). Stanford University, Stanford, CA.

Suchman, L. A. (1987). *Plans and situated actions: The problem of human-machine communication*. Cambridge: Cambridge Press.

Tyler, S. (1978). *The said and the unsaid: Mind, meaning, and culture*. New York: Academic Press.

VanLehn, K. (1988). Student modeling. In M. Polson & J. Richardson (Eds.), *Foundations of intelligent tutoring systems*. Hillsdale, NJ: Lawrence Erlbaum Associates.

Vygotsky, L. S. (1966). *Thought and language*. (E. Hanfmann & G. Vakar, Trans.). Cambridge, MA: MIT Press. (Original work published 1934)

Winograd, T., & Flores, F. (1986). *Understanding computers and cognition: A new foundation for design*. Norwood, NJ: Ablex.

Wittgenstein, L. (1958). *Philosophical investigations*. New York: Macmillan.

# Author Index

# Subject Index